Imagining the American Jewish Community

Brandeis Series in American Jewish History, Culture, and Life

Jonathan D. Sarna, *Editor*
Sylvia Barack Fishman, *Associate Editor*

For a complete list of books in the series, visit
www.upne.com and www.upne.com/series/BSAJ.html

Jack Wertheimer, editor *Imagining the American Jewish Community*

Murray Zimiles *Gilded Lions and Jeweled Horses: The Synagogue to the Carousel*

Marianne R. Sanua *Be of Good Courage: The American Jewish Committee, 1945–2006*

Hollace Ava Weiner and Kenneth D. Roseman, editors *Lone Stars of David: The Jews of Texas*

Jack Wertheimer, editor *Family Matters: Jewish Education in an Age of Choice*

Edward S. Shapiro *Crown Heights: Blacks, Jews, and the 1991 Brooklyn Riot*

Kirsten Fermaglich *American Dreams and Nazi Nightmares: Early Holocaust Consciousness and Liberal America, 1957–1965*

Andrea Greenbaum, editor *Jews of South Florida*

Sylvia Barack Fishman *Double or Nothing? Jewish Families and Mixed Marriage*

George M. Goodwin and Ellen Smith, editors *The Jews of Rhode Island*

Shulamit Reinharz and Mark A. Raider, editors *American Jewish Women and the Zionist Enterprise*

Michael E. Staub, editor *The Jewish 1960s: An American Sourcebook*

Judah M. Cohen *Through the Sands of Time: A History of the Jewish Community of St. Thomas, U.S. Virgin Islands*

Naomi W. Cohen *The Americanization of Zionism, 1897–1948*

Seth Farber *An American Orthodox Dreamer: Rabbi Joseph B. Soloveitchik and Boston's Maimonides School*

Ava F. Kahn and Marc Dollinger, editors *California Jews*

Amy L. Sales and Leonard Saxe *"How Goodly Are Thy Tents": Summer Camps as Jewish Socializing Experiences*

Ori Z. Soltes *Fixing the World: Jewish American Painters in the Twentieth Century*

Gary P. Zola, editor *The Dynamics of American Jewish History: Jacob Rader Marcus's Essays on American Jewry*

David Zurawik *The Jews of Prime Time*

Ranen Omer-Sherman, 2002 *Diaspora and Zionism in Jewish American Literature: Lazarus, Syrkin, Reznikoff, and Roth*

Ilana Abramovitch and Seán Galvin, editors, 2001 *Jews of Brooklyn*

Pamela S. Nadell and Jonathan D. Sarna, editors *Women and American Judaism: Historical Perspectives*

Annelise Orleck, with photographs by Elizabeth Cooke *The Soviet Jewish Americans*

Steven T. Rosenthal *Irreconcilable Differences: The Waning of the American Jewish Love Affair with Israel*

Jonathan N. Barron and Eric Murphy Selinger, editors *Jewish American Poetry: Poems, Commentary, and Reflections*

Barbara Kessel *Suddenly Jewish: Jews Raised as Gentiles*

Imagining the
American Jewish Community

Edited by Jack Wertheimer

Brandeis University Press
Waltham, Massachusetts
Published by University Press of New England
in association with the Jewish Theological Seminary of America
Hanover and London

Brandeis University Press
Published by University Press of New England,
One Court Street, Lebanon, NH 03766
www.upne.com

© 2007 by Brandeis University Press
Printed in the United States of America
5 4 3 2 1

Library of Congress Cataloging-in-Publication Data
Imagining the American Jewish community / edited by Jack Wertheimer.
    p.   cm.—(Brandeis series in American Jewish history, culture, and life)
Includes bibliographical references and index.
ISBN-13: 978-1-58465-669-2 (cloth : alk. paper)
ISBN-10: 1-58465-669-7 (cloth : alk. paper)
ISBN-13: 978-1-58465-670-8 (pbk. : alk. paper)
ISBN-10: 1-58465-670-0 (pbk. : alk. paper)
    1. Jews—United States—History. 2. Jews—Cultural assimilation—United States.
3. Jews—United States—Social conditions. 4. Jews—United States—Intellectual
life. 5. Jews—United States—Identity. 6. Social integration—United States.
I. Wertheimer, Jack.
E184.J5143 2007
305.892'4073—dc22   2007032129

Contents

I. Reappraisals in American Jewish History

II. Community on Display

Preface and Acknowledgments

Since their arrival on these shores over 350 years ago, American Jews who have wished to maintain a Jewish communal life have faced a set of novel challenges. In marked contrast to coreligionists living in Christian and Muslim lands still governed by medieval laws, Jews were free throughout their history in the United States to embrace or eschew communal involvement; to support or ignore Jewish institutions; to associate with other Jews or maintain a distance from them. In time, when the Constitution forbade governments from establishing a state religion, various arrangements of church/state separation further ensured that Jewish communal activities would be based entirely on voluntarism and not external state compulsion, the latter having served as an indispensable prop to Jewish communal organization throughout the medieval era and in most countries inhabited by Jews in modern times—but not in this country.

The dispersal of Jews across so vast a country has also posed serious challenges to Jewish unity. American Jews rarely established unifying national bodies—or if such agencies emerged, they rarely withstood for long periods of time the forces of regionalism and localism eroding their authority. Yet even on the local level, American Jews have struggled to maintain overarching communities. Jewish neighborhoods rarely lasted long, and as Jews decamped to green suburbs—and more recently, exurbs—their institutions found it hard to deliver services or maintain a sense of cohesion. For these and many other reasons, the group existence of Jews in the United States is a tale of efforts to create and re-create community in the face of powerful centrifugal pressures.

It is also a story of creativity and inventiveness. The Internet has spawned much talk about "virtual communities," but in truth, Jews in diverse settings over many eras have formed virtual communities based not necessarily upon physical proximity, a common language, or even shared institutions but often upon less tangible commonalities—an identification with victims of antisemitic persecution, a shared concern for impoverished and homeless coreligionists, a desire to maintain vital religious, educational and cultural institutions, and overarching ideologies.

America's voluntaristic ethos, moreover, provided opportunities for Jews to devise innovative communal arrangements. American society had never hosted Jewish communities in the Middle Ages, and, accordingly, no entrenched traditions governed *how* Jews should organize themselves. Rather, as wave upon wave of Jewish immigrants washed up on these shores, each new group reinvented its own communal institutions and patterns of association to fit its own and the then-prevailing American conception of community. In time, new forms of communal association emerged to address the concerns of men and women, specific age cohorts and generations, urban, suburban, and rural inhabitants, and ideological fellow travelers. Jews with similar religious sensibilities banded together, as did Jews with common political, social, class, and recreational interests. In short, Jewish communal life has never remained static in the United States but continually has been reimagined.

The current moment marks a particularly challenging time in the dynamic history of Jewish community formation. Mounting evidence attests to declining levels of participation in the key institutions of the Jewish community: synagogue membership has dropped by nearly one-third over the past half century; Jewish community centers are relying ever more heavily on non-Jewish members, while others are folding because of decreasing membership; the numbers of donors to federations of Jewish philanthropy have plummeted by some 45 percent over the past thirty years; many major Jewish organizations are struggling to appeal to younger members; and recent research on the attitudes of twenty- and thirtysomething Jews indicates high levels of indifference within this population toward the major institutions of the American Jewish community.

Simultaneously, new types of communities have sprung into existence. Niche synagogues now appeal to particular age cohorts, to gay and lesbian Jews, to nondenominational Jews, to Jews who are primarily concerned with social action rather than worship, and even to secular Jews who gather in humanistic congregations. Jews in many locations are also creating new venues for meeting—salons for cultural exchanges, Jewish film festivals, systematic adult education programs that follow a two-year or longer curriculum. New organizations have proliferated to address the specific concerns of Jewish women, ranging from lobbies to bring about changes in Orthodox divorce procedures to support networks for Jewish women suffering with breast cancer; from organizations to aid women's advance in the workforce to groups designed to shatter the glass ceiling impeding women's promotion to leadership positions in Jewish communal agencies. Socially conscious Jews are gathering under the aegis of environmental agencies, humanitarian service organizations, and political advocacy groups—all of which proudly define themselves as Jewish institutions. And among the more experimental forms of Jewish association are those that harness the Internet to connect Jews to one another through worship, study, debate, conversation—and dating.

Although these new Jewish groupings hold the potential for a renewal of Jewish communal life consonant with the current age, they do not as yet offer overarching messages that might go beyond the interests of subpopulations. Indeed, to some the very notion of *a* Jewish community with a single address seems hopelessly naïve. Large communal agencies are struggling to define a broader mission or purpose that might rally American Jews. Symptomatic of the current mood is the emphasis currently placed on diversity and pluralism—that is, on creating a place for each and every kind of Jew—whereas broader allegiances and calls for sacrifice in behalf of a larger Jewish common good seem less compelling. As subgroups of Jews insist on ever more respect for their own distinctive experiences and practice a form of internal Jewish identity politics, it is harder to identify a collective memory, let alone a shared sense of purpose. The dilemma is directly confronted in these pages when historian Eli Lederhendler notes: "internal diversity in a social system is a historical fact of life. But the sine qua non in the process of community formation is the predominance of collective commitment over sectoral and private self-definitions." Such collective commitments seem more elusive than ever at this historical moment.

These contemporary concerns coupled with a desire to explore the varied character of Jewish communal conceptions loomed large as the Jewish Theological Seminary (JTS) prepared to celebrate the 350th anniversary of Jewish life in the United States. In March 2004, JTS was among the first institutions to mark the impending anniversary by convening a scholars' conference dedicated to an exploration titled "Imagining the American Jewish Community." The essays in this volume are all expanded and revised versions of papers delivered at that conference.

Written by historians, literary critics, anthropologists, and students of Jewish thought and culture, the essays in this volume portray the multiple conceptions of community in the American Jewish imagination. Although some of these essays shed new light on specific forms of communal organization, they are not intended as institutional histories. Rather, they aim to uncover the underlying assumptions and imaginings of Jews who engaged in the act of reconceptualizing Jewish community in the United States. Some essays explore works of fiction to reveal how authors have imagined the nature of Jewish community on these shores; others analyze the works of theologians intent on rebuilding Jewish community. Others focus on the role of iconography—photographs and monuments—that implicitly portrays conceptions of community. Still others examine school records for evidence of the "hidden curriculum" of community building; and others bring a critical eye to the role of language, sports, a board game, museum exhibits, and new media in the making of community. Some essays examine the marketplace as a force for building community, and others the particular role of Jewish women in reconceiving the nature of Jewish community. The essays in this volume range from the first efforts at community building in colonial America to the era of mass migration, and then up to the present day.

. . .

I wish to acknowledge with appreciation the role of an advisory group, consisting of Hasia Diner, David Roskies, Jeffrey Shandler, and Shuly Rubin

Schwartz, who helped me develop the theme of imagined communities. Ismar Schorsch, then chancellor of the Jewish Theological Seminary, graciously supported the conference held at JTS in March of 2004 and offered much helpful encouragement. His successor, Arnold Eisen, is a contributor and has taken a strong interest in this project. I am also grateful for the logistical support provided by my JTS colleagues, Rabbi Carol Davidson, Elise Dowell, Tom Kagedan, and their staffs. My greatest debt is to the sixteen colleagues who remained patient as this volume took shape and entrusted me with their imaginative work.

Contributors

Joyce Antler is the Samuel Lane Professor of American Jewish History and Culture at Brandeis University, where she teaches in the American Studies and Women's Studies programs. She is has written and edited many books on women's and Jewish history, including *The Journey Home: How Jewish Women Shaped Modern America*; *Talking Back: Images of Jewish Women in American Popular Culture*; and *America and I: Short Stories by American Jewish Writers*. Her most recent book is *"You Never Call! You Never Write!" A History of the Jewish Mother* (Oxford University Press, 2007).

Hasia Diner is the Paul S. and Sylvia Steinberg Professor of American Jewish History at New York University and the Director of the Goldstein-Goren Center for American Jewish History. Her most recent book is *The Jews of The United States, 1654–2000*, published by the University of California Press.

Arnold Eisen is the Chancellor of the Jewish Theological Seminary of America. He is the author of, among other works, *Rethinking Modern Judaism: Ritual, Commandment, Community* and (with sociologist Steven M. Cohen) *The Jew Within: Self, Family and Community in America*. His most recent publication is *The Jew of Culture*, an edited collection of the writings of Philip Rieff.

David E. Fishman is Professor of Jewish History at the Jewish Theological Seminary of America and Director of Project Judaica, a joint program of JTS and Russian State University for the Humanities in Moscow. He is the author of *The Rise of Modern Yiddish Culture* (University of Pittsburgh Press, 2005) and coeditor of a guide to Jewish war-trophy collections held in the "Special Archive" in Moscow (Russian State University Press, 2005).

Karla Goldman is historian in residence at the Jewish Women's Archive in Brookline, Massachusetts, where she coordinated the digitization and online posting of the nineteenth-century periodical *The American Jewess* (accessible at http://www.jwa.org). She is author of *Beyond the Synagogue Gallery: Finding a Place for Women in American Judaism*. Her current research project focuses on the history of the Jewish community of Cincinnati.

Jeffrey S. Gurock is Libby M. Klaperman Professor of Jewish History at Yeshiva University. His most recent book is *Judaism's Encounter with American Sports* (Indiana University Press, 2005).

Paula E. Hyman is the Lucy Moses Professor of Modern Jewish History at Yale University. Among her books are *Gender and Assimilation: The Roles and Representation of Women* and *The Jews of Modern France*. She is co–editor in chief of two encyclopedias, *Jewish Women in America* and *Jewish Women: An Historical Encyclopedia*.

Jenna Weissman Joselit is a professor of American studies and of modern Judaic studies at Princeton University who has also actively served as a public historian and a museum curator. Currently at work on a new book about America's fascination with the Ten Commandments, she will be a visiting scholar at the Library of Congress's Kluge Center in 2007.

Eli Lederhendler is Head of the Avraham Harman Institute of Contemporary Jewry at the Hebrew University of Jerusalem, where he holds the Stephen S. Wise Chair in American Jewish History and Institutions. Among his published works are *The Road to Modern Jewish Politics*; *Jewish Responses to Modernity: New Voices in America and Eastern Europe*; and *New York Jews and the Decline of Urban Ethnicity, 1950–1970*.

Riv-Ellen Prell, an anthropologist, is Professor of American Studies at the University of Minnesota. Among her publications are her edited volume, *Women Remaking American Judaism*; *Fighting to Become Americans: Jews, Gender and the Anxiety of Assimilation*; and *Prayer and Community: The Havurah in American Judaism*.

Marianne Sanua is an associate professor in the Department of History and the Jewish Studies Program of Florida Atlantic University in Boca Raton, Florida. She is the author of *Going Greek: Jewish College Fraternities in the U.S., 1895–1945* (Wayne State University Press, 2003) and *Let Us Prove Strong: The American Jewish Committee, 1945–2006* (University Press of New England, 2007).

Jeffrey Shandler is Associate Professor in the Department of Jewish Studies at Rutgers University. He is the author of *Adventures in Yiddishland: Postvernacular Language and Culture* (2005) and *While America Watches: Televising the Holocaust* (1999); the editor of *Awakening Lives: Autobiographies of Jewish Youth in Poland before the Holocaust* (2002); and coauthor/coeditor (with J. Hoberman) of *Entertaining America: Jews, Movies, and Broadcasting* (2003), among other publications.

Holly Snyder is North American History Librarian at Brown University's John Hay Library, where her responsibilities include Judaic studies. Prior to joining the staff of the Brown University Library, she taught American history and Judaic studies at Boston University, Hampshire College, and Smith College, and worked as an archivist at the United States Holocaust Memorial Museum, the American Jewish Historical Society, and the John Nicholas Brown Center (Providence, Rhode Island). She is the author of "Rules, Rights and Redemption: The Negotiation of Jewish Status in British Atlantic Port Towns, 1740–1831," published in the May 2006 issue of *Jewish History*. Her book *Geographical Destinies: Jews, Identity and Social Place in the British Atlantic World, 1654–1831* is forthcoming from the University of Pennsylvania Press.

Daniel Soyer is an associate professor of history at Fordham University. He is the editor of *A Coat of Many Colors: Immigration, Globalization, and Reform in the New York City Garment Industry* (Fordham University Press, 2005) and, with Jocelyn Cohen, of *My Future Is in America: Autobiographies of East European Jewish Immigrants* (New York University Press, 2006).

Beth Wenger is the Katz Family Term Chair in American Jewish History and Associate Professor of History at the University of Pennsylvania. She is the author of *The Jewish Americans: Three Centuries of Jewish Voices in America* (2007) and *New York Jews and the Great Depression: Uncertain Promise* (1996). Wenger is also coeditor of *Remembering the Lower East Side: American Jewish Reflections* (2000) and *"Holy Land": Place, Past, and Future in American Jewish Culture* (1997). Her current book project is titled "History Lessons: The Invention of American Jewish Heritage."

Jack Wertheimer is the Joseph and Martha Mendelson Professor of American Jewish History at the Jewish Theological Seminary. His recent publications include studies of recent trends in synagogue life, the relationship between the Jewish religious denominations, the cultures of Jewish education in a range of local Jewish communities, and the changing structure of leadership in the national American Jewish community. This is his fourth volume in the Brandeis Series in American Jewish History, Culture, and Life.

Hana Wirth-Nesher is Professor of English and American Studies at Tel Aviv University, where she is also the Samuel L. and Perry Haber Chair on the Study of the Jewish Experience in the United States and the Director of the Goldreich Family Institute for Yiddish Language, Literature, and Culture. She is the author of *City Codes: Reading the Modern Urban Novel*; a coeditor of the *Cambridge Companion to Jewish American Literature*; and most recently the author of *Call It English: The Languages of Jewish American Literature*.

I

Reappraisals in American Jewish History

Rethinking the Definition of "Community" for a Migratory Age

1654–1830

In 1993, Leo Hershkowitz wrote an article in which he characterized the notion that Jewish communal life in New York City began in 1654 as "somewhat optimistic and misleading." Although it had long been employed as the beginning date for Jewish settlement in the geographic area that would later become the United States, Hershkowitz argued that 1654 was a problematic choice for a number of important reasons. His examination of the evidence found in records of the Gemeente Archief (Jewish Communal Archive) in Amsterdam revealed that most of the Jews who arrived in New Amsterdam during the summer of 1654 did not remain there for more than a few years. Ten years later, when the colony was transferred to England, there were only four Jews residing there. The New York tax lists for 1676 further indicated that the number did not grow in the intervening twelve years. Only one of the Jews living in New York during this period even seemed to have a wife living with him, and there were no reports of any Jewish children in the colony. A Torah that had arrived in 1655, with merchant Abraham de Lucena, was sent back to Amsterdam in 1663 — a clear signal that a minyan was no longer available for communal worship. The often-cited interpretation of Solomon Pietersen's statement about twenty-three Jews "big and little" as referring to adults with children was, in fact, pure speculation;[1] given common parlance in the seventeenth century, it more likely referred to Jewish heads of household (that is, men and wealthy widows) of "big" and "little" means. Moreover, there were no

3

records of anything that could conceivably constitute a synagogue.[2] In fact, in an earlier piece, Hershkowitz had already reviewed evidence for the physical establishment (and here I refer to rented facilities rather than new construction) of Shearith Israel's first synagogue structure, which, he found, appears not to have existed at all prior to 1703 or 1704.[3]

The idea of the "synagogue community" as the single most important feature of Jewish life in early America has had great cachet during the past half century among scholars of American Jewish history. But as a historiographical concept, I have discovered that it has something of a murky past. None of the historians who have specialized in early American Judaism over the past half century have documented its birth and development. It would seem that the idea first arose about the time of initial planning for the tercentenary celebrations of 1954, although even within that context one cannot be sure of its origins. Notably, it seems to have arisen first among historians whose work focused on the Jewish experience in New York City. In 1949, for example, Hyman Grinstein published an article in the *American Jewish Historical Quarterly* in which he argued the case for what he termed the "synagogue-*kahal.*" Comparing the traditional Jewish communal organization in the European experience, the *kahal*, with the American synagogue, Grinstein suggested that a transformation had taken place in the structure of Jewish communal life during the process of Jewish acculturation to the American environment, of which the first phase comprised "the compression of the entire community into the framework of the synagogue so that *kahal* and synagogue became synonymous."[4] Grinstein had previously delineated this notion in his book on early New York congregations, first published in 1945,[5] but the mention there was fleeting (limited to a page or two in a work of some two hundred pages), and the idea apparently did not immediately register with scholars in the way that he had evidently hoped it would. In this subsequent article, therefore, Grinstein articulated the thesis that the synagogue-community was the essential vehicle for establishing European Jewish culture on American shores, where it was shortly to be reformulated under the influence of "the spirit of American democracy," leading to such innovations in self-government as general membership affiliation. Yet, for Grinstein (himself a traditional Jew), even a little democracy in the synagogue went too far. While nineteenth-century reforms allowed for greater participation and jettisoned the class system by which the synagogue-*kahal* had been rigidly controlled, they sacrificed communal authority over individual members in the process. Significantly, that loosening of strictures led to steep declines in synagogue membership and attendance and a corresponding sense of social isolation for those who remained attached.[6] Like many historians of Puritanism in early New England, Grinstein envisioned a halcyon episode of strong communal identity, followed by a sharp decline in religious commitment and vitality. For Grinstein, the period when the synagogue-*kahal* dominated American Jewish life represented an ideal whose passing was to be much regretted.

Grinstein's appeal was passionate, but it took some time until his arguments found their way into American Jewish historiography—and then without his getting due credit for them. In the 1988 introduction to the bibliography of synagogue histories that he published with Alexandra Korros, Jonathan Sarna pointed not to Grinstein but, rather, to a piece published by Moshe Davis in 1956 as the point of origin for the synagogue-community concept.[7] Davis, excluding any mention of Grinstein's article or book, with which he surely was familiar, and in an even more forceful manner than Grinstein had already done, insisted upon the centrality of the synagogue to the Jewish community in early America. According to Davis, the synagogue was not just "the chief instrumentality to transfer the Jewish tradition from one continent to another"; it also became, in the process, the preeminent institution of American Judaism. As the American Jewish experience evolved, "it was through the Synagogue that the changes in Jewry were expressed," and they were inextricably intertwined in such a way that "[t]o understand the nature of the American synagogue is to understand the meaning of American Judaism." For Davis, the "real drama" of early American Jewish history lay not in the demise of "the monolithic structure of the Colonial Synagogue" but in the creation of new communal forms, including the rise of independent Jewish philanthropic bodies and the formation of multiple synagogues in a single locality that drew on the same population base of American Jews and thus competed for their affiliation.[8]

Perhaps surprisingly, Jacob Rader Marcus, the quintessential historian of early American Jewry from 1950 to his death in 1995, never employed the term "synagogue community" or similar terminology in any of his works (although it does appear that he had adopted the basic concept of the synagogue community sometime in the early 1950s).[9] Moreover, it must be noted that neither of the two scholars most closely associated with the genesis of the "synagogue community" as a historiographical concept were experts in either the colonial period of American history or in early modern European history—the period in which they claimed the "synagogue community" to have been the most important feature of American Jewish life. In fact, neither Grinstein nor Davis cited any primary or even secondary evidence for their claims about the efficacy of the early American "synagogue community." Each man, in turn, assumed the mantle of blazing a new historiographical pathway for American Jewish history while walking on thin ice, and both did so in the context of writing the history of antebellum Jewish New York (Moshe Davis as to a single congregation, and Grinstein as to the evolving congregational scene). Davis, in his study of B'nai Jeshurun, dated the key "watershed in American Jewish history" no earlier than 1810, but Grinstein had earlier dismissed the very idea of writing about the colonial era due to a purported "lack of sources."[10] Indeed, neither had heeded the cautions suggested by Salo Baron's nuanced portrait of Jewish communal life, which outlined the constant tensions among "a concatenation of many external and internal forces" from which early modern European Jewish communities were able to draw their power over individual Jews—tensions that simply did not exist in the same way on the western edge of the British Atlantic world, or even in England itself.[11] Baron himself later noted the absence of communal control over individual Jews in the context of colonial America.[12] So, what are we to make of the nebulous past of an idea that has become one of the bedrock concepts of American Jewish history? The notion of a "synagogue community" appears to have evolved out of shadows—rising not from rigorous examination of the historical evidence, but largely from a sequence of commonsense presumptions about the role played by the synagogue in nineteenth-century Jewish communal life in the United States, projected backward onto the colonial past. These presumptions consisted of three untested theories that relied on a single historical "fact." The historical "fact" (so denoted here, because closer examination reveals it to have been open to interpretation) was that none of the Jewish communities in early America had more than one documented synagogue before 1802, when Congregation Rodeph Shalom became Philadelphia's second synagogue.[13] The assumptions were, first, that the synagogue formed immediately and maintained a continuous existence from the moment of first settlement in a particular place; second, that all organized Jewish activities, both ritual and social, then took place through the institutional agency of the synagogue; and, third, that our current understanding of the Jewish community as geographically fixed would function as a valid measure of Jewish communal life for the seventeenth and eighteenth centuries.

In fairness, I will acknowledge that the evolution of the "synagogue community" paradigm predates by nearly four decades Benedict Anderson's *Imagined Communities*,[14] which has lately generated a new appreciation for the mythic components of ethnic identity in scholarly circles. Yet although the synagogue-community paradigm, for its time, represented an advance in the historiographical treatment of the earliest and most formative period in American Jewish history, its limitations have come to outweigh its utility. American Jewish history as an academic discipline has now reached a crossroads; the time has arrived to reconsider our previous assumptions about Jewish life in early America and expose them to greater scrutiny. Here, I present an extended critique of the synagogue-community paradigm as the sole, or even the best of several, means for understanding Jewish communal life in early America. By pushing at the boundaries of the relationship between synagogues and their communities, I hope to reveal how the synagogue-community paradigm limits our comprehension of Jewish life during the seventeenth and eighteenth centuries. And in addition to exposing its flaws, I will suggest a number of other criteria that might be productive as we consider alternative ways for thinking about Jewish communities and communal life in early America.

The Oscillating Universe of Jewish Life in Early America

Given the existence, in published form, of the early minute books for Congregation Shearith Israel dating from 1728,[15] Grinstein's plea of "lack of sources" to document New York synagogues prior to 1825 was wholly disingenuous— but only as to New York. Had he been writing about any of the early Jewish congregations in North America except New York, his claim would have been validated by the extant documentary record.[16] Still, there are sufficient documents from each community, when examined in conjunction with other types of records, with which to flesh out an argument about the notion that Jewish life in colonial North America was entirely centered in the synagogue.

One of the most difficult issues facing the historian of Jewish settlement in early America is the fact that the population of each site was so small—proportionately far smaller than the Jewish community in America at the dawn of the twenty-first century. At the time of the first federal census in 1790, Jews constituted no more than 1,500 of the nation's 3,929,000 inhabitants.[17] By 1820, the first census for which sufficient records have survived on which to base a complete estimate, the entire Jewish population of the United States numbered no more than 3,000.[18] Even in 1820, Jews constituted no more than 1 percent of the U.S. population.[19] Most historians dismiss these communities as a topic worthy of serious consideration precisely because of their proportionate paucity. Like Grinstein, they have perused the extant documentary record for evidence of large stories and, finding little of that description, have managed to ignore the significance of the fact that there is anything there at all. The historian of Jewish communal life in early America must look beyond the numbers and ask a different set of questions in order to elucidate the importance of these nascent Jewish settlements for American history as well as for the history of Jews in America. In short, we need to examine the very process by which Jews managed to settle and form new communities in a British America that was overwhelmingly Christian and characterized by a limited tolerance for difference.

From the perspective of constructing Jewish community, a far more important factor than size in early America was the wild oscillation in its Jewish population that each place endured over the course of several decades before the community managed to achieve the critical mass that would allow it to establish permanent structures, procedures, and institutions. As Hershkowitz points out so succinctly for New York, the arrival of the *Sainte Catherine* in the summer of 1654 resulted in neither the establishment of a stable community nor the immediate formation of a congregation. Indeed, the initial influx of Jews into New Amsterdam in 1654 was soon reduced to a pitiful number such that a *minyan* could not be formed for decades to come. For many years, there was only one Jew (Asser Levy) residing in the entire colony.

And New York was not unique in this regard. Newport, Savannah, Charleston, Philadelphia, and Montreal all experienced similar oscillations at different points in their early history. In Newport, an initial settlement of Jewish merchants from Barbados during the seventeenth century had completely faded away by the turn of the eighteenth century. A Jewish presence was not reestablished there until 1740, when a number of Jewish merchants arrived from New York; this settlement, too, died in the 1820s, when its last surviving member moved to New York. Savannah was singular because it was the only place in early America where Jews arrived as a group with the specific intention to form a religious congregation.[20] However, in its early years Georgia was a tenuous frontier colony, and when war broke out with Spain in 1740, the town was largely depopulated. As a result, the few remaining Jews had to travel to Charleston to meet religious needs and obligations; the congregation, as such, could not be reestablished until 1774.[21] Jewish life in Pennsylvania swung between coastal Philadelphia and the frontier post of Lancaster until the American Revolution, when an influx of Patriot refugees into Philadelphia from New York, Newport, Savannah, and Charleston (all under British occupation) led to the incorporation of Congregation Mikve Israel in 1782. Although each town had a minyan, neither had a synagogue; the two communities even shared the services of a *shochet* and other religious functionaries.[22] Thus, the idea that the early American synagogue had an immediate and continuous existence is fallacious.

In point of fact, the alternating expansion and contraction of the early Jewish population in seventeenth- and eighteenth-century British America was part and parcel of the ongoing process of European migration into the Western Hemisphere. This was a period of large-scale migrations—migrations proportionately far greater in size and range than historians of nineteenth- and twentieth-century America have previously acknowledged. Recent work by historians on the parameters of the British Atlantic world amply demonstrates that such migrations were extensive in scope, involving not one transatlantic movement over the course of a lifetime but many such transitions from east to west, west to east, north to south, and south to north.[23] Although Jews by themselves did not constitute a significant migration stream, their ebb and flow from British American towns reflected acute perceptions of various factors that Jews required for establishing communal life in a new environment, including the atmosphere of religious tolerance among local Christians, a colonial society that welcomed new participants and overlooked ethnic differences, and multiple opportunities for achieving economic success.

The second premise—that is, that all Jewish activity in early America occurred through the agency of the synagogue—can be similarly exploded, despite the dearth of surviving records that document Jewish activities. Here, there is a fair amount of evidence to support the argument that the synagogue was not the principle or only agent of Jewish religious behavior. Let's take Newport, Rhode Island, as an example. The settlement of Jewish merchants in Newport during the late seventeenth century led to the establishment of a cemetery in 1678, but it was not accompanied by a permanent synagogue structure. By 1702, all Jews had moved away from the town, leaving only the *bet haim* (cemetery) to mark their presence. For nearly four decades, the cemetery thus constituted the town's only Jewish site—culminating in the name "Jew Street" for the roadway that ran past its entrance. In Newport, it was the cemetery, rather than a synagogue, that constituted the symbolic center of Jewish life prior to the dedication of the Touro synagogue in 1763. In every place where Jews would eventually establish a synagogue—as well as in some where they did not—we know that individual Jews managed to maintain kashruth even in the absence of synagogue authority by slaughtering their own meat. Savannah's Mordecai Sheftall even took his slaughtering knives with him when he visited Christian friends in the Georgia backcountry.[24] In fact, the surviving records of Shearith Israel indicate that even after that synagogue's *Mahamad* (governing board) began to regulate kosher slaughtering, the number of members conversant in the rules pertaining to *shechitah* were sufficient that *shochet* and *bodek* were competitive posts.[25] We also know that, although the knowledge was not as widely dispersed as the *shechitah*, the circumcision rites of *brit milah* were regularly performed outside of the synagogue context—sometimes by a father on his own offspring.[26] Such widespread knowledge was a practical necessity to ensure Jewish survival in an environment where there were few Jews and no established communal authority, and where the ritual supervision of a synagogue was either too far distant to be consulted or altogether lacking. The absence of a synagogue, although often deeply regretted by nascent Jewish communities, thus did not preclude the observance of Jewish ritual life in early America.

The third premise, that of the geographical specificity of Jewish communal life, is a peculiarly modern fiction. In fact, Jews were part and parcel of the early modern European world of transatlantic peregrinations, and I will give here two examples to demonstrate how these intrude upon our current notions of communal identity and membership for the seventeenth and eighteenth centuries. Moses Israel Pacheco has been considered one of the founders of the Jewish community of Newport. However, his residence in Newport was but a brief interlude in a long and varied mercantile career. Pacheco originated in Hamburg, where he appears in Sephardi communal records between 1654 and 1660. But by 1662 he was on English soil, petitioning Charles II for denization

as an English subject. By February 1678 he was in Newport, involved in purchasing land for a *bet haim*. In 1680, as Wilfred Samuel has documented, he
appears in the records of Speightstown, Barbados. By 1688, however, he had
died—not in Newport, but back in Hamburg, leaving some property in Newport to be managed by his chief creditor, Gov. Caleb Carr, who won appoint-
ment as executor of Pacheco's Rhode Island estate.[27] Pacheco's peripatetic
lifestyle is echoed nearly a century later by that of Abraham Sarzedas, whose
travels were even more widely dispersed. Sarzedas was raised in Portugal as a
Converso. As a young man, he and his wife became part of a larger influx into
London of *Conversos* seeking to escape the reach of the Portuguese Inquisition. In February 1746, Sarzedas and his wife Rachel were living in Jamaica,
where they applied to be naturalized as subjects of the British Crown.[28] By
1753, Rachel had died and Sarzedas was in New York, where he took as his
second wife the teenage daughter of an Ashkenazi merchant.[29] Abraham's
business interests were far afield, encompassing most of the British colonies
in North America and the Caribbean. He made long and frequent sojourns
in distant places, doing whatever he deemed necessary for the success of his
enterprises, including piloting the ships of other merchants in the dangerous
Caribbean basin.[30] Moreover, as a confident and self-assured trader, he did not
stint to keep hours at his shop more inclined to Mediterranean than English
custom.[31] In the early years of his second marriage, Abraham set up the family household in New York City. But by 1757, Abraham had resettled his family to Savannah, Georgia.[32] Within a decade, the family had removed from
Savannah to Newport, Rhode Island, only to return to Savannah early in 1775.
Abraham's new wife bore him five additional children between 1760 and 1767
and, of necessity, had to fend for her family by herself during the long months
of his extended absences.[33] It was during one of his long trading voyages to
St. Nicholas Mole on Hispaniola (now Cap Haitien, Haiti), where he hoped to
set up a correspondent warehouse, that Abraham Sarzedas suddenly became
ill and died.[34]

These two examples bear witness to the problems inherent in assigning
a specific geographic affiliation to early modern Jewish merchants and their
families. Does Moses Israel Pacheco belong to Hamburg or to Rhode Island,
both of which may claim him as a founder of their respective communities?
And what are we to make of his long sojourns in London and Barbados, where
he appears to have had relations? Portugal, London, Jamaica, New York, Georgia, Rhode Island, and Hispaniola—to which of these places can Abraham
Sarzedas be said to have truly belonged? The problem is much greater than
that presented by the lives of two individuals, because there were many like
them—they are indeed typical of larger trends. Comparing the earliest records
of Congregation Shearith Israel to I. S. Emmanuel's monumental *Jews of the
Netherlands Antilles*, for example, one finds repeated instances of Curacao

merchants who lived in New York for a year or two at a time, most likely in order to develop the knowledge of local markets and the local contacts they would need to successfully pursue the New York trade from Curacao. As resident New Yorkers, they affiliated with Congregation Shearith Israel—but only while living in New York. Some families—notably the Gomez clan of New York—also used marriage to build their mercantile networks. Mordecai Gomez, apprenticed by his father to a New York Jamaica trader, took a Jamaican woman as his first wife before 1716; his younger brother Daniel followed suit, but when his first wife died, Daniel, whose interests had by then transferred to Curacao, took a second wife from that island.[35] Trade drove the need for connections in distant places, and merchants thus formed extensive ties—for business and familial purposes—with other Jews at great geographical remove.

The Jewish world I am describing here was a world in motion. As difficult as travel then seems to our modern sensibilities, the lives of America's earliest Jews revolved around the need to move, and the most successful among them can frequently be found in constant flux. To the extent that we, as historians residing in the twentieth and twenty-first centuries, have attempted to fix them to one geographic place, we have missed large and significant portions of their respective stories. To bring those stories into focus, we will need to move beyond the idea that "community" is fixed to a set of geographic coordinates. The culture of early modern Jews was, indeed, a portable world, and the necessity for motion, whether pushed (due to expulsion or flight from the Inquisition) or pulled (owing to the demands of trade), required that the principal wealth of Jewish communities be invested in things that could be readily carried from place to place—mercantile knowledge, medical skills, gemstones, silver and gold—rather than in things that were fixed in space such as land, houses, and furniture.

All of this is to suggest that if we look more closely at the historical evidence, we will gain a better understanding of these early American Jewish communities than we have had until now. Since we are looking for the critical linkage between the synagogue and the community, the obvious portal through which to enter this world is institutional—that is to say, via the synagogue. So as we begin our brief tour of this world, I will borrow from political scientist Gerald Gamm three terms: membership, rootedness, and authority. These terms represent categories of analysis that we can use both to critique the synagogue-community paradigm and to interrogate (as Gamm did for the religious institutions he studied in twentieth-century Boston) the way in which early American synagogues functioned in the day-to-day lives of ordinary American Jews.[36] This discussion may, I believe, help to illuminate what "synagogue" and "community" meant to Jews living in early America.

Membership

Critical to any understanding of the American synagogue is its membership. Grinstein underscored this understanding of his synagogue-*kahal* model when he claimed that "[a]ll matters of religion, education, philanthropy and even social life" operated as "functions of the synagogue."[37] But what did "membership" mean in the Jewish communities of early America? And can we really say, as the synagogue-community model presumes, that membership in the synagogue was synonymous with membership in the Jewish community at large? I would suggest that our answer to this question depends on whose story we are telling. It is certainly no accident that the notion of a synagogue-centered Jewish community originated among male scholars at a time when historiographical writing on Jewish women in America was virtually nonexistent. Had either Davis or Grinstein had to face the wealth of new scholarly work on American Jewish women that has erupted since Charlotte Baum, Paula Hyman, and Sonya Michel published their groundbreaking book *The Jewish Woman in America* in 1976,[38] such a restricted notion of communal membership would have been impossible to articulate persuasively. We now know, from the work of scholars like Dianne Ashton and Karla Goldman, that women were active participants in the evolution of American Judaism and its central institutions. Karla Goldman's *Beyond the Synagogue Gallery*, to take the most cogent example, demonstrates the degree to which women sought to exercise agency over Jewish affairs even while membership in the synagogue was officially denied to them. From fighting over seats in the women's gallery on the High Holidays, to seat subscriptions, to making their own independent contributions to synagogue funds, to claiming the privileges of a deceased husband, Goldman documents how American Jewish women asserted their religious identity in the antebellum synagogue in ways that openly, if only tacitly, defied the official rules against female membership.[39] In her study of Rebecca Gratz, Dianne Ashton shows us a woman whose activism was, by virtue of her gender alone, forced into building independent institutions, like the Female Hebrew Benevolent Society and the Hebrew Sunday School, that supplemented but existed outside the governance of Congregation Mikve Israel. It was only by virtue of their complete separation from the synagogue hierarchy that such institutions served as places where women could make instrumental contributions to the preservation of Judaism, as the rules of synagogue membership would not allow for female agency.[40] Emily Bingham's recent work on the Mordecai family gives us three Jewish women who, following this trend, made lifelong and paying careers out of teaching in the larger world at the turn of the nineteenth century, some decades before school teaching became a fashionable trade for young women—and even then only prior to marriage.[41] Even earlier than these women was the outspoken Abigail Levy Franks, frequently impatient with the "Supperoregations" of Jewish ritual life, and anxious for the reforms that a Jewish "Calvin or Luther" might bring should he "rise amongst Us."[42] The evolving scholarship reveals a complex picture, suggesting that the lives of Jewish women were invested with religious thought and intention. From what we now know, does it make sense to continue excluding them from our study of the Jewish community in early America by virtue of the fact that they could not be members of the synagogue?

Women may constitute the most obvious example of who is excluded by the presumption that the community is synonymous with the synagogue, but there are other aspects of the Jewish community in early America that have yet to make it onto our historiographical radar. Poor Jews, for example, constituted a fair proportion of the community. The 1750 roster of seat assignments for Shearith Israel tells the story: twenty-four Jews who could pay only the lowest rate for seats (15 shillings) against twenty who paid for the best seats, worth £2 or more.[43] The stories of those twenty are relatively well known—they were important merchants who served on the *Mahamad*, and thus left us records of their experiences: correspondence, court cases, and account books, along with entries in the congregation's minute books. But of the poorest Jews—those who might not have had the wherewithal to subscribe to a seat—we have nothing but a few entries in the accounts of a congregation's *tzedakah* fund. When Mrs. Martha Lazarus Moravia died in Newport on July 12, 1787, Moses Seixas, as *gabay* (treasurer) of the synagogue, noted that she had been a pensioner of the *tzedakah* fund of congregation Jeshuat Israel for six years and nine months, having received total payments in that time of approximately $1,500. Yet apart from the simple headstone in the *bet haim*, her presence was not noted in any other official or public record in the town of Newport.[44] Aaron Pinto is mentioned only twice in the records of Congregation Shearith Israel—first, in October 1765, as a person to "be dispacht as soon as possible," and then a month later, when it was determined "That three Corse Shirts be made & sent" to him "as he is almost naked."[45] An even more significant exclusion consists of those Jews who elected not to affiliate with the synagogue—whether because of distance from a Jewish community or religious apostasy of some type. Levi Sheftall recorded a significant number of such instances in his communal record book for Savannah: Mrs. Moses Nathans, "being very sick, and having a wish to be brot w[h]ere there were Jews"; Lyon Henry, who "removed some time ago with his family to a place called Vainsborough" (an isolated place more than one hundred miles distant from Savannah); a young Jew named Benjamin Jewel, who "after being here some time . . . maried a french woman, none of our profession but is a roman catholic"; Lion Norden, whose "mode of living was such as he kept no [Sabbath] day" and "ought not," in Sheftall's view, "to have been buried amongst the Jews."[46]

In neglecting to study their connection to the Jewish community at large, we fail to address the weak spots in Jewish communal life and blind ourselves to the failures of communal reach.

Rootedness

As a close corollary to the matter of membership we must reconsider the notion of the synagogue structure and its physical location, and in particular the juxtaposition of human capital with architecture. In our passion for finding evidence of Jewish life in colonial times, we have tended to focus on the physical evidence: Shearith Israel's 1728 synagogue on Mill Street; Newport's Touro synagogue, dedicated in 1763; Charleston's 1838 Beth Elohim synagogue and its 1792 predecessor, of which only an engraving remains. But where does the true nature of the "synagogue" lie? In the physical structure itself? Or in the congregation that calls it home? In *Urban Exodus*, his study of neighborhood change in ethnic Boston, Gerald Gamm recalls his 1991 visit to the abandoned Seaver Street synagogue in Roxbury that had once been home to Congregation Mishkan Tefila, since relocated to nearby Newton. As Gamm discovered, Mishkan Tefila continues to have a vibrant communal life—but it has not done so at Seaver Street for many decades.[47] So, which is the true synagogue? The once elegant, but now empty and decrepit, Seaver Street structure—whose current neighbors have had no experience of the congregation that built it—or the lively and expanding structure currently used by Mishkan Tefila in Newton? Here, I think, Gamm's encounter with both the grim remains of Mishkan Tefila's former life and its vigorous present existence leads us to fundamental questions about the role of the physical structure (what we may call the "physical synagogue") in the Jewish experience. Upon closer examination, asking these questions may prove to be as useful for interrogating the character of the synagogue and its role in Jewish communal life during the seventeenth and eighteenth centuries as it is for our own times.

Let's consider a seventeenth-century case that may illustrate some of the distinctions between the physical synagogue and its congregation in the early modern world: resettlement London. Through the careful work of Anglo-Jewish historians, much information has been uncovered about the resettlement of Jews in England during the regime of Oliver Cromwell. The activities of Antonio Fernandes Carvajal in the founding of a small synagogue in the Parish of St. Katherine Creechurch were well documented in the early twentieth century by Lucien Wolf; the location and structure of the private house that was converted into the physical synagogue for the resettlement community were described by Wilfred Samuel at about the same time; A. S. Diamond has more recently analyzed the history of London's first resettlement *bet haim*.[48]

All of these scholars focused their work on the Spanish and Portuguese Jews who formed Congregation Sha'ar HaShamayim, which still owns the synagogue structure at Bevis Marks Place that was constructed in 1703 to replace the outgrown house synagogue on Creechurch Lane. Yet Wolf also uncovered sources that may indicate there were other groups of Jews residing in London during the second half of the seventeenth century who were not affiliated with this congregation. Two informers lists, provided to Cromwell about 1660, suggest that there was a second minyan, probably Ashkenazi, operating near Great St. Helen's—a few streets away from the Creechurch Lane synagogue belonging to the Spanish and Portuguese congregation. The evidence is thin and has not been confirmed by other sources. Still, the appearance of a "Senor David The Pre[a]st" and "Sin. David Mier" on two separate lists is suggestive enough to rattle the historiographical presumption that London had only one minyan for several decades before the Ashkenzi Great Synagogue was built at Duke's Place.[49] Here, what I would point to is the existence of a minyan meeting at a private house instead of in a public place for worship—that is, setting aside the question of public versus private worship, what I want to highlight is the fact that there may well have been a number of groups meeting for Jewish religious worship simultaneously with the congregation of Spanish and Portuguese Jews that (unlike Congregation Sha'ar HaShamayim) did not leave records for historians to analyze.[50] If Wilfred Samuel is correct in his surmise that there were a number of such "oratories" to be found in seventeenth-century London, and in his theories about the secret worship in the house on Creechurch Lane prior to 1657, we will need to rethink the moment of a congregation's "birth." Rather than fixing the birth of the congregation to its first written constitution or the dedication of the physical synagogue structure, we need to ask about the moment when the small minyan meeting in a private home achieves the impetus necessary to call itself a congregation and begins to dream dreams of constructing that physical synagogue. Although early synagogue records for colonial North America are sparse, we do know, for example, that Jews were living in Newport, Rhode Island, for some fourteen years prior to the effort to construct the Touro synagogue and that fundraising efforts for building that structure had begun some nine years prior to the 1763 dedication. One suspects that a group of Jews who were so entirely devoted to the construction of a synagogue building were not living in a state of sin all that time. In New York, Hershkowitz's work shows that Congregation Shearith Israel rented a house for religious purposes for more than two decades prior to the construction of the Mill Street synagogue in 1728. Yet we also face conflicting evidence. Newport's Congregation Jeshuat Israel has oscillated four or five times without moving the Touro synagogue since its dedication in 1763; but Shearith Israel now inhabits its fourth synagogue structure since the dedication of the Mill Street synagogue, each on a different site in

Manhattan. Beth Elohim, formally organized in 1750, rented houses at three different locations in Charleston before it purchased a site in 1791 for its "New Synagogue." Further, some evidence suggests that a secondary minyan broke away from Beth Elohim prior to 1791, although it was unable to maintain sufficient cohesion to become a permanent congregation.[51] Philadelphia's Mickve Israel existed as an informal association without name, rules, or officers and met in a rented house for more than three decades before the influx of Jews from other places spurred the formal commitment to form a congregation and build a synagogue structure in 1782, and Montreal's Shearith Israel had a like experience for the decade between 1768 and 1778.[52] Members of Richmond's Beth Shalome, whose constitution dated from August 1789, rented rooms at two different locations and, after the second of these collapsed, did without for a number of years prior to finally purchasing a lot on which to build a physical structure in 1818. Another four years elapsed before the building was finally dedicated; in 1891 it was sold to another congregation, and Beth Shalome moved elsewhere.[53] Altogether, the physical structure of a synagogue, like the human body, is only a shell for its soul.

Authority

Grinstein read the establishment of American democratic structures within the synagogue as the death knell for synagogue authority over the Jewish community, but the reality of the early American synagogue may not have been quite so simple. Here, we need to give closer attention to the tensions within the synagogue over rules and rule making—that is, to the kinds of challenges made by individual members to the authority of the *Mahamad*, and to the undercurrents of libertarian freethinking that led a number of Jews to disregard synagogue rules. Karla Goldman has made a first step into this arena with her discussion of the battles over seating in the women's gallery,[54] but the discussion needs to be broader. There is much evidence in correspondence (particularly that of the religiously assiduous Manuel Josephson) and in surviving congregational records—particularly the minute books of New York's Congregation Shearith Israel and surviving records of Philadelphia's Congregation Mikve Israel—to detail these disputes.

A critical force behind some of these issues in early America was the necessity for merchants to follow trade, even when that meant having to reside in inland locations where there were no other Jews. David de Sola Pool referred to this movement as "[t]he centrifugal tendency which drew individuals away from the city . . . notwithstanding that these [places] were then accessible only with considerable difficulty." The move inland necessarily meant escape from the constraints of life in an urban Jewish quarter, and in particular removal from the supervisory gaze of one's neighbors and synagogue elders. In 1737, Pool notes, the "tendency" to move out to rural places was sufficiently pronounced that the *Mahamad* of Shearith Israel levied a charge on country dwellers to ensure that they provided adequate annual support for the maintenance of the synagogue even though they deigned to appear only on those occasions when it suited them to be in town. Imposing the fee did not seem to have ameliorated the underlying problem, however; in 1757, the *Mahamad* heard "undoubted Testimony That severall of our Brethren . . . in the Country have and do dayly violate the principles of our holy religion, such as Trading on the Sabbath, Eating of forbidden Meats & other Henious Crimes. . . ." Pool reads these resolutions as evidence that during the eighteenth century Shearith Israel was "the sole center of every aspect of Jewish life in New York, . . . a powerful force in drawing to and . . . holding individuals within the Jewish community."[55] Yet, I think another reading of the same evidence gives us a very different picture: that is to say, rather than regarding the synagogue as the core of their social and religious existence, many Jews by the middle decades of the eighteenth century found it possible, and even desirable, to build their lives according to other criteria. The fact that Shearith Israel had to pass resolution after resolution—each more stringent than the one before—in its attempts to draw outliers back into the fold suggests that the synagogue did not have as much power over the lives of individual Jews as both the *Mahamad* thought it should and the proponents of the synagogue-community model would like us to believe. Even during the eighteenth century, it was possible for Jews to fall away from ritual diligence and yet still maintain some tie to the fold.

Approaching a New Definition of "Community"

With these critiques of the synagogue-community model in mind, let me now suggest some possible ways in which we might reenvision Jewish communal life in early America.

First, we might think of the Jewish community as a series of concentric circles, with the synagogue at the center. The pillars of this expanding community were the successful merchants whose profits funded its activities. These men constituted the *Yechidim* (Elders) who controlled synagogue governance through the *Mahamad* and became the public face of the Jewish community. At the core of the synagogue-community were the learned men engaged to perform ritual tasks within the synagogue: the *hazan*, the *shamas*, the *shochet* and *bodek*, the religious teachers and *mohels*. Beyond these inner circles were women—wives and mothers, widows and spinsters, prohibited by Jewish tradition from playing a full role in the rituals of the synagogue but nevertheless key to Jewish life as the keepers of the important domestic rituals, which were largely responsible for the continuity of Judaism within the home and thus in its transmission from one generation to the next.[56] At the outer margins were the transients, usually merchants, sometimes impoverished, who sojourned in the community for a time but never established a permanent presence; at outermost periphery were those Jews who married Christians or converted to Christianity, who maintained tenuous connections to their observing Jewish brethren and were (upon occasion) buried in the consecrated ground of the *bet haim*. This conception is appealing in two important ways. First, for those wedded to the synagogue-community paradigm, the concentric community paradigm continues to use the synagogue as a key to understanding Jewish communal life, incorporating its significance to Jewish ritual. In this, it echoes the way that New England Puritans described their ideal townscape—a nucleated community with the meetinghouse at its core and the wilderness at its periphery, where the rings represented decreasing degrees of social importance as you moved outward from the center.[57] At the same time, the concentric community paradigm brings into the description of the Jewish community those outside the margins, those who were ineligible or incapable of becoming *Yechidim* in the synagogue yet who continued in other ways to live as Jews—women, the poor, proselytes to Judaism, and those who lived outwardly as Christians (including both Portuguese *Conversos* who continued the practice of the double life and open apostates from Judaism whose sympathies for their former brethren did not entirely evaporate with conversion).

A second possibility, although this requires something of a creative leap, would be to envision the Jewish community as existing without regard to geographical specificity, across the vastness of space, perhaps even extending into infinity, without limitation. The point here is to imagine how a community might exist beyond a particular pair of geographic coordinates, and to extend the concept of community across space and time as a virtual reality. This portable community paradigm, as postmodern as it sounds, would nevertheless allow us to capture a critical element of the Jewish experience in diaspora. Rather than describing Jewish communities as individual islands surrounded by a vast nothingness, it would permit us to document the threads that connected individuals such as Abraham Sarzedas or Moses Israel Pacheco to many communities, and the Jews of one geographical place to other sets of Jews in far distant places. In the context of early America, it would allow us to comprehend the often close connections that bound Jewish Savannah to Jewish Charleston, Newport to New York, Lancaster to Philadelphia, Quebec to Montreal, and Montreal to New York. It also suggests a way of approaching the initial oscillations that each of the early Jewish communities experienced before it took root and became permanent.

Third, we might imagine the Jewish community as plastic rather than encapsulated—that is, as a living, breathing organism within a larger ecosystem, one that has a symbiotic relationship with the other living beings within that system. This approach, which we might call the contingency paradigm, would allow us to examine and describe the dynamism of Jewish interaction with the Anglo-Christian world that was British America. It would enable us to ask new questions: Where and how does the Jewish community restrict itself to "tradition"; when and how does it acculturate? What ideas are embraced, and which ones are rejected? It suggests a means of examining how Jewish communities changed over time. It would also give us a forum for examining the paradoxes of ethnic and class issues, which often pushed Jews to align themselves with Christians rather than with other Jews: how the out-marriage of Phila Franks to the Huguenot Oliver Delancey, scandalous as it seemed to her mother, was closely tied to the ongoing activities and aspirations of the Franks family in elite New York social circles; how the Ashkenazi Benjamin Sheftall came to ask a Salzburger Lutheran minister for help in getting the English authorities to allow Savannah's German Jews to build a synagogue, over the objections of their Portuguese coreligionists; how Judah Monis and Joseph Ottolenghe came to eschew Judaism in pursuit of greater opportunities in a Christian world, even though they would never stop being "Jews" in the eyes of their Christian neighbors.

Fourth, we might think of early American Judaism as a set of parallel systems. The efficacy of domestic Judaism—that is to say, Judaism as practiced in the home—has long been ignored by scholars. Yet we are well aware that the Jewish population of early America was largely composed of Sephardim—that is to say, former *Conversos* raised in an atmosphere where synagogue attendance was impossible and home-based rituals were the only means for both Jewish observance and the transfer of Jewish knowledge. In an age when such families inhabited colonial towns without a physical synagogue, and at times when there was no minyan, how else could Judaism be practiced? In fact, it was the homebound Jewish practices, for many of which women were largely responsible, rather than synagogue attendance that maintained Judaism and promoted its transmission to the next generation in early America.[58] By giving serious examination to the homebound practices of familial Judaism, we may arrive at a clearer understanding of how Jews continued to live Jewish lives in places where they were isolated from a community of other Jews and thus could not participate in public ritual practice. Chava Weissler, for example, has identified a *tkhine* (prayer) in which the woman supplicant compares her position in the home to that of the high priest in the Temple of Jerusalem.[59] We might broaden that notion to encompass several sets of parallel systems—male and female, observant and nonobservant, poor and wealthy, home and synagogue. The parallel-systems paradigm thus would not dismiss the role of the synagogue or downplay the importance of its all-male membership; but would, nonetheless, create a new historiographical structure that embraces the separate role of women and children, the disabled and housebound, the poor, and the religiously marginal in ways that the synagogue-centered focus has long neglected.

Conclusion

In 1983, Benedict Anderson argued that nationalism is an inherently subjective conception, relying on common beliefs and qualities of community and sovereignty that are virtual rather than actual—that is to say, imaginary rather than tangible, or abstract rather than concrete. Although Anderson was concerned with the impact of nationalism during the twentieth century, his conception of an "imagined community" applies equally well as a way of looking at the Jewish experience in the early modern era—at a time when "the Jewish Nation" was the term frequently used, both by non-Jews and by Jews themselves, to mark Jewish self-governance as well as Jewish social and religious separation from the Christians among whom they resided.[60] Unfortunately, in the "synagogue community" paradigm, Grinstein, Davis, and other historians have themselves imagined a cohesiveness and a fixity within the Jewish communities of early America that never existed. In conflating the synagogue with the Jewish community, historians have created a static system, elided many points of conflict and fracture, and discarded much historical evidence that has not fit into the "synagogue = community" framework.

Jonathan Sarna recently remarked that a striking historical theme in American Judaism arises from the creative adaptations that Jews and their communities have repeatedly made in order to preserve Judaism in the American environment.

> Reshaping Judaism in response to challenges from within and without, they have time and again revitalized their faith, strengthening it, sometimes in surprising and unexpected ways that have brought Jews back into synagogues and produced children more religiously knowledgeable and observant than their parents.[61]

By stretching our historiographical reach beyond the notion that communal life was geographically fixed by the location of a synagogue, by considering the establishment of early Jewish communities in North America from the perspective of individual participants, their goals and expectations for Jewish communal life, we allow ourselves to recapture some of the dynamism Sarna finds in American Judaism. Along with a better understanding of the roots of American Judaism, we may also discover surprising new details about the Jewish congregations that gave it its first breath of life.

Acknowledgment

My thanks to Jonathan Sarna, Joyce Antler, Riv-Ellen Prell, Hasia Diner, and Jeff Gurock for helpful comments on an earlier draft of this work.

Notes

1. This interpretation was first suggested by Arnold Wiznitzer in 1954 and subsequently repeated by Jacob Rader Marcus. See Arnold Wiznitzer, "The Exodus from Brazil and Arrival in New Amsterdam of the Jewish Pilgrim Fathers," *American Jewish Historical Quarterly*, vol. 44, no. 1 (September 1954), pp. 92–94; Jacob Rader Marcus, *The Colonial American Jew* (Detroit: Wayne State University Press, 1970), vol. 1, p. 210. Wiznitzer based his figures on extrapolation from the extant records of New Amsterdam. Presuming that the number given for the Jews who arrived on the *Sainte Catherine* (that is, 23) comprised all of the Jews and not just heads of household, and finding only 4 adult Jewish males and 2 adult Jewish females listed in the records, Wiznitzer concluded that these were the only heads of household among the group and that the remaining 17 Jews from the group of 23 must have comprised the wives of the 4 adult Jewish males and 13 "younger people." (The gloss that the 13 "younger people" were children was added by Marcus.)

   I would note that this claim for the demographic structure of the Jewish group in New Netherland does not allow for adult men who were single or widowed, heads of household who did not seek to prosecute claims before the Burgomaster and Schepens, or those who were seen by the record keepers as simply too insignificant to be deemed worthy of recording by name. There is, in fact, no census of the Jews of New Amsterdam in 1654, or at any point during Dutch rule of the colony.

2. Leo Hershkowitz, "New Amsterdam's Twenty-Three Jews—Myth or Reality?" in Shalom Goldman (ed.), *Hebrew and the Bible in America: The First Two Centuries* (Hanover, New Hampshire: Brandeis University Press, 1993), pp. 171–183; Jonathan D. Sarna, *American Judaism: A History* (New Haven: Yale University Press, 2004), pp. 10–11.

3. Leo Hershkowitz, "The Mill Street Synagogue Reconsidered," *American Jewish Historical Quarterly*, vol. 53, no. 4 (June 1964), pp. 404–410.

4. Hyman B. Grinstein, "Communal and Social Aspects of American Jewish History," *American Jewish Historical Quarterly*, vol. 39, no. 3 (March 1950), pp. 270–271.

5. Hyman B. Grinstein, *The Rise of the Jewish Community of New York, 1654–1860* (Philadelphia: Jewish Publication Society of America, 1945, 1947), p. 35.

6. Grinstein, "Communal and Social Aspects," pp. 271–273.

7. Jonathan D. Sarna, "Introduction," in Alexandra Shecket Korros, and Jonathan D. Sarna, *American Synagogue History: A Bibliography and State-of-the-Field Survey* (New York: Marcus Wiener Publishing, 1988), p. 1.

8. Moshe Davis, "The Synagogue in American Judaism: A Study of Congregation B'nai Jeshurun, New York City," in Harry Schneiderman (ed.), *Two Generations in Perspective: Notable Events and Trends, 1896–1956* (New York: Monde Publishers, 1956), pp. 210–213.

9. How do we know this, if, as I have stated, Marcus never used the term? A quick glance at the index to volume 2 of his *Early American Jewry*, published by JPS in 1953, indicates the following *"see, also"* references under the heading "synagogue": "Community, Jewish, Creation of the; Congregations; Religio-communal organization." It is notable that no such cross-references appeared under the same heading in the index to volume 1, published just two years earlier.

10. See Grinstein, *Rise of the Jewish Community of New York*, p. vii.

11. Salo W. Baron, *The Jewish Community: Its History and Structure to the American Revolution* (Philadelphia: Jewish Publication Society of America, 1942), vol. 1, pp. 208–209, 238. Among these forces, as outlined by Baron, were the Catholic Church, the evolving marketplace, and the absolutist state. On Jewish communal life in England, see David S. Katz, *The Jews in the History of England, 1485–1850* (Oxford, England: Clarendon Press, 1996), pp. 107–239; on British America, see, generally, Holly Snyder, "A Sense of Place: Jews, Identity and Social Status in Colonial British America, 1654–1831" (Waltham, Massachusetts: Brandeis University doctoral dissertation, 2000).

12. Salo W. Baron, *Steeled by Adversity: Essays and Addresses on American Jewish Life* (Philadelphia: Jewish Publication Society of America, 1971), pp. 128–129.

13. Edwin Wolf 2d and Maxwell Whiteman, *The History of the Jews of Philadelphia from Colonial Times to the Age of Jackson* (Philadelphia: Jewish Publication Society of America, 1957), p. 225. It should be noted that Kingston, Jamaica, had already experienced such a communal fracture in 1788, when a congregation of Ashkenazim broke away from the Sephardi Cong. *Shangare Shamayim* to form their own congregation; Ashkenazim in Spanish Town followed a decade later and formed Cong. Mickve Israel. See Will of Moses Adolphus the Younger, December 25, 1795 (proved April 16, 1798), Liber of Wills 64, folio 56, Island Record Office, Spanish Town, Jamaica; typescript in Collections of the American Jewish Archives, Cincinnati. It has also been reported that KK Beth Elohim in Charleston experienced such a split between Sephardim and Ashkenazim, albeit temporarily, prior to 1791. Solomon Breitbart, "Two Jewish Congregations in Charleston, S.C. before 1791: A New Conclusion," *American Jewish History*, vol. 69, no. 3 (March 1980), pp. 360–363. By contrast, New York would not have its second congregation until Congregation B'nai Jeshurun split from Shearith Israel in 1825.

14. Benedict Anderson, *Imagined Communities: Reflections on the Origin and Spread of Nationalism*, revised and expanded edition (London and New York: Verso, 1991), pp. 5–7.

15. *Publications of the American Jewish Historical Society*, vol. 21 (1913) (hereinafter, *Lyons Collection I*).

16. The earliest records for KK Beth Elohim (Charleston) apparently burned in the fire of 1838 that destroyed Beth Elohim's 1792 structure. A few letters and scattered accounts survive for the early years of Newport's Jeshuat Israel, but nothing

more. Surviving documentation on these synagogues, along with KK Mikve Israel of Savannah, Philadelphia's Mikve Israel, and Richmond's Beth Shalome, is strongest for the period after 1780. See, e.g., Jacob Rader Marcus, *American Jewry—Documents—Eighteenth Century* (Cincinnati: Hebrew Union College, 1959).

17. Ira Rosenswaike, "An Estimate and Analysis of the Jewish Population in the United States in 1790," *American Jewish Historical Quarterly*, vol. 50, no. 1 (September 1960), pp. 23–24; see, also, Malcolm H. Stern, "Some Additions and Corrections to Rosenswaike's 'An Estimate and Analysis of the Jewish Population in the United States in 1790,' " *American Jewish Historical Quarterly*, vol. 53, no. 3 (March 1964), p. 285, and Ira Rosenswaike, "Comments on Dr. Stern's Additions and Corrections," *American Jewish Historical Quarterly*, vol. 53, no. 3 (March 1964), pp. 289–290.

18. See Ira Rosenswaike, "The Jewish Population of the United States as Estimated from the Census of 1820," *American Jewish Historical Quarterly*, vol. 53, no. 2 (December 1963), pp. 131–132, especially note 3.

19. Rosenswaike, "The Jewish Population as Estimated from the Census of 1820," pp. 147–148. Rosenswaike's figures show a Jewish population of approximately 2,700 out of a total U.S. population of 9,638,000 of which approximately 8,100,000 were white—revealing that Jews constituted far less than 1% of the population in 1820, regardless of whether slaves are included in the population total.

20. See Malcolm H. Stern, "The Sheftall Diaries: Vital Records of Savannah Jewry, 1733–1808," *American Jewish Historical Quarterly*, vol. 54, no. 3 (1965), pp. 246–248, showing that the group of forty-odd Jews who arrived in July 1733 brought with them a Torah and circumcision box "for the use of the congregation that they intended to establish," that they subsequently formed a congregation in July 1735, and that they received from London a second Torah, a Hanukilla, and a number of books "for use of the Congregation" in July 1737.

21. Holly Snyder, "A Tree with Two Different Fruits: The Jewish Encounter with German Pietists in the Eighteenth Century Atlantic World," *William & Mary Quarterly*, vol. 58, no. 4 (October 2001), pp. 864–865, especially note 34; Stern, "The Sheftall Diaries," pp. 250–251; see, also, Saul Jacob Rubin, *Third to None: The Saga of Savannah Jewry, 1733–1983* (Savannah, Georgia: Congregation Mikve Israel, 1983); James W. Hagy, *This Happy Land: The Jews of Colonial and Antebellum Charleston* (Tuscaloosa: University of Alabama Press, 1993).

22. Wolf and Whiteman, *History of the Jews of Philadelphia*, pp. 49–50, 66.

23. See, e.g., Dirk Hoerder, *Cultures in Contact: World Migrations in the Second Millenium* (Durham, North Carolina: Duke University Press, 2002), especially part 2, pp. 135–273; Bernard Bailyn, *Voyagers to the West: A Passage in the Peopling of America on the Eve of the Revolution* (New York: Vintage Books, 1988), pp. 89–103; Aaron Fogelman, "Migrations to the Thirteen British North American Colonies, 1700–1775: New Estimates," *Journal of Interdisciplinary History*, vol. 22, no. 4 (Spring 1992), pp. 691–709; Aaron Spencer Fogelman, *Hopeful Journeys: German Immigration, Settlement and Political Culture in Colonial America, 1717–1775* (Philadelphia: University of Pennsylvania Press, 1996); Alison F. Games, *Migration and the Origins of the English Atlantic World* (Cambridge, Massachusetts: Harvard University Press, 1999).

24. David T. Morgan, "Judaism in Eighteenth-Century Georgia," *Georgia Historical Quarterly*, vol. 58, no. 1 (1974), pp. 45–46.

25. Minute book of Congregation Shearith Israel, *Lyons Collection I*, pp. 13, 26, 45, 46, 47, 64, 108–109.

26. Morgan, "Judaism in Eighteenth-Century Georgia," p. 45; Stern, "The Sheftall Diaries," p. 250; Frank Zimmerman, "A Letter and Memorandum on Ritual Circumcision, 1772," *American Jewish Historical Quarterly*, vol. 44, no. 1 (Sept. 1954), pp. 58–63.

27. Samuel Oppenheim, "The Jews and Masonry in the United States before 1810," *Publications of the American Jewish Historical Society*, vol. 27 (1920) (hereinafter Lyons Collection II), p. 175; Wilfred Samuel, R. D. Barnett, and A. S. Diamond, "A List of Persons Endenizened and Naturalised 1609–1799," *Miscellanies of the Jewish Historical Society of England*, part 7 (1970), p. 114; Rhode Island General Court of Trials, Book A, folio 97, Collections of the Rhode Island Supreme Court Judicial Records Center, published as Jane Fletcher Fiske, *Rhode Island General Court of Trials, 1671–1704* (Boxford, Massachusetts: 1998), p. 152; The Lyons Collection II, *Publications of the American Jewish Historical Society*, vol. 27 (1920), p. 175 (facsimile of the deed to the cemetery), 413; Wilfred Samuel, "A Review of the Jewish Colonists in Barbados in the Year 1680," *Transactions of the Jewish Historical Society of England*, vol. 13 (1933–1935), pp. 26, 95. Pacheco was not one of the named defendants in the 1684–1685 case against "Alien" Jews. See Fiske, *Rhode Island General Court of Trials*, p. 132. However, extant documents do not reveal whether he was excluded from the case because he held endenization papers or because he was no longer in Newport.

28. "A List of persons that have intitled themselves to the benefit of the Act (13th Geo. 2d) intituled 'An Act for naturalizing such foreign Protestants and others therein mentioned as are settled or that shall settle in any of His Majesty's Colonies in America,'" Manuscripts Division, Library of Congress (Mss. copy of original found in Plantations General, C.O. 324/55–56, Public Record Office of Great Britain).

29. Abraham married Katey Hays in 1753. See Will of Judah Hayes, 1764, in Leo Hershkowitz (ed.), *Wills of Early New York Jews (1704–1799)*, Studies in American Jewish History no. 4 (New York: American Jewish Historical Society, 1967), pp. 120–121.

30. In 1766, Sarzedas made two trips to Savannah, Georgia, as master of the sloop *Brotherly Love*, owned by two Jamaican Jews. The first journey was from St. Martin, while the second was from St. Croix. C.O. 5/710, ff. 21, 34, 32, Collections of the Public Record Office of Great Britain.

31. On July 26, 1764, Sarzedas advertised for sale quantities of various provisions from Madeira, the Azores, Martinique and other Caribbean islands, England, New York, and New England from his store on Thomas Lloyd's wharf in Savannah, "where he gives due attendance from eight in the morning until twelve at noon, and from two in the afternoon till six in the evening." *Georgia Gazette*, July 26, 1764. By October, Sarzedas had removed to a house opposite Abigail Minis's tavern, from which he continued to offer provisions "as formerly advertised." *Georgia Gazette*, October 4, 1764.

32. On September 30, 1757, Sarzedas was granted Lot no. 87 in the town of Hard-wicke, and he recorded the deed on November 9 the same year. See *Colonial Records of the State of Georgia*, vol. 28, part 1, Kenneth Coleman and Milton Ready (eds.), *Original Papers of Governors Reynolds, Ellis, Wright, and Others, 1757–1763* (Athens: University of Georgia at Athens, for the Georgia Commission for the National Bicentennial Celebration, 1976), p. 114, reproduced from C.O. 5/646, C40 (Abstract of Grants from July 27, 1757, to January 27, 1758), in the Collection of the Public Record Office of Great Britain.

33. For example, the Rhode Island colony census of 1774 shows Catherine Sarzedas as the head of a household consisting of four children (two sons and two daughters) under sixteen, herself, and four adult household servants (one black man and three black women). See John Russell Bartlett (arr.), "Census of the Inhabitants of the Colony of Rhode Island and Providence Plantations in New England, 1774" (Providence: Unpublished ms., 1858), p. 27, located at the Rhode Island State Archives.

34. Malcolm H. Stern, *First American Jewish Families: 600 Genealogies, 1654–1977*, third revised ed. (Baltimore: Genealogical Publications, 1978), p. 262.

35. Stern, *First American Jewish Families*, p. 85; I. S. Emmanuel, "Notes on the Jews of North America as Found in Divers Manuscripts and Archives in Holland and in Curaçao," typescript, Collection of the American Jewish Archives.

36. Gerald Gamm, *Urban Exodus: Why the Jews Left Boston and the Catholics Stayed* (Cambridge, Massachusetts: Harvard University Press, 1999), pp. 17–21.

37. Grinstein, *Rise of the Jewish Community of New York*, p. 35.

38. Charlotte Baum, Paula Hyman, and Sonya Michel, *The Jewish Woman in America* (New York: Dial Press, 1976).

39. Karla Goldman, *Beyond the Synagogue Gallery: Finding a Place for Women in American Judaism* (Cambridge, Massachusetts: Harvard University Press, 2000), pp. 51–58.

40. Dianne Ashton, *Rebecca Gratz: Women and Judaism in Antebellum America* (Detroit: Wayne State University Press, 1997).

41. Emily Bingham, *Mordecai: An Early American Family* (New York: Hill and Wang, 2003); Emily Bingham, "Mordecai: Three Generations of a Southern Jewish Family, 1780–1865" (Chapel Hill: University of North Carolina doctoral dissertation, 1998); Emily Bingham and Penny Richards, "The Female Academy and Beyond: Three Mordecai Sisters at Work in the Old South," in Susanna Delfino and Michele Gillespie (eds.), *Neither Lady Nor Slave: Working Women of the Old South* (Chapel Hill: University of North Carolina Press, 2002), pp. 174–197.

42. Abigail Levy Franks to Naphtali Franks, October 17, 1739, in Leo Hershkowitz and Isidore S. Meyer (eds.), *Letters of the Franks Family (1733–1748): The Lee Max Freedman Collection of American Jewish Colonial Correspondence*, Studies in American Jewish History no. 5 (Waltham, Massachusetts: American Jewish Historical Society, 1968), p. 66. A new rendering of the letters, edited by Edie Gelles, emphasizes Franks' religious thought. See Edith B. Gelles (ed.), *The Letters of Abigaill Levy Franks, 1733–1748* (New Haven: Yale University Press, 2004).

43. Snyder, *A Sense of Place*, p. 221, note 32.

44. *Lyons Collection II*, pp. 201, 350.
45. *Lyons Collection I*, p. 91.
46. Stern, "The Sheftall Diaries," pp. 251, 255, 265, 268–269.
47. Gamm, *Urban Exodus*, pp. 1–8, 286–287.
48. Lucien Wolf, "The First English Jew: Notes on Antonio Fernandes Carvajal with Some Biographical Documents," *Transactions of the Jewish Historical Society of England*, vol. 2 (1894–1895), pp. 15–28; Wilfred S. Samuel, *The First London Synagogue of the Resettlement* (London: Spottiswoode, Ballantyne & Co., 1924); A. S. Diamond, "The Cemetery of the Resettlement," *Transactions of the Jewish Historical Society of England*, vol. 19 (1955–1959), pp. 163–170.
49. Lucien Wolf, "The Jewry of the Restoration, 1660–1664," *Transactions of the Jewish Historical Society of England*, vol. 5 (1902–1905), pp. 6–10. Wolf refers to this second minyan as a "synagogue," but it did not build a permanent structure, and there is no evidence that it represented a permanent religious society like Sha'ar HaShamayim. For a full discussion of the question of small, informal minyanim in seventeenth century London, see Wilfred S. Samuel, "The Jewish Oratories of Cromwellian London," *Miscellanies of the Jewish Historical Society of England*, part 3 (1937), pp. 46–56.
50. In his recent book on the development of American Judaism, Jonathan Sarna claims that private worship in the seventeenth century became a simultaneous means for Dutch and English authorities in New York to control Jewish behavior in public space and for Jews to avoid provoking their neighbors. Sarna, *American Judaism*, pp. 3, 11. While this may well have been true on one level, such an interpretation removes the Jewish experience from the general context of religious intolerance in the wake of the Protestant Reformation. In fact, dissenting Christian sects faced adverse and even dire conditions in their long struggle to obtain the right to public worship. In both Dutch New Amsterdam and English New England, sects perceived to threaten the social order of the colony's officially established denomination (Puritans in New England and Dutch Reformed in New Amsterdam) were not only prohibited from public worship, but also threatened, exiled, jailed, tried, beaten, and publicly executed for attempting to worship according to their beliefs in private as well as public space. By contrast, no Jews suffered such persecution for seeking to worship as Jews in early America. See, e.g., James Homer Williams, "An Atlantic Perspective on the Jewish Struggle for Rights and Opportunities in Brazil, New Netherland, and New York," in Paolo Bernardini and Norman Fiering (eds.), *The Jews and the Expansion of Europe to the West, 1450–1800* (New York: Berghahn Books. 2001), pp. 369–388; Carla Gardina Pestana, *Quakers and Baptists in Colonial Massachusetts* (Cambridge, England: Cambridge University Press, 1991); Carla Gardina Pestana, "Martyred by the Saints: Quaker Executions in Seventeenth-Century Massachusetts," in Allan Greer and Jodi Bilinkoff (eds.), *Colonial Saints: Discovering the Holy in the Americas, 1500–1800* (New York: Routledge, 2003), pp. 169–192.
51. Barnett A. Elzas, *The Jews of South Carolina, from the Earliest Times to the Present Day* (Philadelphia: Press of J. B. Lippincott Company, 1905), pp. 32–37, 120–122, 209; Hagy, *This Happy Land*, pp. 73–78, 238–241; Breitbart, "Two Jewish Congregations in Charleston, S.C. before 1791," pp. 360–363.

52. Wolf and Whiteman, *History of the Jews of Philadelphia*, pp. 32, 114–118; Sheldon J. Godfrey, and Judith C. Godfrey, *Search Out the Land: The Jews and the Growth of Equality in British Colonial America, 1740–1867* (Montreal & Kingston: McGill-Queens University Press, 1995), pp. 113–114.

53. Myron Berman, *Richmond's Jewry, 1769–1976* (Charlottesville: University Press of Virginia, for the Jewish Community Federation of Richmond, 1979), pp. 43–44.

54. Goldman, *Beyond the Synagogue Gallery*, pp. 51–59; see, also, Holly Snyder, "Queens of the Household: The Jewish Women of British America, 1700–1800," in Jonathan D. Sarna and Pamela S. Nadell (eds.), *Women and American Judaism: Historical Perspectives* (Hanover, New Hampshire: Brandeis University Press, 2001), pp. 16–17.

55. David de Sola Pool and Tamar de Sola Pool, *An Old Faith in the New World: Portrait of Shearith Israel, 1654–1954* (New York: Columbia University Press, 1955), pp. 235–238.

56. See Chava Weissler, *Voices of the Matriarchs: Listening to the Prayers of Early Modern Jewish Women* (Boston, Massachusetts: Beacon Press, 1998), pp. 3–85.

57. John R. Stilgoe, "The Puritan Townscape: Ideal and Reality," *Landscape*, vol. 20 (1976), pp. 16–20.

58. See, e.g., Renee Levine Melamed, *Heretics or Daughters of Israel: The Crypto-Jewish Women of Castile* (Oxford, England: Oxford University Press, 1999), pp. 73–93.

59. Chava Weissler, "Woman as High Priest: A Kabbalistic Prayer in Yiddish for Lighting Candles," *Jewish History*, vol. 5, no. 1 (1991).

60. On this point, see Yosef Haim Yerushalmi, *From Spanish Court to Italian Ghetto: Isaac Cardoso, a Study in Seventeenth-Century Marranism and Jewish Apologetics* (New York: Columbia University Press, 1971), pp. 16–21; Snyder, "A Sense of Place," pp. 98–140.

61. Jonathan D. Sarna, *American Judaism in Historical Perspective*, David W. Belin Lecture in American Jewish Affairs no. 10 (Ann Arbor: Frankel Center for Judaic Studies, University of Michigan, 2003), p. 5.

Buying and Selling "Jewish"

The Historical Impact of Commerce

on Jewish Communal Life

The history of an entity called the "Jewish community," as it existed in America and as it functioned nearly everyplace else, cannot be imagined without considering commerce and consumption. While Jewish communities served historically as places where Jews worshipped together, organized to provide charity, protected each other, and fulfilled basic religiously shaped needs—marriage, burial, circumcision, education, and the like—they also derived much from the fact that they existed as places where Jews bought from other Jews and where Jews sold to their coreligionists. Indeed, once we factor into our understanding of Jewish community life the constant flurry of buying and selling that took place on "the Jewish street" and we consider such activities analytically important, we discern no clear line between the more conventional religious, social, and political definitions of "Jewish community" and the flow of goods among Jews. Rather the commercial transactions, the "buzz" of the Jewish marketplace, made the other, presumably loftier functions possible, at the same time that stores and other kinds of commercial places often did double duty as either formal or informal community centers.

It might not be too great a leap to contend that wherever and whenever Jews coalesced to form communities, they bought and sold to and from each other and made the exchange of goods for money a key form of in-group interaction. What differed from place to place and across time reflected changing Jewish residential patterns, differentials in the size of Jewish communities, technological developments that affected how goods got bought and sold, and the degree to which the state regulated economic activities. But regardless of the historic moment, commerce and consumption helped make community and provided physical locations for the kinds of interactions among people that fostered connectedness.

The twinned processes—buying and selling—lay at the heart of Jewish life inasmuch as Jewish enclaves thrived upon the commercial relationships that brought Jews into constant contact with each other, whereby the marketplace took its basic characteristic from the flow of the Jewish calendar, and according to which Jewish neighborhoods functioned with a tempo set by Jewish merchants who provided goods to Jewish customers, who simultaneously demanded that Jewish entrepreneurs satisfy their yearnings for particular goods, at specified times, and in particular ways. Both consumer and entrepreneur depended upon each other, and they in turn, because of the web of reciprocal relationships that bound them together, created a system that wound nearly all elements of the Jewish place together. While conflict also characterized intra-Jewish commercial transactions, the degree to which Jews depended upon each other for basic (and special) goods invested the entrepreneurial sector with meaning and made it a vehicle for creating and sustaining community.

Whether the commercial transactions functioned smoothly and harmoniously or conflict arose as the two groups sparred with each other vis-à-vis disputes over cost versus quality, their continuous interactions with each other brought each into the other's orbit and as such forged intimate connections that provided the bedrock of community life. Whole histories of Jewish communities could in fact be told from the vantage point of the mundane reality that wherever Jews lived they sold and bought amongst themselves and that the shopping street, no less than the synagogue, the study house, the ritual bath, or the community center, forged the bonds upon which most definitions of community depend.

The sellers and the buyers each played crucial roles in the chain of relationships that made community possible. Those who hoped to make a profit—obviously the merchants—and those who yearned to purchase desired items of the highest quality for the lowest price—the consumers—probably had in mind merely their own instrumental and petty goals when facing each other. Doubtless neither party to the transaction thought "community" when each saw the other across the counters of thousands upon thousands of Jewish-owned shops, nor did they consciously ponder the fact that by purchasing or selling a loaf of bread, a pad of paper, or a pair of socks they were helping sustain the collective life of the Jewish people and that their behaviors constituted historically significant actions. They probably had no reason to see beyond the shelves and the cash registers in the stores and the larders and cabinets of their homes.

But we as scholars should devote some attention to the ways in which the complicated processes involved in the purveying and purchasing of goods within Jewish communities can and ought to be historicized, divided into categories of analysis, and always linked to our imaginings of community. We should not confuse the ordinariness of selling and shopping with historic irrelevance nor should we see such activities as unchanging and without deep social, cultural, and political meanings.[1]

This assertion, that the cultures of communities were reflected in their retail infrastructures and that the shops and stores of any community served larger communal purposes, obviously transcends the history of the Jewish people, in America or anywhere. As one historian of shopping as a factor in English social history noted, "Wherever we live, whoever we are, our shopping is very much a reflection of ourselves."[2] Most of the literature, however, has tended to emphasize the goods up for sale, patterns of consumption, and changing tastes.[3] Few, whether focusing on the United States or elsewhere, and whether historically based or concerned with the contemporary, have brought together the idea of community with that of commerce. Yet shopping streets, wherever and whenever they developed, functioned as common space, places where individuals met, interacted, saw what they shared with each other, and in the process of buying and selling, carved out a zone for public life.

Therefore, how and where Jews bought goods, how they used commercial spaces for communal purposes, and what kinds of relationships existed between merchants and customers ought to be part of our scholarly projects. Opening up the category of community to the ubiquitous issue of buying and selling broadens the analytic framework in general and also makes relatively ordinary Jewish people—women as shoppers and sellers, in particular—key players in the creation of community.

In the context of American history we have examples from a number of subfields as to the importance of retail space in the forging of community ties. Studies of small-town life, both the empirical and the nostalgic, have made much about the country store as a gathering place that bound people together. Lewis Atherton in his 1954 homage to the dying small towns of the Midwest, the "middle border," offered an entire chapter to the shopping areas of the towns, which primarily served farm families. In particular, he pointed to the classic general store, a place where men and women congregated in different areas and where "close to the stove and the conversation" the shopkeeper tallied his ledger and supervised the flow of the shopping. Atherton's *Main Street on the Middle Border* also made emotionally and historically significant the barbershops, hotels, saloons, and livery stables that lined the village thoroughfares and where men and women met, bought, sold, and made community.[4] The Reifel store in Four Corners, Iowa, a town recently analyzed by historian Carol Coburn, provided the men of this rural, heavily German community with "a gathering place at night . . . where they gathered to exchange the latest news." The store emerged in this study as the least problematic common denominator for the men, who in aspects of their community life struggled with each other over matters of politics, religious doctrine, and the lure of American culture.[5]

The histories of all minority communities, like the German enclave of Four Corners, could be told from the vantage point of the ethnic marketplace and the multiple functions served by the buying and selling of goods within the community. No immigrant/ethnic community existed without its own commercial infrastructure, in which group members shopped in stores owned by coethnics and in particular imagined those shops to be key places to fulfill group needs. John Bodnar has elevated ethnic merchants in *The Transplanted* to their rightful place as community leaders, noting in this broad, synthetic book that, "in every settlement a group emerged to pursue entrepreneurial ventures which depended upon the support of the immigrant community." He offered bits and pieces of evidence drawn from numerous histories of various groups that demonstrated how ethnic neighborhood businesses served "neighborhood clienteles," although he did not go much further than that in analyzing the role played by those stores in enabling communities to form.[6]

The historical scholarship on nearly every ethnic group has been replete with listings and descriptions of food establishments, bookstores, music stores, taverns, and clothing stores, which through commerce made it possible to "be" a participant in the ethnic project. The more sophisticated of these studies put such ethnic businesses as record shops and clothing stores squarely into the analytic framework. George Sanchez's *Becoming Mexican American*, for example, showed how merchants and consumers mediated between "old world" formats and American realities and how the stores functioned as meeting places for Mexicans in Los Angeles, thereby creating sites for growing community. In Sanchez's Boyle Heights record shops, merchants arbitrated between the many musical formats derived from various regions in Mexico and between music defined as Mexican versus American, while the music emanating from the shops drew customers in, put them in conversation with the merchants and each other, and solidified notions of Mexicanness and community membership.[7] Lizabeth Cohen's *Making of a New Deal* charted the close relationships that existed in Chicago's immigrant neighborhoods between shopkeepers and customers, coethnics. The former (grocers, for example) not only provided needed goods to the latter but also, by offering credit to struggling families, became brokers in the political and economic life of the communities.[8]

Notably, though, few historians studying any ethnic community in the United States have done more than mention in passing the vast amount of commerce that linked merchants and customers of the various enclaves. Histories of one group or another contain what might be seen as an obligatory paragraph or two on the range of stores that community members favored and sustained, drawing attention to which goods shoppers preferred. The historians have, by and large, not paused longer to actually study the phenomenon directly, systematically, or thoroughly.

Rather, political scientists and sociologists studying the post-1965 immigration have drawn our attention to the analytic gravitas of entrepreneurship (and consumership) in the construction of ethnic communities. Ivan Light and Edna Bonacich, for example, in their study of Korean immigrant entrepreneurs in Los Angeles have provided a theoretical model that identifies an entity they call "the ethnic economy," which, unlike the "ethnic enclave economy," does not require "locational clustering of ethnic firms, nor does it require that ethnic firms service members of their ethnic group as customers or buy from coethnic suppliers."[9] Like sociologist Alejandro Portes in his numerous studies of the Cuban enclave economy of Miami, Light and Bonacich invested analytic significance in the social, economic, and political implications of the clustering of Korean-owned businesses located in the heart of Los Angeles' "Korean Town," and the almost inexorable draw of those stores for the residents of the neighborhood.

Historians of ethnic communities in the United States might indeed learn much from the work of the social scientists who focus now on the contemporary processes of immigration and ethnicization. The latter observe these developments as they unfold and see how crucial a role the ethnic markets play in the streets of America's new immigrant neighborhoods. Those of us who concern ourselves with the past, scholars of American Jewish history included, ought to attempt to replicate their work but in a historical perspective, by asking how commerce and consumption made community and how the hum of the marketplace provided more than just background music to the realities of membership in the enclave. We can transfer some of their questions to our sources and incorporate their larger point that shopping in the ethnic enclave and selling on the ethnic street represented powerful acts of community building.

This paper represents an attempt, exploratory and episodic in nature, to highlight what we already know about the historic significance of Jewish enclave commerce and the intricate links between it and the ways in which American Jews lived in their Jewish communities. It asserts that not only did the buying and selling of Jewish "stuff" have long historic roots—this is surely well known—but also that those quotidian commercial acts lay close to the heart of what it meant for American Jews to live in their Jewish communities. American Jews invested meaning in their marketplaces, and defined them as key sites in the construction of both identity and lived life.

In terms of types of Jewish commercial transactions as they lay at the center of the history of Jewish community life, a number of categories suggest themselves. First, some of the goods that flowed along the Jewish commercial chain fell clearly in the domain of what has commonly been assumed to be essential to the practice of Judaism. As such, the commercial sector never stood apart from the religious. Merchants who sold kosher foods, those who marketed particular delicacies associated with Sabbath and holidays, those who enticed customers with new clothing for festivals, as well as the merchants who displayed pots and pans, crockery and cutlery in the weeks before Passover, provided the material underpinnings that enabled holy time to be marked. Likewise, the sellers of books, almanacs, greeting cards, magazines, candles, and various objects that carried religious or ethnic valence acted through the medium of their commercial transaction as religious functionaries. Their displaying and selling of particular "things" on a weekly or seasonal basis fostered a Jewish tone and helped infuse the streets with a sense of Jewish time.

For those who purchased these goods, their many and repeated acts of shopping and the range of merchants they depended upon to secure these goods all made possible such sacred acts as marking the Sabbath, making the holiday, and fulfilling a continuous set of other religious mandates. Indeed, given the degree to which Judaism functioned first and foremost as a home- and family-based religious system, the masses of Jews depended more upon merchants and their stores in order to perform Jewish rituals than they did upon synagogues and rabbis. As such, not only can the commercial life of the Jewish street not be distinguished from the performance of religious obligations, but rather that life stood at the forefront of getting ready for ritual activities.

The literature as it exists now, despite the fact that few scholars have devoted much specific attention to the web of relationships that linked Jewish shops to Jewish community life, already offers many examples of how places of Jewish commerce served simultaneously as places that dispensed Jewish news, fostered Jewish interactions, and made possible the provision of Jewish services. Ewa Morawska in her study of the small Jewish enclave in Johnstown, Pennsylvania, described how the kosher butcher shop, which opened up in 1903, stood next to the railroad station. She detailed how it "served as a referral service for passengers just off the train. If they were transients, travel assistance was provided by women of the *Hakhnoses Orkhim*, a society constituted to provide aid to wayfarers." The implications of this small detail bear thinking about as we imagine community.[10]

If we understand the making of "community" to be an abstract concept indicating the process by which a set of individuals consider themselves responsible for others with whom they share some characteristic, transforming them from being merely "a set of individuals" to a collectivity with mutual obligations and expectations, then the butcher shop in Johnstown played a key role for numerous Jews who passed through this western Pennsylvania steelmaking and coal-mining town. The Jews of Johnstown supported the butcher shop by spending their money there on food that they believed Judaism obliged them to consume, and the women of Johnstown banded together to create a formal society that ministered to the needs of Jews in transit from one place to another. Placing the butcher shop near the railroad station may not have been done specifically to fulfill a communal obligation—*hachnassat orchim*—but rather it may have been just good business sense. But its physical location, a prominent place near the depot, made possible the intricate fusion of economic, philanthropic, and religious needs, all of which sustained the community of Jews in Johnstown and which by implication made the Jewish community of Johnstown a player in the creation of a larger American Jewish community.

While some kinds of business establishments, like kosher markets, clearly depended upon Judaism and Jewish law, as well as on a network of Jewish religious functionaries, other stores such as those that sold household wares, clothing, stationery, and the like also served Jewish functions. Stores that lined the Jewish street did not have to sell specifically Jewish goods to at times play a role in the creation of Jewish community life. Again a small detail in the scholarship winks at us, pointing out that the entrepreneurial sector intersected with the communal, indeed fostered it.

In 1909 a group of Jewish women in Boston's South End, mostly poor mothers, met at Hyman Danzig's Three and Nine Cent Store. No doubt they exchanged information about a whole range of subjects in this otherwise obscure neighborhood store, which served as a convenient gathering place. Among the issues they noted was the fact that no medical facility existed in the neighborhood. They spontaneously formed themselves into a committee, which later that year came up with "a novel fund-raising scheme," constructing and selling "miniature bricks at fifty cents a piece to pay for the building of an entire hospital. . . . They made the most of nickels, dimes and quarters. By September, 1911, the little group of women had grown into a fund-raising society known as the Beth Israel Hospital Association."[11] Although the women might have gone about the business of creating a hospital anyhow, even if they had not tended to gather at Hyman Danzig's store in the normal course of life, the store and its role in this story constituted a crucial element in the history of this project and this community.

That the women used this commercial space as a social space should draw the attention of historians. It should highlight to us how community in the broadest sense of the word depends as much on the street as on the formal institutions designated as such. This same point has emerged as an analytic detail in writing about Boston at the other end of the century. Historian Gerald Gamm, in a study subtitled *Why the Jews Left Boston and the Catholics Stayed*, documented the entrepreneurial infrastructure of the community that the Jews were about to abandon. After ticking off the number of kosher butcher shops supported by the Jews who shopped along Blue Hill Avenue, as well as the bakeries, groceries, and fruit markets, Gamm put the G&G delicatessen onto historic center stage, as *the* place that "gave the district its special character." Quoting from a local newspaper, Gamm offered an insight into the close connection between the making of a Jewish community and the existence of particular commercial establishments. The article deserves to be quoted here at some length. Thus, referring to the delicatessens of the neighborhood:

> Of all the fortresses only one reached the proportions, could claim palatial ame-nities that testify to high culture, that immense landmark which any traveller who has passed down Blue Hill avenue will smile in recognition of, the G&G. On the tables of the cafeteria talmudic jurisprudence sorted out racing results, politics, the stock market, and the student could look up from his "desk" to leer at the young girls sipping cream soda under the immense wings of their mothers; watch the whole world of Blue Hill avenue revolve through the G&G's glass gate.

The dissolution of the Jewish neighborhood of Dorchester—a dense Jewish residential community by all accounts—according to Gamm, can be marked less by the moving of the synagogues—his core interest in the book—than by the final closing of the "glass gate."[12]

Gamm's reference to this quite ordinary restaurant did not constitute the first scholarly valorization of it as a dense, powerful, and magnetic Jewish communal institution. Hillel Levine and Lawrence Harmon in their 1992 study of Boston Jewry, aptly titled *The Death of an American Jewish Community*, also focused on decline, following "the glory years" of Blue Hill Avenue. They placed the delicatessen at the center of the Jewish community's politi-cal and social history and went so far as to declare that it "enjoyed the great-est drawing power of any institution in the Jewish community." Politicians, Jewish and non-Jewish, eager to win the Jewish vote made an obligatory pil-grimage to the G&G, for example. Indeed, so central a role did it play in bring-ing Jews together and providing them with a place to be and be with other Jews that "If asked to free-associate about Jewish Boston, former residents [would] invariably utter "the G&G" . . . a place to dine, cut deals, and evalu-ate prospective sons-in-law." (Levine and Harmon asserted, suggestively, that the intellectual and religious leadership of the community expressed disdain for the G&G and resented the fact that it competed with schools, synagogues, and more refined places of Jewish communal life. "Those charged with shap-ing the community" actually "struggled for ways to get people off the Avenue and into the classroom or clubhouse." To no avail, since, at least in the realm of meaning and memory, while many Boston Jews did attend classes as the Hebrew Teacher's College, "few former residents think first of Hebrew College when reminiscing of the old neighborhood." That place of honor belonged to the G&G.)[13]

Whereas Gamm, and before him Levine and Harmon, identified a few dozen Jewish food establishments as key places in the community's self-conception of itself as distinctive and as providing for its own needs, other and larger Jewish enclaves supported even more retail establishments where Jews sold to each other, congregated, and did business in a dense Jewish environment. New York obviously stood in a category by itself, as a mammoth and complicated place for Jewish marketing and Jewish community. An 1899 survey of New York's Eighth Assembly District, which encompassed parts of the immigrant neighborhood, listed no fewer than 631 food establishments that

> catered to the needs of the inhabitants of this area. Most numerous were the 140 groceries which often sold fruits, vegetables, bread and rolls, as well as the usual provisions. Second in number were the 131 butcher shops which proclaimed their wares in Hebrew letters. The other food vendors included 36 bakeries, 9 bread stands, 14 butter and egg stores, 3 cigarette shops, 7 combination two-cent coffee shops, 10 delicatessens, 9 fish stores, 7 fruit stores, 21 fruit stands, 3 grocery stands, 7 herring stands, 2 meat markets, 16 milk stores, 2 matzo . . . stores, 10 sausage stores, 20 soda water stands, 5 tea shops . . . 11 vegetable stores, 13 wine shops, 15 grape wine shops, and 10 confectioners.[14]

If to every one of these places a steady stream of Jewish women and men came in and out, stopping to talk to the shopkeeper and to the other customers, exchanging news, finding out about each other's fortunes and misfortunes, then we can see how the profusion of retail establishments on the Jewish street created a thick space for making community. The photographic record of that Eighth Assembly District, that is, the Lower East Side, testifies to the intensity of the street life and the degree which commercial activities drew Jews out of their apartments and into the public spaces, talking as well as buying, interacting as well as inspecting merchandise, and in the process creating community.

Likewise, for decades Jews who had once lived on the Lower East Side but then moved out to newer areas in the Bronx and Brooklyn trekked back to the "old neighborhood" to shop. Memoirs told and retold the details of Jews from other parts of New York coming to the Lower East Side before Passover to buy nuts, dried fruit, and wine, returning on Sunday mornings for bargains on clothing as well as for pickles and "appetizing"; and finally, in a nearly religious act tantamount to a pilgrimage, fathers brought their pre–bar mitzvah sons to the "sacred space" to purchase a tallith in anticipation of their thirteenth birthday. Each one of these acts of Jewish shopping not only helped make the Lower East Side the crucible of American Jewish memory culture but also, in the process, helped create the key narrative of community in its most authentic form.[15]

Jewish commercial life sustained ritual practice and provided the spaces where Jewish socializing and community-building activities could happen, but the ways in which different groups used those places reveal to historians some of the fissures that divided communities. No issue demonstrates this more sharply than that of gender. That is, Jewish women and Jewish men had different, albeit linked, histories of commerce and community.

To what degree did the small-business sector, the shops along the Jewish main street, employ the labor of all family members versus function as the sole domain of male or female entrepreneurs? What role did married women play in these stores, and how did their entrepreneurial activities enhance their authority within the family? How did Jewish women's involvement in these shops and stores limit their options? Here we certainly have a vast range of firsthand accounts that bear witness to the ways in which Jewish women as shopkeepers blurred any kind of line between the public and the private and between the work of business and the business of home. Countless numbers of Jewish shops doubled as places of residence inasmuch as families lived above and behind "the store." Mary Antin, for example, offered a description in her lyrical autobiography of how her mother tended the store and "in the intervals of slack trade, she did her cooking. . . . Arlington Street customers were used to waiting while the storekeeper [her mother] salted the soup or rescued a loaf from the oven."[16] Hers may be the most famous depiction of a phenomenon that predominated among Jewish entrepreneurial families. To what degree did this pattern affect women differently than men and how did the fusion of family and shop leave its mark on community life?

Additionally, the shopping districts of Jewish neighborhoods brought out both Jewish women and men in search of goods. Some sources indicate that they divided their responsibilities as to who bought what. Louis Wirth in *The Ghetto* declared that in the Chicago Maxwell Street market, "Thursday is 'chicken day,' when Jewish customers lay in their supplies for the Friday evening meal. Most of the purchasing is done by the men, who take a much more active part in the conduct of the household and the kitchen than is the case among non-Jewish immigrant groups. The man sees that the chicken is properly killed for if something should go wrong, he, as the responsible head of the household, would have to bear the sin." Buying the fish, however, he observed, fell more squarely in the woman's domain on this particular Jewish street. As such, Wirth suggested that a gendered shopping world existed, and this in turns offers us another way of seeing how the world of consumption in Jewish neighborhoods throbs with analytic possibilities.[17]

Statements like these provide tantalizing hints that indicate that gender and gender relations underlay the commercial life of the Jewish street. They lead us to seeing that full-scale histories of Jewish communities as places where Jews bought from and sold to each other have to be refracted through the lens of gender. That Jewish women and men have experienced migration, adaptation, and the process of community building differently now resides, as an analytic statement, at the center of our historic understanding. That they experienced

America as a place of conflict now figures prominently as an accepted element in our understanding of the past.[18]

The commercial zone can provide yet one other place where this gender struggle played itself out. Paula Hyman has certainly shown this in her now classic article on the kosher meat boycotts in New York at the turn of the twentieth century. Those food fights pitted Jewish women, the consumers who considered themselves and their families to be entitled to the right to consume meat at a price within their means, against Jewish male merchants, the butchers, who had behind them the communal leadership, the slaughterers, and the rabbis. As the women saw it, the merchants, as Jews, had a responsibility to the women and their families, and prices and goods did not exist outside the scope of communal obligations. Rather the women's demands underscored the degree to which marketing and community functioned as fused categories. The drama that played out in front of the butcher shops—and in the pages of Hyman's article—demonstrates the degree to which commerce, community, gender, and conflict all need to be considered as pivotal forces in Jewish history.[19]

The size of a community as well as the gendered nature of community life reflected itself in the realm of Jewish shopping. From the early twentieth century onward, Jewish visitors who came to New York from the "hinterlands" commented in awe about the great metropolis as a place to buy Jewish goods. The sheer size of New York's Jewish community made possible a diversity of markets whereby Jewish "things" could be consumed. *The Jewish Catalog*, perhaps the key text in the Jewish counterculture spawned in the 1970s, offered its readers explicit advice on how to shop for Jewish goods in New York. The array of items that Jewish merchants in New York could sell to Jewish consumers eager to acquire Jewish "things" demonstrated the city's significance, particularly the Lower East Side. Thus, the *Catalog*, after suggesting, for example, to those eager to buy Jewish books to try bookstores in their local communities, directed them to "the Lower East Side . . . a visit to which calls for the time-tested Jewish skills of haggling and striking a bargain with the booksellers." For shoppers in search of a ram's horn for Rosh Hashana, it noted, "it helps a lot to be in close proximity to either Jerusalem or (not to mention the two in the same breath) New York. If you are so situated, head for Meah Shearim or its diasporic equivalent, the Lower East Side." The ability to buy Jewish goods—books, ritual objects, and pickles—on the Lower East Side added to its sanctity and made it in the process a metaphor for the image of an organic and dense Jewish community.[20]

Likewise, in any number of memoirs or autobiographical fragments American Jews who had grown up and lived outside New York described, as did art historian Alan Schoener, how a visit to the Lower East Side evoked a sense of Jewish connectedness through what could be bought on its streets. "I found myself," he wrote, "roaming around Delancey Street and Second Avenue, eating food that my mother never cooked." He connected emotionally to a metaphoric sense of Jewish community through those rambles and through those acts of consumption. In order to eat that food, which transported him to a time when the neighborhood had been a dense Jewish enclave, he had to pay money to a merchant, be it a vendor with a cart, the owner of a restaurant, or the proprietor of a store. Schoener, like so many other voyagers to the old immigrant enclave, reconnected to a mythic community by means of a commercial transaction. (Schoener went on to curate the Jewish Museum's exhibit Portal to America, itself a powerful text in the furthering of the idea that the Lower East Side constituted a formative site in the construction of American Jewish communal identity.)[21]

These commercial transactions between Jews, in whichever century they took place, had tremendous impact on the nature of community life and community self-understanding. Although Jews sold to non-Jews historically more often than they sold to Jews, the close connections that developed between Jewish merchants and local Jewish buying publics helped sustain Jewish space and Jewish community. By patronizing neighborhood merchants and transforming shopping places into community spaces, Jewish consumers in concert with the merchants, whom they may at times have conflicted with over quality and price, nevertheless helped make the personal public, and the private communal. Memoirs, autobiographies, as well as a vast number of journalistic sources described often in exquisite detail the ways in which Jews in cities and towns in many lands and several continents congregated in Jewish stores and shops. Here they mixed together their buying of fish, meat, wine, bread, hats, and socks with the spreading of community news, the selling of notions with debates over notions of community priorities. The stores and shops provided places to gossip, sites for planning public activities, as well as venues for getting the goods defined as both necessary and desirable.

Examples of the connections between community and commerce have been strewn throughout the American Jewish history literature, both primary and secondary, as well as in the literary, photographic, and artistic sources. While no historian has as yet specifically isolated this issue and attempted to historicize the dense connection between community and commerce, the number of references to it points to the possibility that such a study (or better, studies) can be undertaken and would enhance and enrich the scholarship.[22]

For one, the literature as it already exists points to a number of crucial eras in the history of the American Jewish community as a place where Jews obtained the goods they needed to lead a Jewish life as they defined its parameters. The first era in American Jewish history, the one that extended into the early decades of the nineteenth century, relied on the imposition of a premodern European Jewish (and also colonial-style) model of high levels of community control in which Jewish merchants who served the Jewish public had to submit to community control.[23] Those goods which Jews saw as crucial to the practice of Judaism—kosher wine, kosher meat, and matzah in particular—rather than flowing to customers through independently owned and operated stores, which needed to woo the public to come and buy in competition with others selling the same goods, instead functioned as the monopoly of the congregation. Congregations could withhold goods from Jews who deviated from community standards of behavior, and enterprising entrepreneurs had no chance of setting up their own businesses. That the goods came from the congregations also made for a kind of hidden Jewish market. We have no evidence that shops with Hebrew letters, marked with words like "kosher" or "Jewish," graced the streets of early America.[24] While the Jewish women and men who inhabited these early communities made a living primarily in commerce, in the selling of various kinds of goods to the general public, Jewish goods came to Jews through the regulated world of the congregations.

Hyman Grinstein in his pathbreaking history of the Jews of New York, the first of the notable community biographies that dominated the scholarship in earlier times, introduced the community-commerce nexus as early as the third page of the book. Grinstein asserted in this introduction that the key moment in the history of the community, a moment that presaged later community diversification, seen by some as disunity and the decline of authority, came about in 1812 when a brief, unsuccessful breakaway group from Shearith Israel, the only congregation in the city, went out and hired its own *shochet.* Although the "rift was soon healed" and "Shearith Israel continued to supervise the sealing and sale of kosher food," a powerful trajectory had been established. The universal practice that had prevailed in America since the end of the seventeenth century—that the one and only congregation existing in each city with an organized Jewish presence maintained total control over the selling of kosher food—began to unravel. Instead, under the "broad concept of liberty which existed in America," commercial individualism flourished, and competition between congregations and merchants and among those who wanted to be merchants became the norm. The communities unraveled in the face of the "climate of freedom," and a culture of enterprise infused the Jewish commercial world no less than it came to suffuse nearly all aspects of American life.[25]

With that unraveling there ensued a long period of time, from the 1820s through possibly the 1960s, in which Jewish community life derived much of its impetus and structure from the vibrant and flamboyant tone of the commercial transactions of the street. In that extended history, in one city after another, Jewish neighborhoods became distinctive in large measure because of what got sold and bought on their streets, and how. Jews went out onto streets in the ordinary course of life, making the purchases of necessities and luxuries in company with other Jews, shopping at stores owned by their coethnics. Street, store, and living spaces flowed into one another, as being Jewish in large measure meant shopping and consuming Jewish. That marketplace culture flowered in every city where Jews lived, and it existed in its particular way until the age of suburbanization, when the rise of the low-density automobile culture put in place a set of new realities.[26]

In the years that the streets of Jewish neighborhoods functioned as Jewish marketplaces, merchants had to court the Jewish buying public. The signs, advertisements, hawking, and pulling in, all tactics designed to attract customers, gave the Jewish streets their particular appearance, announcing to all that these streets constituted Jewish space. Alfred Kazin, describing his Brownsville of the 1920s, remarked looking backward from the late 1940s how the "electric sign . . . lighting up the words Jewish National Delicatessen" made him and the others who used Pitkin Avenue as their turf feel "as if we had entered into our rightful heritage."[27]

The needs of ordinary Jewish women and men to buy particular goods and the desire of the Jewish shopkeepers—also quite ordinary Jewish women and men—to win over the consumers meshed. In that meeting place between Jewish consumers and Jewish entrepreneurs—although conflict between the two groups flared with frequency—community flourished.

We can narrate that history of community-through-commerce from the narratives of every community that has heretofore been written about. We can see the communal power of buying and selling Jewish in the primary documents that have survived from each Jewish enclave regardless of where it was. Let me offer a few examples, just to demonstrate the breadth of the material already available.

Thinking back about all that he had seen in his life, Isaac Mayer Wise remembered in his 1901 *Reminiscences* the Jewish community that had taken shape on the east side of Baltimore in the early 1850s as a place where "there seemed to be many Jews . . . although everything [was] very primitive. Women in the small shops carrying children in their arms, or else knitting busily. Young men invited passers-by to enter this or that store to buy. . . . M'zuzoth, Tzitzith, Talethim, Kosher cheese and Eretz Yisrael earth were on sale."[28] Here, in Wise's recollections, family life and entrepreneurship, community and consumption, overlapped in a visible if unappealing way.

In his sociological analysis of Chicago's Jewish community of 1928, Louis Wirth may have avoided the word "primitive" and eschewed the kind of judgmental tone that Wise indulged in, but he offered a similar kind of observation, which put the world of retail squarely into the making of Jewish community. "The description of the ghetto," opined Wirth, "would be incomplete without mention of the great number of other characteristic institutions that give it its own peculiar atmosphere and mark it as a distinct culture area." Here Wirth included "the Kosher butcher shops, where fresh meats and a variety of sausages are a specialty . . . the basement fish store to gratify the tastes of the connoisseur with a variety of herrings, pike, and carp, which Jewish housewives purchase on Thursday in order to serve the famous national dish of *gefülte fish* at the sumptuous Friday evening meal . . . Kosher bake-shops with rye bread, poppy-seed bread, and pumpernickel daily . . . the bathhouse, which contains facilities for Turkish and Russian, plain and fancy, baths . . . basement and second-story bookstores, cafes, and restaurants . . . the cigar stores, and the curtained gambling houses . . . the offices of the shyster lawyers, the *realestateniks*, and sacramental wine dealers. . . ." Wirth's monograph, published by the University of Chicago Press, came adorned by a series of woodcuts by the artist Todros Geller, which included a depiction of the "Horseradish grinder" who sat "on the sidewalks in front of butcher shops and fish stores . . . bowed and bearded," selling to the women and men who walked by, and which included as well as an artistic rendition of the Maxwell Street Market, streaming with people scurrying around buying goods of various kinds.[29]

That same tone pervaded much of the imaginative literature that grew out of the immigrant communities. Anzia Yezierska's 1923 *Salome of the Tenements* positioned her protagonist Sonya Vrunsky—a fictional stand-in for Rose Pastor Stokes—on New York's Essex Street. Yezierska depicted, with decidedly negative tones, the "jostling throngs, haggling women, peddlers and pushcarts. The smell of fishstalls, of herring stands," all of which gave the neighborhood its distinctive quality. Yezierska peopled her fictional world with Jews who used the streets to provide and consume goods they understood to be crucial to Jewish life. "Holiday hats! Shine yourself out for Passover! Everything marked down cheap!" blared a "puller-in" to Sonya, who, lured by the lights of Fifth Avenue, found the life of Essex Street a dismal combination of "the sordidness of haggling and bargaining—all she had ever known till now"—with the essence of the immigrant Jewish community.[30]

In their history of the Jews of Buffalo, a product of the tercentenary commemorations, Selig Adler and Thomas Connolly provided yet another example of how thinking about Jewish community cannot be divorced from considering the role of retail. In charting how "Buffalo's first distinctly Jewish neighborhood" came into being, the two historians noted that it coincided with the rise of the community's first "shops and business institutions." In particular they noted the centrality of "Rosenblatt's Bakery," where at 268 William Street "Jews met as they picked bagel, honey-cake and *hallah* out of the bins in the store windows." The opening up of Rosenblatt's stimulated competition, so Joseph Cohen "went into the same business." With his purported "secret recipe" brought from Warsaw, Cohen opened up shop on Strauss Street, and "here his son, Albert, made 'Cohen's rye bread' a household word in Buffalo." The upstate New York city's Jewish entrepreneurial nerve center extended beyond just bread, and "by the turn of the century, kosher butcher shops throughout the area had multiplied rapidly. There were Jewish barber shops in the neighborhood, a bicycle shop operated by Levi Russlander at 136 William Street, and a number of Jewish shoe repair shops."[31]

The rabbis, the sociologists, historians, and novelists as well as journalists, reformers, and memoirists have all made a crucial point (each in their separate way, reflective of the genres in which they worked and the projects they pursued) that offers scholars of community and of American Jewish history a direction for research. They each saw, like so many other observers, the profound reality that Jewish communities in the United States functioned not just as places where Jews prayed, acted politically, and furthered some worthy social goal such as providing for the poor, sustaining education, or supporting Jewish culture. Jewish communities also served as sites for buying and selling, and the entrepreneurial infrastructure of Jewish spaces operated in tandem with the construction of Jewish identity and meaning.

The Jewish streets of Baltimore, Chicago, and New York, and all the other places where Jews settled and lived—the commercial hubs of the neighborhoods where Jews planted themselves—provided more than sites for supplying ordinary Jews with ordinary necessities. Rather these streets offered Jews informal and organic ways to interact with other Jews. Although the world of Jewish commerce never existed independent of politics and ideology, the reality that some Jews, the shopkeepers among them, needed these stores to make a living while others, the consumers, needed them to feed, clothe, and supply themselves with a range of goods made for reciprocity and connectedness, essential elements of the idea of community. The relatively mundane commercial activities recorded by Wise, Wirth, Yezierska, and the others, the realities they saw of Jews selling and Jews buying, represented a foundational element of Jewish communities. Existing in an intermediate zone between the formal structure of communities (the synagogues, associations, societies with their charters, bylaws, and elections of officers) and the informal (the groups of friends, relatives, neighbors, and even strangers whose very presence shaped everyday life), stores and shops, the merchants and their customers, made possible Jewish public space.

The businesses that made up the entrepreneurial infrastructure of the "street" played a crucial role in the history of Jewish communities, and of all ethnic enclaves, in the United States and elsewhere. In these stores, which could be found in close propinquity to where community "members" lived, the mundane acts of buying and selling emerged as elements in the construction of community life.

The commercial nexus offers us then a historically rich and analytically complicated vantage point from which to see changing patterns of Jewish community life. While the reality of Jews buying from and selling to each other (both the goods that they believed Judaism demanded of them as well as the ordinary stuff, both basic necessities and luxuries) has run continuously through Jewish history, each place and each era reflected differences in context. Those contexts—and in this case the American one—offer historians a new and relatively untapped mine of material from which to imagine community, communities, and their histories.

Notes

1. A quite robust literature on the history of consumption and the significance of shopping has already been developed. A few of the key works of recent years include Susan Porter Benson, *Counter Cultures: Saleswomen, Mangers, and Customers in American Department Stores, 1890–1940* (Urbana: University of Illinois Press, 1986), Gary Cross, *An All-Consuming Century: Why Commercialism Won in Modern America* (New York: Columbia University Press, 2000), and Lizabeth Cohen, *A Consumer's Republic: The Politics of Mass Consumption in Postwar America* (New York: Alfred A. Knopf, 2003).
2. Molly Harrison, *People and Shopping: A Social Background* (London: Ernest Benn, 1975).
3. See Grant McCracken, ed., *Culture and Consumption: New Approaches to the Symbolic Character of Consumer Goods and Activities* (Bloomington: Indiana University Press, 1988).
4. Lewis Atherton, *Main Street on the Middle Border* (Bloomington: Indiana University Press, 1954), p. 44.
5. Carol Coburn, *Life at Four Corners: Religion, Gender, and Education in a German-Lutheran Community, 1868–1945* (Lawrence: University of Kansas Press, 1992), p. 22.
6. John Bodnar, *The Transplanted: A History of Immigrants in Urban America* (Bloomington: Indiana University Press, 1985), pp. 131–138.
7. George Sanchez, *Becoming Mexican American: Ethnicity, Culture and Identity in Chicano Los Angeles, 1900–1945* (New York: Oxford University Press, 1993).
8. Lizabeth Cohen, *Making a New Deal: Industrial Workers in Chicago, 1919–1939* (Cambridge: Cambridge University Press, 1990).
9. Ivan Light and Edna Bonacich, *Immigrant Entrepreneurs: Koreans in Los Angeles, 1965–1982* (Berkley: University of California Press, 1988), p. xi.
10. Ewa Morawska, *Insecure Prosperity: Small Town Jews in Industrial America, 1890–1940* (Princeton: Princeton University Press, 1996), p. 51.
11. Susan Ebert, "Community and Philanthropy," in Jonathan Sarna and Ellen Smith, eds., *The Jews of Boston: Essays on the Occasion of the Centenary (1895–1995) of the Combined Jewish Philanthropies of Greater Boston* (Boston: Combined Jewish Philanthropies of Greater Boston, 1995), p. 225.
12. Gerald Gamm, *Urban Exodus: Why the Jews Left Boston and the Catholics Stayed* (Cambridge, Massachusetts: Harvard University Press, 1999), pp. 198–199.
13. Hillel Levine and Lawrence Harmon, *The Death of an American Jewish Community: A Tragedy of Good Intentions* (New York: Free Press, 1992), p. 13.

14. Quoted in Moses Rischin, *The Promised City: New York Jews, 1870–1914* (Cambridge, Massachusetts: Harvard University Press, 1962), p. 56.

15. Hasia Diner, *Lower East Side Memories: The Jewish Place in America* (Princeton: Princeton University Press, 2000).

16. Mary Antin, *The Promised Land* (1912) (New York: Penguin, 1997), pp. 155–156.

17. Louis Wirth, *The Ghetto* (1928) (New Brunswick, New Jersey: Transaction Publishers, 1998), p. 237.

18. Riv-Ellen Prell, *Fighting to Become American: Jews, Gender, and the Anxiety of Assimilation* (Boston: Beacon Press, 1999).

19. Paula Hyman, "Immigrant Women and Consumer Protest: The New York City Kosher Meat Boycott of 1902," *American Jewish History* 70, 1 (September 1980), pp. 91–105. See also Dana Frank, "Housewives, Socialists and the Politics of Food: The 1917 New York Cost-of-Living Protests," *Feminist Studies* 11, 2 (Summer 1985), pp. 255–285. What is particularly notable in Frank's article is that Jewish women were among the most assertive housewives in New York in demanding that the merchants of their neighborhoods respond to their consumer needs.

20. Sharon Strassfeld and Michael Strassfeld, eds., *The Third Jewish Catalog: Creating Community* (Philadelphia: Jewish Publication Society of America, 1980), 205–206.

21. Quoted in Hasia Diner, *Lower East Side Memories: A Jewish Place in America* (Princeton: Princeton University Press, 2000), pp. 98–99, 80.

22. The one work in American Jewish history that has given the marketplace its due as an analytic construct is Andrew Heinze, *Adapting to Abundance: Jewish Immigrants, Mass Consumption, and the Search for American Identity* (New York: Columbia University Press, 1990).

23. The scholarship on the premodern period in Jewish history has stressed the degree to which business and commerce within the ghetto operated under the control of, and with strict regulation by, the formally sanctioned community. Rabbis and wealthy elites controlled the commercial sector no less than they controlled the religious sector or the relationship between the community and the larger non-Jewish world. See, for example, Jacob Katz, *Tradition and Crisis: Jewish Society at the End of the Middle Ages* (Syracuse: Syracuse University Press, 2000), where the power of the elite in the economic activities of the community is a major subject of discussion. Katz noted, for example, that the leadership took upon itself the question of "how to regulate competition among Jews" and how to limit the rights of "strangers," although they were Jews, settling and doing business in the community. See, for this, p. 49.

24. Eli Faber, *A Time for Planting: The First Migration, 1654–1820* (Baltimore: Johns Hopkins University Press, 1992), pp. 69–70.

25. Hyman Grinstein, *The Rise of the Jewish Community of New York, 1654–1860* (Philadelphia: Jewish Publication Society of America, 1947), p. 3.

26. A full-scale history of Jewish consumption and Jewish community would have to deal with the late twentieth century and the massive suburbanization of American Jewry as an analytically different era. The impact of low-density, automobile-driven suburban life on Jewish shopping needs to be probed. In essence the

realities of suburban design changed the basic nature of "the street" as a place where people walked into and out of stores, congregated on corners, met casually in the mundane course of activities. The development of Internet shopping and the privatization of consumption further changed basic patterns and would need to be analyzed in its own terms.

27. Alfred Kazin, *A Walker in the City* (New York: Harcourt Brace, 1952), pp. 33–34.

28. Quoted in Isaac Fein, *The Making of an American Jewish Community: The History of Baltimore Jewry from 1773 to 1920* (Philadelphia: Jewish Publication Society, 1971), p. 78.

29. Louis Wirth, *The Ghetto* (1928) (New Brunswick, New Jersey: Transaction Publishers, 1998), pp. 224–228.

30. Anzia Yezierska, *Salome of the Tenements* (1923) (Urbana: University of Illinois Press, 1995), pp. 12–142

31. Selig Adler and Thomas E. Connolly, *From Ararat to Suburbia: The History of the Jewish Community of Buffalo* (Philadelphia: Jewish Publication Society of America, 1960), pp. 186–187.

Transnationalism and Americanization in East European Jewish Immigrant Public Life

There was a fundamental tension in East European immigrant Jewish life between the drive to integrate more fully into American society and the inclination to maintain active ties to people in the immigrants' places of origin. These two seemingly contradictory tendencies, "Americanization," on the one hand, and "transnationalism," on the other, manifested themselves on a variety of levels—personal, familial, and communal. Focusing on the communal level, this paper will examine one crucial arena in which this tension played itself out: the thousands of hometown societies, *landsmanshaftn*, established by the immigrants. Before World War I, the landsmanshaftn played an important role in their members' Americanization. During and after the war, however, they became vital centers of transnational activity, as they undertook relief work for their war-ravaged hometowns and even sent "delegates" to supervise the distribution of aid directly.

The paper will argue, first, that despite tensions between the two tendencies, Americanization and transnationalism were compatible. Second, it will advocate a nuanced view that recognizes that transnationalism is not a monolithic phenomenon. Rather, it can wax and wane depending on circumstances. Moreover, the concept might describe the experience of some members of a given community better than that of others. These are not particularly original observations, but I hope to show that the Jewish case provides important evidence to support these perspectives on transnationalism.

"Americanization" is something of a loaded term, having been applied to the often coercive effort to detach immigrants from their native cultures and allegiances and force them to conform to Anglo-American standards.[1] I use it, though, to describe the process by which Jewish immigrants, on their own, turned their attention away from the old country and toward the new. In so doing, they sought to strike roots in American soil, acquiring property, establishing businesses, building families, and founding communal institutions. They also came to identify themselves, often enthusiastically, as Americans, and embraced what they saw as the fundamental American values of freedom, democracy, equality, and voluntarism. This definition of Americanization leaves much room for the construction of a distinctive ethnic identity, as the immigrants themselves determined the terms of their hybrid culture. Nevertheless, to the extent that the immigrants devoted their efforts to life in the United States, it seems likely that they would have had less time, energy, and emotional commitment to devote to their places of origin.

The process of Americanization has concerned U.S. scholars of immigration for decades, but in recent years some scholars have identified the phenomenon of "transnationalism" in immigrant life. More than simply the retention of ethnic cultures, the term refers to "the processes by which immigrants build social fields that link together their country of origin and their country of settlement."[2] These "fields" encompass political and economic activities, familial structures, personal relationships, emotional commitments, and any other social patterns that cross national boundaries and bind immigrants together with compatriots still in their countries of origin (and, it may be added, in other countries of settlement) in an ongoing and active way. Remittances of funds to family back home, correspondence, travel between the country of origin and the country of settlement, the involvement of emigrants in homeland politics, relief work, and business ventures that span borders are all examples of transnational ethnic activities. Transnational migrants thus live in two places and two societies at once, no matter where they actually spend most of their time. A transnational perspective leads away from a focus on how immigrants become American to an emphasis on how they negotiate the complex interactions across borders and develop an identity that transcends those of both host and home society.[3]

The Jews make an interesting test case precisely because they can be viewed as both the quintessential transnational people *and* the quintessential Americanizers among the wave of turn-of-the-twentieth-century immigrants. On the one hand, they arrived in the United States with a stronger consciousness of peoplehood than did many of the European peasant peoples who crossed the ocean at the same time. Moreover, their sense of peoplehood had easily spanned state borders in the "old country" before their migration, as much as it did after migration. (It should be noted that the "national" in transnational refers to the crossing of state borders and not to national consciousness, cultural unity, imagined community, community of fate, or whatever else, besides political sovereignty, might be seen to constitute nationhood.) It should therefore not be surprising that transnational Jewish consciousness survived the journey across the ocean and that American Jews continued to identify closely with Jews in other places.

On the other had, Jews generally came to the United States to stay, and had a much lower return rate than members of other important immigrant groups to which they might be compared. As permanent settlers, they committed themselves to life in the United States, sending their children to public schools, establishing businesses, acquiring property, and identifying strongly with certain aspects of the American ideology. In some ways, then, immigrant Jews in America were stronger Americanizers and led far less transnational lives than did those immigrants who, for example, came to the United States to make money so that they could return to their countries of origin to buy land or pursue other goals.

American landsmanshaftn were active agents of self-Americanization, in which immigrants helped each other settle into their "new home" and taught each other the norms of American-style democracy and organizational life, especially in the period before World War I. Indeed, a close examination of how the landsmanshaftn operated demonstrates the degree to which Jewish immigrants eagerly adopted and elaborated an American Jewish identity different from the East European identity they had brought with them. This is so despite the organizations' dependence for their definition on their members' shared nativity in a given town in Europe, a definition that would seem at first glance to have been a prime expression of transnational consciousness.[4]

But how can this account of enthusiastic Jewish immigrant Americanization be reconciled with the intertwined phenomena of continued hometown consciousness, massive relief campaigns, and, especially, travel to the country of origin, much of it sponsored by the landsmanshaftn in the 1920s and 1930s? These visits home on the part of well-settled immigrants constituted a clear expression of the continued involvement and direct contact across borders that defines transnationalism. Only a small percentage of immigrants actually made return visits, of course, but their trips often had wider implications for the community. Particularly in the half decade following the end of the First World War, many landsmanshaftn sent delegates collectively carrying millions of dollars for relief of their compatriots still in the old hometowns. Even when their visits were purely personal, travelers often transported letters and money for *landslayt* (fellow townspeople) and reported back to their landsmanshaftn, formally and informally, on conditions in the old hometown on their return to the United States.

The premise here is that transnationalism did exist among early twentieth-century immigrants as it does among those of the early twenty-first century. In contrast, some of the original theorists of transnationalism have argued forcefully that it is a new trend that differentiates today's immigrants from their predecessors. According to this view, previous waves of immigrants quickly lost all contact with their sending communities as they or their children assimilated into the Anglo-American population. Since the late twentieth century, on the other hand, economic globalization, technological advances in communication and transportation, the increasing availability of dual citizenship, and other factors have led to a new kind of migrant who moves easily and frequently back and forth between societies and cultures. This Handlinesque perspective ignored several decades of historical research on the experiences of previous generations of immigrants, as several more historically minded proponents of modified transnational theory have pointed out.[5]

Along with a more historically informed version of the transnational perspective comes a more nuanced one. Anthropologist Robert Smith provides just such a nuanced account of transnationalism when he argues that the phenomenon should not be seen as an absolute condition but as "one of several important spheres of life to which immigrants can belong and in which they can participate."[6] It is not the case, according to Smith, that an individual or group is either transnational or not. Rather, transnationalism should be seen as an aspect of immigrant life that can coexist with others. An individual might, for example, open a business and become involved in local politics (indicating an orientation toward America) at the same time as she raises money for relief work and makes frequent visits to her country of origin (indicating an orientation toward transnationalism).

Once transnationalism is not viewed as absolute and mutually exclusive of other processes, several arguments can be made. First, transnationalism might wax and wane over time in response to changing conditions in the sending and receiving countries.[7] In the East European Jewish case, periods of intense transnational activity alternated with periods in which the immigrants concentrated their efforts on establishing themselves in their new American homeland. Ironically, during the years of peak immigration before World War I, when one might think that transnational connections were strongest, the immigrants and their organizations were focused on America. (This is not to say that there was no transnational activity, particularly on the personal level, just that there was less than in other periods.) From about 1919 to 1924, the tremendous dislocation in Eastern Europe in the aftermath of World War I prompted an upsurge in transnationalism on the communal level as landsmanshaftn undertook massive efforts to provide relief to their landslayt still in Europe. As the situation in Eastern Europe stabilized, relief efforts declined, only to revive again in response to recurrent crisis in Europe in the mid- to late 1930s.

Second, as Smith and sociologist Peter Kivisto both point out, members of a given ethnic group might vary in the degree to which they are transnationally oriented.[8] It may be that some individuals or subgroups lead very transnational lives while others are more embedded in either the sending or receiving society. In fact, there may be an infinite gradation in the degree to which individual immigrants or organizations expressed transnational concerns. Landsmanshaft delegates and relief committee leaders, for example, may have been deeply involved in transnational networks and experiences — their lives largely defined by their cross-border social relations. Among broader circles of immigrants, some may have provided money for the delegates to bring over to relatives or general relief funds. Others may have read travel accounts in the newspaper or attended meetings where delegates reported on their face-to-face encounters with the old hometown. These also constituted forms of transnational activity, though less intensive than the delegates' trips home. Still other immigrants may not have participated in transnational networks at all, even when transnationalism defined communal life.

Most importantly, the Jewish case supports Kivisto's argument that expressions of transnationalism can coexist with a strong drive toward Americanization.[9] Indeed, transnational activities may even have reinforced the immigrants' sense of themselves as Americans, and therefore as different from their friends and family who remained in the place of origin. Those who visited their hometowns often found, to their surprise, that they now viewed their former homes through American eyes and were dismayed by what they perceived as the primitive and backward conditions and attitudes that they saw. Their trips confirmed for them that they had made the right choice in emigrating and settling in the United States. On an organizational level, relief delegates often brought pragmatic American sensibilities to their work and imposed them on ideologically charged and highly fractured local communities. In so doing, they helped to further the revolution in authority that was already underway in Jewish Eastern Europe.

Landsmanshaftn and Americanization

During the peak of mass immigration from the 1880s to World War I, Jewish immigrants from Eastern Europe formed thousands of associations based on their members' common town of origin. These landsmanshaftn, as they were known in Yiddish, were perhaps the most basic form of immigrant communal organization, often arising from informal networks of landslayt. Ranging from tiny, unstable groups of ten or twenty to long-lasting organizations of a thousand or more, the landsmanshaftn provided their members with important material benefits as well as a place to socialize with familiar faces from the "old home." The landsmanshaftn, however, were hardly purely spontaneous creations. Rather, they reflected all the political, religious, and social divisions within the community. Even a small town might be represented by several societies, one made up of religious Jews, one of Socialists, and so on. There were women's societies and mixed societies, but most landsmanshaftn were open only to men.

Both contemporary observers and later historians sometimes criticized the landsmanshaftn for being old-worldly and backward looking, but they were actually intensely American institutions. Even the principle according to which they were organized—origin in a specific East European town—turns out, at second glance, to have been less old-worldly than it seems at first, since it only made sense once the members had left their native places. The act of emigration thus made much more salient an identity that would have had little effective meaning in the hometown itself. Associations based on town or region of origin have been common in migrant societies in many places and periods, but the Jewish landsmanshaftn in the United States took a peculiarly American form.

The landsmanshaftn's organizational structure and benefits signal their American character. The societies operated according to constitutions and bylaws patterned on American models. With their democratically elected presidents and other officers, they very closely resembled, not only typical Anglo-American mutual aid associations and fraternal orders, but those of other immigrant groups as well. Conversely, their organizational structures differed greatly from those of traditional Jewish societies in Eastern Europe. This was true even of conservative, religiously observant landsmanshaftn that adopted traditional-sounding names. The American inspiration for society governance was quite explicit. Immigrants learned the ins and outs of organizational leadership from Yiddish-language manuals that sometimes included translations of popular American manuals of parliamentary procedure. According to one such manual, "The government of this great republic is run exactly the same way as a society, like a big society. It also has its constitution and officers: the president with his secretaries. . . . Congress is the meeting place of the entire people, and since it is impossible for the whole people to meet in person, everyone sends a delegate which he elects."[10] The influence worked both ways: not only did the immigrants pattern their societies after the republican form of government they admired; they also learned citizenship skills in their societies.

During the main period of immigration before World War I, the landsmanshaftn's primary role was to help their members cope with life in the United States, rather than to help them maintain links with family and friends in the old country. This may seem ironic, since during this time the immigrants had not yet had time to settle into their new situation in America and one would expect them still to be very emotionally involved in the life they had left behind. But, on further consideration, it makes sense; gaining a toehold in the new home took a lot of energy and resources, and so the immigrants looked to their organizations for help with the basic material and social needs that arose from this struggle. Of course, expressions of transnationalism took place all the time outside the formal workings of the societies: new arrivals brought news of the hometown, letters were exchanged, remittances were sent to families, and the Yiddish press reported on events in Europe. The radical societies also sometimes raised money for revolutionary movements in Russia. But even they devoted most of their efforts to providing mutual aid to their members.

The landsmanshaftn were, essentially, mutual aid societies of the sort that were widespread among all immigrant groups in the United States, as well as among native-born workers. The benefits provided by the Jewish groups fit the general mold, a further indication that the societies functioned along American lines and manifested their members' Americanization. Societies generally provided a set weekly payment to members who could not work because of illness or injury; the services of a doctor contracted to serve the members at reduced rates; a funeral and burial; and a payment to the survivors of deceased members. Some also provided interest-free loans. In addition to benefits officially determined by the societies' constitutions, the organizations offered occasional ad hoc financial aid to needy members, as well as informal sorts of assistance in finding jobs and housing. Not only the benefits themselves but also the procedures involved in procuring them were standard in American mutual aid associations across ethnic lines.

The hometown societies also furthered the Americanization of the immigrant Jewish population by helping to build the local Jewish communal infrastructure. Hundreds of landsmanshaftn became branches or lodges of Jewish fraternal orders such as the Independent Order Brith Abraham and the Workmen's Circle. To varying degrees, they supported such efforts as HIAS (Hebrew Sheltering Immigrant and Aid Society) and the New York Kehillah, and, through their regional federations, even established hospitals, old-age homes, and other social welfare institutions. The societies were mainstays of support for the Yiddish theater, and, depending on their ideological orientation and class composition, assisted strikes and unions as well. All these activities helped establish a tangible East European Jewish presence in American cities and towns, and gave the members a substantial collective investment in their country of settlement.

Perhaps most importantly, the landsmanshaftn demonstrate the degree to which their members adopted the American ethos of democracy, egalitarianism, and voluntarism. They symbolized the transformation in status and fortune that their members underwent in the course of migration and settlement from downtrodden, poverty-stricken subjects, oppressed not only by the Gentile authorities but also by the oligarchic Jewish community, to free, equal, and, in many cases, upwardly mobile citizens of a free republic and members of independent organizations. One immigrant, Jacob Sholtz, recalled how a meeting of his society changed his feelings about America and led him to abandon thoughts of returning to Russia:

> Something happened, something extraordinary, that affected me very strongly and completely knocked out of my head the idea of going back. This is what happened. During the months that I was hanging around . . . , my landslayt brought me into a society. And there I was, sitting at a meeting when one of the members—a man with a very good appearance—was addressing a question very intelligently, nicely, and logically, in good Yiddish. I asked who this man was. When I was told his name my mind was changed completely—my thoughts about going back disappeared.
>
> What had happened? Here I must tell a little of the past of the man, the speaker at the meeting, who had made such an impression on me. He was a childhood landsman of mine, from the same street and from the same synagogue. As children we kept far away from each other. He was very poor, of a bad, even ugly, appearance—dirty, raggedy. He studied neither in a *heder* nor in a school. It is likely that he could not even read the prayers, though he used to hold the prayer book open. I quickly left him behind and forgot about him until this encounter at the meeting.
>
> So my whole way of thinking took a turn. A poor boy there! A fine, intelligent householder here, with a nice family and fine children! Dirty there! How clean and neat he is here! Of ugly appearance there! How nice and respectable he is here! In my ears I can hear the words as he would have actually pronounced them: "Do not scorn me because I am swarthy." And, of course, David's verse: "The stone forsaken by the builder has become the cornerstone."
>
> How could all of this have happened—this change from there to here? Then and there, I decided no longer to think of going back. Here in America, in the free land with all its opportunities for everyone equally, here is my home. I shook off the last bit of dust from the old country.[11]

This "shaking off" of the "last bit of dust from the old country" took place in a society made up entirely of compatriots from one town in Eastern Europe! Clearly, these associations served as an arena of Americanization, even if this Americanization took place on the immigrants' own terms.

Crisis and Transnationalism

Despite their earlier orientation toward America, the landsmanshaftn became active organs of transnationalism during World War I and, even more so, in the years immediately after. Not only did they facilitate communication between relatives and acquaintances on each side of the Atlantic, but they also funneled large sums of money from American landslayt to their fellow townspeople still in the old hometown. Most spectacularly, many—perhaps hundreds of—

landsmanshaftn sent representatives to their hometowns to supervise personally the distribution of aid. The amount and intensity of transnational activity on the part of the societies varied throughout the interwar period in direct proportion to the degree of crisis faced by the Jews of Eastern Europe. The way in which this activity waxed and waned helps to demonstrate that transnationalism, far from being an absolute and unwavering characteristic of certain ethnic groups as opposed to others, might fluctuate within in a given group over time.

At the outbreak of World War I, American Jews responded to the crisis of European Jewry on a number of levels. Three different national relief organizations arose to raise money from different constituencies: Orthodox elements organized the Central Relief Committee for the Relief of Jews Suffering through the War (CRC), the American Jewish Relief Committee (AJRC) represented primarily wealthy Americanized Jews, and the People's Relief Committee (PRC) worked with the labor movement and Socialist sector of the immigrant community. Together, these groups formed the Joint Distribution Committee (JDC) to deliver in a professional and efficient manner the funds they had collected.[12] Meanwhile, thousands of landsmanshaftn, alarmed at reports of violence and dislocation in and around their members' hometowns, banded together to form their own relief committees.

The history of the United Brisker Relief illustrates both the possibilities and the limits of transnationalism for Jews during and after World War I. According to the organization's longtime leader, the Brisker Relief first took shape after a landsman received a "heartrending" letter in 1914 with disturbing news of events in Brisk (Brest Litovsk or Brzesc nad Bugiem). This instance of private transnationalism led to a communal response: the Brisker branch of the Labor Zionist Jewish National Workers Alliance and the anti-Zionist Brisker Bundist Fareyn took the lead in forming the United Brisker Relief committee, which spanned the religious and political spectrum from the Bundists to the Brisker Shul Tifereth Israel. (This ecumenicalism was, in fact, a common attribute of the American landsmanshaft relief committees.)[13]

Like other similar committees, the Brisker Relief initiated a discourse of relief that emphasized its constituency's close relationship with the people of the town who remained in Europe and called on the American landslayt to accept responsibility for supporting the unfortunate war-torn inhabitants of Brisk. "We, the fortunate Briskers, who are here in this free country," it insisted, must take an interest in "our Briskers" and "our brothers and sisters" suffering from the war. It criticized the American landslayt—"well-fed, well-dressed, and cheerful"—for not doing enough for their relatives overseas and tried to entice people to its meetings by promising them news from home received through special channels.[14]

But external factors stemming from the war itself put major obstacles in the way of the development of a transnational field of activity, and perhaps even of a transnational consciousness for some Brisker. First, since all civilians had been expelled from Brisk, an important Russian garrison town, at the beginning of the war, the American landslayt found it difficult to reach the townspeople who were now dispersed as refugees in various parts of Poland and the Russian Empire. Some, the older elements, according to activist Jacob Finkelstein, argued that there was no point in relief work for a city with no one in it. The younger people disagreed, and continued to collect money. In late 1916, they managed to send $700 to a Brisker committee in Warsaw, but when the United States entered the war the following year, it became impossible to send any more. By the end of the war the committee had sent only $748, although it had channeled many more private communications between Briskers on opposite sides of the ocean.[15]

The end of World War I enabled American landsmanshaftn to reestablish direct contact with their hometowns, although war conditions continued in much of Eastern Europe. Relief committees, including the United Brisker Relief, sprang back to life, now collectively sending millions of dollars to Jewish communities in Eastern Europe, especially Poland. Much of this aid was sent through the JDC, HIAS, the Red Cross, and other agencies that established offices in Poland and other countries of Eastern Europe and sent occasional missions from the United States. But relations between the professional relief agencies, which sought to distribute aid in a dispassionate and efficient way, and the landsmanshaft relief committees, which had a more emotional and personal approach, were often strained.

Dissatisfied with the work of the professional social workers, the relief committees began to send their own "delegates" overseas. Each carrying tens of thousands of dollars in personal remittances and general aid, hundreds of these delegates went to Europe between 1919 and 1921. The feverish activity spanned national boundaries as American relief workers, professional and amateur, departed from New York and traveled through Paris and Warsaw on their way to their individual towns. As they did so, they personally entered a transnational space that involved them intensively in the affairs of their hometown communities. Their involvement, in turn, affected the communal structures of both the hometown and the immigrant colonies in the United States.

Along with a colleague, Harry Berger traveled to Minsk, then controlled by Poland, in 1920, representing a coalition of Minsker societies in the United States. Upon his return to America, he published an account of his trip in the *Forward*. His story, later reprinted in book form, illustrates the perils of such a mission.[16] Berger, after leaving New York on April 16, arrived in Warsaw via Plymouth, London, Le Havre, and Paris, on May 8, by which time he had already learned the value of bribes in clearing the road to Minsk. After eight days in Warsaw tracking the exchange rate and seeking a pass to travel in the

Russo-Polish war zone, Berger and his partner left Warsaw with $20,000 in cash and a bank account containing some 24 million Polish marks ($120,000). Stepping off the train in Minsk, they were immediately detained by drunken officers of the gendarmerie, who accused them of carrying Bolshevik propaganda and funds, confiscated private letters they were carrying—and demanded a bribe. Released, the delegates shuttled among civil and military officials seeking the release of the letters and permission to start work. When they finally began to distribute the money without official approval, they were "besieged by hundreds and thousands of people who were supposed to receive money from their American relatives, and also by those who only hoped to receive money." [17] Near the end of their mission, Berger was arrested again by officials who hoped to extort some money from him, but he bought their goodwill with a contribution to the Polish Red Cross.

The extent to which this post–World War I period was a transnational moment is demonstrated by the fact that, even under such trying conditions, Berger and his friend were not alone. Significantly, there were "several" other American Jewish landsmanshaft delegates in Minsk at the time, representing immigrants from nearby towns. Some of these delegates were purely "private entrepreneurs" hoping to make money by manipulating exchange rates, but others were legitimate delegates. [18] In addition, "uniformed representatives" of the American Young Men's Christian Association were on hand to help Berger resolve a problem with his bank. As Berger reported, the presence of these emissaries went far, not only in ameliorating the physical needs of the local inhabitants, but also in boosting their spirits. Those who received assistance from their families knew that they were not forgotten. In addition, communal aid from abroad bolstered several important institutions.

Delegates to Brisk had similar experiences. In 1920, in response to appeals from Brisk, the revived United Brisker Relief sent former chairman Philip Rabinowitch to Brisk with some $80,000. He too faced danger, nearly turning back in fear of antisemitic bands operating near the city. But the transnational Brisker network was pressed into service to keep the delegate on track. After Rabinowitch wrote of his hesitation to Jacob Finkelstein in New York, Finkelstein dispatched Brisker landsman and journalist Pesach Novick, who had lived for a time in New York and was then in Vilna, to encourage Rabinowitch and help him carry out his mission. Once in Brisk, Rabinowitch found crowds of desperate landslayt grateful for the assistance from America. [19] The success of Rabinowitch's mission, and renewed appeals from Brisk, prompted the Brisker Relief to send another delegation, consisting of Jacob Finkelstein and H. Kleinberg, in 1921, this time with $110,000 for their beleaguered hometown. [20]

As Smith points out, transnationalism must be measured not only by the effect that it has on the immigrant community but also by its impact on the community of origin.[21] The relief missions certainly left their mark on their respective landsmanshaft communities in the United States. Rebecca Kobrin has shown in the case of Bialystok, for example, that relief activity helped to make the United States and, more specifically, New York, the capital of a transnational community that included other places of emigration as well as the home city itself.[22] On the local level, the missions also served as a focal point of activity, prompting fund-raising campaigns accompanied by mass meetings before and after the trips. As the leaders understood, nothing would promote giving so much as direct reports—by returning delegates, or in personal letters from relatives—from the old country. In addition to enhancing the prestige of the organizations that sponsored the trips, the missions undoubtedly also helped to raise the status and consolidate the leadership positions of the individuals who made them.

But transnational activity probably had a greater impact on the impoverished hometowns that received the aid—an impact obscured in the Jewish case by the subsequent disappearance of those communities. As Smith has argued, emigrant intervention in local affairs can have the effect of upsetting traditional hierarchies of power, but only if challenges to those hierarchies are already under way. In Jewish Eastern Europe, of course, such a challenge had begun decades before, mounted by the nineteenth-century Haskalah or by later secular movements such as socialism or Zionism. During the war, as Steve Zipperstein has demonstrated, relief agencies, often staffed by young radicals, became a new center of authority in the Jewish community.[23]

The American relief missions furthered this transition. Conservative traditionalists and radical labor elements in the receiving communities often had very different ideas of what constituted proper priorities for relief. In Brisk, for example, radical elements condemned charitable aid to individuals and called for funds for institutions that they believed would treat all segments of the population equally and perhaps effect structural change in the communal hierarchy. They thus favored public kitchens, schools, and clinics. The town rabbi, on the other hand, pointed out that respectable individuals who had been ruined by the war were reluctant to take advantage of such general public agencies. He requested more money for discreet individual assistance—the kind of assistance that the radicals feared would be doled out unequally between the fallen bourgeoisie and proletarian poor.[24]

In some places, the JDC and the landsmanshaftn cooperated with local rabbis and kehillahs. But the American agencies often appointed their own "American relief committees" to represent them on the local level, bypassing the traditional communal authorities. When JDC representative Boruch Zuckerman (a Labor Zionist) came to Brisk in 1919, he inserted himself into the struggle between the "young" radicals and the "old" members of the traditional establishment, bypassing the local kehillah and setting up a new

relief committee that included leftist elements. He also mandated that a specified amount of aid money go to the radicals' favored institutions. As one letter writer reported, the traditional leaders "had to do this against their will,
because Mr. Zuckerman said so [*hot geheysn*]." But now that he had left the
scene, the "reactionaries" [*shvartse*] were "exploiting" his absence to reassert
themselves.[25]

Sometimes, the Americans threw their weight behind "workers' relief
committees" representing youthful radical forces in the towns, but often they
sought to impose an American spirit of pragmatism and nonpartisanship on a
highly ideologically charged and fractious situation. When delegates Finkelstein and Kleinberg arrived in Brisk two years after Zuckerman, they met with
a wide spectrum of communal leaders, from the chief rabbi to the leaders of
radical factions. Despite their own radical inclinations, they strove to be stu-
diously nonpartisan in their distribution of the $15,000 entrusted to them for
general communal aid. Using the power that their control over such large sums
of money gave them, the Americans attempted to force the locals to create a
united relief committee representing all factions. While they had limited success in getting Zuckerman's American Committee to work with the rabbi and
the kehillah, they did manage to bring feuding radical factions into a "united
workers' committee," on which the New York relief committee was to have
representation.[26]

Indeed, during their stays the delegates wielded tremendous power directly
due to their control over discretionary funds. Most of the money that Berger
brought to Minsk, for example, was in the form of personal remittances sent
by American Jews to their families in Europe. Nevertheless, the Minsker delegate had tens of thousands of dollars to distribute as he saw fit. Some of
this money he gave to needy individuals whose relatives had not sent them
anything. But he also contributed large sums to such institutions as the Jewish hospital and the children's colony, with whose work he was impressed
as he investigated local conditions. The delegates also provided a number of
patronage jobs, though, as Berger reports, not as many as the locals hoped or
expected.[27] Likewise, the Brisker delegates Finkelstein and Kleinberg carried
with them $15,000 in general relief funds (in addition to $95,000 in personal
remittances). These they distributed to the Talmud Torah, the old-age home,
the Jewish hospital, the pharmacy and clinic, the orphanage, the Great Synagogue, several smaller study houses, the schools of the Young Zion movement,
and the Workers' Relief Committee.[28]

By the mid-1920s, the crisis had ebbed in Eastern Europe, and with it the
flurry of transnational activity in the United States. Judging its mission to be
over, the JDC even prepared to shut down. It did not do so, of course, and
both the JDC and the landsmanshaftn continued to send aid abroad. Private
contact also continued. But the amounts of money collected and sent by the

organizations fell, and the delegate movement quieted down. Many relief committees became dormant.

Other forms of transnational activity continued, sometimes encouraged and sometimes discouraged by the governments of the countries of origin. While government sponsorship of transnationalism among emigrants has been widely discussed in the literature, official antagonism has not. The example of Poland, however, shows that governments might discourage transnationalism or promote it, depending on circumstances. During the delegate movement, the Polish government expressed hostility toward the Jewish relief workers, viewing them, at best, as a nuisance and, at worst, as Bolshevik agents. As the American minister to Poland, himself no friend of the landsmanshaft delegates, put it, "The [Polish] government appears to proceed on the assumption that it is a privilege for foreigners to spend their money on relief in Poland, and that foreign relief organizations must be prepared to put up with all sorts of affronts, difficulties and delays in return for being allowed the privilege of carrying on their charitable activities."[29] What applied to professional relief agencies such as JDC and HIAS was even truer of the landsmanshaft delegates, many of whom were harassed or even arrested while carrying out their missions.

But in the late 1920s, under the regime of Marshal Jósef Piłsudski, and at the urging of a new consul in New York, the Polish government actually courted American Jews of Polish origin, viewing them as more capable and wealthier than non-Jewish Polish Americans.[30] The Poles hoped not only to attract Jewish capital but also to gain American Jewish support in their public relations efforts and, not incidentally, in their conflicts with Polish Jewish leaders. Accordingly, the Polish government established good relations with the Federation of Polish Jews in America, several of whose leaders participated in joint goodwill committees. The federation sponsored at least one group tour of Poland with the encouragement of the Polish government.[31] The Polish effort to cultivate the support of Polish Jews abroad soon faltered, however, against the backdrop of rising popular and state antisemitism in Poland. The Federation of Polish Jews broke off relations with the Polish government in 1931.

In the mid- to late 1930s, there was a revival of transnational activity among Polish Jews in America in response to the increasingly menacing international situation and deteriorating conditions in Poland. General agencies such as the JDC increased their funding, and landsmanshaft relief committees reactivated after a period of dormancy. In response to the pogrom in Brisk in May 1937, for example, secretary Jacob Finkelstein called a meeting of the United Brisker Relief, which had been inactive for ten years. The relief reorganized to protest antisemitism in Poland and to raise funds to help those suffering from the depressed Polish economy.[32] While the expression of solidarity with the Jews of Brisk by the Brisker Relief included an undertone of anger at the Polish regime, the Federation of Polish Jews was pulled in the opposite direction by the international threat, once again drawing closer to the Polish government in the face of German and Soviet aggression.[33]

Communal and Personal Dimensions of Transnationalism

Transnationalism was clearly an important aspect of immigrant Jewish public life in the World War I and interwar periods. It provided a focus of activity not only for landsmanshaftn but also for general relief agencies. Mass meetings, fund-raising campaigns, organized tours to the old country, reports by delegates and private travelers, the reading and writing of official communications, and so on all contributed to the buzz of communal life. So too did the heated arguments that revolved around geographic expressions of differing political ideals as adherents and opponents of the Soviet experiment and the construction of a Jewish homeland in Palestine vied in the public arena for support. American Jews helped to fund both these endeavors, and eyewitness travelers' reports found eager readers in the Yiddish press as partisans of the various camps enlisted them for their respective causes.

Likewise, the delegates and leaders of these organizations lived in an intensely transnational space. In order to carry out his mission, for example, Minsker delegate Berger negotiated the bureaucracies of two different governments and participated in three or four different, though overlapping, civic cultures (American, American Jewish, Polish, Polish Jewish). An activist like Brisker Jacob Finkelstein retained a lifelong attachment to his birthplace, which he expressed through his unwavering commitment to the United Brisker Relief, even after the destruction of Jewish Brisk in World War II. He had helped organize the relief committee during the First World War and traveled to Brisk as a delegate in 1921. He revived the committee in 1937 after receiving news of the pogrom in Brisk and remained in its leadership into the postwar period. He visited Brisk again in 1969.[34] Finkelstein's role in the transnational Brisker community was central to his self-definition.

But this apparent transnationalism on the communal level and in the lives of certain communal leaders really says little about its role in the lives of the majority of immigrants. One might posit a variety of levels or degrees of transnational involvement, ranging from visits to the old country (even frequent visits on the part of a very few people) to the sending of remittances and letters to relatives still in Europe to attendance at meetings at which reports were read and funds raised for the community of origin to the reading of travel accounts in the newspaper. It also seems likely that individual levels of transnational involvement fluctuated over time. But to confirm these suspicions, much more research is needed.

Jocelyn Cohen's analysis of immigrant autobiographies provides some clues to the way people thought, or did not think, about their places of origin.[35] According to Cohen, immigrants were caught up, to greater or lesser degrees and often inconsistently, in various "discourses" that shaped their sense of identification with both the old and new homes. The "radical" and "traditional" discourses, for example, encouraged a continuing feeling of attachment to the old hometown, according to Cohen, while the "dominant" or "upwardly mobile" discourse promoted a focus on life in the United States. Certainly, the landsmanshaft relief committees pushed a discourse of intimate connection with communities left behind, and this must have influenced many people to varying extents.

Transnationalism and Americanization

Perhaps the most important conclusion regarding transnationalism that can be drawn from the American Jewish case is that transnationalism is not at all incompatible with Americanization. This can be seen in the reactions of the landsmanshaft delegates to their old hometowns. Even as they engaged in a deeply transnational enterprise, traveling personally across borders to deliver aid and help reorganize communities, they indicated that the standards by which they measured the world had shifted from east to west. Despite his emotional commitment to the Jews of Minsk, for example, Harry Berger could not help seeing the Belorussian metropolis through the eyes of a Westerner. He compared his native city with the larger and richer cosmopolitan cities through which he had traveled: "Coming from New York, and having traveled through such gigantic cities as London, Paris, and Warsaw, I felt, as I traveled through the streets of Minsk as if I had fallen into a cellar. The houses, which I thought I knew so well from before, now looked to me to be strangely small, low, and insignificant."[36] His sensibilities were thus no longer those of a Minsker Jew, but those of the Philadelphian he had become.

Paradoxically, a visit to the *old* home could also convince the visitor that her or his *true* home was the new one. Some accounts demonstrate a shift in identity during the course of a trip. Sidney Herbst, for example, kept a diary during his 1935 trip to Sedziszow on behalf of the First Sedziszow Galician Society. As he leaves Warsaw for his town of origin, he expresses his happiness at heading "for home." But the tone shifts very quickly after his arrival in his destination, which he perceives as cold, shabby, horrible, and altogether wretched. Within days, he writes, "Can't wait 'til I leave. Counting days like in a prison." The only time he felt "sort of at home" in Poland was at the American consulate in Warsaw![37] Similarly, when Rose Schoenfeld returned "home" to New York from a private trip to her hometown of Drohobycz in 1932, she "thanked God properly for the first time for leading me on the right path to America, the land of freedom, where I could make decent people of my children."[38] Her transnational venture thus confirmed for her that she had made the right decision in emigrating and committing herself and her children to America.

Moreover, although they were ostensibly in their hometowns as landslayt bringing aid to brothers and sisters, the delegates often found it necessary or expedient to emphasize their American identity. As Berger explained to officials who were demanding to see a list of aid recipients during one of his detentions, "We had been elected by a huge number of American citizens in order to carry out our relief mission here, our work had also been authorized officially by the American government, which had issued us special relief passports, and we considered our relief mission to be a confidential and private matter, according to the American custom." Berger thus managed to invoke his American credentials and values three times in one sentence, concluding with a demand to be allowed to contact the U.S. ambassador.[39]

Ironically, the emotional commitment that brought the immigrants in America into closer contact with their landslayt abroad also emphasized the cultural distance that had arisen between them. One member of the United Horodyszczer Relief Organizations expressed it this way: "We look at things and people a little differently than they do. They don't understand our way of thinking. Their psychology is very different."[40] In civic terms, the material and political security of Jews in the United States contrasted so starkly with the hostility, poverty, and instability encountered by Jews in Eastern Europe that it would have been hard for even the most transnationally involved immigrant to resist the pull of Americanization.

Conclusion: Transnational Aspects of American Jewish Life

Immigrant relief work and travel represent just one transnational moment in American Jewish history. One could also focus on travel to Israel for the post–World War II generations, or on activism concerning Israel or Soviet Jewry. Transnationalism is also apparent in the *haredi* communities that freely circulate among cities in the United States, Canada, Europe, and Israel. Indeed, the near complete destruction of Jewish Eastern Europe obscures the degree of involvement that American Jewry had with its East European homeland and renders it impossible to tell what the long-term effects of that involvement would have been on either community.

Rebecca Kobrin demonstrates the complexity of the Jewish transnational constellation in her recent dissertation on the Bialystoker diaspora.[41] She shows that transnational communities were more than bipolar. Rather, emigrant colonies in many different places interacted regularly with each other and with the hometown. Moreover, the American center, especially New York, supplanted the city of origin as the metropolis of this far-flung community, by dint of its material wealth, political stability, and the psychology that these engendered. But, as this formulation itself indicates, transnationalism was not only compatible with a degree of adjustment to American life. It may have been dependent on it.

Acknowledgment

Thanks to Jack Wertheimer for inviting me to present this paper at "Imagining the American Jewish Community: An Academic Conference," at the Jewish Theological Seminar in March 2004. Thanks also to the other participants for their comments.

Notes

1. See Gary Gerstle, "Liberty, Coercion, and the Making of Americans," *Journal of American History* 84:2 (1997): 524–558.
2. Nina Glick Schiller, Linda Basch, and Christina Blanc-Szanton, "Transnationalism: A New Analytic Framework for Understanding Migration," *Annals of the New York Academy of Sciences* 645 (1992): 26.
3. For overviews of transnationalism see also Steven Vertovec and Robin Cohen, "Introduction," in Vertovec and Cohen, *Migration, Diaspora and Transnationalism* (Cheltenham, U.K.: Edward Elgar, 1999), xxiii–xxiv; Peter Kivisto, "Theorizing Transnational Immigration: A Critical Review of Current Efforts," *Ethnic and Racial Studies* 24:4 (July 2001): 549–597.
4. See Daniel Soyer, *Jewish Immigrant Associations and American Identity in New York, 1880–1939* (Cambridge, Mass.: Harvard University Press, 1997).
5. Ewa Morawska, "Immigrants, Transnationalism, and Ethnicization: A Comparison of this Great Wave and the Last," in Gary Gerstle and John Mollenkopf, eds., *E Pluribus Unum? Contemporary and Historical Perspectives on Immigrant Political Incorporation* (New York: Russell Sage Foundation, 2001), 175–212; Kivisto, "Theorizing Transnational Immigration"; Robert C. Smith, "How Durable and New Is Transnational Life? Historical Retrieval through Local Comparison," *Diaspora* 9:2 (2000): 203–233; Nancy Foner, "What's New about Transnationalism? New York Immigrants Today and at the Turn of the Century, *Diaspora* 6:3 (1997): 355–375.
6. Smith, "How Durable and New Is Transnational Life?" 204.
7. Morawska, "Immigrants, Transnationalism, and Ethnicization," 184–190.
8. Kivisto, "Theorizing Transnational Immigration," 556; Smith, "How Durable and New Is Transnational Life?" 209–210.
9. See also Smith, "How Durable and New Is Transnational Life?" and Morawska, "Immigrants, Transnationalism, and Ethnicization."

10. Bernard Modell, *Parliamentarishe gezetse. Klalim un erklerungen vi tsu orga-niziren sosayetis, vi tsu zayn prezident oder sekretar, es erklert oykh iber di far-valtung fun der Amerikaner regirung, ales daytlekh erklert un in a ontsiender shprakhe geshriben* (New York: Printed by E. Zunser, n.d.), 4.

11. Jacob Sholtz, autobiography #5, American Jewish Autobiographies Collection, RG 102, YIVO Institute for Jewish Research Archives, pp. 8–10. Incidentally, Sholtz's American-born cousin, David Sholtz, served as governor of Florida, a fact that must have reinforced Jacob Sholtz's impression that anything was pos-sible in America.

12. On the JDC and its constituent groups, see Oscar Handlin, *A Continuing Task: The American Jewish Joint Distribution Committee, 1914–1964* (New York: Ran-dom House, 1964), 19–47; Yehuda Bauer, *My Brother's Keeper: A History of the American Jewish Joint Distribution Committee, 1929–1939* (Philadelphia: Jewish Publication Society, 1974), 3–18.

13. Jacob Finkelstein, "Di landsmanshaftn un di geshikhte fun fareyniktn Brisker relif," in *Entsiklopedie fun di goles-lender: Brisk D'Lite* (Jerusalem: Farlag fun Entsiklopedie shel Galuyot, 1955), 612–615; Jacob Finkelstein, "50 Years United Brisker Relief," *50th Anniversary of United Brisker Relief, 1915–1965* (New York, 1965), 3.

14. "Tsu ale Brisker," in *Brisker Relief for the War Sufferers* (New York, 1917), n.p.

15. Avrom Kaplan, *Der khurbn fun Brisk in der velt milkhome* (Breść nad Bugiem, 1925); Jacob Finkelstein, "Geshikhte fun Brisker relif" (manuscript), 6, folder 12, Records of United Brisker Relief, RG 898, YIVO Institute for Jewish Research; Finkelstein, "Di landsmanshaftn," 615–617; Finkelstein, "50 Years," 4; "Yerlekher finans berikht," 1917, folder 10, Records of United Brisker Relief, YIVO Institute for Jewish Research; "Unzer thetigkayt," in *Brisker Relief for the War Sufferers.*

16. Harry Berger, "A rayze durkh gehenom," in *Fun fraynt tsu a fraynt: a matone Heri Berger'n tsu zany 50ten geburtstog* (Philadelphia: Jewish Labor Movement in Philadelphia, 1936), 101–148.

17. Berger, "A rayze," 109.

18. Berger, "A rayze," 114.

19. Letters from Beril Farber and L. Muliar to Jacob Finkelstein, July 25, 1919; Rabbi Isaac Ze'ev Soloveichik to Nisn Liberman, Heshvan 2, 5680 (October 26, 1919); Kooperatywa to Corn [*sic*] Relief Committee, April 8, 1920; Philip Rabinowitch to Jacob Finkelstein, June 28[, 1920], all in folder 2; "A grus fun Brisk," June 15, 1920, in scrapbook, folder 3; Finkelstein, "Geshikhte," 15–16, in Records of United Brisker Relief; Finkelstein, "Di landsmanshaftn," 619–620, 623.

20. Letters, Levengard et al. to Jacob Finkelstein, November 8, 1920, and Sol Weiss to Jacob Finkelstein, January 17, 1921, folder 6; "Hilf oyf Pesakh durkh di Brisker shloykhim," folder 6; financial summary for "Yor 1921," folder 1; letter of credit, Bank of the United States to United Brisker Relief, March 9, 1921, in scrapbook, folder 3, Records of United Brisker Relief; "Brisker relif komite," unidentified, undated clipping, folder 82, Archives of the American Jewish Joint Distribution Committee, 1919–1921.

21. Smith, "How Durable and New Is Transnational Life?" 209.

22. Rebecca Kobrin, "Conflicting Diasporas, Shifting Centers: Migration and Identity

in a Transnational Polish Jewish Community, 1878–1952" (PhD dissertation, University of Pennsylvania, 2002).

23. Steven J. Zipperstein, "The Politics of Relief: The Transformation of Russian Jewish Communal Life During the First World War," *Studies in Contemporary Jewry* 4 (1988): 22–36.

24. Farber and Mulier to Finkelstein, July 25, 1919; Soloveichik to Liberman, Heshvan 2, 5680 (October 26, 1919), folder 2, Records of United Brisker Relief.

25. Farber and Mulier to Finkelstein, July 25, 1919. See also Samuel Kassow, "Community and Identity in the Interwar Shtetl," in Yisrael Gutman, Ezra Mendelsohn, and Chone Shmeruk, *The Jews of Poland between Two World Wars* (Hannover, N.H.: Brandeis University Press/University Press of New England, 1989), 202–203, 213–214.

26. Finkelstein, "Geshikhte," 18; Finkelstein, "Landsmanshaftn," 624–625; Petition of Jewish Artisans' Union, May 2, 1921, folder 2; "Reglamin fun a.h.k. in Brisk," folder 14/9–10, Records of United Brisker Relief; Memo, JDC Warsaw to Landsmannschaft Department, New York, June 23, 1921, folder 123, Archives of American Jewish Joint Distribution Committee, 1919–1921.

27. Berger, "A rayze," 135, 139–140.

28. See receipts from various organizations to the delegates of the Brisker Relief, April–May 1921, folder 2, Records of United Brisker Relief.

29. Zosa Szajkowski, "Private American Jewish Overseas Relief (1919–1938): Problems and Attempted Solutions," *American Jewish Historical Quarterly* 57 (March 1968): 302.

30. Daniel Stone, "Polish Diplomacy and the American Jewish Community between the Wars, *Polin* 2 (1987): 73–94.

31. "Di ekskoyrshon keyn Poyln ayngeordnt fun der federeyshon a groyser erfolg," *Farband*, June 1930; Roman Kwiecien to Gustave Eisner, 23 September 1933, Eisner Papers, RG 316, YIVO Institute for Jewish Research.

32. J. Finkelstein, "Di landsmanshaftn un di geshikhte fun fareyniktn Brisker relif," in *Entsiklopedie fun di goles lender: Brisk-Dlite*, ed. Eliezer Steinman (Jerusalem: Encyclopedia of the Jewish Diaspora Co., 1955), 628–629.

33. Stone, "Polish Diplomacy," 89.

34. J. Finkelstein, "Ayndrukn fun mayn ershtn un tsveytn bazukh in Brisk," in Kopl Novik, *Di shtot Brisk* (New York, 1973), 33–35.

35. Jocelyn Cohen, "Discourses of Acculturation: Gender and Class in East European Jewish Immigrant Autobiography, 1942" (PhD dissertation, University of Minnesota, 2000).

36. Berger, "A rayze," 106.

37. Diary of Sidney Herbst, entries for 1/14, 1/15, 1/23, Herbst family file, Collection on Family History and Genealogy, RG 126, YIVO Institute for Jewish Research.

38. Rose Schoenfeld, autobiography #110, p. 30, Collection of American Jewish Autobiographies, RG 102, YIVO Institute for Jewish Research.

39. Berger, "A rayze," 118.

40. *Horodishcher barg* (New York: United Horodyszczer Relief Organizations, 1920), 21.

41. Kobrin, "Conflicting Diasporas, Shifting Centers."

Community and the Discourse of Elegy

The Postwar Suburban Debate

American Jewish communal life was a pressing topic for Jewish commentators throughout the 1950s. Intellectuals and academics who wrote for *Commentary* and other Jewish publications of opinion debated these issues as regularly as did activists, rabbis, social services professionals, communal leaders, and laypeople in their journals and magazines. In one way or another they all addressed the viability of postwar American Jewish life.[1] The world of Jewish print fostered broad and intense debates on the subject.

These communal conversations were played out in a specific register that questioned whether Jews and Judaism could thrive or even survive in the nation's newly settled suburbs. Could American Jews live as Jews outside the dense urban centers created by the Jews of the second generation? Could this new and largely alien suburban world make young Jews into Jewish adults? The debate was lively; all positions had their advocates.

Commentary magazine, in fact, marked the tercentenary year of Jewish settlement in North America by featuring a number of articles on suburbanization. The editors compared the internal migration from the metropolitan center to the suburbs to the earlier waves of Jewish immigration to the United States. Both transplantations promised to create "the American Jewish story." These "new communities" were developing "the mold of living," according to the editors. Their plan was to feature a series of articles to provide "informal studies of development."[2]

Commentary did not misjudge the importance of suburbanization. Many scholars have demonstrated that it was one of the single most important changes in American Jewish life following World War II, as it was for the nation as a whole and for American religion as well. Jews suburbanized to a far greater degree than other Americans. In the decades following World War II Jews left Boston, Newark, Chicago, Cleveland, and ultimately Manhattan, as well as other urban areas, for suburbia. One Jewish journalist termed this movement immediately after the war "a stampede."[3] During the 1950s the Jewish population of suburban Chicago increased by 100,000.[4] In that same period the Jewish population of Newark declined by nearly 20,000, and a number of New Jersey's Jewish enclaves in suburbs increased by the thousands.[5] That same decade Roxbury (a part of Boston) lost nearly 13,000 Jewish residents, largely to suburbs.[6] One scholar writing about Jewish education for the *Journal of Educational Sociology* asserted that "Jews make up a substantial part of the suburban population in the largest metropolises of our nation."[7]

Some Jews moved to new suburbs, most famously Levittown, which drew Jews from New York, Philadelphia, and New Jersey. Some moved to established suburbs like Highland Park, Illinois, that became increasingly Jewish. Some "towns" became suburbs after the population expansion following World War II, and Jews moved there to join, and usually overtake, the small Jewish communities that they found there.

These examples simply illustrate the central demographic fact that Jews as a group tend to move from their place of birth, and in the 1950s and 1960s they tended to move to suburbs.[8] The causes of suburbanization for Jews and others have been documented elsewhere. They include a housing shortage, white flight, increased transportation and roads, as well as other factors. I am less concerned with the cause than the effects in this essay.

Those, however, who wrote about suburbanization did not focus their anxiety on "community," let alone, with a few exceptions, even use the word. Ironically, the danger of suburban life for many writers lay in the *abundance* of communal organizations and Jews' zeal to join them. What preoccupied the period's commentators was instead the question of American Jewish life itself. Who defined and who controlled Jewish life? What was the relationship between postwar Jewish life and the older, immigrant, often left-wing or Orthodox urban Jews who had personified it previously? What would become of the generation of Jews born in the suburbs? The debates evinced a free-floating anxiety about Jewish life in the very period largely perceived as triumphant for American Jews. The Jewish age of optimism, from one perspective, was weighted with anxiety from another.

These anxieties were hardly resolved as Jewish residential patterns continued to move Jews a greater distance from cities and their ethnic enclaves. As "community," "identity," and "continuity" became the language of Jewish "crisis" in the 1970s, 1980s, and 1990s, suburbanization lost its saliency as a central cause of these problems. This debate, nevertheless, continues to merit our attention. Jewish historians of this period remain divided about the impact and significance of suburbanization on American Jewish life. The mordant tone of much of the popular literature of this time has found its way into historical writing. What the historiography appears to share with the 1950s discourse about American Jewish viability is the inability to envision the extent to which change is organic to culture and how communities develop in response to those changes. The elegiac mode offers a language of nostalgia and limits the ability to envision a vital future. The replication of this discourse in historical writing raises questions about how culture and community are conceived by scholars who reflect on American Jewish history and culture.

The Suburban Paradox

In 1953 Morton Sterne, who described himself as "an executive director of a large suburban temple outside of New York City," weighed in on the impact of suburbanization of Jews in the very title of his article, "Country Club Judaism." Sterne wrote:

> We start with a paradox. Jewish life in the suburbs is at once more Jewish and yet less Jewish. The institutions command loyalty and support. They thrive; their buildings are imposing. A much higher percentage of Jews in the suburbs are affiliated than in New York City. And yet Jewish suburban living seems diluted and pallid. In New York City one can feel Jewish and yet not belong to the Jewish Center; in the suburbs one belongs to the Jewish Center and yet is dogged by a sense of losing Jewish identity.[9]

Sterne argued that a suburban Jewish life, in contrast to life in the city, led Jews to "modify their folkways and curb their personalities in an effort not to offend." Hence suburban Jews did Jewish things, joined Jewish groups, particularly synagogues, but they did not feel Jewish, and according to some commentators they were really not Jewish.

The suburban Jewish "paradox"—doing more but feeling less Jewish—is a culturally rich discourse. It is engaging not because it accurately or inaccurately described what happened in new suburbs and in suburbs new to Jews, but because it provides us a language and logic through which we can analyze an important and even transformational moment in American Judaism and Jewish life.[10] What did these writers mean by declaring that less was more, that membership denoted a lack of authentic connection, and that suburban connections were exercises in futility? How could an abundance of "social capital," to use Robert Putnam's term—the active membership in (Jewish) civic organizations that bound people to one another and the collective—spell the doom of Jewish life?[11]

Certainly, some writers of the period, particularly from the Conservative and Reform movements, made a case for the emergence of a new religiosity and innovative social connections in the suburbs. Nevertheless, the "paradox" suggested that these forms of Jewish life lacked "authenticity." Jews may have assembled, spent time together, and acted in relationship to one another, but that did not constitute a Jewish culture that, according to one national lay leader, was "organic" with history, received through "our mother's milk and our father's prayers."[12]

The suburbs, according to their critics, lacked Jewish languages, foods, many traditional institutions, and especially a majority of Jews. Hence, suburban Judaism was a community without a "culture." The substitute offered in the suburbs for the city's rich cultural life was the synagogue, the only address for suburban American Jews.[13] Not surprisingly, it too was the subject of an even more heated debate, which questioned the authenticity of the religious revival linked to the explosion in synagogue building and the increase in synagogue membership. Both synagogue membership and Jewish communal life were typically dismissed as expressions of conformism and association.

A Spatial Judaism

The suburban Jewish paradox encodes what might be read as the key trope of Jewish life before and shortly after World War II in the United States. It was lived within a spatial dimension. Jews were Jews because of where they lived. Jews lived their lives in urban streets, air, and public spaces. Even stores that catered to Jewish needs became a version of a Jewish civic square. These neighborhoods took on meaning as important "places," but in effect what was most significant about them was the shared space they created. Brooklyn was Brooklyn only because Jews settled and lived there; otherwise, it was unmarked by unique meanings.

For example, Boston's urban Jewish area, particularly Roxbury and Dorchester, counted about seventy thousand Jews as residents in the 1940s and 1950s. The neighborhood had forty synagogues, only two of which were non-Orthodox. Sixty kosher butchers, and shops, bakeries, pharmacies, and stores lined Blue Hill Avenue, a main thoroughfare of the area. One commentator quipped that a resident could not walk past three storefronts without running into a friend or former tenant.[14] Another memoirist recalled the local G&G delicatessen as the center of life on the avenue. He wrote,

> On the tables of the cafeteria Talmudic jurisprudence sorted out racing results, politics, the stock market and the student could look up from his "desk" to leer at young girls sipping cream soda under the immense wings of their mother; watch the whole world of Blue Hill Avenue revolve through the G and G's glass gate.[15]

Mark Mirsky captured the ways in which space and culture were inter-twined. He linked the images of the house of study to the experience of gathering in a commercial/public space. Conversation topics like politics and racing were approached with the same sharp logic and complexity as Talmudic discourse. He glossed the delicatessen table as the *shtendar*, or the study desk, and imagined a young man eyeing a young woman from it. Study houses still existed of course, although they were not the dominant mode of American Jewish life. Nevertheless, in Mirsky's memory the neighborhood constituted Jewish space.

The discourse of space and place implied a second logic as well. Urban Jewish life did not require self-conscious choices, membership, or necessary activity. It was about being in a place rather than participating in any particular facet of it. One did not have to go into a synagogue, a union hall, or a mikvah; one had simply to be in their orbit. That these Jewish institutions existed was hardly incidental; they marked the spaces as overtly Jewish. They had their devoted members. However, one who was not a member was no less Jewish, because what defined the Jewishness of the area was the dominance of Jews. A majority Jewish neighborhood constituted a "natural," or "normative," Jewish setting.

Harry Gersh, a Jewish professional in community relations, wrote one of *Commentary*'s reflections on the suburbs in 1954:

> The places we lived were ghettos, no matter how well concealed. . . . In those days we were the majority in our community and we reacted as a majority. We were not hyper-conscious of our Jewishness. It was not that we were indifferent to it. Things Jewish were ingrained in our lives.[16]

It would be stretching the logic only slightly to suggest that in the period prior to World War II, when Jews were "racialized " by the larger society, Jews reflexively understood themselves as "spatialized." The spatial dimension of their lives certainly implied all sorts of institutional relationships, but they implied contiguous neighborhoods as well. Spatial relationships were unself-conscious; "memberships" were often based on different loyalties or ideologies—religious, political, hometown ties, and cultural outlooks. Community, then, was a web of connections constituted by where one resided. Density not only defined the spatial dimension but sheer numbers as well.

Those spaces depended less on formal membership than on the presence of kin and the overlapping relationship of work, family, and a variety of communal organizations. Jewish culture was diverse, polyvalent, and bounded primarily by space. Jewish life was not constituted by a shared worldview in a religious sense, though certainly other values and outlooks were key.[17] Fundamentally, Jewish life rested on the fact that Jews were in the majority of those paradigmatic urban neighborhoods, and Jews defined the norms.[18]

Ties of family and the *Yiddishkeit* of Ashkenazic Jewry filled the cultural spaces of urban life and fueled a commitment to achievement and mobility. The left-wing politics of most Jews of these areas could be traced to the dominance of its residents' working-class roots and union loyalty. The shared experience of antisemitism heightened the sense of a bounded world that divided Jews from others. For reasons of income or perceived lack of alternatives, these neighborhoods appeared to be the only choices for the Jews who lived there.

Not surprisingly then Jewish neighborhood life was often cast as prisonlike for the generation that abandoned it. Many characterized it as suffocating. The yearning to flee certainly marked the lives of native-born Jews. One *Commentary* author wrote candidly about her feelings about the Bronx when she was a student at Hunter College in 1942:

> Everything I thought and did was part of an effort to get away from the family, the neighborhood, the whole city if such a thing was possible. I plotted and planned and went to concerts, lectures, dances at the American Labor party headquarters, talks on Zionism.[19]

Eve Gordon, the Bronx-born subject of a study of an American postwar family, recalled her anticipated move to the suburbs with her new family as "liberation from the extended family." She judged that fact as almost as compelling a reason to leave as the "danger" she experienced on Bronx streets in 1951.[20]

It was often the case, though not for Eve Gordon, that parents encouraged their children to find a "better" life outside their neighborhood. Mobility involved leaving urban neighborhoods for many Jews, and little American Jewish literature has been devoted to generational struggles over leaving the city. The process was remarked upon in a work like *Goodbye Columbus*; it was not marked by loss. In the end, the neighborhood had little hold on the lives of Jews even if, according to the "suburban paradox" and other commentators, it created an unselfconscious Jewish world.

One has only to contrast the experience of American Catholic suburbanization to Jewish patterns to understand the meaning of the spatial trope. Like Jews, prior to World War II Catholics lived in a subculture that was religiously marked. Even following the war 50 percent of Catholics said that half of their neighbors were Catholic.[21] Yet the period after the war initiated a radical transformation, as it did for Jews and other urbanites. A Catholic writer noted that in one year following the war more Catholics moved to suburbia than came to the United States during any decade of the nineteenth century.[22]

Neighborhoods changed for both Jews and Catholics; however, the centrality of the suburban synagogue constituted a more dramatic change for Jews.[23] For Catholics a growing emphasis on national and international interests as the focus of prayer suggested to scholars that suburban Catholicism reflected a waning emphasis on the neighborhood. Catholics were, bluntly put, more "religious" or more volitional about their participation than Jews, for whom the suburban synagogue functioned as a communal gathering place and the substitute for the neighborhood.[24]

Catholics joined parishes. Jews lived in neighborhoods and brought synagogues along. The Catholic hierarchy protected its urban institutions for newcomers to the city. Lacking a comparable hierarchy, urban Jewish institutions disintegrated.[25] The parish was continuous in cities and suburbs. Synagogues took on a new role in the suburbs where, for Jews, the meaning of space was radically altered.

Those who contested the mordant view that "more" would be "less" in suburban Jewish life laid claim to a new logic. Again, what is of interest is not primarily whether they were correct but the emergence of a discursive logic that marked a redefinition of American Jewish life. The relationship between city and suburb emerged as a new polarity in defining postwar American Jewish life. Hence, the elegiac tone that marks some of the writing of both historians and the period's "experts" suggests that the abandonment of shared space constituted the end of a viable American Jewish life. Many, though not all, used the image of declension. For them the world left behind could not be replicated in a "new" world.[26]

Jewish Life as Association and Affiliation

Urban Jews who moved to suburbia entered a new world. They found not only the unfamiliar backyards, in which so many delighted, but a world that was not populated primarily by Jews. Morton Sterne's paradox thus followed. In his elegy for Jewish life he viewed suburban Jews as people who founded and joined all sorts of organizations. However, their memberships failed to make them "feel" Jewish, since they no longer set communal norms. For Sterne and others who shared his view membership was compensatory, a necessarily inadequate replacement for a vibrant Jewish neighborhood.

Advocates for Jewish life in the suburbs challenged that assumption and therefore signaled the emergence of a new logic. Following World War II Jewish life was for them built increasingly on affiliation, and synagogue affiliation in particular constituted one, if not its key, form in the 1950s and 1960s. Harry Gersh, a former union educator and a 1950s Jewish professional, wrote:

> The synagogue symbolizes the most important change in the move to suburbia. The closest thing to a Jewish community in the United States is a suburban synagogue. True, its power is only psychological. It is nonetheless, real. The Jew is perforce a member of his religious community. Even if he refuses to accept formal membership, he does not openly dispute the synagogue's right to speak for him.[27]

The synagogue was for Gersh the suburban American version of the *kehillah*, the communal organization that regulated European Jewry in pre-Enlightenment Europe. Though they were radically different from one another, Gersh reached for an analogy to suggest that in suburban America Jews were represented to their neighbors through a vehicle of religious affiliation.

Few of these communal organizations were invented after the war. They simply mushroomed and became the medium of Jewish life. Detractors, however, suggested that affiliation offered a spurious and inadequate culture. They predicted doom for the Jewish people. Advocates touted the superiority of affiliation. What was the logic of affiliation? Its advocates suggested that membership involved a degree of commitment and identification that was lacking in urban life. It fostered a sense of identification in an enterprise that was thoroughly Jewish: to live among Americans as Jews who were members of vibrant, democratic, and young organizations created by Jews in their new neighborhoods.

Simon Glustrom, a layman and founder of his synagogue, argued in 1957 in the journal *Conservative Judaism* that half the Jews who lived in the suburb of Fair Lawn, New Jersey, joined the new synagogue center. In cities, he stated, "they felt no pressure [to affiliate]" to what he described as "the synagogue around the corner." However, in the new suburbs they sought a closer identification with "Jewish community life."[28]

Abraham Fleischman, a member of the New York Metropolitan section of the Jewish Welfare Board, made a similar argument in *The Reconstructionist* in 1953. He wrote about the "changing characteristics of the Jewish individuals as they take root in the suburbs." Those from the Bronx, Brooklyn, or the Lower East Side were "conscious" of being Jews, but in their new environment they developed a "self-consciousness" of this fact. He noted that they joined organizations—"service groups, clubs, country clubs, and others had they stayed in their old neighborhoods they would have never dreamed of doing." He might have added to his list, as others frequently did, synagogues. Fleischman, while not uncritical of suburban Jewish life, suggested that the suburban Jew "feels the new institutions, which he helped create and finance, to be more a part of him."[29]

Rabbi Golovensky similarly defended "country club" Judaism when he described Jews' investment in their associations. He wrote that Jews' experience of the suburbs challenged the ways they had "felt" Jewish in the city. They made the person aware of "the vacuity of the vague feeling Jewish." For him the suburban alternative created " a feeling of solidarity and cohesiveness, the support that a sense of belonging confers." The "pressure from without and compulsion from within" to join a synagogue motivated Jewish suburbanites. The self-consciousness of membership, he argued, was a positive development.[30]

Affiliation, according to one participant in Marshall Sklare's ethnographic study of a Chicago suburb, emphasized his "personal identification" with a congregation. He commented, "It's the first synagogue I've belonged to that I feel I'm a part of. The rabbi calls me Al. The president calls me Al. It never happened before."[31] This new Jewish suburbanite suggested both a yearning for and satisfaction with membership that he felt was lacking in urban Jewish life. In this sense affiliation constituted the opposite experience of unselfconscious membership in a neighborhood and reformulated Jewish life as membership and personal relationships.

The logic of affiliation implied "American" values, particularly egalitarianism and democracy. In the early years of Jewish suburbanization these writers noted a democratic spirit of youth and new leadership in communal life. Suburbanites also claimed that Jewish life in cities had closed off participation for young men. They complained that they had been confronted with the "iron curtain of the older generation," the established leadership cadre who would never let them become leaders.[32] Commentators held up equality and innovation as positive and new Jewish values that were well suited to American postwar life.

For example, Simon Glustrom, a founder of the Fair Lawn Jewish Center in New Jersey, commented on another dimension of the synagogue's "openness." "The newcomer," he wrote, "is particularly impressed with the number of women who serve on the board. He is convinced that this is a significant step forward when women are given the same privileges and responsibilities in the synagogue that they have earned in government, finance, and education."[33]

These "native texts" suggest that the logic of affiliation linked organizational life to a series other issues. Membership was self-conscious, democratic, innovative, and inclusive. It was rooted in American life and drew on what America had to offer. It was often contrasted not only with the city but also with Europe. Perceptions of urban Jewish life underlined dominance by an "old guard." Jewish life in suburbia was associated with a more inclusive Jewishness that was less likely to create barriers to participation.[34] It was "forward looking," and its logic implied a lack of ideology. Ideology was associated with urban Jewish life whether it was political or religious.

Glustrom, for example, noted that in 1950 Fair Lawn's synagogue of 750 members was drawn from a total Jewish population of 1,500 families. Members originally hailed from both New York City and New Jersey cities. Of these members, he noted, 150 were Reform and 175 were Conservative. Suburbanites praised a Jewish life characterized as fluid rather than rigid. Similarly, historian Jeffrey Gurock found a high degree of similarity between Orthodox and Conservative synagogues in this period as well.[35]

Certainly a persistent theme in the logic of affiliation was the centrality of religion and synagogue, during a time that Judaism was undergoing a revival following World War II. In the early years of postwar suburbanization in particular, the promise of what would be called a "religious revival" was as potent in the Jewish community as it was in its Christian counterpart.[36] Robert Gordis, editor of the new journal *Judaism: A Quarterly Journal of Jewish Life and Thought*, declared in 1952 in the first issue that American Jews were experiencing a "renascence" of Judaism, or what he also termed a revival of interest. Though he did not allude to the suburbanization debate, he focused instead on the events of the war, the birth of Israel, and the inability of science to answer key questions, in order to explain this dramatic change. These issues, particularly the first and the last, were widely believed to shape the perspectives of those settling the suburbs.[37]

If there was a "renascence," a matter discussed below, the synagogue was indeed central to the logic of affiliation. It was where self-consciousness about being a Jew led young suburbanites. While initially some choices were made between building religious schools and synagogues, or federations and synagogues, ultimately these communities all built synagogues.[38]

The logic of affiliation was, of course, grounded in a social reality. Suburban Jews were a highly affiliated group, as were most Americans of the period. Suburban Jews, for example, were more likely to belong to synagogues than the Jews of Brooklyn. Marshall Sklare found that 66 percent of his respondents were members of a Chicago suburb's synagogues, and 83 percent were past or present members. About 88 percent of residents were affiliated with a Jewish voluntary organization and 91 percent with a nonsectarian one, most likely the PTA.[39]

In contrast, the large synagogue centers of Brooklyn drew their membership from a larger geographic radius because the lower middle class could not afford to join. Class mobility, which made it possible to move to the suburbs facilitated synagogue membership and advanced the logic of affiliation.[40]

The Vulnerabilities of Postwar Logics

The logic of space was challenged by the logic of affiliation. Harry Gersh wrote, "Still in seeking a less 'Jewish' existence no matter how subtly expressed, we find in Suburbia a more 'Jewish' existence." He inverted the paradox of country club Judaism. Indeed, less was more in a world where self-consciousness about being a minority created a far higher affiliation rate than in the city.[41]

However, the critique of suburban life persisted among American Jews throughout the 1950s and 1960s, just as it did generally in America. Writers continued to insist that a suburban Jewish life was inauthentic and empty—or, in the case of Oscar Handlin, the historian of immigration and the nation, that its content was irrelevant. He wrote for *Commentary* about "American Jewish patterns" on the occasion of the tercentenary celebration. He wrote approv-

ingly about American Jewish life and also provided a straightforward definition of the apparent turn toward religion. About Judaism he wrote, "religion
in that sense meant the pattern of activities that drew the group together and
located it in the universe that drew its children onward and cemented family
relationships."[42]

Handlin claimed that American Jews did not trouble themselves about the
"Jewish content" or the "American environment" that "moved them" to their
involvement in adult education, or benefit card parties, dances, or brother-
hoods. Rather, they found "peace of mind" in the company of their fellows
and emotional satisfaction for the whole personality.[43] His only explanation for
the pleasure and tranquillity that resulted was the failure of any prior vision
such as Zionism or universalism or radicalism or liberalism. Indeed, he concluded that as "men matured" after the 1920s they discovered that "America
was not, after all, a land of unaffiliated men. The children's questions [to their
fathers about why they were not members of a religion] could not be answered
if everyone else did somehow belong."[44]

For Handlin, a passionate advocate for Jews to accommodate to the larger
society by fitting in, affiliation was the answer to how Jews could best become
Americans. Affiliation became an end in itself. There was no difference
between a card party and a religious service. Both served the ends of involvement. Affiliation was a rejection of the Jew as critic or even visionary.

Robert Ellwood, an important scholar of American religions, claimed
that the American turn toward religion in the 1950s was complex and nicely
explained why the debate around affiliation was intense and protracted. He
argued that American religion, whether "popular" or the "elite" version of
theologians and intellectuals, was caught in the great conundrum of the period.
Mass society presented dangers on two fronts. Communism and totalitarian-
ism on the one hand, and "Madison Avenue" and the world of advertising
on the other, had the capacity to manipulate the individual in an impersonal
bureaucracy. Because, according to Ellwood, crowds were dangerous, membership was suspect. Thus church and synagogue membership could well be
construed as a sort of capitulation to mass society.[45]

Therefore it is no surprise that the "affiliation anxiety" Ellwood outlined
dominated the first article in the *Commentary* series on suburbia. In this article Evelyn Rossman described the parade of visitors who came to see her when
her family moved to Northrup, her pseudonym for her northeastern suburb.
Women from Jewish women's organizations arrived with gifts such as candy
dishes to welcome her. As they exited they always provided her with a membership form on which she felt obligated to pledge a year's membership to
this or that Jewish women's organization. She questioned the value of such
groups, and above all what she experienced as their coercive expectation that
she would of course join them.

Indeed, she was anything but triumphant about suburban Jewish life. For all the communal activity, she focused primarily on the struggle between the suburb's "masses" of Jews and the "serious" Jews who wanted more for themselves and their children in the way of Jewish learning and life. What she observed in suburbia—in contrast to her Bronx, immigrant, Orthodox home—was "the loss of Jewish values, the disrespect for study, for social conscience, culture and charity."[46] Like other writers, she emphasized the hollowness of affiliation.

The logic of affiliation was open to suspicion, and its critics, from within and without the suburbs, cast such a community as dangerous. Jewish experience is rarely a simple reflection of the larger society. The criticism of the new logic of affiliation was not only about the danger of capitulation to conformism and mass society but about inauthenticity as well. Those critiques revealed a larger concern for the viability of American Jewish life.

The emergent postwar logic, therefore, came under constant attack in the popular Jewish press, particularly as the first near-utopian years of the 1950s yielded to the realities of the burgeoning suburbs and established patterns of Jewish life. Building organizations and recruiting members did not guarantee their Jewishness. Adjectival epithets modifying Judaism—"country club," "juvenile," and "dancing school"—suggested that all sorts of critics believed that there was little Jewish content to suburban Jewish life.

Affiliation as Divided Selves and Culture

The suburban critique turned on issues of authenticity. The language of the divided self emerged regularly, as much for suburbanites as for the scholars who began to study them. The integrity of culture and self was not only under scrutiny but also raised the problem of what it meant to be a Jew in relationship to the nation in the logic of affiliation. Harry Gutmann, a synagogue board member from New Rochelle, New York, appraised suburban Judaism in 1955 for the journal *American Judaism*. "Suburban life . . . stabs a searching light beam upon us and reveals us to ourselves for what we really are: tentative, groping, dichotomized American Jews.[47]

Gutmann was not the only person writing on Jewish life in suburbia who evoked the term "schizophrenia" to capture the experience. Dr. L. H. Grunebaum, chair of his temple's education committee, evaluated the religious school and provided the results for "private consumption" within the temple. His evaluation found its way, however, to the pages of *Commentary*. He suggested that "the children suffer from a kind of mild schizophrenia. Here are the rabbi, director, cantor and teachers; there are the parents. Here is supernaturalism, prayer, the Ten Commandments. There is science, atomic facts, sex and Mickey Spillane, American ways and values. . . . So it comes about that the attempt to make children more secure as members of the Jewish community has in many cases the opposite result."[48] It was in the language of division, and even pathology, that affiliation raised the problem of authenticity. Could Jews be members of organization and institutions but not share a culture, a way of life, or at least a neighborhood world? Suburbanites might have fled their parents' world, but they were loath to deny its authenticity.

Not surprisingly, Irving Howe, the socialist literary and cultural critic, fired the first salvo in this idiom in 1948 in *Commentary* about the pseudonymous Spruceton, a rural town in Connecticut with a longtime Jewish presence. He juxtaposed an old man, father of a friend, with the newer generation. The elder practiced, for Howe, what was a real Judaism. His leftist politics and his Yiddish marked that authenticity. According to Howe, his own younger generation had intermarried and left the town. They were replaced by an invasion of newcomers. A new wave of suburbanites migrated to Spruceton. Howe dismissed them as "alrightniks," evoking those who betrayed the immigrant Jews by their mobility in the previous generation. They wanted to fit in and be like those around them; they lacked any of the values, sensitivities, or politics of their elders. In short, they were Jewish without being Jews. Howe pondered "how to explain the fact that the group that knew least about and cared least for Judaism became the most active and sustaining section of the Jewish community." His conclusion was that the "old-timers' group was disintegrating with time. Their sons left. The alrightniks were the only ones who cared, and they created an inoffensive and empty Judaism."[49] In Howe's view the new suburbanites established a bourgeoisie that became coterminous with community. The "real" Jews were working class. The bourgeois wore their Judaism without authenticity. This elegy for Jewish life suggested that what would remain would not be real.

The elegiac tone was not only directed toward the passing of an older generation. More frequently it was the suburbanites' hyperfocus on children that was used to puncture the emptiness of affiliation. By the 1970s Marshall Sklare, the leading scholar of postwar sociology of American Jews, wrote confidently that in the Conservative synagogue ties of ethnicity really brought Jews together under the guise of religion.[50]

However it was children more than ethnicity that provided the logic of affiliation. Even as synagogue building was booming, families struggled both with what it meant to be an American and what it meant to be a Jew, and their relationship to one another. The Jews who had felt suffocated by the urban centers seemed more than a little uneasy with the religious affiliation that the suburbs appeared to demand.

Many scholars, beginning with the sociologist Herbert Gans, established the child-oriented nature of suburban Judaism.[51] The language of affiliation was, for Jews, grounded in that relationship. Child orientation connoted for the larger society such matters as consumption patterns. For Jews, it also implied that children participated in a Judaism that the parents would not embrace. Judaism was far more a matter of religious school and synagogue than home, the precise inversion of the spatial Judaism of the second settlement. Indeed, the early suburbanites often protested against the expectation that they should keep their children home from school on Jewish holidays. Christmas was strenuously debated in the suburbs. Many families claimed that they had Christmas trees and celebrations for their children, while others stopped celebrating Christmas because they were convinced by synagogues and religious schools that Christmas was not good for their children.

In the institution of the religious school, the authority of Judaism became the rope in a tug-of-war precisely because the focus on affiliation, as a logic and a reality, moved people into the sphere of religious authority. Parents pulled in one direction; rabbi, teachers, and school often pulled in another. There were contradictions created by affiliation as a medium of identity when those joining wanted to contain the power of the institutions.

Rossman recounted that at her children's Hebrew school meetings parents asked: "How can I teach my child to believe things he knows I don't believe?" "How can my child be proud of being a Jew when I'm not sure that I'm so proud?"[52] A psychologist writing for the *United Synagogue Review* in 1959 thundered in print that Jewish parents, perfectly capable of giving children gender identities, were stumped by giving them Jewish identities because the parents were so uncertain about their own feelings about being Jews.[53] Another reported on a parent-teacher meeting at a Hebrew school in a New England town about an hour outside Boston. A parent expressed his outrage that the Hebrew school had informed the public schools about the dates of Jewish holidays, when children would miss class. He reportedly said, "Why don't you take a poll? Why don't you find out how people feel before you send notices?" He declared his need to protect himself from a community that pressured him and his children to observe holidays of no interest to them.[54]

The logic of affiliation was fraught with danger. Membership implied connection, belief, even sincerity. Although affiliation organized the experience of the new suburban world, it challenged the logic because participants joined for the sake of others, joined religious institutions for other than religious reasons, and were pressured by others to behave in ways consistent with membership. If space could be fled, as Jews had fled urban centers, then memberships could be dropped or minimized as Jews pondered their dangers for themselves and their children as they sought to become more fully American.

The Suburb as the Nation

Jews joined the suburbs in part to escape what was perceived as the suffocation of growing up in urban neighborhoods—the lack of choices and the dominance of the anxieties of mothers and fathers. They yearned, in short, for the America of houses, yards, and new neighbors. Sam Gordon, the subject of a study of postwar family life, left the Bronx and purchased his first home on Long Island in 1952. He recalled looking across the sand at his new lot and thinking that he "was seeing democracy for the first time, democracy un-tempered as it was meant to be."[55] Suburban affiliation implied, then, not only association with other Jews but a form of citizenship in a newly accessible America.

In the end, nevertheless, many suburbs became sites of "reterritorialization," and took on the territoriality and boundaries of urban enclaves. By design of developers, by the choices of some Jewish families, and by the lack of choices given to others, Jews began to be part of identifiably Jewish neighborhoods within suburbs. Rossman expressed her dissatisfaction with isolation from Gentiles as clearly as the absence of community.

> The desire to be like everyone else seems quite separate from the wish to be with them. . . . The Jewish community seems to be developing alongside, separately, rather than within the larger community. Most of the Jews accept this development as a perfectly natural one. The fears we sometimes hear expressed that organized Jewish community life of the kind that is building in our town makes for separation and clannishness seems not at all groundless.[56]

Affiliation, therefore, raised the problem of where Jews should and could live. The same concern over coercive membership underlined debates in Jewish venues over where Jews would live in these new residential developments. Were Jews really entering a democratic landscape of young families? Were they being forced to live with one another, or were they realizing their ideal by being surrounded by other Jewish families? Those who advocated the latter found in suburbia a utopian paradise, at least in the early 1950s, fairly free of class differences. But the evidence falls on the side of coercion.

One article from 1958 in *Commentary* was devoted to yet one more person writing under an assumed name, recounting his effort to sell his home in a Jewish section of a suburb to a non-Jew. "I sell my house: One Man's Experience with Suburban Segregation" made clear that suburbs were not neutral spaces despite the invisibility of their boundaries. The author was, contrary to the expectations of such a title, not trying to racially integrate his block. He could not find a Christian who was willing to purchase his house.[57] His article reflected on why suburbs of Long Island and Westchester County were becoming religiously divided. Some blamed brokers who enforced religious homogeneity; some blamed Jews for their clannishness and irrational fears. The point was clear, however: Jewish suburbia was becoming reterritorialized in New York, Chicago, Boston, and throughout the country.[58]

As the private musings of a synagogue member cited above made clear, Jews had fewer choices than they imagined. Some affiliated reluctantly and defensively.

The Logics of American Jewish Lives

How best to explain the anxious tone of American Jewry's golden era of the 1950s? Why was the register of Jewish social life focused on its viability? Why was communal self-reflection, at least in print media, so often written in the language of elegy? The doomed country-club-Judaism debate, or Howe's yearning for authenticity, or the fear that no revival was authentic or, if it was heartfelt, it was because Jews were losing their values—all were elegies for a lost past and an inadequate future.

Eli Lederhendler argued, following Marshall Sklare and others, that urban ethnicity had little power to act as the cultural glue of American Jewish experience. It was the immigrant generation who constituted their experience through the powerful connections of ethnicity as a shared destiny and outlook.[59] Suburbanization was simply an artifact of upward mobility, and the ties of class trumped other forms of affiliation. Indeed, the work on Jews and whiteness suggests that the suburbs were the setting for the consolidation of whiteness as an effect of class mobility.[60]

While one would not want to dispute such straightforward sociological observations, the terms of the debate ask for more. I self-consciously use the notion of "cultural logic" in order to emphasize the centrality to these debates of ideas about ordering experience, situating oneself in social relationships, and receiving and transmitting fundamental notions of who one is. The cultural logics of American Jewish association that I document are not solely cognitive, as the term *logic* might imply. Nor are they a simple matter of personal choice. To the contrary, these processes are complex, neither matters of "mere" nostalgia nor rationalizations for class mobility. Indeed, to return to the original "suburban paradox," to explore why an American Jew *feels* more or less Jewish because he or she *lives* in one or another neighborhood is to ask the central questions of culture. In what social settings are American Jews made Jews? What must they do and with whom must they do it to become Jewish and American? What authenticates their experiences, and what denies them?

The debates from which I draw these cultural logics are important for a second reason. They demonstrate simultaneously the extent to which they are embedded in American culture of the period and reshape it. The publication of David Riesman's work on "inner-" and "outer-directed" Americans in 1950 marked an American preoccupation with the dangers of suburbanization and conformism.[61] Gordon Allport similarly judged religious authenticity according to its motivations for connection to outer or inner experience.[62] America was awash with fears of mass society, bureaucracy, and the manipulation of desire by anonymous corporate forces.

It is, therefore, no surprise that Jews writing for a variety of publications, whether they were social workers, rabbis, writers, or social scientists, would reflect similar concerns about young Jews in new suburban settlements. However, they wrote about these problems as Jewish ones related to their exit from the city. They linked the problem of conformism to the viability of American Jewry, and the language of authenticity shaped the ways in which they reflected on a specific relationship to their own parents and families. These cultural logics were the medium for imagining Jewish life, its past and its future.

I use the concepts of logic, culture, and discourse in order to de-center the study of the postwar period from a focus on declining community, broken social relationships, and inauthentic religion. In its place I want to heighten the sense that residence, space, place, authenticity, and even women's leadership are not self-evident sociological truisms. They are the stuff of culture and contestation. They reveal a period in American Jewish culture of change and transformation, not death and decay.

The historian Edward Shapiro writes:

> The problems of postwar American Jewry were primarily the problems of suburbia. The diffusion of Jewish population into the suburbs and exurbs diluted Jewish identity. In the compacted Jewish neighborhoods of the cities, Jewish identity was absorbed through osmosis. In suburbia it had to be nurtured.[63]

His history of the postwar period, not unlike many others, uncritically posits and repeats these orthodoxies without exploring what any of the basic terms meant in this time or that they were the subject of active debates. This is not to dispute that suburbanization was both the product of and a contributor to a transformation in American and American Jewish life. Both Deborah Dash Moore and Arthur Goren address this point with greater precision and accuracy.[64] It is to seek instead to understand the nature of the conflict and why a mordant tone dominated these logics.

Space and affiliation, the two logics of American Jewish life, constituted different ways of imagining Jewish community and, perhaps, a notion of Jewish citizenship. Neither used the language of community, I would argue, for two reasons. First, "community" was not a key term in the social criticism of the period. "Prejudice," "status," "conformism," and "role" dominated the social sciences of the period, only to more or less disappear within two decades. Community was not to take center stage in social thought until well into the 1960s. The term did not resonate, because community was not an issue: Jews continued to live near other Jews. Even if the new settlers of postwar suburbia were few in number initially, their isolation appeared to be short-lived. There were Jews who wished to flee the tight-knit world of Jewish settlement. Those who sought community could find it easily. There were debates about whether or not it was "authentic," not whether or not it existed.

However, there were powerful Jewish terms that were not shared with the wider society that did appear in this period in reflective essays and books. "Ethics," "belief," and "authenticity" were among them. "Community" appeared infrequently other than as a noun modified by "the Jewish."

The most powerful contrast between the logics of affiliation and space nevertheless concerned the nature of community. One has reason to question whether community really can be constituted by "osmosis." When writers suggested they became Jews through "our fathers' prayers and our mothers' milk," to contrast the urban center to the suburb, they did posit community as overlapping sets of relationships grounded in a shared culture that appeared to have defined margins. It appeared that Jewish normativity was actually central. The logic of space assumed a majority Jewish world.

Urban Jewish neighborhoods were of course built upon a huge variety of forms of association, "secular" and "religious." The reasons for "joining," what one joined, and why were quite different than in the suburbs. Ironically, the emphasis on community as "natural" or transmitted by "osmosis" or requiring no commitment appeared to be the perspective of the younger generation. They left, both before they joined adult organizations and, for some, because they could not yet belong to power brokers of other groups. As Irving Howe famously wrote, "Growing up in the Bronx I didn't feel Jewish nor did I not feel Jewish."[65] The logic then, at least in part, was a discourse of exodus and nostalgia, a memory about another world used as a critique of a new one. Space loomed large as the alternative to affiliation.

Affiliation was straightforward. Jews brought a variety of organizations to the suburbs, fraternal and religious, and joined them in order to establish connections to one another. Many suburbs were an age- and class-homogeneous environment in their early years. They established networks of relationships among Jews. The criticism of them as redundant groups of the same people doing the same things is the very definition of community.

The elegiac tone of a great deal of postwar writing was shaped by the logic of affiliation. In contrast to space, or to the density of Jewish urban organizational life, suburban affiliation raised the questions of authenticity, content, meaning, and choice. The anxiety of conformism made any membership suspect, as Robert Ellwood argued. That was all the more the case in a dramatically new residential setting where Jews were redefining the nature of Jewish life and community. Those new definitions were in the hands of returning soldiers and their wives, members of what all scholars would agree was the least educated Jewish generation in history. They were pioneers in drawing new boundaries around Jew and non-Jew, self and other, and Jew and Jew. Whether this enterprise would work or could work or should work are questions that are shot through with both a longing for authenticity and anxiety about its possibility.

In the suburban context the language of affiliation was a language of integration and to some extent of cultural pluralism. Americans joined things, in contrast to ethnic Catholics and Jews—who were a religion and, in another time, a nation or a political/cultural entity. Religion seemed an especially good medium for integration. "We have one and they have one." One writer for *Commentary* suggested that Jewish ethical readings included William James, John Dewey, and a host of other Western philosophers. Robert Gordis, like so many other Jewish writers and intellectuals, linked Jewish thought to Western thought. Judaism really was presented as seamless with America if not Americans. The counterpart in the logic of affiliation was the anticipation that the Jewish communal connections would be well integrated into a hospitable world of other Americans. No wonder that some of the elegies for Jewish life raised the problem of why Jews were not joining non-Jewish organizations and asked why they were separating themselves from their non-Jewish neighbors.

The suburban paradox of doing more and feeling less is then not only about a logic of affiliation. It also underlines a second paradox. Jews went to the suburbs to become Americans and found themselves back in Jewish neighborhoods. They were different types of neighborhoods and communities. Some wanted precisely that experience, but it is unlikely that any of them wanted to be denied access to the America for which a war had been fought.

Did the elegies mask deeper anxieties about their rejection? Did they displace their fears about the near destruction of European Jewry onto leaving urban Jewish neighborhoods? Was the concern for a Jewish future fundamentally about how to go about living a truly new formulation of Jewish life, or did it underline the waning hold of the Jewish community on young Jews?

The suburban logic of affiliation was short-lived in at least two senses. Affiliation did not remain coercive, nor did it remain the medium for integration into the larger society by the end of the 1960s. Indeed, in retrospect it can be seen as transitional, even briefly experimental. Not unlike Jewish urban centers, it held the fascination of one generation, meeting their needs, articulating their vision, and solving their problems about how to be a Jew in America. Just as the logic of bounded space could not contain a new generation, the logic of affiliation as the path to America did not draw the baby boom generation, who radically challenged the form and nature of community.

However, that is precisely the point about cultural change. Its experiments are constantly transformed. One would not have predicted during this period the high degree of polarization between observant Jews and nonaffiliated ones that would mark the present moment. When scholars of American Jewry adopt the mordant tone of the "natives," they lose sight of the long view, of tracking change and transformation.

For example, in a provocative and important book, *New York Jews and the*

Decline of Urban Ethnicity, 1950–1970, Eli Lederhendler argues the following about New York Jewish life in the 1960s:

> To cherish what had been lost and to retrieve some of it, even while acknowledging its irretrievability, became the cultural credo of the Jewish community. The contrast between this posture and the general urgings of American culture in the sixties with its emphasis on "the torch being passed" to a new generation, on kicking over the traces of the Eisenhower years, on the abstract and the sensual, on the experimental in both outer and inner space, on the new could scarcely be greater. Self-validation in the American idiom turned toward the future while self-validation in the Jewish idiom turned toward the past. The utopian possibilities of an urban Jewish culture were finally relinquished—one is tempted to say forfeited. Possibly for this reason, those who tried to define the quality of Jewishness in New York were hard pressed to identify it with anything that was actually present.[66]

For Lederhendler memory becomes the cudgel that affiliation was for another generation. Because precisely when American culture was kicking over the fifties, other Americans were viewing ideas about politics and justice through the lens of remembered pasts. Women were recalling suffrage and an earlier women's culture; Latinos, African Americans, and Asian Americans were looking to ties of nationalism and histories of oppression. And some Jews drew on such memories to ground new formulations of religious community, study, American progressive politics, and more. One could find literary, musical, and artistic movements developing among younger Jews in just this period as a black arts movement was developing among younger African Americans. Memory and affiliation share complex cultural terrains.

There is no world easier for scholars, pundits, and artists to caricature than the suburbs. In retrospect, there is no cultural logic more naïve and even banal than the 1950s idea that joining Jewish organizations with little Jewish content could produce Jewish children and open the way to integration with Protestant neighbors. There is little grandeur in a world of anxious Jews trying to figure out how to be Americans and pressuring Jewish schools and rabbis to minimize and reshape Judaism. "Feeling Jewish," as Mr. Sterne posed in the opening paradox, is as weak a foundation for community as any that one could choose. What other tone would one adapt than an elegy to write about such a time?

If I see dynamic cultural processes, contestation, and even pioneers in those suburbs, perhaps it is because I want to understand this time as one in which a new American Judaism was taking shape. As scholars like Michael Staub argue, an important political debate was under way among Jews in this period.[67] New ideas about community emerged, were tried, and were superseded. The mordant tone misses that as well as the dynamic nature of American Jewish culture. I have argued for the need to treat community as culture, to understand how it laid out its own terrain in a particular historical moment, and to closely attend to its contradictions.

Notes

1. Letters to the editor allowed readers of these publications to respond to and often disagree with writers and one another about the nature of Jewish life. Whatever filters editors placed on those letters, or whatever the biases of editors, the topic of community persisted.
2. Editorial comment, *Commentary*, vol. 18 (5), November 1954, p. 393.
3. Philip Rubin, "Two Million on the Move," *National Jewish Monthly*, vol. 73, July 1959, p. 4.
4. Irving Cutler, *The Jews of Chicago: From Shtetl to Suburb* (Urbana: University of Illinois Press, 1996), p. 256.
5. Edward S. Shapiro, *A Time for Healing: American Jewry since World War II* (Baltimore: Johns Hopkins University Press, 1992), pp. 144–145.
6. Gerald Gamm, *Urban Exodus: Why the Jews Left Boston and the Catholics Stayed* (Cambridge, Mass.: Harvard University Press, 1999).
7. Edwin Simon, "Suburbia—Its Effect on the American Jewish Teen-ager," *The Journal of Educational Sociology*, Vol. 36, November 1962, p. 125.
8. On the importance of suburbanization in the United States see Kenneth T. Jackson, *The Crabgrass Frontier: The Suburbanization of the United States* (New York: Oxford University Press, 1985). On the impact of suburbanization on American Jews see Shapiro, *A Time for Healing*; Arthur A. Goren, "A Golden Decade for American Jews: 1945–1955," in Jonathan Sarna, ed., *The American Jewish Experience* (New York: Holmes and Meir, 1997), second edition, pp. 294–313.
9. *Congress Weekly*, May 4, 1953, p. 5.
10. Scholars have begun to study the presence of Orthodox Jews and Judaism in postwar suburbs. See Etan Diamond, *And I Will Dwell in Their Midst: Orthodox Jews in Suburbs* (Chapel Hill: University of North Carolina Press, 2000), and Jonathan Sarna, *American Judaism: A History* (New Haven: Yale University Press, 2004), pp. 290–306.
11. Robert Putnam, *Bowling Alone: The Collapse and Revival of American Community* (New York: Simon and Schuster, 2000), pp. 18–26.
12. William Haber, "The Question Is," *The National Jewish Monthly*, September 1960, p. 22.
13. The Jewish community center also served as a gathering place for Jews. It tended to follow the synagogue.
14. Hillel Levine and Lawrence Harmon, *The Death of an American Jewish Community: A Tragedy of Good Intentions* (New York: Free Press, 1992), p. 16. Gerald Gamm, *Urban Exodus: Why the Jews Left Boston and the Catholics Stayed* (Cambridge, Mass.: Harvard University Press, 1999), pp. 196–199. Ironically, this area of Boston began as a suburb in the 1920s but ultimately became part of urban

Jewish life, to be supplanted by the new suburbs such as Brookline. This process is described in both books cited.

15. Cited in Gamm, *Urban Exodus*, pp. 198–199, from a 1971 article in the Sunday *Boston Globe*.

16. Harry Gersh, "The New Suburbanites of the 50's," *Commentary*, vol. 17, March 1954, pp. 211–212.

17. Discussions of those values in New York City can be found in Deborah Dash Moore, *At Home in America: Second Generation New York Jews* (New York: Columbia University Press, 1981), and Beth Wenger, *New York Jews and the Great Depression: Uncertain Promises* (New Haven: Yale University Press, 1996). Politics and communal responsibility for those in need usually figure prominently in such a recounting, although they certainly do not describe any specific individuals or families.

18. The parallels to Zionism are obvious.

19. Evelyn Rossman, "The Community and I: Belonging: Its Satisfactions and Dissatisfactions," *Commentary*, vol. 18 (5), November 1954.

20. Donald Katz, *Home Fires: An Intimate Portrait of One Middle Class Family in Postwar America* (New York: Harper Collins, 1992), p. 56.

21. John T. McGreevy, *Parish Boundaries: The Catholic Encounter with Race in the Twentieth-Century Urban North* (Chicago: University of Chicago Press, 1996), p. 79.

22. Cited in McGreevy, *Parish Boundaries*, p. 83.

23. See McGreevy, *Parish Boundaries*.

24. McGreevy, *Parish Boundaries*, pp. 82–84.

25. Gamm, *Urban Exodus*, pp. 261–262. In Boston Jews did maintain a relationship to former synagogues by continuing to support them, belonging to one in the new area and the old one as well. Gamm argues that this pattern kept urban Jews from developing their own leadership cadre.

26. Deborah Moore noted that this language was also used for those Jews who left the Northeast for new regions of the United States following World War II. Deborah Dash Moore, *To the Golden Cities* (New York: The Free Press, 1994).

27. Gersh, "The New Suburbanites of the 50's," p. 217. Gersh argues that many organizations argue about who represents the Jews, such as the American Jewish Committee, Jewish Labor Committee, Workmen's Circle, or others, but none of them represents suburban Jews.

28. Simon Glustrom, "Some Aspects of a Suburban Jewish Community," *Conservative Judaism*, Winter 1957, pp. 27–28.

29. Abraham A. Fleischman, "The Urban Jews Goes Suburban," *The Reconstructionist*, vol. 19, March 6, 1953, pp. 22–23.

30. Golovensky, "Defense of Country Club Judaism," *Congress Weekly*, November 9, 1953, p. 9.

31. Marshall Sklare and Joseph Greenblum, *Jewish Identity on the Suburban Frontier: A Study of Group Survival in the Open Society* (Chicago: University of Chicago Press, originally published 1967), second edition 1972, p. 203.

32. Glustrom, "Some Aspects of a Suburban Jewish Community."

33. Glustrom, "Some Aspects of a Suburban Jewish Community," p. 27. His observa-

tion was not entirely accurate. Women probably had more opportunities for leadership in synagogues than in government or finance. However, his perception was that the presence of women brought parity between Jewish institutions and American ones. In fact, the presence of women in the synagogue was also the source of considerable debate in this period, and their leadership was a source of concern. See Riv-Ellen Prell, *Fighting to Become Americans: Jews, Gender and the Anxiety of Assimilation* (Boston: Beacon Press, 1999), chapter 5.

34. For example, Marshall Sklare argued in his study *Conservative Judaism: An American Religious Movement* (New York: Schocken, originally 1955), 1972, pp. 58–59, 79, that in Chicago in the 1920s and 1930s the old guard resisted religious change and sought to keep younger, American-born men out of leadership. He argued, by contrast, that in the third settlement, at the city's edge or in the suburbs, synagogue members welcomed changes in worship styles and activities. Sklare suggested that because the Jews in these areas were already acculturated to American society, they sought to avoid the further assimilation of their cohort or the next generation. Affiliation was the best way for Jews to maintain their Jewishness, more important perhaps than maintaining certain practices and traditions.

35. Glustrom, "Some Aspects of a Suburban Jewish Community," p. 27. See Jeffrey Gurock, "From Fluidity to Rigidity: The Religious Worlds of Conservative and Orthodox Jews in Twentieth Century America," David W. Belin Lecture in American Jewish Affairs, Frankel Center for Judaic Studies, University of Michigan, 1998, for an important analysis of the connection between Orthodox and Conservative Jewish practice in this period.

36. See Sarna, *American Judaism*, pp. 278–282, for a discussion of a postwar Jewish revival as well as a decrease in observance.

37. Robert Gordis, "Toward a Renascence of Judaism," *Judaism: A Quarterly Journal of Jewish Life and Thought*, vol. 1 (10), January 1952, pp. 3–10.

38. On one such debate over the priority of institutions, see Herbert Gans "The Origins and Growth of a Jewish Community in the Suburbs: A Study of the Jews of Park Forrest," in Marshall Sklare, ed., *The Jews: Social Patterns of an American Group* (Glencoe: Free Press, 1958).

39. Sklare and Greenblum, *Jewish Identity on the Suburban Frontier*, pp. 97, 253.

40. Moore, *At Home in America*, p. 128.

41. Gersh, "The New Suburbanites of the 50's," p. 209.

42. Oscar Handlin, "The American Jewish Pattern, after 300 Years," *Commentary*, vol. 18 (4), October 1954, p. 303.

43. Handlin is clearly addressing pre- and postwar Jewish enclaves in this description, particularly in the 1940s, and as part of what he described as "the religious redefinition" that Jews underwent, pp. 304–305.

44. Handlin, "The American Jewish Pattern," p. 302.

45. Robert Ellwood, *The Fifties Spiritual Marketplace: American Religion in a Decade of Conflict* (New Brunswick: Rutgers University Press, 1993).

46. Rossman, "The Community and I," p. 404.

47. Harry Gutmann, "We Suburban Jews: An Appraisal of Suburban Judaism and Where It Is Going," *American Judaism*, vol. 5 (2), November 1955, p. 5.

48. Theodore Frankel, "Suburban Jewish Sunday School: A Report," *Commentary*, vol. 25, June 1958, pp. 490–491.
49. Irving Howe, "Sprucetown Jewry Adjusts Itself: Portrait Sketch of a New England Community," *Commentary*, vol. 5, June 1948, pp. 555, 558.
50. Sklare, *Conservative Judaism*.
51. While the importance of children to the synagogue building boom is indisputable, it would be an error to understand synagogues in solely those terms. Judith S. Goldstein's study of Great Neck, New York, a postwar synagogue, emphasizes the importance of adult participation in Reform and Conservative synagogues. She notes both the development of leadership and adult education as among their central features. *Inventing Great Neck: Jewish Identity and American Dreams* (New Brunswick: Rutgers University Press, 2006), pp. 132–135.
52. Rossman, "The Community and I," p. 404.
53. Earl X. Free, *United Synagogue Review*, Spring 1959, pp. 10–11.
54. Evelyn N. Rossman, "The Community and I: Two Years Later," *Commentary*, March 1956, p. 236.
55. Katz, *Home Fires*, p. 62.
56. Rossman, "The Community and I," 1954, p. 405.
57. Alan Wood, "I Sell My House: One Man's Experience with Suburban Segregation," *Commentary*, vol. 26, November 1958, pp. 383–389.
58. See Albert Gordon, *Jews in Suburbia* (Boston: Beacon Press, 1959); Joseph Ringer, *The Edge of Friendliness: A Study of Jewish Gentile Relationships* (New York: Basic Books, 1967).
59. Eli Lederhendler, *New York Jews and the Decline of Urban Ethnicity, 1950–1970* (New York: Syracuse University Press, 2001).
60. Karen Brodkin, *How Jews Became White Folks* (New Brunswick: Rutgers University Press, 2000).
61. David Riesman, *The Lonely Crowd: A Study of the Changing American Character* (New Haven: Yale University Press, 1950).
62. Gordon W. Allport, *The Individual and His Religion: A Psychological Interpretation* (New York: Macmillan, 1950).
63. Shapiro, *A Time for Healing*, p. 147.
64. Moore, *To the Golden Cities*; Goren, "A Golden Decade for American Jews."
65. Cited in Moore, *To the Golden Cities*, p. 6.
66 Lederhendler, *New York Jews and the Decline of Urban Ethnicity*, p. 66.
67. Michael Staub, *Torn at the Roots: The Crisis of Jewish Liberalism in Postwar America* (New York: Columbia University Press, 2003).

II

Community on Display

Chapter 5   Beth S. Wenger

War Stories
Jewish Patriotism on Parade

For centuries, American Jews have made painstaking efforts to demonstrate their devotion to the United States, their loyalty as citizens, and their willingness to make the supreme sacrifice for the nation in times of war. Like other minorities in this country, Jews found a particular need to underscore their military commitments as a way to prove the extent of their devotion and belonging to America. As historian David Lowenthal has observed, "Willingness to die for a collective cause is the supreme seal of national faith," and Jews joined in the chorus of ethnic minorities proclaiming that faith through the sacrifices of war.[1] Jewish efforts to document and celebrate war service have generally been interpreted as signs of defensiveness, motivated by a need either to prove loyalty in xenophobic times (as times of war often are) or to respond to antisemitic claims that Jews would not fight for their country. In fact, these unsettling fears often lurked, not so subtly, behind Jewish expressions of patriotism. But public and often self-congratulatory assertions of Jewish patriotism were more than the defensive reactions of an immigrant group; they were also part of the remaking of Jewish identity in America. As they celebrated Jewish patriotism and war service, Jews crafted a public image of the Jewish citizen, redefined Jewish masculinity (and sometimes femininity), created occasions for sociability, and actively engaged in a process of self-conscious transformation.

Generations of European Jews experienced firsthand the harmful repercussions that accompanied familiar accusations that Jews shirked military service, a charge that emerged regularly during the debates over Jewish emancipation. From East to West, ruling authorities questioned both Jewish fitness and willingness to fight for the countries in which they lived. For centuries, Jews were considered "incapable of being soldiers because of their physical weakness, cowardice, religious fanaticism, and suspect loyalty." In the Russian Empire, Tsar Nicholas I attempted to transform Jews and indeed ultimately force conversion through conscription, believing that military service would remake the Jews of the East.[2] During the emancipation debates in the West, such drastic measures were not imposed, but legal toleration and citizenship brought to forefront the issue of Jews' obligation to serve in the army. In the wake of French emancipation, Napoleon's questions to the Parisian Sanhedrin directly inquired whether Jews would be willing to fight for their country, and the Assembly of Notables replied affirmatively, emphasizing the sacrifices Jews had already made on behalf of France.[3] The questions surrounding Jewish military service, which recurred constantly throughout modern Europe, encapsulated deep-seated uncertainties about Jewish loyalty and about the fundamental nature of Jewish personality and behavior. Doubts about whether Jews could or would fulfill their duty as soldiers remained part of public debate for more than a century after Jewish emancipation, growing stronger at the outbreak of military conflict. During World War I, for example, German Jews mounted little effective opposition to the so-called Judenzählung, the census of Jewish soldiers ordered by the Prussian war ministry in 1916. The government ordered the survey supposedly to determine whether Jews were evading the draft and dodging frontline service, but never released the results, leaving the lingering impression that the charges had merit.[4] Such unsubstantiated accusations haunted European Jews throughout the nineteenth and twentieth centuries, and remained in the consciousness of Jewish immigrants and on the agendas of Jewish organizations after arrival in the United States.

American Jews never faced the potent antisemitism that Jews had encountered in Europe, and while doubts about Jewish ability and readiness to serve in the military did sometimes emerge, they never received any official government sanction or reached the pervasiveness or virulence of such attitudes in Europe. This altered the ways that Jews framed and defended their military contributions in the American context. Although responding to detractors remained a constant part of the agenda, documenting and celebrating Jewish war service in the United States contained a much greater internal mission. Within all their public discussions about participation in American wars, Jews repeatedly made references to the ways that they had been reinvented and reinvigorated as a result of their American citizenship and service to the country. The defensive posture never completely disappeared when Jews recounted their military accomplishments, but it blended with expressions of pride and assertions that something had dramatically changed from the experience of Europe.

Embedded in the rhetoric about Jewish military contributions was a palpable desire to overcome the European past. In the late nineteenth and early twentieth centuries, American Jews regularly filled their newspapers, speeches, and public ceremonies with declarations about how much the United Stated had freed them to reach their full potential as citizens in ways that had been impossible in Europe. War service, long a stigma of inferiority for European Jews, emerged as the most powerful evidence of the fundamental makeover in Jewish opportunity, behavior, and even personality produced by immigration to America. When Jews talked abut their renewed commitment as soldiers, they testified to their faith in America and in Jewish ability to "assimilate" and become loyal citizens. There is ample evidence to suggest that non-Jewish Americans wanted to be reassured that Jews in their country would differ from those in Europe. In 1904, a New York newspaper celebrated the 250th anniversary of Jewish settlement in the United States by praising American Jews for their transformation. "The American Jew," the paper noted with the best of intentions, "is already a type clearly distinguishable from that of any of his European brethren."[5] American Jews understood the need to project their "improvement" in the eyes of the public, but the self-assured proclamations about their military contributions in the United States also testified to the tone of superiority that American Jews began to assert over their European counterparts by the turn of the twentieth century. Because of its symbolic value as the supreme act of national loyalty, military service emerged as a useful prooftext both for the level of acceptance that Jews enjoyed in their adopted homeland and for the extent of Jewish self-transformation that had occurred in America. Achieving that transformation remained an abiding concern within a Jewish community that remained deeply tied to Europe but also determined to chart a new course.

The dynamics of a perceived identity shift from Europe to America lay beneath virtually every discussion about Jewish military contributions in the United States. War service became a primary means for Jews to demonstrate their newfound military prowess, purportedly fostered by the American environment, and to underscore the distance they had traveled from their European past. These sentiments emerged cogently in Jewish rhetoric about the Spanish-American War, as pride in service to the American military commingled with revealing reflections back toward Europe. In 1930, an article in the *Reform Advocate* recalled the reasons that Jews had supported and served in America's war with Spain:

> When war was declared in the Congress of the United States against Spain, the Jews of this country were instantly aroused. The reasons ascribed for their interest were two-fold . . . to demonstrate their patriotism and loyalty to the country which had given them a home and a place of refuge; and they would take part in a war to help two oppressed nations, Cuba and Porto Rico [*sic*] in their struggle for liberty and independence, against the yoke of Spain. But back of the two obvious reasons there was a third one which was not openly admitted by the Jew, even to himself; namely a secret desire to avenge the thousands of Jewish

martyrs who perished during the days of the inquisition. These three reasons, each of which was sufficient to stir the heart of every Jew, who was able to bear arms, and give his life in a conflict for his beloved United States and against his old foe, Spain. It enkindled a flame in the hearts of American Jewry which broke out into a conflagration. Three violent passions of the human heart were now at play in the soul of the American Jew: patriotism, love of liberty, and revenge.[6]

In this formulation, a patriotic Jewish community, fiercely loyal to its adopted homeland, was also capable of conquering (albeit metaphorically) its legacy of European oppression. According this scenario, the reinvigorated Jews of America emerged to vanquish the memory of the European past and to exert a level of power that their ancestors could never have wielded. In this particular retelling of Jewish war service, that power had both physical and spiritual dimensions, reflecting both a newfound military prowess and, as the article stated, "the great change wrought in the soul of the Jew" upon becoming American.[7] While this article appeared three decades after the war, the deep feelings about American Jewish abilities to triumph over a European foe that had once cast them out were present among Jews during the time the war was fought. In 1899, a year after the conclusion of the Spanish-American War, Jewish members of New York's Republican State Committee issued a circular in Yiddish, urging Jewish immigrants to support Theodore Roosevelt's gubernatorial bid. The document reminded Jews that it had been Roosevelt who fulfilled the "long Jewish desire to see Spain fall" and vanquished the country that had betrayed its once loyal Jewish population by sending them "to the dungeons of the Inquisition and to the fires of the auto da fe."[8] The handbill emphasized that many Jewish soldiers had served among Theodore Roosevelt's Rough Riders and that he had supported and promoted them. The political campaign to get out the Jewish vote for Roosevelt contained pointed messages about both the enduring memory of the Inquisition and the capacity of American Jews to write a new ending to that chapter in Jewish history:

> Spain now lies punished and beaten for all her sins. But the Party which brought Spain her defeat, and the man who fought against her, now stand before the citizens of this State and ask whether they are satisfied with their work. . . . Every vote for Roosevelt's opponent . . . is a vote for Spain. . . . Can any Jew afford to vote against Theodore Roosevelt and thereby express his disapproval of the war against Spain?[9]

The Yiddish circular testified to the power of the immigrant vote and the tactics of group interest employed in American politics, but it also revealed the profound meaning that Jews attached to the newfound strength they possessed to conquer an old enemy.

In many of the narratives about Jewish military contributions, American Jews appear as newly capable of becoming successful soldiers, reclaiming their physical toughness in a land that offered them freedom and opportunity. The American Jewish Committee, which documented Jewish service during World War I, kept in its files the statements of U.S. Army major LeRoy Eltinge, who asserted that Jews did not possess the physical or psychological makeup to be good soldiers. "[The Jew] has not been a soldier for over two thousand years," insisted Eltinge in his 1915 book *The Psychology of War*. "For the same length of time he has preferred trading to doing work with the hands. The soldier's lot is hard physical work. This the Jew despises." According to the author, the Jew could become a successful soldier only if "the latent mainsprings of character that twenty-five hundred years ago made him a soldier to be respected" were somehow reactivated.[10] According to many American Jews, that was precisely the transformation that had occurred. In assessing Jewish contributions during the First World War, Lee Levinger, author of the earliest American Jewish history textbook, claimed that the freedoms of America had gradually altered the disposition of Jews. "The Jewish immigrant," he insisted, "fleeing from a land of oppression to one of freedom, was in the vast majority of cases ready to break with his unwarlike tradition to defend his chosen country. The American-born Jew, product of American institutions rose to their defense exactly like every other native American."[11] According to the many articles and reports that took note of the remaking of Jews in America, the combination of opportunities afforded Jews and their deep loyalty to the nation had resuscitated long-dormant Jewish military convictions and fundamentally altered Jewish behavior. "In the land of the Czars," boasted one Jewish author, "[the Jew] made every effort to escape military service; in the new land he made every effort to give his very life in return for the privileges which he received."[12]

But more than simply Jewish behavior had changed in America; the American Jew, or more accurately in these narratives, the American Jewish man, had been essentially transformed in the United States, reclaiming his masculinity. Within Jewish history, the "new man in the new land" trope has generally been posited as an element of the Zionist project. Zionist thinkers and pioneers asserted that the physical weakness associated with Jewish men in the Diaspora could be restored only when Jews built their own civilization, in their own nation.[13] In the United States, the notion of remaking the Jew never emerged with the frequency or the ideological potency that it had in the Zionist movement. Yet the same sort of assertions appeared with surprising regularity in American Jewish writings. In his commentary on Jews and World War I, Lee Levinger remarked that one positive outcome of the war had been its opportunity to provide a model of the "ideal of American manhood toward which we are constantly trying to train and urge our people."[14] In their efforts to rehabilitate the image of Jewish men, American Jewish authors often linked the heroism of Jewish soldiers to the long tradition of Jewish bravery through the ages. Simon Wolf's *American Jew as Patriot, Soldier and Citizen*, published in 1895 as a defense against claims that Jews had shirked their duty during the Civil War, not only documented Jewish service during American wars but also connected their valor to the history of Jewish fighting men "from the earliest Biblical records, emblazoning the era of the Maccabees, signalizing the Roman period and illuminating the Dark Ages." Wolf, like so many other Jewish authors, peppered his description of Jewish soldiers with words like "bravery," "undaunted courage," and "faithful service"—characterizations that may well have been accurate but also reflected a conscious effort to paint a new portrait of American Jewish men.[15] In 1932, a *Collier's* magazine article portrayed Judah Benjamin as "The Gallant Rebel," both brave and highly intelligent. "Not for Judah Benjamin the pliant knee and fawning eye," its author wrote.[16] Similar language emerged surrounding Samuel Dreben, the highly decorated World War I soldier whose exploits were popularized by the poet Damon Runyon, best known for his work on the musical *Guys and Dolls*. His tribute to Dreben, "The Fighting Jew," appeared in a volume titled *Poems for Men*. In a poem that directly confronts existing prejudices against Jews and celebrates Dreben's heroism, Runyon also includes the following lines: "[T]here's a heart beneath the medals/That beats loyal, brave and true. . . . He's a he-man out of Texas/And he's all man through and through."[17] Blending bravery and patriotism with other valued characteristics of masculinity in middle-class America, a much earlier Jewish newspaper article titled "Yes, the Jews Can Fight" quickly dismissed as absurd any notion that Jews could not be good soldiers, adding that Jewish men possessed an even more admirable quality—their supreme devotion to family life. Notwithstanding the fact that this particular turn-of-the-century article made that point by asserting that a Jewish husband always remained devoted to his wife no matter how old she became and how much her beauty faded, the portrait of the Jewish man as both dedicated soldier and loyal family man created an ideal masculine type in the commercial age.[18]

Documenting Jewish War Service

While Jews consciously reconstructed their own image as part of an effort to reinvigorate Jews and Jewish life in America, some of the earliest accounts of Jews in the military were undeniably motivated as defensive responses to defamatory remarks. In 1891, one letter writer to the *North American Review* replied to an article about Jewish service during the Civil War with a claim that in his year and a half in the military he had neither seen nor heard of a single

Jewish soldier.[19] Answering the challenge from the letter's author for some documentation of Jewish military contributions, Simon Wolf produced an almost six-hundred-page treatise that attempted to chronicle every Jewish soldier who had served the United States. Proceeding war by war from the time of the Revolution, listing officers and enlisted men, and documenting medals and distinguished service, the book was a clear attempt to refute claims that Jews had not served their country, by amassing historical evidence to the contrary. "This timely work on a timely topic," declared an advertisement for Wolf's book, "called forth by recent magazine discussions regarding the position of Jewish citizens as patriots and as soldiers, contains an alphabetical register and numerous detailed notices of American citizens of the Jewish faith who have been enrolled in the armies of the country from the earliest period of American history to the present time."[20] Wolf, like other Jewish leaders at the turn of the century, felt a need to counter the antisemitic, anti-immigrant backlash that accompanied the mass arrival of East European Jews and was especially potent during the economic hardships of the 1890s. Moreover, like other Jews of his era, he couched his defense of Jews with an eye toward the longue durée of Jewish history, the current conditions facing Jews in Eastern Europe, and the faith in America as different. Offering the observation that "the ghastly tragedy that marked in Spain the opening year of American discovery is being rehearsed in Russia with modern aggrandizement," Wolf concluded his book with a declaration of Jewish devotion to American ideals: "To no others of the Old World denizens was the New World more completely new: for no other people has the promise of the Columbian epoch been more completely fulfilled than for the Jews."[21] For American Jews, the issue of military service was always bound up with the larger attempt to construct a new home and new self-definition as Jews in the United States.

The cycle of defamatory accusations and defensive reactions recurred in subsequent generations, but the rehearsal of military contributions also became part of internal discourse within the Jewish community, emerging as a standard element in popular narratives of American Jewish history. A litany of Jewish service to the United States appeared regularly in the earliest accounts of American Jewish history, usually illustrated through the contributions of individual soldiers. Every survey of Jewish history began with a detailed description of Jewish participation in the Revolutionary War. Demonstrating that Jews had been instrumental in the nation's founding remained an abiding concern for the authors of popular Jewish texts. "The Patriot cause had its Jewish advocates everywhere," declared a 1931 publication.[22] Most narratives contained accounts of Jews who aided the Revolutionary cause in a variety of ways, including ubiquitous references to the broker and financier Haym Salomon, but they all recounted the deeds of Jewish soldiers. The list included Salisbury and Isaac Franks, Mordecai Noah, Benjamin Nones, the

Pinto brothers, just to name a few; Simon Wolf named forty Jews who served in the Revolution, and his account became a primary source for most later texts.[23] But popular narratives also tended to dramatize the historical record. A play written in the 1930s for use in the Sunday schools of the Union of American Hebrew Congregations recounted the deeds of Mordecai Sheftall, a Jewish soldier who fought in Savannah, Georgia, during the Revolution. In the play, Sheftall responds with an eloquent speech to charges that as a Jew, he could not be trusted and was a traitor to the cause. "I am a Jew by religion and ancestry," he tells his detractors, "but I am also an American, born on American soil, and loving American liberty better than life itself."[24] Chronicling the Jewish role in the creation of the United States held special significance for American Jews who wanted to lend legitimacy to their connection to the nation's origins, but popular narratives also detailed Jewish contributions to subsequent wars. Lee Levinger's textbook, first published in 1930 and issued in revised editions through the 1950s, detailed Jewish service not only during the Revolution but also in the War of 1812, Mexican War, Civil War, Spanish-American War, as well as the two world wars.[25]

While popular Jewish writings narrated the history of Jews and American wars, Jewish organizations concerned themselves more somberly and systematically with collecting statistics about Jewish military contributions. Documenting war service was a constant theme in modern Jewish history. Throughout modern Europe, Jewish sociologists and organizations worked feverishly to collect statistics about Jewish participation in the military, attempting to counteract accusations that Jews failed to fulfill their duties as citizens. The drive for documentation grew out of a desire to gather irrefutable proof of Jewish willingness to serve the country, particularly during wartime. Providing evidence—counting each Jewish soldier, comparing the total number who served to the percentage of Jews in the general population—were the tools of protection and pride, an effort to provide indisputable confirmation that Jews were indeed loyal citizens, willing to fight to protect the nation. Simon Wolf's influential study represents precisely this sort of endeavor, with a large portion of the book consisting literally of lists of Jewish soldiers who served in various wars, and his amateur efforts were followed in subsequent generations by more scientific attempts to gather statistics.

When the United States entered World War I, the American Jewish Committee's Office of Jewish War Records determined not to leave it to historians to document Jewish war service. "[T]his time," the Committee declared, "no effort should be spared to preserve in permanent and authentic form the full story of Jewish service and sacrifice."[26] The desire to keep a record of Jewish war service was long-standing, but when the United States entered World War I, the Jewish community was both larger and better organized than it had been during previous wars, and more capable of carrying out a thorough statistical analysis of the community's efforts. Moreover, Jews may have felt a particular need to document their commitment to the war effort because the Jewish community had been deeply divided about supporting military intervention before the United States officially joined the conflict.

When fighting first erupted in Europe, American Jewry's most prominent leaders expressed a range of opinions about the war. Most of the Jewish Left, including the leading figures in the Jewish labor movement and *Jewish Daily Forward* editor Abraham Cahan, vocally opposed the war, joined in their dissent by pacifists and antiwar activists such as Judah Magnes and Lillian Wald. For immigrant Jews, resistance to the war had less to do with a particular stance toward United States policy than it did with the abiding concern for the situation in Russia. The antipathy toward the Russian tsar, fed by lingering memories of anti-Jewish policies, led many East European immigrants to support Germany's bid to defeat permanently the tsarist government. While some Jews opposed war in principle, most Jewish immigrants from Eastern Europe simply could not conceive of siding with the Russian forces that continued to persecute Jews. At the same time, Jews of German descent, such as prominent communal leader Jacob Schiff, found themselves deeply torn by the war. Schiff retained a profound loyalty to Germany and to his own German heritage. In the early years of the war, he expressed hopes for a speedy resolution to the conflict and insisted that the United States had little to gain by joining the fight. But by 1917, with the continued increase in Germany military aggression, Schiff reversed his position and came to support American entry into World War I.[27] By this time, other well-known leaders of the established community, including Cyrus Adler and Louis Marshall, along with organizations as diverse as the American Jewish Committee, Hebrew Educational Alliance, and the Orthodox Yiddish press, all supported American intervention in the conflict. With the fall of the tsar in 1917, the tide turned for most American Jews, who more comfortably sided with the Allies and rallied behind the war effort.[28]

As long as the United States maintained a policy of neutrality toward the war, Jews aired their differing opinions in dueling speeches and in the press, but once America entered the conflict, even most of the strident opponents conceded the issue. "As if by magic," declared an article in the *Jewish Daily Forward*, "the debates and discussions on the Jewish street about whom the Jews should sympathize with in the present war have disappeared. There is nothing more to discuss."[29] The *Yiddishes Tageblatt* confirmed that assertion, assuredly proclaiming that "If anyone ever thought that there was a Jew in America who was pro-German, then he has made the greatest mistake possible. . . . The Jews were anti-tsarist, but never pro-German."[30] After the United States was embroiled in the conflict, only a few pacifists within the Jewish community held out opposition. Most Jews shared the sentiments of the widely read *Jewish Daily Forward*, which enjoined its primarily immigrant readers not to "give anyone occasion to doubt that the interests of this country are not our interests, that the good name of this country is not dear to us. Let us act as natives, not as foreigners."[31]

When the United States joined the conflict, the American Jewish Committee initiated a comprehensive project to count every Jewish soldier serving in the war and blanketed the community with information about its ambitious survey. Because the military never recorded the religious or ethnic affiliation of servicemen, the Jewish community had to gather the information on its own. Publicizing the effort in synagogues, fraternal organizations, colleges, public and parochial schools, and throughout the Jewish press, the Committee's Office of Jewish War Records distributed thousands of war record cards in every possible venue.[32] Most Jews seemed eager to participate in the survey, writing letters to the Committee and requesting additional cards to distribute. One young man sent in two cards from his friends at the front and requested a batch of cards to take with him as he and his two brothers shipped out for Europe.[33] Requests and completed cards came in from individual Jews, communities, and organizations across the country, suggesting that many Jews shared the desire to record their military participation.

However, not all Jews greeted the survey with such enthusiasm. "I entirely resent this movement to separate the soldiers of the Jewish faith as in any way differing from any other American," wrote one Jewish soldier. Another man who received a standard form letter from the Committee, soliciting information, returned the letter with the words "in error" written in large red letters. One committee staff member noted on the returned letter that this particular man was known to one worker in the office and was indeed Jewish, but obviously did not want to be counted as such.[34] Julian Leavitt, director of the project, responded to each of these letters, explaining to each writer: "You have completely misunderstood the spirit and purpose of our work. It is *not* an attempt at self-glorification, but an authentic record of Jewish service, which has served, and will serve for a generation to come, as an effective answer to those who could deny the value of the Jewish contribution to American civilization."[35] The Committee's staff maintained a special file for all those who refused to be counted in the survey, labeling it "Maranhos" [*sic*], an indication of the extent of disdain they elicited.

In the three years that it functioned, the Committee's Office of Jewish War Records worked feverishly to document every Jewish soldier who served, count commissioned officers as well as enlisted men, and highlight the accomplishments of those who were honored in any way for their service.[36] Its final report, issued in the fall of 1919, concluded that 150,000 Jews participated in the war and 2,200 lost their lives in the conflict. Important for its particular mission in compiling these statistics, the office calculated that although Jews represented only 3 percent of the American population, they comprised approximately 4 percent of the military during the war.[37] (Later estimates increased those figures, counting about 250,000 Jews in the service, numbering about 5 percent of all those in armed forces.)[38] The American Jewish Committee proudly boasted that Jews had served their nation "a generous margin beyond their quota" and had "enlisted cheerfully, fought gallantly and died bravely for the United States."[39] Throughout the survey process, the Committee repeatedly stated that its purpose was to provide an accurate historical record in order to respond to potential detractors, yet its language also suggests obvious stirrings of ethnic pride and a quest for communal self-definition. Sharing a similar dual agenda, the Jewish War Veterans, the leading representative of Jews in the military and an organization that also engaged in many tabulation projects, exhibited its findings through a graphic illustration, complete with portraits of "representative" Jewish soldiers from each American war, relevant statistics about aggregate Jewish participation, and citations of individual Jewish heroism (see figure 1). This frequently republished document informed readers that "the Jew has done his share in the American armed forces from its inception," while also using these soldiers to paint a desired collective self-portrait. Exhibiting "coolness, courage and daring," proving to be "second to none, but superior to many," the Jewish soldier emerged as an icon of Jewish communal aspirations.[40]

Even in later years, when Jews were far more secure in the United States, when the majority of American Jews were native born, and when antisemitism had markedly declined, Jews continued to make an effort to document their war service. During World War II, more than half a million Jews served in the armed forces, and the organized Jewish community again undertook a systematic campaign to count the precise number of Jews in the military. This time the effort was sponsored by the National Jewish Welfare Board's Bureau of War Records, which went about culling available records and establishing local committees in cities across the country. The result was a two-volume study that again consisted of state-by-state lists of Jewish soldiers, medals awarded, casualties incurred, and a host of other detailed information.[41]

In the context of 1940s America, the director of the Bureau of War Records, Samuel Kohs, couched the need for a systematic study of Jewish war service in scientific terms and in the interests of both the Jewish people and the nation. Kohs stressed that all minority groups, not only Jews, could be vulnerable to unfounded charges. "Unless each minority group is prepared with facts and figures to answer these innuendos and groundless accusations," he explained, "it places itself in an extremely weak position in relation to the majority group."[42] Kohs further maintained that the Jewish community should gather such information to gain a better understanding of its "own group needs and own group purposes." The knowledge obtained would benefit not only Jews, he claimed,

THE JEW IN AMERICA'S WARS

The following pictures and statistics show very briefly, but graphically that the Jew has done his share in the American armed forces from its inception. He has carved himself a patriotic niche in our History of which every Jew may be proud.

REVOLUTIONARY WAR 1776

CIVIL WAR 1861

Total population 3,000 Jews. Many States disbarred Jews as soldiers, yet over 160 fought on the Colonial side. Col. Issac Franks and Col. David S. Franks were prominent. Although not a soldier, Haym Solomen did much to help the Cause. He gave to it $658,007.13, not a penny of which was ever repaid.

Jews fought with equal bravery on both sides—over 8,000 took part, out of a total population of 150,000. Of this number there were 750 officers and numbered among them 9 Generals. 7 in the Blue Army received medals from the hands of President Lincoln.

WAR OF 1812

WAR WITH SPAIN 1898

No complete statistics of number of Jews who fought, but History records several prominent names: Col. Nathan Meyers, Capt. Meyer Moses, Adjt. Issac Myers, Samuel Noah, Benjamin Gratz, David Metzler, and last but not least Judah Tuoro. The building of Bunker Hill Monument was made possible by the latters donation of $10,000.00 toward its erection.

More than 5,000 men joined—far more than their numerical proportion to the population. The first volunteer was a Jew, the first soldier to fall was a Jew. Not less than 150 Jews dashed up San Juan Hill with Roosevelt.

WAR WITH MEXICO 1846

WORLD WAR 1917-18

About 70 men and of them 15 officers served. General David De Leon was twice voted the thanks of Congress. Other distinguished soldiers, Surgeon General Moses Albert Levy, Colonel Leon Dyer, Major Alfred Mordecai, Samuel Henry and Sgts. Jacob Davis, and Corporal Jacob Hirschborn.

250,000 served during the World War. This was almost 5% of the armed forces of the U. S. A. whereas Jews form but 3% of the population. Of those in the service, 20% were VOLUNTEERS. No less than 1100 citations for valor were awarded to Jews. Of the 78 Congressional Medals of Honor awarded, 3 were conferred on Jews. There were about 10,000 Jewish Commissioned Officers in service. Jewish casualties were 14,000, of which more than 2,800 made the supreme sacrifice.

From the earliest period of the Republic to the present time, the Jew has been a conspicuous figure in our regular army and navy, and in every branch of the service he has made an honorable record. On the battlefields of Europe and America, the Jew has certainly shown by his coolness, courage and daring that he is a soldier second to none, but superior to many, and has proved his patriotism by offering his life as a sacrifice on the altar of the country that gives him shelter and protection. Every Jew may well be proud of our military record.

Figure 1. The Jewish War Veterans regularly reproduced this image to document Jewish service in American wars. *The Jewish Veteran*, August 1935. Courtesy of the National Museum of American Jewish Military History.

but also contribute to "the unity of our American people through understanding based on facts, rather than misunderstanding based on myths, rumors, and falsehoods."[43] By the World War II era, the tenor of discussion surrounding the survey of Jewish war service had changed somewhat, informed by the rhetoric of scientific data analysis, but the motivations for it continued to contain a measure of defensiveness as well as an internal mission.

Commemorating Jewish War Service

Celebrating Jewish war service and honoring military heroes provided many occasions for public gatherings and opportunities for communal reflection. Memorials for fallen soldiers became communal exercises as early as the Civil War era. In 1866, Jewish women in the South created the Hebrew Ladies' Memorial Association, an organization devoted to caring for the graves of Confederate Jewish soldiers. The Jewish women's society joined other women's associations in the task of maintaining Confederate burial plots, but its members also envisioned a particular communal purpose for their work. They intended the graves of Jewish soldiers to serve as proof of Jewish loyalty to the Confederacy in the face of "the malicious tongue of slander." If anyone should question Jewish service, the women wrote, "then, with a feeling of mournful pride, will we point to this monument and say: '*There* is our reply.'"[44] Honoring Jewish military service had both an internal and external purpose, stirring pride within the Jewish community and serving as a sign to potential detractors.

In 1904, in the midst of a nationwide building flurry of Civil War monuments, the Jewish community dedicated the first monument to Jewish soldiers, built in one of New York's largest Jewish cemeteries. As other Americans began to erect memorials to Civil War soldiers, the Hebrew Union Veterans' Association (a precursor to the Jewish War Veterans) commissioned a monument to memorialize the Jewish community's Civil War veterans. Erected in Salem Fields cemetery in Cypress Hills, New York, the starkly designed monument stands fifty feet tall with a bronze eagle on the top.[45] On the sides are four bronze memorial tablets listing the names of Jewish soldiers. The inscription on the monument reads:

To the memory of the Soldiers of the Hebrew Faith who responded to the call of their country and gave their lives for its salvation during the dark days of its need so that the nation might live.[46]

The unveiling ceremony, like many of its kind, contained a fair share of pomp and circumstance, including a parade led by the Hebrew Orphan Asylum Band

Figure 2. Monument to Jewish Civil War Veterans, Salem Fields cemetery, Cypress Hills, New York. Photograph by the author.

and two hundred Jewish veterans marching in line. The program featured many dignitaries, both Jewish and non-Jewish, allowing the event to serve simultaneously as an occasion for Jewish collective pride and an opportunity to articulate a shared, interfaith commitment to the nation. The featured speaker, Nathan Straus, denounced the evils of war, but he made a point to cite the numbers of Jews who fought in American battles. Relying on the familiar trope of numerical calculation, Straus explained that during the Civil War "the Jewish population furnished one brave soldier to every twenty-nine persons of its entire population, and more than ten thousand of the flower of its manhood enlisted in the civil and Spanish wars."[47] Standing in one of the country's largest cemeteries, this monument became, over the years, a site used to memorialize Jewish soldiers who lost their lives in subsequent wars and a permanent testimony to Jewish loyalty and sacrifice.

Such commemorations of Jewish war service occurred in virtually every city in America, providing a window into some of the more grassroots campaigns to memorialize Jewish veterans. For example, in 1935, the local Jewish

War Veterans Post in Portland, Maine, dedicated a small memorial to Jacob Cousins, the first Jewish soldier from the city killed in World War I. The local post donated a stone with a bronze plaque to the city, with an inscription that detailed the soldier's service and stated simply that "[h]e was the first soldier of Jewish faith from this city to make the supreme sacrifice in the line of duty during the World War."[48] The dedication ceremony was a community event, involving elected officials, Jewish veterans who traveled in from neighboring cities, as well as both Jews and non-Jews from the Portland area. The Jewish community wanted to create an elaborate spectacle. The national office of the Jewish War Veterans sent out a letter inviting veterans from nearby states to attend the event. "We hope a large delegation from your post, in uniform if possible, will turn out for this function," declared a letter sent to members.[49] As part of the performance of patriotism, some of the children of Jewish veterans dressed in service uniforms for the parade.[50] This event, like most others of its kind, also had meaning for the city's non-Jewish residents. The significant numbers of non-Jewish citizens who participated in the dedication seized the occasion to declare their support of the Jewish community and the nation's commitment to equality. "America," declared Portland's mayor in his address to the crowd, "is great only because she is the melting pot of the world but she needed the blood of the Jew and the Gentile to make her the great nation she is."[51]

Figure 3. Jacob Cousins memorial, Portland, Maine. Photograph by the author.

Figure 4. Memorial Day Parade outside New York's Park Avenue Synagogue, May 1934. Jewish War Veterans Collection, American Jewish Historical Society. Courtesy of the National Museum of American Jewish Military History.

The Jewish War Veterans, which took the lead in commemorations of military service, consistently made the Jewish community visible in national celebrations. Every Memorial Day, local JWV posts participated in parades across the country, consciously focusing attention on Jewish military contributions. In the small Jewish community of Buffalo, New York, in the mid-1930s, JWV representatives described how their unit marched "[w]ith heads erect and eyes front, with flags fluttering," noting that "[e]very American of Jewish descent who stood on the side lines of this Parade must have felt a thrilling glow within his heart as our Unit passed by."[52] In New York City, Memorial Day parades regularly attracted large crowds, sometimes with ten thousand or more Jewish participants. The 1934 parade featured an address by Samuel Untermeyer, five bands, and a fife and drum corps. Before almost every Memorial Day parade, some of the participants gathered at the city's large congregations, such as Temple Emanu-El and the Park Avenue synagogue, for brief services before joining the parade, lending a tone of religious sanctity to the civic observance.[53]

For all the bravado of the parades, many of the JWV's activities remained quite solemn. Members of Jewish War Veterans considered it their duty to

Figure 5. Service conducted in New York's Park Avenue Synagogue before the Memorial Day Parade, May 1934. Jewish War Veterans Collection, American Jewish Historical Society. Courtesy of the National Museum of American Jewish Military History.

decorate the graves of each Jewish soldier on Memorial Day, and the organization constructed detailed rituals for the ceremony. Similarly, the organization designed elaborate rituals for the funeral of any Jewish veteran, with precise instructions about how all commanders and participants should march and stand, and exactly what words should be recited during the ceremony.[54] Every Fourth of July, after Congress designated the date as Jewish War Veteran Day at the Tomb of the Unknown Soldier, JWV representatives conducted annual exercises there, asking nearby members to attend whenever possible.[55]

The Unknown Soldier held particular significance for the JWV, which saw in the anonymity of the death of one soldier the possibility to define the American soldier as a member of any race or religion. Created after World War I, the idea of the Unknown Soldier emerged first in Europe and later in the United States as a means to honor the contributions of ordinary soldiers and to illustrate the tremendous loss of so many human lives. Government officials intended the Unknown Soldier to foster national unity and to bring together America's many ethnic and religious groups. The first ceremony memorializing the Unknown Solider in 1921 included the Jewish Welfare Board and

Figure 6. Funeral Service for Daniel Harris, the last surviving Jewish Civil War veteran, 1945. Jewish War Veterans Collection, American Jewish Historical Society. Courtesy of the National Museum of American Jewish Military History.

the Jewish War Veterans, along with African American, Catholic, and other hereditary organizations. As many critics observed at the time, the Unknown Soldier depicted in official ceremonies was usually imagined, despite the symbolism, as white and Protestant.[56] In fact, as one historian of American memory has noted, a few years after the initial ceremonies, "when the Jewish Welfare Board learned that a proposed monument for the Unknown Soldier's tomb contained a cross, they had to remind the Commission of Fine Arts that this anonymous individual may well have been a Jew."[57] Yet, while the dominant culture envisioned the Unknown Soldier as a reflection of the majority, the Jewish War Veterans tenaciously continued to interpret the symbol in its own image. Demonstrating its investment in the idea of the Unknown Soldier, the JWV chose to celebrate its fiftieth anniversary in 1946 with an historical pageant titled "The Unknown Soldier Speaks." Produced by Isaac Van Grove, who also worked on "The Eternal Road" and "The Romance of a People," the pageant in Chicago Stadium reenacted the participation of Jewish soldiers in battle beginning with the Revolutionary War and moving forward in time.[58] This event, like many others, blended entertainment and pageantry with a selective historical narrative designed to elicit Jewish communal pride.

Despite its undeniably self-congratulatory posture, the Jewish War Veterans retained a keen sense of the power of history to forge collective identity and a determination to perform that history through ritual. In 1945, as World War II drew to a close, the JWV held an elaborate funeral procession for Daniel Harris, presumed to have been the last surviving Jewish Civil War veteran.[59] Marching through the Sailors and Soldiers Monument in Brooklyn, the Jewish War Veterans connected the long tradition of American Jewish sacrifice to contemporary events in the nation, allowing the funeral to narrate a history of American Jews and to broadcast its lessons to both the Jewish and non-Jewish communities. In the mid-1950s, the JWV looked to fulfill that same mission with a tangible and permanent marker on the American landscape, moving its headquarters from New York City to Washington, D.C. The organization called its new building a National Shrine to the Jewish War Dead, and included within its walls a chapel, museum, library, record rooms, and a Hall of Heroes. In fund-raising material, the organization defined the structure as "a testament to the patriotism of the Jews of America . . . eloquent evidence of love of country and the free way of life, a monument to the fallen, an inspiration to the living."[60]

In a lighter vein, the Jewish War Veterans also marketed a variety merchandise in order heighten the visibility of Jewish war service and to provide tangible reminders of the meaning and purpose of the organization. The JWV's insignia, which graced its membership medallions and the cover of its magazine, reflected the organization's conscious self-definition. According to the words of the membership oath, the emblem represented the relationship between Jews and United States:

> Upon the face of emblem appears the Star of David, historical reminder of our origin as Jews, within the wreath of American victory. Superimposed thereon is the American Eagle, symbolic of freedom, while in the center are inscribed the initials U.S., both of which are emblematic of the highest rights of free men. The entire arrangement typifies the interwoven histories of our steadfast religious belief and continuing loyal citizenship to our nation."[61]

Figure 7. The insignia of the Jewish War Veterans displayed on the cover of the organization's magazine. *The Jewish Veteran*, April 1934. Courtesy of the National Museum of American Jewish Military History.

That emblem appeared on a host of JWV materials, from military caps and watch chains to automobile reflectors, all designed to raise the profile of the organization. Not surprisingly, many of the items were geared to a male audience, such as the "JayVee" razor blades, advertised as American made, "with a finer, harder steel and a smoother, keener shaving edge."[62]

Men, of course, occupied center stage in the Jewish War Veterans, since the organization revolved around the legacy of military service, but women also

Figure 8. Advertisement for the Jewish War Veterans automobile reflector. *The Jewish Veteran*, July 1935. Courtesy of the National Museum of American Jewish Military History.

participated quite regularly and vitally. The Ladies Auxiliary, which admitted any close relatives of JWV members, performed many of the behind-the-scenes organizational tasks common to most ladies' auxiliaries—planning events, cooking, decorating, and a host of other activities. But these women never conceived their roles as menial. The auxiliary crafted its own constitution and bylaws that outlined the organization's objectives, which included such lofty goals as maintaining allegiance to the country, encouraging liberty

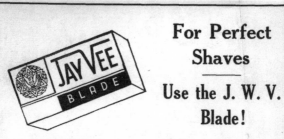

Figure 9. Advertisement for "JayVee" blades, sold by the Jewish War Veterans. *The Jewish Veteran*, July 1935. Courtesy of the National Museum of American Jewish Military History.

and equality, combating bigotry, and assisting veterans and their families. Like the men, the women retained elaborate rituals for conducting meetings and inducting new members. At times, they also demonstrated a certain consciousness of the historical role of Jewish women; one of the auxiliary's members authored an article in the *Jewish Veteran*, "Daughters of 1776," that chronicled the contributions of Jewish women during the Revolution. While this particular essay, written in the 1930s, reflects a sophisticated perception about

Figure 10. The Ladies Auxiliary of the Jewish War Veterans. *The Jewish Veteran,*
October 1934. Courtesy of the National Museum of American Jewish Military History.

women's historical importance, it also reveals very traditional notions about
gendered behavior. The "Jewish daughters of 1776" described in the article
included "the beautiful and light-hearted Rebecca Franks . . . the tragic Rachel
Solomon . . . the self-sacrificing Mrs. Sheftall; the pious Bilhah Franks; the
cultured Reyna Touro; and the home-loving and practical Miriam Gratz."[63]
Just as celebrations of war service reflected changing notions of Jewish masculinity, so, too, did they reveal Jewish women's embrace of American ideas
about proper feminine behavior.

For all the solemnity of some formal Jewish War Veterans commemorations,
other events organized by the JWV, like those of so many other Jewish associations, often revolved around occasions for sociability. Some of those activities
were homosocial—Jewish men marching in parades and conducting rituals,
with Jewish women organizing events and holding meetings of their own. Others involved dances, banquets, and parties where men and women socialized
together. According to one JWV report, the necessary ingredients for a successful military ball included "[p]omp, ceremony, beautiful women, brave men,
[and] delightful music."[64] Advertising an upcoming annual convention (always
called an encampment), the JWV promised "[d]ances, banquets, country fairs,
sports of every type, trips around the city, and country, parties, games, contests."[65] Ensuring that Jewish war service received proper respect and recognition remained the central purpose of the organization, but that effort was never
divorced from the more mundane happenings of a Jewish association.

In many ways, the frequent refrains about Jewish military contributions belong within the framework of Jewish associational networks, as part of the acculturation process and the construction of a distinct sort of Jewish identity in America. To be sure, rhetoric about the willingness of Jews to fight for their country emerged in virtually every modern nation where Jews lived. But not with the precise tenor that it had in the United States. The defensive posture that characterized the Jewish desire to document war service in other countries did exist in the United States; so many American Jewish efforts to create a record of Jews in the military were precipitated by attacks on Jewish loyalty and purported lack of military contributions. Yet Jews seemed to want the record for themselves as much as for their detractors. The surveys, the textbooks, the children's stories, and the parades did serve to represent Jews to the nation, but at least equally important, they told a story about Jewish experience in America, one that began in the Revolutionary period with the birth of the United States. These stories allowed Jews to place themselves at the founding of their country, fighting for America's creation. Although Jews certainly declared their patriotism in other Diaspora nations, they could never craft that kind of narrative about being a part of their country's historical origins. The American Jewish discourse about Jewish military contributions and heroism, no matter how self-serving or defensive, posited Jews as part of the organic fabric of the nation, even if the effort to make the case sometimes seemed more forced than natural. War so often defines national consciousness, and for American Jews, celebrating and documenting war service gave shape and weight to their own history as Jewish Americans.

Notes

1. David Lowenthal, *The Heritage Crusade and the Spoils of History* (London and New York: Viking Press, 1997), p. 57.

2. Michael Stanislawski, *Tsar Nicholas I and the Jews: The Transformation of Jewish Society in Russia, 1825–1855* (Philadelphia: Jewish Publication Society of America, 1983), p. 14.

3. For a brief account of both the questions posed and replies offered by the Assembly of Notables on this issue, see Paul Mendes-Flohr and Jehuda Reinharz, eds., *The Jew in the Modern World: A Documentary History*, 2nd ed. (New York and Oxford: Oxford University Press, 1995), pp. 126, 130.

4. Jürgen Matthäus, "Deutschtum and Judentum under Fire: The Impact of the First World War on the Strategies of the Centralverein and the Zionistische Vereinigung," *Leo Baeck Institute Yearbook* 33 (1988): 139–40.

5. "Jew in American Life," *New York Journal of Commerce and Commercial Bulletin*, text included in *The Two Hundred and Fiftieth Anniversary of the Settlement of the Jews in the United States* (New York: New York Co-operative Society, 1906), p. 224.

6. *Reform Advocate*, 31 May 1930, p. 431.

7. Ibid.

8. "Hanokem Et Nikmatenu" [He Who Takes Revenge for Us], New York, 1899, as cited in Abraham J. Karp, *Haven and Home: A History of the Jews in America* (New York: Schocken Books, 1985), p. 138.

9. Ibid.

10. Major LeRoy Eltinge, U.S. Army, "Psychology of War," Records of the American Jewish Committee–Office of War Records, I-9, box 1, folder 2, American Jewish Historical Society, Newton Centre, Mass., and New York, N.Y. An excerpt from his book, *The Psychology of War*, with notes is contained in the AJC files. LeRoy Eltinge, *The Psychology of War* (Fort Leavenworth, Kans.: Press of the Army Service Schools, 1915), p. 43. Eltinge's book was reprinted in several subsequent editions. In a distinguished military career, he rose to the rank of brigadier general.

11. Lee J. Levinger, "American Jews in the World War," a paper read before the AJHS on May 6, 1923, p. 12. Microfilm no. 1097, American Jewish Archives, Cincinnati, Ohio.

12. *Reform Advocate*, 31 May 1930, p. 431.

13. One of the many works on Zionism to discuss this theme is Michael Berkowitz, *Zionist Culture and West European Jewry before the First World War* (Chapel Hill and London: University of North Carolina Press, 1993), pp. 99–100, 116–18.

14. Levinger, "American Jews in the World War," p. 12.

15. Simon Wolf, *The American Jew as Patriot, Soldier and Citizen* (Philadelphia: Levytype Company, 1895), p. 12.

16. George Creel, "Gallant Rebel," *Collier's*, 22 October 1932, p. 30.

17. Damon Runyon, "The Fighting Jew," in J. George Fredman, ed., *Jews in the World War: A Study in Jewish Patriotism and Heroism* (New York: Jewish War Veterans of the United States, 1941), p. 22.

18. "Yes, the Jews can fight—Everybody knows that," 1904, box 3, folder "Loose Newspaper Clippings," Jewish War Veterans Collection, I-32, American Jewish Historical Society.

19. Article cited in Wolf, *The American Jew as Patriot, Soldier and Citizen*, p. 1.

20. Advertisement copy reprinted in the last page of the book. Ibid., n.p.

21. Ibid., p. 566.

22. Anita Libman Lebeson, *Jewish Pioneers in America, 1492–1848* (New York: Brentano's Publishers, 1931), p. 212.

23. Ibid., pp. 205–41; Peter Wiernik, *History of the Jews in America* (New York: The Jewish History Publishing Company, 1931), pp. 87–97; Lee J. Levinger, *A History of the Jews in the United States*, from 19th ed. (1930; rpt. New York: Union of American Hebrew Congregations, 1959), pp. 115–18; Wolf, *The American Jew as Patriot, Soldier and Citizen*, pp. 44–52.

24. Edith Lindeman Calisch, *The Jews Who Stood by Washington: A Play in One Act* (Cincinnati: Department of Synagogue and School Extension of the Union of American Hebrew Congregations, 1932), p. 8.

25. Levinger, *A History of the Jews in the United States.*

26. *The War Record of American Jews: Plans and Suggestions for the Organization of*

Community Surveys (New York: Office of War Records, American Jewish Committee, 1919), p. 3.

27. Naomi W. Cohen, *Jacob H. Schiff: A Study in American Jewish Leadership* (Hanover, N.H.: University Press of New England, 1999), pp. 189–95.

28. Christopher M. Sterba, *Good Americans: Italian and Jewish Immigrants during the First World War* (Oxford and New York: Oxford University Press, 2003), pp. 62–67.

29. *Jewish Daily Forward*, 30 March 1917, p. 6.

30. *Yiddishes Tageblatt*, 20 March 1917, p. 4.

31. *Jewish Daily Forward*, 12 June 1917, p. 4.

32. *The War Record of American Jews*, pp. 7–8.

33. Letter from Louis Silverman to Bureau of Jewish Statistics, 9 October 1918, Records of the American Jewish Committee–Office of War Records, box 1, folder 5.

34. Letter from Saul Schectman to Office of War Records, 20 October 1920, and letter from Office of War Records to Sam Blackman, 15 December 1919, Records of the American Jewish Committee–Office of War Records, box 1, folder 10.

35. Julian Leavitt to Irwin Auerbach, 13 November 1919, Records of the American Jewish Committee–Office of War Records, box 1, folder 10. The basic template of this letter remained consistent, with a few variations, and was sent to all those who wrote to the Committee refusing to participate in the survey.

36. *The Jews of America in the World War: A Memorial of Jewish Service and a Contribution to American and Jewish History*, compiled by the Office of War Records of the American Jewish Committee in Cooperation with the Jewish Welfare Board (New York, 1919), Records of the American Jewish Committee–Office of War Records, box 1, folder 2.

37. *The War Report of American Jews: The Thirteenth Report of the Office of War Records, American Jewish Committee* (New York: American Jewish Committee, 1920), pp. 50–53.

38. J. George Fredman and Louis A. Falk, *Jews in American Wars* (New York: Jewish War Veterans of the U.S., 1942), p. 78.

39. *The War Report of American Jews: The First Report of the Office of War Records, American Jewish Committee* (New York: American Jewish Committee, 1919), p. 28.

40. This graphic image was republished frequently in Jewish War Veterans materials. See, for example, *The Jewish Veteran*, Convention Number (August 1935), n.p.

41. Bureau of War Records of the National Jewish Welfare Board, *American Jews in World War II: The Story of 550,000 Fighters for Freedom*, 2 vols. (New York: The Dial Press, 1947). This essay explores the public dialogue about Jewish war service. For a study of the impact of World War II on the Jews who served and on Jewish culture in the United States, see Deborah Dash Moore, *GI Jews: How World War II Changed a Generation* (Cambridge, Mass.: Belknap Press, 2004).

42. Samuel C. Kohs, *Jews in the United States Armed Forces* (New York: Yiddish Scientific Institute, 1945), p. 4.

43. Ibid., pp. 5, 4.

44. Cited in Jonathan D. Sarna, *American Judaism: A History* (New Haven: Yale University Press, 2004), p. 123.

45. *American Hebrew*, 12 May 1905, pp. 760–62.

46. Ibid., p. 760.

47. Ibid., p. 762.

48. Inscription on monument.

49. Benjamin Sperling, Adjutant General, National Headquarters Jewish War Veteran of the United States, to "Dear Sir and Comrade," 17 September 1935, Jacob Cousins file, Jewish War Veterans, Washington, D.C. Provided to the author by Sandy Cohen, archivist, Jewish War Veterans.

50. *Portland Press Herald*, 23 September 1935, p. 7.

51. Ibid., p. 16.

52. *The Jewish Veteran* (June 1935), p. 24.

53. Photograph of 1934 services at Park Avenue Synagogue in Jewish War Veterans Collection, box 5, folder 2. Many other similar examples are contained in the collection.

54. *The J.W.V. Manual* (1947; rpt. New York: Jewish War Veterans of the U.S.A., 1952), Jewish War Veterans Collection, pp. 35–51, box 3, folder "Printed Materials"; *The Jewish Veteran* (April 1934), p. 4.

55. *The Jewish Veteran* (June 1935), p. 10.

56. G. Kurt Piehler, *Remembering War the American Way* (Washington, D.C., and London: Smithsonian Institution Press, 1995), pp. 120–21.

57. Ibid., p. 121.

58. "The Unknown Soldier Speaks," program leaflet, 1946, Jewish War Veterans Collection, box 3, folder "50 Years of the JWV."

59. Description of the funeral procession included with photograph, Jewish War Veterans Collection, box 2.

60. Jewish War Veterans, "National Shrine for the Jewish War Dead," Jewish War Veterans Collection, box 1, folder "National Shrine to Jewish War Dead," n.p., n.d.

61. *The J.W.V. Manual*, p. 22.

62. For an example of this advertisement, see *The Jewish Veteran* (July 1935), p. 2.

63. Anne Ruth Selstal, "Daughters of 1776," *The Jewish Veteran* (July 1937), p. 3.

64. *The Jewish Veteran* (July 1934), p. 16.

65. Ibid., p. 12.

Chapter 6

Jeffrey S. Gurock

Orthodoxy on Display in the Arena of Sports, 1920–2000

In January 2001, a Yeshiva University newsletter highlighted the achievements of its Stern College for Women's "first NYC Marathoner" who completed the 26.2-mile trek in under four hours, a very respectable time for a novice. The profiled runner, reportedly, liked the idea that her community knew of her personal triumph, but she demurred when school publicists wanted to print an action shot of her in shorts. She was concerned with the issue of *tzniut* [modesty] as she sought respect in the worlds of both Orthodoxy and sports.[1]

Ten months later, another Stern College athlete approached the university's athletic director with a comparable religious-sports problem. As Dr. Richard Zerneck would soon explain to the National Collegiate Athletic Association (NCAA), the governing authority of university sports in this country, this young woman "is an observant member of the Orthodox Jewish religion, and as a married woman, must cover her hair when in public. She plans on covering her hair during basketball games with a tight fitting cloth tied in such a way to stay securely on her head. No pins or fasteners will be used." To accommodate his athlete, Zerneck asked for relief from the NCAA's rule that prohibits players from wearing "head decorations, head wear, or jewelry" during games. Quick to cast his request as not a uniquely Jewish appeal, Zerneck noted strategically that "I would imagine that similar requests have been made for other student athletes of faiths that have similar restrictions [Muslims etc.]." Within less than a week's time, Zerneck received an affirmative response from these tolerant sports officials even as he was advised that "a copy of this [waiver] letter should be taken to all games should the officials or opponents question . . . [the] attire." This student's principled stance was of no real moment to a sports community that prided itself on diversity.[2]

At just about the same time, one of my favorite athletes was a young woman fencer at that same all-women's college. Like her schoolmate, she too had no problem with public praise and exposure for her prowess with a foil. However, she expressly refused to strut her stuff before male spectators. Understand this: fencing outfits are as unrevealing and unfetching as athletic uniforms can get. She was covered from head to foot, mask included. Yet as a product of her own times, this student's early twenty-first-century religious values directed her toward this very conservative decision. Not incidentally, she also had no interest in watching men at play. When I once asked her why she and other sports-minded "Stern girls"—her terminology not mine—did not clamor to have the university charter buses to facilitate their attendance at men's varsity meets and games, as undergraduate females did just a few years ago, her unapologetic response was: "We are a *frum* [punctiliously observant] generation. My father always talks about how he used to meet girls at YU ball games. But that's not the way we do things today."

Of course, given Yeshiva's position as a diverse, "centrist" Orthodox institution, not all students shared the fencer's point of view. Some of her fellow Stern College basketball players, including possibly the married woman who covered her hair during play, loved to have Yeshiva College fans cheer them on. But very few guys showed up at their games, except maybe the husband of that varsity member. And, for that matter, only a committed coterie of coeds turned up regularly for the men's games. The attitudinal arrow was pointing away from such coeducational endeavors.

If, through these words and inactivities, that flashy foilist and her friends—both boys and girls—were putting distance between their parents' and grandparents' religious value system and their own, over in another modern Orthodox sports venue, also in Greater New York, public policy already dictated that men—even fathers and grandfathers—could not watch young women at play. As early as the mid-1990s, the Metropolitan Yeshiva High School League began running its women-only "B League." There, all the players, coaches, referees, scorekeepers and timekeepers, and of course the fans would have to be female. Significantly, other local Orthodox schools that did not subscribe to this strict code of gender separatism could, and did, compete in their own longer-standing league where no one stood at the door except a ticket taker. But the dual athletic association system meant that from then on, solidly coeducational schools would have no athletics-based relationship with girls-only operations. For a while, Yeshiva University's Central High School for Girls, like its parent Yeshiva and Stern Colleges, oscillated left and right to meet its community's centrist proclivities and fielded teams in both leagues. Its better players, and/or girls from families who were not overly concerned about dads in the stands, suited up against the coed schools. Meanwhile, other athletes did battle in half-empty gyms. As of the 2002–2003 academic year and basketball season, this school was comfortable in the so-called "A League." Male relatives could attend games. And no one stood at the door to check lineages. Still, an active effort was made to discourage fraternization among unattached males and females before and after action takes place on the court.[3]

And then there was the Jewish Educational Center (JEC) of Elizabeth, New Jersey, which demonstrated that it too is of several minds over whether to conform to strict gender separation at athletic activities. JEC's girls' school, Bruriah, found an enduring comfort zone playing in both leagues. If Bruriah's principal had her druthers, she would have only "all-girl teams," even as her school was staunchly vigilant against a "social scene" at the games: no meeting of boys and girls. Still, Bruriah remained responsive to its "demographics" and accommodated not only families that are soundly in tune with the sirens of separatism but also those who were aligned with a different set of Orthodox social values.[4]

Meanwhile, as of 2004, the New York Orthodox trend toward gender separation during athletic events could also be found as far away from the metropolis as Boca Raton, Florida. In February of that year, the e-mail newsletter of the Weinbaum Yeshiva High School announced that "not all games are open to the public" at its Third Girls Invitational Basketball Tournament. Usually, this coeducational school's teams "play in the Florida High School Athletic Association, a league in which all public and private high schools" in the state participate and "there are no restrictions whatsoever on who may attend the games as spectators." However, for its girls' tournament, where teams are invited "from yeshivot throughout the country, some of [which] will not play in front of men," an "accommodat[ion]" is made to "their requests."[5]

These present-day vignettes immediately suggest how a community's attitudes toward the incursions of American sports culture into its life—with all its trappings—reflect changing Orthodox social norms over several generations and highlight the tensions that today exist among its variegated constituencies.

What follows takes this conversation to the next level. For more than eighty years now, engagements with the life of American athleticism have pointed up the social and cultural differences that have existed and evolved within the most committed segment of the Orthodox community: American yeshiva students and their families. But, before discussing variances and nuances and their implications, an essential word about what this contingent consistently has had in common when it came to admitting the most basic of sports activities—the realm of recreational pastimes—into its world and what that acceptance of American games says about its affinity for this country's way of life. For now it makes no difference whether the educational institutions that Orthodox students and families attended, led, or supported were called mesiftas, yeshivas, or day schools. All these schools had many youngsters who, in the off hours, took to the streets and played the informal games—like stickball or punchball or association, a game akin to two-hand touch football, and most certainly basketball—that were so much part of the cities' scene. And these kids did so with at least the tacit approval of their parents and even their rabbis. As such, this "new breed" of American yeshiva community showed how different it was from Old World counterparts of its immediate past.

Back in the East Europe of the late nineteenth to early twentieth centuries, not only were formal sports unknown within the Orthodox community; informal games were also frowned upon, and even physical fitness—no matter what Maimonides once said about a sound mind and body—was hardly emphasized. Or to put it another way, while on their own some children played primitive forms of baseball called "Oina" and "Myatch," in which balls and sticks were hit for distance, yeshiva youngsters did so without their elders' blessing. In that society, whiling away time as a ballplayer was no way for a kid to move up in class.[6]

A distinguished East European rabbinical visitor who showed up at Mesifta Torah Vodaath (TVD) in the late 1920s readily observed how different the American yeshiva scene was from the one at his home base. Reportedly, Rabbi Shimon Shkop, rosh yeshiva (Dean) of Shaarei Torah Yeshiva in Grodno, Poland, was troubled to see that during "recess time . . . the boys were playing a game of baseball in the yard. And when he saw this, he was astounded and full of wonder and did not want to believe his eyes." He was chagrined that "students of the yeshiva, who study God's Torah could spend their time in such folly."[7] And this was a yeshiva that was on a mission to sustain the religious civilization of East Europe on foreign American soil without, as its chroniclers have told it, "strategic retreats and compromises."[8] Yet, what would have been counted as, at best, unconventional behavior back in Poland was a commonplace in Brooklyn.

There is no record of Rabbi Shkop upbraiding Rabbi Shraga Feivel Mendlowitz over this aspect of school policy. However, we can reasonably project that had he been confronted, Mendlowitz would have answered that recreational activities—from ball playing to hiking to swimming, even to acrobatics/gymnastics—helped produce a more physically fit *bochur*, possessed of sufficient stamina to spend the largest part of his long school day in productive Torah study.[9] Besides which, if pressed, he might have acknowledged that there were far worse types of pursuits that might entice youths with some spare time on their hands in the wide-open American city.

Similar attitudes and policies toward street games—not to mention minimal adherence to government demands that their schools have "P-T" programs—also obtained at TVD's brother schools, Yeshiva Chaim Berlin (YCB) of Brownsville, Brooklyn, and the Lower East Side's Mesifta Tifereth Yerushalayim (MTY), institutions that also had their eyes fixed squarely on the East European past.[10]

If, in Brooklyn and downtown, yeshiva student interest in fun and games was only accommodated, up in Washington Heights at the Rabbi Isaac Elchanan Theological Seminary's (RIETS) high school, the Talmudical Academy, and its Yeshiva College, athleticism was cultivated in consonance with that institution's affirmation of American culture. The games that "Team Torah U-Mada" played, and the reasons the competitions took place, reflected, on a very basic level, a different set of American Orthodox community values.

At RIETS, informal games drew no comments and raised no eyebrows, and its physical education courses were established parts of school curriculum. Indeed, intramural sports—including student-faculty baseball games—were part of student life, and ultimately the institution's best ballplayers found out how good they really were on the diamond or hardwood when they formed varsity teams. All this activity was in keeping with the school's avowed mission of raising up generations of all-American yeshiva boys.[11]

RIETS president Bernard Revel, who had received his rabbinical training in East Europe, had no personal affinity for sports activity. He certainly had no interest in participating in school sports events. Nor, for that matter, did any of his old-line Orthodox Talmud faculty ever roll up their own gartered sleeves, substitute a ball cap for a fedora, and attempt to get on base. The yeshiva's secular faculty, and sometimes young rabbinical students, manned the faculty team. However, Revel did have a sense, in keeping with his reading of Jewish tradition, that the promotion of physical fitness was part of a school's job in molding an integrated American Orthodox personality. So he wrote in 1926 that "the ultimate aim of [Jewish education] is not the mere acquisition of knowledge or skill or the mere preparation of an individual for a particular task in life, but the building of character and the harmonious development of man's physical, mental and spiritual faculties." Athletics could be part of the message of "synthesis" that he always preached.[12]

For Revel's students, sports met an even more basic need. What other activity proved so decisively that they were "with it," just like other American kids, and that they attended an up-to-date American institution? Maybe student newspaper editorialists said it best when, in 1935, they declared that "more than any college organization, the Yeshiva College basketball team has been instrumental in uprooting [the] misconception . . . that Yeshiva College . . . is an eastern anachronistic product transplanted artificially to a soil totally inimical to it."[13]

We do not know whether Revel ever had to defend this part of his modern yeshiva program to those like Rabbi Shkop, who, by the way, also visited his school for a while in 1928–1929. (We also wonder what the Grodno rabbi thought if, and when, he observed Revel's students at play.) But, had questions been raised within the ranks, Revel had at least one esteemed contemporary colleague in his corner. For at the very moments when the American yeshiva was affirming the role of athletics, Rabbi Abraham Isaac Kook, the famous chief rabbi of Palestine, was advocating the value of physical fitness, and even of sports, among Orthodox Jews.

Kook's religious Zionist four-square stance was basically in response to Max Nordau's hard backhanded swipe, of some years earlier, at the sedentary, and decidedly noncompetitive, lifestyle of religious East European Jews. In 1898, Nordau, a secular Zionist, had called upon the Second Zionist Congress to raise up a new, "muscular" Jew and Judaism. He had prayed that his movement would enlist proud, athletic Jews who would help their people fight against all comers and earn for them respected places within the modern world. Nordau's stand-up guy was lionized as Judaism's best. Indeed, his very buff appearance was contrasted with "the underdeveloped and frail body of Jewish men . . . produced by the experience of studying in a yeshiva."[14]

For Kook, it was a fundamental article of faith and a lifelong point of emphasis that Orthodox Jews had to take part in the incipient political revival of the Jewish people. As he saw it, to ultimately bring libertine Zionism under the rule of the Torah required that Orthodox Jews—even the most intellectually inclined yeshiva student—had to develop sound bodies to complement their bright minds and holy souls. For Kook, the "physical-mental restoration . . . [of] frail Torah scholars . . . represents a cardinal religious obligation."[15]

Rabbi Kook's activist views did not sit well with most of Palestine's old-line Orthodox rabbis. He also had more than his share of outspoken detractors back in East Europe and even in America. But his call to athletic arms received a respectful hearing in Revel's realm because precisely at that point, in the early 1920s, the yeshiva's president linked his school institutionally with the nascent American branch of Mizrachi (Religious Zionists). Later on in Yeshiva's history, Rabbi Kook's teaching would be explicitly evoked to support the expansion of sports' presence at the New York Torah institution.[16]

Until the mid-1940s, the leaders of the downtown and Brooklyn-based yeshivas could sit blithely by, maybe bemused and certainly unconcerned about sports' status within that libertine institution in Upper Manhattan. That equanimity ended when the most athletic types at their schools, presumably emulating the lifestyle of the RIETS boys, sought to create varsities that would represent their own alma maters. These prime-time initiatives did not sit well with their roshei yeshiva (deans) on several critical counts. To begin with, while wins and losses in pickup games had no residual impact upon the atmosphere of a yeshiva, triumphs and failures in competition against other schools had a disquieting ripple effect within the student body. In the schoolyard, the daily "choose up" contests meant constantly shuffled lineups. Yesterday's winners were tomorrow's losers. Not so when two schools met in a formal engagement. Here, the fear was that star players might be lionized, inferior performances roundly criticized, and outcomes incessantly analyzed. Such excitements would set, in their wake, a wrong tone for institutions where the true heroes were supposed to be the boys who focused only on Torah study.[17]

But, to get to the heart of the matter. Road games thrust these youngsters into uncontrolled social environments where they would encounter players and ultimately fans that did not share all their strict Orthodox religious attitudes. What the rabbis saw as a troubling prospect points to a second, more substantial difference in values that then existed within the community of American yeshiva students and their families.

To set the scene for some worst-case scenarios. If, in the mid-1940s, a TVD squad accepted a challenge from the TA "Talmuds," they would be matched against another all-boys school, composed of youngsters who like themselves were, presumably, Sabbath observers and were otherwise religiously devout. However, when the TVD guys arrived at a Manhattan venue, maybe to play a preliminary to a Yeshiva College game, they would come face to face with a decidedly different Orthodox cultural milieu. Players and fans from the Americanized school might have brought dates to the contests and "gone out" afterward. Social mixing of the most innocent of kinds was rampant. The home teams' community values, so much in line with the American way of life, deemed it kosher to have your girl at a game conducted under Orthodox auspices. In fact, occasionally, a "girls' game" preceded a Yeshiva College match.[18]

The decidedly coeducational environs and other extracurricular activities that attended uptown Manhattan games were no place for the TVD crowd. At least that was Rabbi Mendlowitz's and his successors' view. Nonetheless, that decade witnessed a subterranean sports culture emerge within that school, which only suggests that some athletes did not share the full range of their rabbis' strict religious attitudes. Athletes from Brooklyn opposed the Talmudical Academy in 1944 and 1948, most likely before coed audiences. More significant, in the early 1950s, squads of TVD ballplayers joined the fledgling Metropolitan Jewish High School League (MJHSL) of New York. What went on in that umbrella loop, which sought to link in athletic competition and fellowship not only the long-standing yeshivas and mesiftas but also such modern-day schools like the Flatbush Yeshivah, the Ramaz School, and the Hebrew Institute of Long Island, reflected a very different set of American Orthodox values.[19]

The behavior patterns that were routinely on display at MJHSL games stemmed from the maturation within an increasingly variegated American yeshiva community of a new constituency that was deeply committed to intensive Jewish education—otherwise they would have been part of this country's Jewish public and private school crowd—but it was not necessarily sold on the importance of punctilious religious observance.[20] At this constituency's even newer breed of institutions, schools that were wholeheartedly coeducational, boys and girls took all their general and religious studies classes together, separating only at gym time or when boys were taught to lead religious services. In addition, at least in the case of Ramaz, these day schools included a significant number, if a not a majority, of youngsters who were far from scrupulously observant of such Orthodox basics as the Sabbath and kashruth laws. So when it came to sports—that fine reflector of community attitudes—it was a given that boys and girls from these schools would attend the games. Some of the spectators and all the ballplayers would not be wearing yarmulkes. Maybe some coeds would serve as cheerleaders. And, possibly, the boys' varsity games would be preceded by a girls' preliminary.[21] It was also a point of cultural emphasis that after Ramaz home games—single matches or doubleheaders—that the school would sponsor social dances open to both its students and visitors alike. From the perspective of Ramaz's principal, Joseph Lookstein, it made abundant sense to encourage such a social scene. For unless his "academy," as he initially called his school, strongly embraced American mores, he would have no chance of attracting to Ramaz those "discriminating," marginally Orthodox students who would never opt for a "ghetto school" that smacked, in any way, of a "European . . . atmosphere, culturally isolate[d] and tempte[d] by religious sectarianism."[22]

TVD officials could not conceive of their charges participating in the MJHSL. Everything it stood for, and almost everyone it invited in, offended TVD's religious sensibilities. But, evidently, the social mixing with girls in the stands and the perceived immodesty of boosters on the sidelines, not to mention those postgame dances at this decidedly American sports venue, did not exercise those boys in the school who surreptitiously accepted the loop's invitation. What was essentially a rogue operation within TVD lasted two years, from 1951 to 1953, until word got back to school officials about these transgressions and the sportsmen's scheme was scotched.[23]

Rabbi Isaac Hutner of YCB was also less than sanguine about the social scene that accompanied MJHSL games. Still, when the league was established, he permitted his players to participate so long as they adhered to a strict code of conduct after the athletic encounters. He drew an indistinct line on the sidelines and thus defined his community's values differently than did those at TVD. It was a subtle variance in attitude that could not have been lost on TVD's erstwhile varsity boys. Meanwhile, the deal at YCB was that roundballers could officially wear the colors of the "Mesifta High School" against all comers so long as they would discipline themselves and not hang around for postgame dances and parties.

When that tacit agreement was first reached, there were some elements within the school who would have liked the administration to have taken a harder line on this issue. As one player from that era has recalled: "as a matter of fact, there was a point where some of the older *bochrim* in the *beis medrash* wanted to stop it because we played Saturday night and would come into contact [with girls] whether there were dances or not." (It seems that within this religious culture there always are some senior students ensconced within the traditional house of study who regularly oppose all pragmatic social accommodations. Here again, attitudes toward all that sports entails marked off differences in community emphases—even within one specific school. But, let the former YCB athlete continue.) "A couple of us went to the Rosh Yeshiva and he permitted it so long as the restriction on dances at Ramaz held and that was it. At Chaim Berlin, nothing happened unless the Rosh Yeshiva allowed it . . . and we had his approbation."[24]

Left unresolved—and, maybe, unspoken of—when Yeshiva Chaim Berlin boys were permitted to play in the MJHSL was the question of the perceived immodesty of female cheerleaders who performed on the court during stoppages in play. Ramaz inaugurated this ancillary activity in 1951 with girls in longish skirts. Short skirts appeared in 1954 and remained the style for a generation or more. As important, what Ramaz did became a model not only for its sister coed schools. An increasingly Americanized RIETS community, now part of an expanding and expansive Yeshiva University, tacitly followed the lead at its own girls-only high schools established after the Second World War. The organizer of Brooklyn Central's "first cheering squad" said as much in her 1953 high school yearbook when she noted that "she stole all the 'trade secrets' from Ramaz."[25]

In time, Rabbi Hutner came to the conclusion that notwithstanding his youngsters' apparent adherence to his rules, the social scene all around them, particularly those "jumping and prancing" cheerleaders talked about in his school's beis medrash, was inappropriate for his disciples. So when here two Orthodox worlds clashed socially, the YCB contingent decided to retreat to a more clearly marked sideline. At the close of the 1956–1957 campaign, after six years of participation, Yeshiva Chaim Berlin resigned from the MJHSL. It was, in its own right, another subtle Orthodox community-defining moment.[26]

Although the MJHSL regretted losing a charter member—the move ran counter to its mission of being an all-inclusive Orthodox sports association—YCB's exit had no substantive impact on the league. If anything, the late 1950s–early 1960s were a heyday for member schools. The league embarked upon a new era of expansion when, in 1962, it admitted the Jewish Educational Center (JEC) of Elizabeth, New Jersey, to competition. That team quickly became an athletic powerhouse and, in time, its school officials became highly influential in setting MJHSL policies. Meanwhile, natural rivalries between the two TAs and among Ramaz, Flatbush, and HILI (Hebrew Institute of Long Island) were the talk of the modern Orthodox community. For example, on every Washington's Birthday, Ramaz played a triple-header against Flatbush. The boys' junior varsities, urged on by their female boosters, opened the proceedings.

They were followed by girls' and boys' varsities that were inspired by their cheerleaders, under the watchful eyes of appreciative coed crowds. And post-game dances remained part of the Ramaz home game scene.

But, even as Yeshiva University's high schools teams, the JEC (which had its separate boys and girls divisions), and the fully coed schools were then quite content with their approach to sports and to American-style fraterniza-tion, one of the league's charter members was slowly beginning to feel uncom-fortable with these very modern Orthodox practices. Beginning in the early 1960s, voices were heard within the study halls of the Rabbi Jacob Joseph School (RJJ) calling upon their yeshiva to emulate the strict social-religious culture of TVD—and now of YCB—by leaving the MJHSL. And the sports program became a major point of entry for an attempt to interject this spirit within the Henry Street school. For its most militant religious leaders, the effort to separate RJJ youngsters from "association with 'Hebrew culture schools'" [viz., Ramaz, Flatbush, et al.]—a derisive and dismissive charac-terization—that were deemed "derogatory influences on the Yeshiva's repu-tation" was part of a plan to position that school more definitively within the rising so-called "yeshiva world" community. Here, a community's leaders dis-played their newest colors through trying to ban its youngsters from participa-tion in a sports arena.[27]

For much of its early history, RJJ's mission and constituency had been very much akin to that of the TA or of YC. Indeed, until it established its own high school program in 1940, RJJ was a prime feeder school to Revel's high school. And in the 1940s and 1950s, even as it competed with the two TAs (Manhat-tan and Brooklyn) for secondary school students, the downtown institution was still sending many of its youngsters to Yeshiva College. Given its orien-tation as a single-gender school, but with a religious outlook not so different from Yeshiva University's high schools, it was no surprise that it would join the MJHSL. And everyone liked playing against the competitive and combat-ive Rabbi Jacob Joseph School "Raiders."[28]

For the most part, until the 1960s, the school's rabbinical faculty and admin-istrators did not concern themselves with their sports program. Unlike TVD, YCB, or for that matter Ramaz, which had its own strict, if different, disci-plinary codes, RJJ students were not closely monitored. Besides which, some of the ballplayers were also excellent Talmud students who had proven that "learning and ball playing could go hand in hand."[29]

This laissez-faire attitude toward the sports scene at RJJ ended in 1963. Stu-dents of that era have recalled that the school's Hebrew principal, Rabbi Hersch Ginsberg, was especially militant in trying to align the school not only with TVD, YCB, and MTJ but ultimately to have his best students attend advanced Torah institutions like the Beth Medrash Govoha of Lakewood. For Ginsberg, RJJ's man on his own mission, one step in the *right* direction was to end RJJ's participation in a coed sports league. And school officials did so—at least they made their first move to leave the loop—in the fall of 1963.[30]

However, much of the RJJ student body did not share its rabbi's religious fervor, and the aggrieved youngsters, in good American style, quickly formed protest committees aimed at reversing the administration's unilateral decision. A suggestive cartoon that appeared in the student newspaper dramatically depicted rank-and-file sentiment. In this caricature, a faceless, fedora-wearing administrator is shown attempting to close a coffin containing the "RJJ Varsity." But two youthful, muscular hands, rising up from within the coffin, bearing the name "school spirit," stymie his efforts to shut the lid. The cartoon was provocatively labeled "We Shall Overcome," as student protesters analogized their parochial concerns with the most critical American social crisis of their times.[31]

RJJ's battle over the varsity would last four years. And all through this turmoil over membership in an Orthodox sports league, the subtle variances in religious values within this one school's community—between students and their rabbis and even within the faculty and administration—were constantly on display. During the 1963–1964 academic year—and basketball season—the administration threatened, but did not follow through on, its plan to withdraw from the coed sports league. Protests and student promises to stay away from girls at coed games then held the line. Student agreement with the school's demand that all Raider players "wear yarmulkes during the games" also helped the situation even as it suggests that those who at RJJ looked toward YCB, TVD, and beyond to Lakewood as their models really had a long way to go in transforming their school's culture. However, the next year, 1964–1965, brought renewed pressure from the school's most religious elements to end Raider association with the MJHSL. The now familiar canards were repeated—"the mixing of sexes at games"—or they said that "coed Yeshivas who were members of the league presented a downgrading influence on RJJ students." And now student activists were not persuasive enough and/or did not find enough sympathetic ears within school leadership to stem the tide. RJJ would stay out of the league for two years.[32]

During this hiatus, RJJ athletes were given the option of playing in the Mesifta High School Athletic Association, a callow, strictly Orthodox version of the MJHSL. The alternative loop, founded for the 1962–1963 season, was the brainchild of a graduate of RJJ's high school who was then a rabbinical student at MTY. Back in the 1950s, MTY had been a member, for two years, of the MJHSL and had competed, without clash, canard, or controversy, against the coed schools. However, in 1954, MTY left the league primarily because this very small, if elite, school could not field a representative squad.[33]

A competitive sports spirit was revived at the East Broadway institution a decade later, when a contingent of students became "interested in organized sports." So much for total uniformity of interests within another Orthodox institution. But, given the changed tenor of the times, the administration, headed still by the eminent Rabbi Moses Feinstein, would not countenance rejoining the MJHSL. This renowned decisor of Jewish law had not spoken out against the coed league in the 1950s. But times had changed! In any event, the slight accommodation to sports-minded students was for MTY's unpaid, volunteer coach to contact YCB and five other similarly minded schools to form a league of their own. This athletic association would play as all other leagues did, with uniforms, scoreboards, playoffs, and certified officials. It even rented the same public school gyms that the coed league frequented. However, the athletic association explicitly and consistently barred women — even the mothers and sisters of players — from watching their yeshiva boys at play. This closed-door athletic association model would prove worthy of future emulation.[34]

Back at RJJ, Rabbi Ginsberg probably would have been happiest if his students had had no sports program. But, if RJJ boys had to play, if they still felt the urge to compete, Ginsberg could not question the company these athletes were now keeping. If anything, arguably, when the Raiders lined up against students from YCB, the Yeshiva of Eastern Parkway, the Chofetz Chaim Yeshiva, the Kamenetz Yeshiva, or the Yeshiva Samson Raphael Hirsch, their school was making yet another community-defining statement. Through the sports venue, that highly unorthodox sports arena, RJJ joined up — in a semi-official way — with the expanding "yeshiva world." The school was certainly buying into the spreading spirit of gender separation.[35]

The battle to "crack the adamant refusal of the school's administration" to accede to student wishes to be part of the coed league was rejoined during the 1965–1966 season. A "Bring Back Basketball" campaign was organized, and, in a repeat of the 1963–1964 scenario, talks resumed about of addressing "one of the chief problems . . . the mixing of the sexes at the games."[36] The crucial question once again was, would RJJ boys stay away from girls in a monitored coeducational environment? To test whether "students [could] behave in an orderly manner," the administration permitted the booking of an exhibition game against BTA (the Brooklyn Talmudic Academy). And when students seemingly lived up to their end of the bargain, "an element of trust" began to be "built between the administration and student leaders that suggested that the young men" understood the values of the school and would protect those values."[37]

In the fall of 1966, RJJ reentered the MJHSL. A deal was struck that the Raiders could play in the coed league but they would stay away from the feared fraternization. In many ways, it was a protocol that was reminiscent of the deal that had existed at YCB a decade or so earlier. The agreement also reminds us that, in the end, RJJ community attitudes — notwithstanding Rabbi Ginzberg's hopes and efforts — were not the same as TVD's, YCB's, most certainly

Lakewood's, and even those of its own close downtown neighbor MTY, situated just a few blocks away on East Broadway. However, not all aspects of this student-administration social contract, which also called for good, gentlemanly behavior in the stands—were always in force. Certainly, from the point of view of how outsiders, such as Ramazites, defined appropriate deportment, Raider rowdies often seemed to be up to their old tricks. For example, during their first year back, they would chant *sonei yisroel, sonei yisroel* (lit. antisemites, fig. you are less religious than us) whenever the Ramaz team had the ball in its possession. But these catcalls of Orthodox community dissonance were sounded as most RJJ guys sat in their own section of the bleachers, in keeping with the letter of the unwritten law. RJJ remained in that loop for another decade until "the decline of the lower East Side affected RJJ," causing "a painful reversal in [its] fortunes" and leading the then seventy-five-year-old institution to close its high school.[38]

The 1960s ended with the teams and schools that remained in the league comfortable with the religious values of all athletic competitors. It helped that, by that time, Ramaz's "Fall Frolic" and other such dances were socially passé. It wasn't that current students were more religious than their predecessors. They just saw themselves as having concerns more pressing than tuxedos, corsages, and how to cut in properly on a lacquered floor. In that very special month of June 1967, the idea of a senior prom was considered a particularly frivolous indulgence.[39]

But, over the long haul, it was the gradual conformity of schools like Ramaz and Flatbush to stricter league definitions of proper female "on court" dress and demeanor that maintained unity, for the next generation, among rival institutions. Slowly but surely, the social rigors of "Brooklyn" Orthodoxy that came to influence, if not permeate, more modern segments of the American yeshiva community played themselves out in the athletic realm. In the late 1970s, the MJHSL began moving against the long-standing tradition of cheerleading performances on the floor during stoppages in play. JEC's Rabbi Elazar Teitz, who led the charge versus those who wore their short skirts in front of men and boys, has recalled that initially his forces pushed for the right of a school that was offended by the "gyrations" to prohibit such routines in their building. Flatbush and Ramaz girls could cavort all they wanted when their schools played each other. But never at JEC. Rabbi Teitz did allow his girls to cheer on their male friends in street clothes from the sidelines, a concession of sorts that did not sit well with even more traditional elements within his own community. Over time, league officials extended their ban to games where visiting teams might be offended. Ultimately, gymnastic-style cheerleading was prohibited entirely from all yeshiva league contests.[40]

The 1980s also witnessed the promulgation of a dress code for female athletes. No longer would girls be permitted to run downcourt in short gym shorts and short-sleeved shirts in front of grown men and pubescent boys. Sweatpants and long-sleeved uniforms would be the required way to go. Once again, the ban was implemented in stages, with Ramaz and Flatbush, for example, initially retaining the right to dress as they chose when they met each other. Actually, here too, for Rabbi Teitz, this policy constituted a middle ground between those within the Orthodox community who would have banned men totally—fathers and brothers included—from observing girls in action and those for whom watching what unfolded on the court was just good, clean American sports fun. Still, the sweats and sleeves rule constituted a dramatic departure from past custom or practice. Those who had run RJJ had to have smiled ruefully once they learned of the direction the league had taken. Too bad for them, their school had not survived long enough for its leaders to vote now with the majority in support of increased social separatism.[41]

Clearly, Rabbi Teitz's personal determination to repaint long-standing out-of-bounds lines was a major factor here. The young rabbi carried the ball effectively for his father, the eminent Rabbi Mordecai Pinchas Teitz, who, from his perch as unofficial—if highly influential—chief rabbi of Elizabeth, made the call that modern Orthodoxy, even when played out here on the hardwood, had to position itself somewhere between the strict separatism of the "yeshiva world" and the more laissez-faire attitudes at Ramaz and even at Yeshiva University's high schools. In keeping with this creed, the senior Teitz encouraged school administrators "to attend basketball games and other athletic events." For him, reports his family biographer, "sports and a spacious gymnasium were necessities, not extras." Indeed, Rabbi Mordecai Pinchas Teitz believed that "if you let the boys know the results [of the World Series], you'll have a good relationship with them." Rabbi Hutner over at Chaim Berlin never thought in those terms. But Rivkah Teitz Blau also asserts on behalf of her father that "the exciting sports program served Torah," at least her father's and brother's definition of the Torah's views on proper dress and deportment at games. What is most significant for us is that the other schools' principals—most of whom were also Orthodox rabbis—the men and some women who now ran the league, acceded to the Teitzs' calls. It was their acquiescence that made these decisions stick.[42]

Before the start of the 1978–1979 basketball campaign, Flatbush abruptly pushed its cheerleaders to the sidelines, ending a generations-old tradition at that school. Anxious still to publicly express their "school spirit," the sidelined pep squad members channeled their abundant enthusiasm for Falcon athletics—and their dissent from the school's decision—into a coed group of "Rabble-Rousers." From then on, a very vocal group of Flatbush's boys and girls stood in the bleachers and "faithfully cheered on the Falcons at every game." Mixing of the sexes at big ball games would continue to be part of the Flatbush social scene for years to come.[43]

At Ramaz, full compliance with league rules moved much slower. Through the mid-1980s, cheerleaders—"their marching army," as its yearbook put it—continued to do their thing on the court at home games. However, they were dressed now in sweatpants and long-sleeved shirts. And as of 1991, cheerleading was a thing of the past even at that Yorkville school. But no school rabbi forced these girls out of their outfits and away from their routines. Rather, to hear members of Ramaz's last cheering squad tell it, by the late 1980s, "it was not as exciting an activity. . . . It was cooler to be on an actual athletic team." Besides which, with no other schools fielding squads, they felt themselves out of step.[44]

On the girls' basketball front, in 1986 Ramaz students made some noise about "preserv[ing] the Renegades right to wear shorts" in defiance of the "demand" of the "league's teams who refuse to wear shorts that all other squads wear sweatpants." Two years later, in 1988, girl athletes reportedly "did defy the Yeshiva League dress code," somewhat more subtly "wearing cut off sweats above the knee." League officials took notice of Ramaz's deviance but adopted, for a while, a passive approach toward punishing violations—unless, of course, an offended team complained. However, by the early 1990s, Ramaz too fell, or was pushed, totally into line. Howard Stahl, the girls' varsity coach at that time, has recalled that league referees were instructed not to permit an improperly dressed female competitor from taking the floor.[45]

But that era of common religious values among competitive schools would come to an end during the 1990s. The palpable, irresistible force of gender separatism was bumped to a new level as some league schools now formally objected to men and boys watching girls at play, no matter how modestly they were dressed. And that dynamic now brings us to our most contemporary day, where girls-only leagues reflect the adoption within much of the American yeshiva community of a larger set of social protocols that originated in—and was, fifty years ago, restricted to—an Orthodoxy that held sway only in select sections of Brooklyn and the Lower East Side.

Notes

1. Hedy Shulman, "SCW Student Is School's First NYC Marathoner," *Yeshiva University Today* (December/January 2001), pp. 1–5. Interview with Shulman, January 5, 2001.
2. Richard Zerneck to Amy Rule, October 25, 2001; Barbara Jacobs to Richard Zerneck, October 31, 2001. Letters are in the possession of the Yeshiva University Athletic Department.
3. Interview with Richard Hagler, director of the Metropolitan Yeshiva High School League, March 27, 2003; interview with Rochelle Brand, principal of Yeshiva University's Central High School for Girls, July 2, 2003.

4. Interview with Chaya Newman, principal of Bruriah High School, March 13, 2003.
5. *Yeshiva High-lites: The Weekly E-mail Newsletter of the Weinbaum Yeshiva High School*, February 27, 2004, p. 1. E-mail communication between Rabbi Perry Tirschwell and Jeffrey S. Gurock, October 11, 2004.
6. For retrospective studies of the socialization and education of children in the shtetl, with emphases on idealizing the scholar, see Mark Zborowski and Elizabeth Herzog, *Life Is with People: The Culture of the Shtetl* (New York: Schocken Books, 1952), pp. 74–77, 341–43, 353, 391, and Emanuel Gamoran, *Changing Conceptions in Jewish Education* (New York: Macmillan Company, 1924), pp. 112–13. For a discussion of sources that describe in unromanticized ways the lack of physical training available to students in the stultifying heder atmosphere, see Steven J. Zipperstein, *Imagining Russian Jewry: Memory, History, Identity* (Seattle and London: University of Washington Press, 1999), pp. 42–45. By the same token, Diane K. Roskies and David G. Roskies, in *The Shtetl Book* (New York: KTAV Publishing House, 1975), pp. 150, 158, 211, and passim, note that the games children played during their heder years were of the nonphysical type, like tic-tac-toe, memorization games, "IT," etc. They do, however, note, p. 150, that sometimes in heder youngsters "yelled or fought with each other," we imagine outside the purview of their teachers. For another vision of traditional Jews as nonsportsmen in East Europe, see Chaim Bermant, *The Jews* (New York: New York Times Books, 1977), p. 180. See also Cary Goodman, "(Re)Creating Americans at the Educational Alliance," *Journal of Ethnic Studies* (Winter 1979): 19–20, for references to primitive forms of baseball played by kids in East Europe. It should also be noted that as the twentieth century unfolded, Zionists and Bundists developed their own sports clubs. But these modern Jewish groups came out of a culture quite different from the traditional religious environment that is under discussion here.
7. For a brief biography of Rabbi Shkop, see Aaron Rothkoff, *Bernard Revel: Builder of American Jewish Orthodoxy* (Philadelphia: Jewish Publication Society, 1972), p. 119. On the report on the East European rabbi's visit to TVD see D. B. Schwartz, *Artzot HaHayim* (Brooklyn, 5752 [1992]), p. 16b, noted in Aaron Ahrend, "Physical Culture in Rabbinical Literature in Modern Times," *Korot: The Israel Journal of the History of Medicine and Science* 15 (2001): 61.
8. For a discussion of Mendlowitz's and TVD's agenda by a sympathetic chronicler, see Yonoson Rosenblum, *Reb Shraga Feivel: The Life and Times of Rabbi Shraga Feivel Mendlowitz the Architect of Torah in America* (New York: Mesorah Publications, 2001), pp. 78, 90.
9. It should be noted that Mendlowitz's view of recreation as rounding out the training of religious students was in the spirit of Rabbi Samson Raphael Hirsch, whose thought he had studied while still a yeshiva student in Hungary, See on this aspect of Mendlowitz's background, Alexander S. Gross and Joseph Kaminetsky, "Shraga Feivel Mendlowitz," in *Men of the Spirit*, Leo Jung, ed. (New York: Kymson Publishing Co., 1964), pp. 553–61. For sources on Rabbi Hirsch's Central European Orthodox attitudes toward physical fitness as part of the total *mensch-yirsoel* see Samson Raphael Hirsch, *Horeb: A Philosophy of Jewish Laws and Observances*, vol. 2, Dayan Dr. I. Grunfeld, trans. (London: Soncino Press, 1962), p. 408. For a

rare source from East European Orthodoxy in support of physical fitness activities to round out a yeshiva student's daily pursuits see a statement made by Rabbi Israel Meir Ha-Cohen Kagan, Chofetz Chaim, noted by R. P. Mankin in *Shaarei Tziyon* (Tammuz-Elul, 5694 [1934]), quoted in Ahrend, "Physical Culture," p. 63.

10. On the availability of facilities for recreation at YCB and MTY, see interviews with Abraham Sodden, September 5, 2000, Rabbi Sheldon Steinmetz, September 6, 2000, and Rabbi Daniel Mehlman, August 3, 2000. On Rabbi Moses Feinstein's (head of MTY) fundamentally positive attitudes toward physical fitness see *Igrot Moshe, Even Ha-Ezer*, vol. 3, 61, 1, pp. 119–20; *Orach Chaim*, vol. 5, 40, 26, p. 69. On handball at MTY see Hanoch Teller, *Sunset: Stories of Our Contemporary Torah Luminaries zt"l and their Spiritual Heroism* (New York: New York Publishing Company, 1987), p. 55.

11. On the role physical education and sports were intended to play at RIETS in producing well-rounded high school students see Shelley R. Safir, "Our Next Step," *The Elchanite* (June 1925): 13–14. On the qualifications of the school's first "P-T" instructor see "Annual Report of the Board of Trustees of Talmudical Academy for the School Year Ending July 31, 1919, to the University of the State of New York" (Norman Abrams Collection, Yeshiva University Archives). For a report on a faculty-student ball game see *The Annual Elchanite* (1923): 86.

12. See Bernard Revel, "Jewish Education," *Jewish Forum* (March 1926): 10–11. For more on Revel's views of "harmonization" or "synthesis" as a goal of education at his modern yeshiva see Jeffrey S. Gurock, *The Men and Women of Yeshiva: Orthodoxy, Higher Education and American Judaism* (New York: Columbia University Press, 1988), pp. 90–91 and passim.

13. *Commentator* (hereinafter *Comm*) (December 19, 1935): 2.

14. See Arthur Hanak, "The Historical Background of the Creation of the Maccabi World Union," in *Physical Education and Sports in the Jewish History and Culture*, Uriel Simri, ed. (Netanya, Israel: International Seminar on Physical Education, 1973): pp, 149–52, for a discussion of Nordau's statement and its impact upon the evolution of Zionist sports in Western and Central Europe.

15. Zvi Yaron, *The Philosophy of Rabbi Kook* (Jerusalem: Department for Torah Education and Culture in the Diaspora of the World Zionist Organization, 1991), pp. 104–7.

16. For a discussion of ideological and political opposition to Rabbi Kook's views on sports see Ahrend, "Physical Culture," pp. 73–77. See Gurock, *The Men*, pp. 67–81, for the history of the integration of a Mizrachi-initiated Teachers Institute within Revel's American yeshiva community.

17. Interviews with Moshe Mendlowitz, September 19, 2000. Moshe Mendlowitz conversations with Rabbi Samuel Mendlowitz and other "TVD alumni" reported to Gurock, September 19, 2000. Interview with Roy Chavkin, September 8, 2000; interview with Rabbi Nesanel Quinn. See below for further discussions of these attitudes.

18. For a report on an event of this sort that had taken place just a few years earlier see "Seminary Loses to Yeshivaites at Noar Affair," *Comm* (January 13, 1937): 2.

19. For results of early Talmudical Academy games versus TVD see *The Elchanite* (1944): 59, (1948): 61. On the founding of the MJHSL and its mission see an un-

titled Yeshiva University press release, November 11, 1952, in the Yeshiva University Public Relations Office. Although there is a reference in *The Elchanite* (1946): 71 to a "recently founded Yeshiva League," the founding of the permanent MJHSL dates from the spring of 1951, when Yeshiva University sponsored "the first Jewish High School Invitational Basketball Tournament" involving the [Manhattan] Talmudical Academy, Yeshiva University's recently founded Brooklyn Talmudical Academy, YCB, TVD, and the Rabbi Jacob Joseph School (RJJ). See "Basketball Tourney Molded by Yeshiva," *Comm* (April 16, 1951): 3. Some months later, in 1951–1952, the league played a full schedule with Ramaz included. Flatbush and HILI (also known as Far Rockaway Yeshiva) entered in the 1952–1953 season, giving the league five all-boys' schools and three coeducational schools. See *Comm* (March 6, 1952): 3 for league standings. In 1953, MTY entered the MJHSL. See *Comm* (October 26, 1953): 3.

20. The history of these even more modern schools dates back to the 1920s. See Gurock, "Jewish Commitment and Continuity in Inter-War Brooklyn," in *Jews of Brooklyn*, Ilana Abramovitch and Seán Galvin, eds. (Hanover, N.H.: University Press of New England, 2001), pp. 231–41, for a discussion of the lifestyle of students who entered what were then elementary-level day schools, most notably the Flatbush Yeshivah. After the Second World War, Flatbush and her younger sister schools expanded into the high school realm and began playing interscholastic sports.

21. It is unclear precisely when boy-girl doubleheaders came into vogue. Certainly this was the case by the late 1950s. It is nonetheless possible that the inaugural Central-Ramaz games were "prelims" to boys' varsity games. What is certain is that as early as 1952 the Ramaz yearbook mentions a "tremendous crowd" that attended the Ramaz-Central game and comments that "it could have been [due] to the novelty of the game." Evidently, Ramaz boy fans attended this games. See *Pioneer* (1952): 40–42. In all events, there was a yeshiva league for girl players as early as 1956, and Central cheerleaders were at boys' games as early as 1951. Their presence and performances, as we will presently see, would become a cause celebre. See *Elchanette* (1952): 41, (1957): 51.

22. On Ramaz's mission and how it defined itself differently from other schools, as well as the religious culture that Rabbi Lookstein acknowledged and worked with see Gurock, "The Ramaz Version of American Orthodoxy," in *Ramaz: School, Community, Scholarship and Orthodoxy*, Gurock, ed. (Hoboken, New Jersey: KTAV Publishing House, 1989), pp. 40–42, 62–68. On the religious values harbored by Ramaz students see Nathalie Friedman, "The Graduates of Ramaz: Fifty Years of Jewish Day School Education," in *Ramaz*, pp. 83–123.

23. For information on TVD's short-lived involvement with the MJHSL see Moshe Mendlowitz conversation with Ronald Greenwald reported to Gurock, September 25, 2000. Tape recording of the Mendlowitz-Gurock communication in the possession of the author.

24. For evidence of YCB's early involvement in the MJHSL see *Comm* (March 6, 1952): 4. On Rabbi Hutner's expressed approbation for the team see Gurock interview with Sheldon Steinmetz, September 6, 2000. For more on Rabbi Hutner's reputation for being an all-knowing leader of YCB see William Helmreich, *The*

World of the Yeshiva: An Intimate Portrait of Orthodox Jewry (New York: The Free Press, 1982), pp. 34–36. See also, for recollections of experiences as YCB basketball players in the early 1950s, Gurock interviews with Abraham Sodden, September 6, 2000, and Leonard Polinsky, September 12, 2000.

25. On the history of cheerleading at MJHSL games in the 1950s see Gurock, "The Ramaz Version," pp. 80–81, note 42. See also *Elchanette* (1953): n.p., (1955): 82, 84–85.

26. The dating for YCB resignation from the MJHSL is derived from *The Elchanite* (1957), which lists that opponent's participating in the league for the last time. It is unclear precisely when, and how, the decision was made at the Brooklyn school to exit the league because of cheerleaders. Leonard Polinsky has contended that while he was a student—before the end of 1953—"one of the rebbeim got wind of the fact that the game that we played against MTA and BTA, the Central girls cheering squad came to the game and they were prancing around and jumping around in short skirts and they banned us from the league." He recalls being in the beis medrash—that hotbed of debate—when he heard that the team had been banned. However, Daniel Mehlman, who played at YCB through 1954, recalls that the team was still in the league during his time with the "implicit proviso that there would be no cheerleaders at the games." From these sources, it may be suggested that the cheerleading issue was "in play" at YCB until a final decision was made in 1957 to exit the MJHSL. See Gurock interview with Daniel Mehlman, August 3, 2000.

27. For characterizations of MJHSL schools as "Hebrew culture schools" see "Raider Report," *R.J.J. Journal* (December 1963): 2.

28. On the early history of Rabbi Jacob Joseph School see Alvin Irwin Schiff, *The Jewish Day School in America* (New York: Jewish Education Committee of New York City, 1966), pp. 58–59; Helmreich, *World of the Yeshiva*, p. 46.

29. Gurock interviews with former RJJ students Benjamin Mandel, August 3, 2000, and Ira Steinmetz, August 3, 2000.

30. For retrospective student impressions that Rabbi Ginsberg was influential in this attempted change of attitudes see Gurock interviews with Eli Feit, November 13, 2000, and with Barry Schwartz, November 16, 2000. See also Gurock interview with Rabbi Ginsberg, January 15, 2001. Ginsberg asserted that he had the support of the roshei yeshiva of RJJ. For an in-house appreciation of RJJ's succesful attempt at linkage with Rabbi Kotler and his institution see Marvin Schick, *RJJ Dinner Journal* (n.d.): n.p.

31. "Raider Report." See also cartoon entitled "We Shall Overcome," *RJJ Journal* (December 1963): 2.

32. On the repeat of canards against participation in the MJHSL see Noah David Gurock, "Yeshiva Sportsman," *The Jewish Press* (December 24, 1965): 26. See also *The Tablet: Rabbi Jacob Joseph School Yearbook* (1966–1967): 44.

33. On MTY's early involvement with the MJHSL see *Comm* (October 26, 1953): 3, which notes the school's entrance into the league and an untitled Yeshiva University press release, April 3, 1954. See also Gurock interviews with Rabbi David Feinstein, November 14, 2000, Robert Berezon, November 14, 2000, and Gershon Berezon, November 14, 2000. The Berezons were players at MTY in the 1950s.

34. Gurock interview with Rabbi Moshe Snow, November 27, 2000.
35. Gurock interview with Rabbi Ginsberg.
36. Noah David Gurock, "Yeshiva Sportsman," 26; Gurock interview with Michael Rhein, January 15, 2001. Rhein is identified in the 1966–1967 *Tablet* as G. O. president of RJJ and as a leader in the battle for the return of the team to the MJHSL. Of somewhat lesser moment, but also an issue in play, was RJJ officials' unhappiness that MTA, still awaiting the building of a real home gym on Washington Heights, sometimes used Catholic school facilities where crucifixes adorned the walls. From RJJ's somewhat stricter religious point of view, Jews should not be present in such Christian religious venues. MJHSL officials did not agree.
37. Gurock, "Yehiva Sportsman," 26; Gurock interview with Rhein, January 15, 2001.
38. Gurock interview with Rhien, January 15, 2001. On the decline of RJJ as a downtown-based institution and its move to Staten Island and Edison, New Jersey, see Schick, *RJJ Dinner Journal*.
39. By the way, some thirty years later, circa 2000, a different set of values permeated Ramaz, indicative of the tenor of the times. Proms were back—with all the trappings, including stretch limousines.
40. Gurock interview with Rabbi Elazar Teitz, March 13, 2003.
41. Gurock interview with Rabbi Elazar Teitz; interview with Mrs. Chaya Newman. Regrettably, owing to the absence of records from the league's Principals' Council, which ran the league beginning in the late 1970s, it is impossible to determine precisely when these strictures were implemented. But, as we will immediately see, we can logically date these changes from the late 1970s–1980s through an analysis of responses to the edicts by coed schools like Ramaz and Flatbush. For the record, Mrs. Ruth Ritterband, formerly an administrator at Ramaz, has said that there was no "official rule," at least not one while she was at the Yorkville school. She worked at Ramaz from 1977 to 1988. However, Richard Hagler, who began serving as league director in 1979–1980, has recalled that as early as the 1983–1984 season that there was a dress code for female athletes. See e-mail communication between Gurock and Ruth Ritterband, February 6, 2003, and Gurock interview with Hagler, March 27, 2003.
42. For an authorized biography of Rabbi Pinchas Teitz, which includes notes on the rabbi's interest in sports and use of sports metaphorically to promote Orthodoxy, see Rivkah Blau, *Learn Torah Love Torah Live Torah: Harav Mordecai Pinchas Teitz the Quintessential Rabbi* (Hoboken, New Jersey: KTAV Publishing House, 2001), pp. 138–39, 232–33.
43. An examination of the Flatbush yearbook, *Summit*, from 1970 to 1980 revealed that, until the academic year 1978–1979, cheerleaders in athletic garb were part of the school's scene. Information on when, and how, that contingent was disbanded was derived from interviews with female "Rabble Rouser" leaders Risa Levine and Debbie Reichman Auerbacher on March 18, 2003, and March 19, 2003, respectively. The "Rabble-Rousers" actually date back to 1974. However, *Summit* (1979) states, p. 134, that Debbie Reichman "transformed a once forgotten club into a popular and explosive commission." For more on the "Rabble Rousers'" impact see *Summit* (1985): 142.

44. *Ramifications* (1987): 81, (1989): 90, (1991): 75. See also Gurock-Ritterband e-mail communication.
45. Ramaz's patterns of defiance and conformity to the league rules can be traced through notes in *Ramifications*. See for example, *Ramifications* (1986): 103, (1987): 81, (1988): 87, (1989): 90, (1991): 75, (1992–1993): 134–135. See Gurock interviews with Howard Stahl, March 18, 2003, Hagler, and Tael McLean, March 20, 2003. See also Gurock-Ritterband e-mail correspondence.

Chapter 7

Jenna Weissman Joselit

Best-in-Show

American Jews, Museum Exhibitions, and the Search for Community

Ever since the late nineteenth century, we have come to expect a lot from our museums. We look to them for diversion, spectacle, education, pleasure, and, increasingly over the course of the twentieth century, for community and fellowship as well, especially when it comes to those institutions that traffic in the art, culture, and history of America's minorities such as New York's Jewish Museum. True, the type of community the Jewish museum offers is not quite the same as that provided by a synagogue, a landsmanshaft, a social club, or a JCC, those representative lineaments of Jewish communal life in America. Where they demand steadfastness, fidelity, and financial commitment from their members, the Jewish museum, in contrast, has tended to be a voluntary, intermittent affair, which, apart from requests for a few dollars here and there, does not ask much of its visitors, many of whom are not even members. Where the synagogue has been bound up with faith, the landsmanshaft with geography, and the social club and the JCC with the wholesale pursuit of pleasure, the Jewish museum offered none of these things, at least not until recently. More of a temple of scholarship and contemplation than anything else, it has, for most of its history, successfully stood aloof from the clamor of communal demands.[1] And yet, growing numbers of contemporary American Jews have found that their local Jewish museum constitutes a singularly modern and increasingly attractive form of community, one that they probably seek out far more than they do those institutions that have traditionally made up the American Jewish landscape. A place to assemble with other Jews, to affirm one's identity, to define one's values, to take stock of the present, and to contemplate the past, Jewish museums, of late, have also become the venue of choice for weddings and other ritual moments.

Some observers may see this trend as an inevitable—and woeful—consequence of deracination, as both a rupture with tradition and as proof that something is rotten at the very heart of contemporary American Jewish culture. From this perspective, the latter-day success of the Jewish museum seems predicated on the failure of the community's once-representative institutions. But I take a different, more positive view. By historicizing American Jewry's relationship to museums and their continuously changing roster of exhibitions, I see the current prominence of the Jewish museum as yet another in a long series of institutional innovations characteristic of the American Jewish experience. Like the congregational synagogue or the JCC, the landsmanshaft or the havurah before it, each of which redefined both the terms and the terrain of Jewish communal life, contemporary Jewish museums represent an alternative, yet equally viable, way for modern-day American Jew to belong to something larger than themselves.

American Jewry's affinity for the museum formally dates back to the late nineteenth century, to March 1891, when thousands of New York's Jewish residents lent their name to a petition urging the Metropolitan Museum of Art to open its doors on Sunday. Bearing an estimated 100,000 names, nearly half of which were said to be those of immigrant Jews, the petition made the rounds of the city's stores, offices, cafes, and street corners. A small, square piece of pasteboard with room for anywhere from 50 to 100 signatures per page, the document was circulated by volunteers from the Museum Opening Committee, a grassroots organization determined to expand the cultural franchise of museum-going to New York's poorer citizenry. Though petitions were not uncommon in the New York of the late nineteenth century, this one was no run-of-the-mill petition. For one thing, most of those who signed it were not just Havemeyers, Hewitts, or Vanderbilts but ordinary citizens, many of them immigrants. For another, this petition, unlike so many others that energized urban dwellers of the 1900s, did not call for housing reform, say, or an additional hour of garbage pickup. Drawing unhesitatingly on the imperatives of democracy, it called on the Metropolitan Museum of Art—then, as now, the city's preeminent museum—to open its doors on Sunday: "The undersigned, citizens of New York, join in the petitioning of the Trustees of the Metropolitan Museum of Art, to open the Museum to the public on Sunday afternoon."[2]

While some residents of the city believed, almost as a matter of course, that one or another women's group was "behind it," the petition was actually the handiwork of Charles Stover, the civic-minded manager of the Neighborhood Guild, a social settlement house located at 147 Forsyth Street, in the heart of the Lower East Side.[3] Determined to improve the tenor of life downtown and to expose its residents to something other than the "sordid and vicious surroundings" in which they lived, Stover expended considerable energy in persuading the city's leading cultural institutions, from Cooper Union to the Metropolitan Museum of Art, to welcome the tenement dweller.[4] Having had considerable success a few years earlier in getting Cooper Union to sponsor free Sunday afternoon concerts when he headed the grandly named Movement for the People's Free Sunday Concerts at Cooper Union, Stover now trained his sights on the mighty Met.

Some of those who joined with Stover in clamoring for admission sought, in part, an alternative, a corrective, to the saloon or the biergarten, where many New Yorkers, immigrant men especially, spent much of their free time and extra dollars. "If this desire for innocent and healthful pleasure is not grati-fied," they cautioned, referring to the accessibility of museums like the Met, "the overworked mind and body find relief in more vicious ways and means which, on Sunday, are as easy as the museum is difficult of access."[5] Others, equally mindful of the museum's growing importance as an agent of aesthetic and moral uplift, a vehicle of "public education," wanted, as one of their num-ber put it, to "avail themselves of the privilege of visiting."[6] Were the museum not opened on a Sunday, explained the petitioners, the "great mass of New Yorkers" would lose out on what was rapidly becoming a perquisite of moder-nity and a mark, even a ritual, of urban citizenship: a public encounter with art.[7] "We want it open," they said, "so that the 'industrial classes' can have a chance to go there and be instructed."[8] Besides which, traveling all the way uptown to the Met on a Sunday afternoon transformed what, at night, was a "formidable" undertaking into a "little pleasure journey" during daylight hours.[9]

The Met was not terribly keen on the idea of opening its doors to satisfy the logistical and cultural needs of the body politic; the latter's happiness, after all, was surely not the most important item on the museum's agenda. Unable to make that point directly without giving considerable offense, at least not at first, the Met offered instead a number of different excuses as to why the Sunday venture simply wouldn't do. Some of these excuses were financial in nature, others had to with religion, and still others with a generalized sense of cultural anxiety. Opening the Met on a Sunday was a costly proposition, one that the museum could ill afford, explained its trustees, hoping this admis-sion would quell further talk of Sundays at the Met. It did not. In an attempt to force the Met's hand (We "will leave no stone unturned"), the Museum Opening Committee offered to raise the funds necessary to defray the costs of Sunday openings from June through September 1891.[10] When that offer was rejected, it became increasingly clear that the museum's objection to a Sunday opening had less to do with money than with religion or class bias. Opening the museum on a Sunday would give the Sabbath a "black eye," the trustees eventually acknowledged, insisting that museum-going would "impair popu-lar reverence for the Lord's Day."[11] Horrified at the prospect that Americans, much like their European cousins, might soon spend the day at leisure rather than in prayer, they could not see their way clear to violating the Sabbath by establishing a new precedent. But then, irreligion was not the only thing on their minds. Opening the museum on a Sunday, they also feared, would surely bring in the wrong class of people, those given to misbehavin' and "troublesome" behavior, those with "vandal hands."[12] A museum, they intimated, was no place for the masses.

As public sentiment in favor of a Sunday opening grew louder and louder, the trustees could no longer turn a deaf ear and decided reluctantly to embark on a "perilous experiment": to keep the building open, on a trial basis, for a couple of hours, between 1:00 p.m. and sunset, on several successive Sundays in May and June, after which point a final decision would be reached once and for all.[13] This gesture, cheered a champion of Sunday openings, will "prove whether the working people want to go to a place where they can be educated as well as entertained. It will prove whether the charge . . . that the Sunday crowd would deface the art treasures, is true or false."[14]

Ever-anxious, the Met took great pains to prepare for the occasion, hiring more guards, making sure additional police would be on hand in Central Park, and opening extra checkrooms where visitors could deposit their canes and umbrellas but not their lunch baskets, lest they turn a day at the museum into a real picnic. Curious about the type of people who would choose to spend a Sunday looking at paintings rather than attending church, the Met also made sure to station its staff throughout the galleries, where they were instructed to take notes on who came in and who went out.

The Met's curators and trustees were not the only ones who indulged in a "great deal of speculation" about how things might turn out in the end.[15] So, too, did the metropolitan press, which devoted considerable coverage to the event. Thanks to its lively imagination, the historical record is rich in detail about what ultimately turned out to be not quite so perilous an experiment, after all. For starters, reported the press, visitors came in droves, setting the turnstiles awhirling. "A throng . . . seldom seen in the Metropolitan Museum of Art poured into the building," reported the *New York Times* on its front page, pegging the rate of entry at fifty people per minute or three thousand per hour.[16] What's more, said throng was extremely well behaved and respectful. "A more orderly crowd never entered the building," continued the newspaper, noting that even the harshest critic of a Sunday opening could find fault with very little, if anything. "Those who expected to see Essex Street Polish Jews and 39th Street and Eleventh Avenue hod carriers in ragged clothing and dilapidated hats were agreeably disappointed." They came all dressed up. So, too, did "smart-like colored women with marvelously decorated male companions," whose appearance at the Met "showed that they appreciated the opportunity to visit."

Sunday visitors also came as a family. While here and there individual clerks and saleswomen could be seen, the largest number of visitors by far consisted of parents and their children. "Gleeful voices were heard through the corridors," related one reporter obviously tickled by the sight of "mites in pinafores . . . trott[ing] among the paintings, looking with wondering awe at Laocoon and Hercules. Boys tagged at their mothers' heels and laughed at the queer-shaped pottery of Egyptians." Now and then a few young boys could not "help putting a hand on a piece of statuary," but that kind of behavior, allowed the journalist, happened as much on a weekday as on a Sunday.[17]

As for telltale instances of vandalism, they, too, failed to materialize. "No iconoclastic movements were discovered," wittily observed one eyewitness.[18] Instead, Sunday visitors dutifully went about their business, their hands at their sides. "Group after group stopped to study the passive features of the mummy cases and examined with wonder and intense interest the swathed forms of those who had been living creatures two thousand years ago. All the antiquities had an irresistible charm for the visitors."[19]

For the most part, museum-goers left the building buoyed by what they had seen; those who came away unhappy were in the minority. To be sure, those visitors who came bearing lunch baskets only to be turned away at the door left grumbling, as did those "Kodak camera fiends" forbidden to photograph the Met's treasures. The occasional visitor, "apparently not of the working class," who, having entered the museum with a dog under her arm, was politely refused entry also found herself at loose ends.[20] Everyone else, though, had themselves a grand time. "All looked pleased," reported the *Times*. "They had good words to say for the trustees and the friends of the Sunday opening movement."[21] As for the museum's board, the *Jewish Messenger*, one of New York Jewry's leading weeklies, could not help but poke fun at its prejudices. "Some of the Sabbatarians must have wondered why the obelisk did not fall in dismay or the earth did not yawn and swallow one or two newspapers' offices when two Sundays were thus desecrated, but they are probably satisfied that worse things can happen to a community than that the means of improving their tastes should be at their disposal on their only leisure day," it remarked, cutting the Met's anxious officialdom down to size.[22]

Hailed as a resounding success, a tribute to the power of "popular opinion unmistakably expressed," those early Sunday afternoons at the Met attested to both the seductive power of art and its ability to bring disparate people together.[23] The citizens of New York, otherwise differentiated by religion, ethnicity, social class, neighborhood, and language, were now able to assume a new, more inclusive identity: that of museum-goers. When hod carriers and camera fiends, East Side housewives and Harlem swells, even mites in pinafores, gathered to look at antiquities, mummies, and sculptures, they not only "assert[ed] their rights" to participate fully in all that the metropolis—and its gifts—had to offer; they also became a kind of community, if only for a couple of hours on a Sunday afternoon—a community bound together through the shared experience of contemplating art.[24] Absorbing all these members of the body politic, the Met, in turn, became a "great public institution," a modern expression of the commonweal.[25]

. . .

New York's Jewish Museum, meanwhile, developed over time into a modern expression of the Jewish commonweal, its history a testament to how American Jewry increasingly made the museum its own. In its earliest years, the Jewish Museum functioned more as an extension of the Jewish Theological Seminary's storied library than as an autonomous institution; the scholar, rather than the community at large, was its intended audience, and subdued consideration of the glorious past of the Jews, a past largely understood in intellectual terms, fueled the entire enterprise. Upon relocating in 1947 from the Seminary to Fifth Avenue, a few blocks away from the Met on what has come to be called "Museum Mile," the Jewish Museum changed its stripes. It now embraced art—a resolutely modern art—with a vengeance, rendering a once sleepy, even marginal, institution into a beehive of activity whose comings and goings were widely chronicled by the contemporary press. Much, in fact, has been written about the Jewish Museum's role in advancing a modernist aesthetic in the America of the late 1950s and early 1960s.[26] The institution's curators, keenly attuned to the latest developments in the postwar art world, transformed the Jewish Museum into one of the city's preeminent venues for the exhibition of Abstract Expressionism, a novel, demanding form of visual expression. But then, they were innovative in other areas as well. Mounting a series of interpretive historical exhibitions that compelled American Jews at the grass roots to take a hard and searching look at their own history, they enlarged the museum's capacity for emotional engagement even as they deepened its role as a sophisticated purveyor of ideas.

Take, for instance, the museum's 1966 exhibition The Lower East Side: Portal to American Life. A lively inquiry into the Jewish immigrant experience, this exhibition, curated by Allon Schoener, received especially high marks from the critics. Enthralled by its unabashed theatricality, they allowed how Portal to American Life was to "museums what 'Fiddler on the Roof' was to theater," a bold endorsement, if ever there were one, of the newfound relevance of historical exhibitions to the Jewish civic imagination.[27] Like the wildly successful play, this newfangled kind of exhibition also galvanized its audience, who, enraptured by the stuff on display, brought their grandchildren in tow, generating long lines waiting to get in. So enthusiastic, in fact, was the public's embrace of the show that the Jewish Museum took the then-unprecedented act of extending the exhibition's run by several months.

In one gallery, drawings and paintings by Jacob Epstein, John Sloan, and Abraham Walkowitz took pride of place; in another, "enormously" blown-up photographs—freestanding photomurals, we now call them—and detailed street maps of the Lower East Side's institutions captured the visitor's attention.[28] So, too, did a panoply of colorful Yiddish theater posters, song sheets, and tools of the garment industry, artistically arrayed along a wall. The "raucous" sounds of peddlers hawking their wares added "to the din," or so we are told, while, housed in a tidy little kiosk, a film of Zero Mostel reading excerpts from *Der Bintel Brief* gave voice to Yiddish.[29] "Is it art?" one critic wondered. "Is it Jewish? Who cares? Whatever it is, it is long overdue."[30]

A turning point in both the internal history of the Jewish Museum and the larger world of museology, Portal to American Life set traditional modes and conventions of presentation on their ear, theatricalizing them. By deliberately eschewing a traditionally static, bookish installation in favor of one that more closely approximated a stage set, it broke new ground. No longer could exhibitions make do with a limited aesthetic vocabulary dominated by vitrines and derived from the library paradigm of display; from now on exhibitions had to be as visually arresting as the stuff they displayed. In the process, Portal also redefined the notion of history, claiming it as a visual medium, not just a textual one. Thanks to Portal, bringing history to life was no longer the province of books, the academy, or the solitary imagination; it had become a mandate of the museum as well. This exhibition, remarked the *New York Times*, "evokes the sights and sounds—everything but the smell—of the chunk of Manhattan that was the immigrants' first stop in the New World."[31] "Wandering through the exhibition," related another eyewitness, is "like entering a time machine and exiting into an era which saw a fabulous flowering of Jewish life. For a vivid lesson in living history, run, don't walk, to the Jewish Museum."[32]

Coming full circle, the most immediate impact of Portal to American Life was felt down the block, at the Met, whose director, Thomas Hoving, was so energized by Schoener's use of multimedia and his novel approach to history that he hired him to mount Harlem on My Mind, that colossally controversial show of 1969. Through the deployment of large-scale photomurals and the widespread use of music, the exhibition celebrated the vitality of New York's largest African-American community, hoping to demonstrate that its history was as much a function of internal needs and aspirations as it was a product of racism. Despite its good intentions and sizable audience of both black and white museum-goers, Harlem on My Mind was soon mired in racial politics. Its detractors charged the Met with acting paternalistically by hosting the exhibition in the first place and, more damning still, by mounting it in ways that ran counter to the museum's traditionally restrained conventions. Its supporters, in turn, argued that Harlem's history merited special treatment. And on and on it went, without resolution. In the end, Harlem on My Mind came to be seen as a "molotov cocktail" of an exhibition, one that ensured that "Harlem was on everyone's mind," at least for the duration of its run.[33]

Despite this temporary setback, Portal went on to have an enduring and far-reaching impact on the way Jewish museums and their audiences approached the presentation of history. Through its detailed, sympathetic evocation of the Lower East Side and its vernacular culture, Portal made clear that the past mattered, especially the not-so-distant immigrant past of ordinary mortals named Menachem Mendel and Rochel Leah. Suggesting that it was high time for American Jews to take themselves—and the multiple strands of their own history—seriously, this exhibition and those that followed held out the very real possibility that the modern Jewish museum, rather than the synagogue or the community center, might well be the most effective venue for doing just that. In fact, free of the constraints that hobbled other American Jewish institutions, Jewish museums could offer American Jews something they could not find elsewhere: a neutral Jewish space where they could experience an entirely novel and singularly modern form of belonging based not on geography, religious ritual, or the paying of dues but on a shared appreciation of the varied manifestations of Jewish art and history, an appreciation rooted in the kind of seeing and witnessing that culminated in a heightened sense of affirmation.

For all these reasons, Portal changed the terms of engagement that bound the Jewish museum to its public—a public increasingly made up of families rather than clusters of art enthusiasts or, for that matter, the individual scholar. From now on, Jewish audiences came to a Jewish museum, any Jewish museum, expecting to be moved, heartened, and uplifted by their Jewish identity, not just dispassionately educated about one or another facet of the Jewish experience or exposed to new ways of thinking about art. The overwhelming success that the 1966 exhibition enjoyed made it clear that, from now on, a Jewish museum and its curators had the potential to be, and could successfully serve as, an agent of community rather than its ornament, an active, deliberate force in the shaping of Jewish life rather than merely a passive recipient—and custodian—of its patrimony, as it had long been.[34] To put it another way, the Jewish museum was well on its way to becoming a public institution in the fullest sense of the word.

In the years that followed, the Jewish Museum made good on its promise. Its ambitious roster of exhibitions, from The Dreyfus Affair, curated by Norman Kleeblatt, to Bridges and Boundaries and Berlin Metropolis, to name just a few, firmly established the Jewish Museum both as a center of scholarship and as a place for American Jews at the grass roots to engage responsibly with history and, in the process, with one another. Getting Comfortable in New York, which I had the good fortune to curate together with Susan Braunstein in 1991, also considerably advanced the association between history and community.[35] The last exhibition to be housed in the Jewish Museum, itself the former home of the Warburg family, before it closed for renovations, Getting Comfortable once again underscored the museum's capacity for generating pride and consensus in equal measure.

Picking up where Portal left off, this exhibition followed the lives of Lower East Side residents as they and their children made their way from the slums to well-appointed apartment houses and then on to spacious private homes in the suburbs. While upward mobility was part of the story Getting Comfortable sought to tell, its greater mandate by far was to highlight the role that domesticity played in the fashioning of modern Jewish identity. An ideological construct as well as a physical container, the American Jewish home, the exhibition argued, was central to how American Jews from the late nineteenth century on through the post–WW II era made sense of themselves. Within its walls, they learned how to marry the abundance of consumer culture to the discipline of traditional Jewish practice, giving rise to a distinctive American Jewish identity.

To get that point across, Getting Comfortable constructed a series of environments or tableaus—the exterior of an early twentieth-century tenement, the interior of an interwar kitchen, a '50s "rec room"—whose faithfulness to detail underscored their historicity. And yet these were no "period rooms," as the Met or Winterthur might have it, no eye-popping monuments to the decorative arts. Standing that concept on its head, these humble installations of kitchen cabinets, floral wallpaper, worn linoleum tile, faux wood paneling, and amoeba-shaped tables were designed deliberately to generate recognition rather than to provoke awe and admiration, to engage memory rather than to stun the senses. In this, they succeeded wildly, well beyond our expectations. Visitors by the droves pointed, chuckled, exchanged reminiscences with complete strangers, and, in contravention of museum protocol, even touched the items on display, setting off countless alarms in the process, both ambient and internal.

Getting Comfortable, I suspect, triggered such a powerful emotional response in its viewers precisely because so many of the individual objects on view, along with the built environments that contained them, had once been a part of their daily lives or that of their parents and grandparents. Commonplace, familiar items rather than precious commodities, the Passover dishes, home movies, toys, advertisements, appliances (the icebox was a particular favorite), lighting fixtures, furniture, cookbooks, chromium *chanukiot*, food containers, bar mitzvah paraphernalia, and photographs that inhabited the exhibition represented their patrimony, not someone else's.

This was no accident, no inadvertent consequence of our curatorial vision, but rather a deliberate, conscious strategy. From the outset, Ms. Braunstein and I made a concerted effort to go far beyond the Jewish Museum's holdings, to turn on its head the top-down model of research in favor of one that celebrated the serendipitous find, the everyday object rather than the rarified *objet*. In search of American Jewry's material culture, the two of us visited abandoned tenements and little-frequented attics, flea markets, and matzoh factories. We also advertised in the museum's newsletter and beseeched our friends, family members, and the museum's dedicated cadre of volunteers for stuff. Much like YIVO's *zamlers*, those amateur collectors of prewar Europe who, with a keen eye for the ethnographic and the folkloric, gathered all manner of artifacts for the Vilna research center, our latter-day, American *zamlers* went through their homes with a fine-tooth comb, eager to entrust their things, hundreds of them, to the museum. It is a testament to their zeal and determination, not to mention their museological good sense, that much of what they found ultimately made its way into the vitrines and galleries of the exhibition. But then, the *zamlers'* considerable contributions to Getting Comfortable went far beyond demonstrating the intersection of past and present. Their unstinting efforts on the exhibition's behalf also made clear just how much they cared for and about the Jewish Museum; after all, it was *their* institution. In the end, it's no surprise that Getting Comfortable proved to be such a resounding success. Revelatory in its impact, the exhibition, as one docent turned *zamler* put it, showed as few institutions could that ordinary American Jews "have a history, too."

Trusting in its curators to do right by them, audiences put their faith in the Jewish Museum—and held it accountable. That trust came undone, however, in the spring of 2002 when the Jewish Museum made plans to install Mirroring Evil: Nazi Imagery/Recent Art, an exhibition that explored the impact of the Shoah on contemporary artists. Several years in the making, Mirroring Evil sought to raise "troubling questions" about the relationship between contemporary culture and its fascination with or distance from the Holocaust, a relationship explored through the prism of photography, sculpture, and video installations.[36] "If we dare engage in this discomfiting art, we are forced to confront the very process of moral and ethical decision-making," explained its curator, Norman Kleeblatt, taking the high road.[37] Toward that end, the exhibition displayed, among other things, two renditions of a concentration camp, one fashioned out of Legos and a second, "pop-up death camp," made out of a Prada hatbox ("I'm using the iconography of the Holocaust to bring attention to fashion," its creator, Tom Sachs, explained); a gun created from a Manischewitz matzoh box; busts of the infamous Mengele; and an oversized photograph of inmates at Buchenwald in which the artist inserted an image of himself holding a can of Diet Coke.[38]

If the idea was to generate controversy and, with it, publicity for the museum, the exhibition succeeded beyond its wildest expectations. Editorials in the *New York Times* and other metropolitan dailies denounced the exhibition as did a vicious, mocking *New Yorker* cartoon from the pen of Art Spiegelman. On the street, long lines of pickets, claiming that the exhibition made a mockery of the Holocaust, threatened to make noise ("Don't go in! Don't go in!" they chanted) unless the museum agreed to shutter the exhibition; elsewhere, heated conversations at dinner parties erupted throughout the city, followed in due course by panel discussions and academic conference papers. While the art world, for the most part, welcomed the exhibition, characterizing it as "daring," "uncommonly thoughtful," and as an example of "postmodernity at its best," many members of the general audience were stunned first by what they read in the catalogue, which had been released a couple of months before the exhibition's debut, and then by what they actually saw in the museum's galleries.[39] Some accused the museum of trivializing the Holocaust; others of callous insensitivity. "I broke into tears," said one survivor. "This is very, very painful. The museum has brought this pain to the fore, and I have to live it every day."[40]

As events threatened to spiral out of control, the Jewish Museum sent a letter to its members, hoping to mollify them. Insisting equally on the integrity of the exhibition and the museum's concern for its constituents, the letter sought to reassure them that in mounting Mirroring Evil, it had no intention of "making light of the Holocaust." On the contrary, explained Joan Rosenbaum, the Jewish Museum's longtime director, "The Jewish Museum's mission is to deal with issues of concern . . . and to do so in a thoughtful, balanced and responsible way."[41] When that overture failed to quiet things down significantly, officials of the museum met several times with protesters—which, initially, they had been reluctant to do. What resulted from these meetings was the decision to station a series of "warning signs" throughout the exhibition to alert visitors that they were in the vicinity of some of its more upsetting artworks and should proceed with caution. The text read: "Some Holocaust survivors have been disturbed by these works." Placating some, this strategy only added to the anger of others. "It's moving anthrax from one part of a building to another," declared Menachem Rosensaft. "For Holocaust survivors, it's not less morally repugnant because people are warned. What's objectionable is that they're in the Jewish Museum at all."[42]

In the end, the show went on—as planned. Those who anathematized Mirroring Evil stayed away; those intrigued or puzzled or simply curious came to see it for themselves. Some museum-goers who emerged from Mirroring Evil scratching their heads in confusion no doubt agreed with the assessment of the *New York Times*: "Few exhibitions of contemporary art have come into the world more shrouded in exegesis than Mirroring Evil," it observed in a scathing editorial titled "The Art of Banality," a pointed reference to Hannah Arendt's equally scandalous account of the Eichmann trial of 1963. "The catalog is a briar patch of rhetorical questions and explanatory negotiations and that spirit is echoed on the wall text in the gallery rooms." And that was only the half of it. "Many people," continued the editorial, "have worried that the show would offend. But the only thing offensive about it is the way its creators have self consciously positioned it in a tradition of 'scandalous' exhibitions."[43]

Whether or not Mirroring Evil was deliberately provocative or unintentionally so remains to be seen; the jury is still out on that one. What is certain, though, is that the hullabaloo that resulted from the display of dollhouse-sized death camps underscored the centrality of the museum to the modern American Jewish experience, making it clear that when it came to exhibitions, a lot was at stake: enlightenment and education, yes, but also moral responsibility. Over the years, Jewish audiences had come to envision the Jewish museum as an institution whose primary mandate was to renew them, to affirm them in their Jewishness, to show cause as to why Jewish culture mattered. Mirroring Evil did nothing of the sort. Throwing precedent to the wind, the exhibition purposely challenged and incited its audiences, deliberately rendering them uncomfortable, ill at ease, baffled. Caught off guard by this about-face, which reversed decades of accommodation and consensus building, audiences did not know what to make of it. And in their confusion, they responded with anger.

In the end, the ensuing brouhaha raised lingering questions about the museum's relationship to its constituents. Ought the Jewish Museum or, for that matter, any of its counterparts serve as an agent of community or stand apart from it? What of its mandate? Was it to shock, provoke, and disturb or to comfort, embrace, and affirm? And, finally, to whom was the museum truly beholden? The artists whose work it displayed? The trustees who supported the institution? Or its audience?

For the latter, the issues attending Mirroring Evil were as black and white as some of its artwork. No longer did American Jews of the twenty-first century, the descendants of those who had urged the Met to first open its doors at the turn of the twentieth, regard the museum as an exalted institution, a palace of fine arts, or themselves as poor but worthy supplicants knocking at its door. By 2002, having prospered in America, they had come to see the Jewish Museum as an extension of the American Jewish community and of themselves—their shared values, mutual interests, common sensibilities. But, as it happened, the object of their affections didn't see things quite that way. Charting its own course, one that placed a barrier between itself and its audience, the Jewish Museum threatened to undermine that civic bond, that tacit social contract, between a museum and its constituents. Simply put, it broke faith with what the *Times*' chief art critic Michael Kimmelman called a relationship of "mutual respect."[44] Out of touch with many of its members, the Jewish Museum put on an exhibition that, wrote Kimmelman, "leaves much of the public feeling confused, excluded and finally bored if not pained and offended, which is of course the point."[45] Under those circumstances, was it any wonder that tempers ran high?

. . .

Between 1891, when New Yorkers first demanded greater accessibility to the city's museums, and 2002, when they demanded greater accountability of them, the museum world transformed itself from a preserve of the elite to the meeting ground of the masses, from a custodian of culture to its representative. Over the span of a century, this institution changed course. Initially it held itself at arm's length from the public, but over time, largely in response to the latter's increasingly vocal concerns, the museum evolved into a new kind of public space, as much agora and public square as temple of beauty. No longer simply a steward, answerable to the internal, institutional imperatives of collection, preservation, and presentation, it became something much larger: an arm of the community answerable to its constituents, whose emotional needs had to be acknowledged and met if the museum were to consider itself a proven success. In 1891, at the height of the brouhaha over opening the Met on Sunday, one supporter of the proposition was asked what he and the other petitioners hoped to accomplish by putting pressure on the Met. We want the museum open on Sunday, he replied, so that underprivileged New Yorkers can "go and be made happy."[46] Much the same can be said of contemporary, affluent American Jewish museum-goers who, upon crossing the portals of Jewish museums everywhere, look forward eagerly to standing shoulder to shoulder in the galleries in solidarity with one another and the objects on display. They, too, want to be made happy.

Notes

1. For more on the history of Jewish museums and their collections, see Grace Cohen Grossman with Richard E. Ahlborn, *Judaica at the Smithsonian: Cultural Politics and Cultural Model* (Washington, D.C.: Smithsonian Institution Press, 1997).
2. *New York Times* (hereafter *NYT*), March 20, 1891, p. 4. See also Roy Rosenzweig and Elizabeth Blackmar, *The Park and the People* (New York: Cornell University Press, 1992), pp. 359–363.
3. *NYT*, March 20, 1891, p. 4.
4. "Open the Museum—And Perhaps the Saloon Will Do a Lighter Sunday Trade," *NYT*, March 7, 1890, p. 8.
5. Ibid.
6. "The Masses Will Speak," *NYT*, May 6, 1891, p. 8; "It Was A Grand Success," *NYT*, June 1, 1891, p. 1.
7. "Open the Museum." See also Carol Duncan, *Civilizing Rituals: Inside Public Art Museums* (New York: Routledge, 1995).
8. "The Masses Will Speak."
9. "They May Be Open Sundays," *NYT*, September 25, 1890, p. 9; "Open the Museum."
10. "The Masses Will Speak."
11. "It Was A Grand Success"; "Victory Is Won At Last," *NYT*, May 19, 1891, p. 1.

12. "The Museum of Art," *NYT*, January 1, 1892, p. 8; "The Metropolitan on Sundays. How the Movement for the Opening Was Successful," *NYT*, August 7, 1892, p. 16.
13. "Victory Is Won At Last."
14. "The Masses Will Speak."
15. "It Was A Grand Success."
16. The observations which follow were drawn from "It Was A Grand Success."
17. "It Was A Grand Success."
18. Ibid.
19. *NYT*, June 8, 1891, p. 8.
20. "It Was A Grand Success"; *NYT*, June 8, 1891, p. 8.
21. "It Was A Grand Success."
22. *Jewish Messenger*, June 12, 1881, p. 1.
23. "The Metropolitan on Sundays."
24. *The World*, March 21, 23, 1892, quoted in Rosenzweig and Blackmar, *The Park and the People*, p. 368.
25. "Must Have More Money. Else the Museum of Art Will Not Be Open Sunday," *NYT*, November 1, 1892, p. 9.
26. Julie Miller and Richard I. Cohen, "A Collision of Cultures: The Jewish Museum and JTS, 1904–1971," in Jack Wertheimer, ed., *Tradition Renewed: A History of the Jewish Theological Seminary* (New York: The Jewish Theological Seminary of America, 1997), pp. 341–346.
27. Richard Shepard, "Jewish Museum Depicts American Ghetto," *NYT*, September 21, 1966, p. 44.
28. Alfred Kazin, "The Writer and the City," *Harper's*, December 1968, p. 110.
29. "Seminary Bulletin," October 1966, p. 1, Records of the Communications Department, RG 11, box 46, Jewish Theological Seminary.
30. Shepard, "Jewish Museum Depicts American Ghetto."
31. Ibid.
32. "The Lower East Side: Gateway to the New World, " *World Over*, vol. 28, October 1966, p. 8.
33. Michael Kimmelman, "Culture and Race: Still on America's Mind," *NYT*, November 19, 1995, H1. See also John Canaday, "Getting Harlem Off My Mind," *NYT*, January 12, 1969, section 2, p. 25, and "Art: Harlem on My Mind—Two Views," *NYT*, January 26, 1969, section 2, p. 31.
34. Under these circumstances, curators emerged as key figures in the construction of community. Although at times they chafed under that mantle of responsibility, preferring to view their role in far more dispassionate, intellectual terms not unlike those of academicians, the heightened importance of the Jewish museum endowed them, willy-nilly, with the authority to preserve, interpret, and ensure the continuity of American Jewry's patrimony—just like rabbis.
35. What follows is drawn from the author's personal files on the making of Getting Comfortable, as well as from Susan L. Braunstein and Jenna Weissman Joselit, eds., *Getting Comfortable in New York: The American Jewish Home, 1880–1950* (New York: The Jewish Museum, 1991).
36. "Dear Jewish Museum Member," March 4, 2002.

37. Norman Kleeblatt quoted in Michael Kimmelman, "Evil, the Nazis and Shock Value," *NYT*, March 15, 2002, E35.
38. "Designer Death Camp," *New York Times Magazine*, March 10, 2002, p. 19.
39. Quoted in Ron Rosenbaum, "Mirroring Evil? No, Mirroring Art Theory," *New York Observer*, March 18, 2002, p. 11; Linda Nochlin, "Mirroring Evil: Nazi Imagery/Recent Art—Critical Essay," *ArtForum*, summer 2002, p. 1 in online version.
40. Barbara Stewart, "Museum May Rethink Three Works in Holocaust Show," *NYT*, February 28, 2002.
41. "Dear Jewish Museum Member."
42. Barbara Stewart, "Jewish Museum to Add Warning Label on its Show," *NYT*, March 2, 2002, B1–2.
43. "The Art of Banality," *NYT*, March 22, 2002, A24.
44. Kimmelman, "Evil, the Nazis and Shock Value," E35.
45. Ibid., E33.
46. "The Masses Will Speak."

The "Be Virtuous!" Board Game

"Monopoly" in Contemporary Yiddish

for Satmar Hasidic Girls

When Charles Darrow, an unemployed heating engineer from Germantown, Pennsylvania, brought the first version of his "Monopoly" board game to the Parker Brothers Company in 1935, he had no idea that his product was going to go on to become one of the most popular board games of all time. By the turn of the twenty-first century the company noted that its game was being sold in eighty countries in twenty-six languages and an estimated 200 million sets had been sold since its inception.

In the mid-1990s an enterprising Satmar Hasid from Williamsburg, Brooklyn, can be said to have made it twenty-seven languages when he translated the game into Yiddish for the entertainment and edification of the young girls in his community. In doing so, however, he translated not just words but the entire culture of the game. In Handl Erlikh, which takes its name from an idiomatic phrase that can be loosely translated as "do business honestly" or "be virtuous" or "live piously," the goal is not property acquisition but scrupulous adherence to Satmar laws and customs (*erlikhe yidn*, or virtuous Jews, is the name that those Jews known as Haredim use in reference to themselves).[1] The game is written specifically for girls ages eight and older because Satmar boys are still supposed to be studying Torah constantly and it is unacceptable for them to waste time on such frivolities as board games. Consulting with Satmar rabbis, religious leaders, and educators, the author transformed this ultimate capitalist property-trading game into an alternate imagined world of the community's deepest religious and spiritual values. The game is deliberately designed to serve as an agent of social control and to shore up the foundations of the Satmar enclave. At the same time it reveals some of the anxieties and very modern pressures that are undermining that enclave, especially those pressures relating to the role of girls and young women.[2]

Background to the Satmar

A Jewish journalist from the *Village Voice*, writing a book about Hasidim around the world, observed, "What Pat Buchanan is to the Republican Party, Satmars are to other Hasidim. In the ultra-Orthodox world, it just doesn't get any more religious than this."[3] The right-wing Satmar, named for the Hungarian village of Satu Mare, where the group originated, is the largest Hasidic court in the New York metropolitan area and one of the largest internationally. Of all the Hasidim they are among the most resistant to the pressures of acculturating to the modern world. Their family and communal life, their reading matter, and their schools are written and conducted entirely in Yiddish, a language that serves as a barrier between them and the non-Jewish world. Their total worldwide population at the present time is approximately 100,000, with half of these living in New York. The Lubavitch Hasidim, who can be said to be the Satmar's greatest rivals (one observer refers to Satmar and Lubavitch as "the two Superpowers of the Hasidic world") number a distant second or third. The Satmar are known for their animosity and violence against the Lubavitch, who differ significantly in outlook and philosophy; feelings run particularly high when, as has occurred, some Satmar Hasidim desert the fold and go over to the Lubavitch court. Even reading the Yiddish weekly *Die Algemeine Zeitung*, which is sympathetic to Lubavitch, is considered a sin among the Satmars.[4] In general Hasidim are divided into twenty-five to thirty separate communities or courts, ranging in size from one hundred families to more than five thousand, each court bound to a particular charismatic leader or rebbe.[5] These communities were reconstituted in the United States after World War II—as well as Israel, Canada, and parts of Western Europe—with the arrival of survivors from the Nazi Holocaust who were determined to rebuild the shattered world they had left behind.[6]

While the vast majority of Hasidic Jews in the world were destroyed during the Holocaust, timing and geography influenced the relative number of Satmar and related Hungarian Hasidic adherents who survived. Poland fell to the Nazis in September 1939, and only approximately 300,000 Polish Jews survived the war, almost none of them Hasidim. As a result there are virtually no Hasidim of Polish origins among the New York communities.[7] In contrast Hungary, including the remote corner of Europe where the Satmar lived, was not occupied by the Nazis until March 1944. The time under Nazi control and the length of imprisonment in camps was shorter, and thus proportionately more Hungarian Jews survived. Similarly, more Jews living near the Russian border, including remnants of the Lubavitch Hasidim, were able to flee to the relative safety of the Soviet Union.[8]

The original Satmar Rebbe, Rabbi Joel Teitelbaum, was born in the town of Sighet and left in 1932 to establish his own congregation in the town of Satu Mare. He was ransomed from the Bergen-Belsen concentration camp in December 1944—ironically with the aid of Zionist leaders—along with a trainload of several hundred other Hungarian Jews.[9] After short stays in Switzerland and Palestine, he arrived in New York in 1947 at the age of sixty-one and settled in Williamsburg, Brooklyn, where, because of his great prestige and active leadership, surviving Hungarian Hasidim flocked to his congregation.[10] The first and main congregation, Yeter Lev D'Satmar, was founded in 1948 with a few dozen families. Weddings soon followed, originally of older men (who had lost their first wives and all or most of their children) to younger women, and the congregation began to grow.[11]

Indeed, of all the features that the Satmar Hasidim are famous—or notorious—for, their fecundity is one of the most notable. Pressures from their population explosion and the shortage of resources to support it are among the gravest problems facing the community. Like other fervently Orthodox Jews around the world, the Satmar take literally the commandment to "be fruitful and multiply." A free suburban rest home for the recuperation of mothers who have just given birth, known as *kimptorins*, and a network of older women who will come to the home to help overwhelmed new mothers, are important parts of the community's extensive social welfare system. Having as many children as possible despite all obstacles is both a religious obligation and a conscious effort to undo what Hitler did. "We do practice family planning," said one Satmar Hasid in Kiryas Joel, the group's satellite community in upstate New York's Monroe Township, defending his group's attitude toward birth control. "We plan to have families—of sixteen or eighteen kids."[12]

The birthrate among these Hasidim is possibly the highest of any group in the United States. Even the Amish, who are frequently compared to the Hasidim, average only seven children per family, and number about fifteen thousand in their main region of Lancaster, Pennsylvania.[13] Originally six to eight children per family, the average birthrate in Kiryas Joel has risen in recent years to eight to ten. Furthermore, the Satmar Jewish school system is the largest in the United States, encompassing twenty thousand children in the 1998–1999 academic year, equivalent to half of all Hasidic children and one in ten of all the Jewish children in the nation attending a Jewish day school.[14] Each year approximately five hundred Satmar couples in New York marry—weddings number four or five each day except the Sabbath and holidays—and each week at least two dozen children are born, all adding to an exponential rise in the number of Yiddish speakers. With them the Yiddish language, far from being dead, is actually alive and growing. Dancing at weddings is a major form of entertainment in a group that shuns TV, radio, and almost all forms of media except the community's own Yiddish publications and audiotapes of religiously approved Torah learning and music. The names of all the boys who have been circumcised that week are announced every Friday night at the main Satmar congregation, and once in a single Sabbath in 1989 the number rose to thirty-two.[15] At the current rate the school population is doubling every seven to eight years, and new classes must be added every few months.[16] Having, raising, protecting, and educating all these children is a central preoccupation of Satmar life. In the view of Satmar leaders, everything possible must be done to guard their fragile souls from the evil influences of the modern world and to assure that they stay within the boundaries of the community.[17]

How well the Satmar will hold on to this population remains to be seen. Contemporary observers of the community note that the community is not monolithic and that some fragmentation and gradations of opinion are increasingly taking place, especially as the order of succession of the Satmar Rebbe is not clear and adherents splinter into groups supporting different candidates. However, it is biologically possible that adherents of these groups and their descendants could number in the millions. At the very least, a group that has always been on the periphery of American Judaism might well turn out someday to be a dominant element.[18]

In comparison with other Hasidim, the Satmar have been known for the extremism of the attitude they take toward the modern world. For example, unlike the Lubavitch, who wear modern suits and fedora hats and wear caftans only on the Sabbath and holidays, Satmar men at all times are supposed to dress exactly the way they did in Hungary a hundred years ago. Girls must wear long-sleeved dresses and stockings from the age of three. Another characteristic mark of the Satmar is opposition to Zionism and the modern State of Israel, something that was nearly an obsession of Rabbi Joel Teitelbaum while he was alive. While other fervently Orthodox Jews ultimately came to terms with a secular Jewish state and learned to cooperate with it—the Lubavitcher Rebbe considered aspects of the state's existence miraculous—to the Satmar Rebbe and his followers, Israel was an ally of Satan.[19] The Nazi Holocaust in Rabbi Joel Teitelbaum's view was God's punishment for the blasphemy of modern political Zionism. He also believed that the state was actively keeping the Messiah from coming as he should have in the wake of the greatest destruction the Jews had ever witnessed.[20] The Satmar anti-Zionist view is clearly evident in the Handl Erlikh game.

In the Satmar world, schools and teachers are the partners of the parents in properly socializing the children. The system is deliberately designed to keep the children off the streets as much as possible until they are safely married, ideally at the age of eighteen. School is in session almost the entire year and continues in summer camps in the Catskills for most of July and August. The day starts early and ends late—until four o'clock for the girls and until six o'clock for the boys, with children receiving both breakfast and lunch there—one of the factors that greatly alleviates pressure on the families and makes employment outside the home a possibility and even a norm for women without preschool children. All religious studies are conducted entirely in Yiddish with a growing number of Yiddish textbooks.

In Europe formal Jewish schooling for girls was unknown, and in the early 1950s there was much anxiety and ambivalence over the necessity of setting up schools for them in the United States. Many Satmar Hasidim did not accept the idea until the Rebbe came out in favor of it.[21] The resulting Bais Rukhel Satmar girls' school system abides by a traditional prohibition against teaching Torah to girls.[22] After learning their Hebrew prayers, they do not even use the standard Hebrew texts of the five books of Moses; this they learn from Yiddish workbooks. The superior position in which the Lubavitch Hasidim place the Jewish education of girls and women has been cited as one of the motivations for former Satmar to join the Lubavitch faction.[23] There is no twelfth grade, so it is impossible to get a New York City high school diploma, and going to college is not even an option without further education outside the community; for Satmars, further secular schooling is considered unnecessary and even undesirable too far past the legal dropout age of sixteen, when girls are expected to go to work to earn money for their marriage two or three years later. While they are in school, an important part of the curriculum consists of vocational topics such as home economics, sewing, and secretarial skills, along with religious topics such as the details of the "family purity" laws, rules for married life, and "proper" conduct at home and in public.[24]

Paradoxically, the gender inequalities of the Satmar school system have also led to some advantages to the girls in the possibilities of acculturation to the outside world. One is vocational: since boys must be taught by men and girls by women, becoming a teacher in the Satmar system and thus gaining more economic power within the household became an option, something that did not exist in Europe. It is reported that teachers in the community are relatively well paid, have twelve-month contracts, and receive many fringe benefits, including free school and summer camp tuition for their children, free staff quarter bungalows in the Catskills, and discounts at the community's stores. While boys discontinue most secular studies after the age of their Bar Mitzvah, the girls' schools have good general studies departments complete with vocational training. The girls are subject to boredom and restlessness in their religion classes, where past the third grade the prohibition on teaching them Torah leads to simplified teachings that are below their abilities; the gap is filled by secular studies, where they obtain a better knowledge of English than the boys and become qualified to work at a wider variety of jobs. As one observer of the community noted, "The girls find relief and an outlet in the secular class where they are taught interesting material that suits their respective age levels and where both they and their teachers are not continually suspected of subversion."[25]

The girls are also at an advantage when it comes to their appearance. A young girl in a conventional long dress and uncovered head or even a young woman in a fashionable wig appears far less bizarre to the outside world than her brother, who in addition to black Hasidic garb also has a shaved head and side curls. Females can thus more easily move about and evade the community's restrictions. Girls can more easily wander into forbidden zones such as the public library, where they may read uncensored books, or a movie theater or indeed anywhere around the city. New York City after all is not Lancaster, Pennsylvania, and all the temptations of one of the greatest metropolitan centers in the world are only a short subway or bus ride away. Controlling the children's behavior and ensuring that they abide by Satmar norms is a concern for all, but it is a greater challenge for the girls than for the boys.[26]

Not every waking hour can be spent in school; on Sabbaths and holidays and perhaps for an hour or two between coming home from school and helping to prepare dinner there is an opportunity for the girls to enjoy some leisure, which opens the door for play and games. With no TV, radio, videos, electronic games, or any of the modern media permitted to them, there is the problem of what to do (TV in particular is branded as the *ayin hara* box, or the *shmutzige* or *treyfene keilah*—a source of the evil eye or the dirty and impure instrument). It should be noted that this can be a challenge in observant Jewish families of all backgrounds. Long Sabbath and holiday afternoons, particularly in the summer, create a wide market for pastimes that are G-rated and do not use electricity. Thus in the twenty-first century Orthodox Jewish homes may be one of the few places left in the United States where young people play board games, checkers, chess, dominoes, scrabble, cards, and so forth on a regular basis.[27]

Since the 1960s the specifically Jewish entertainment and leisure repertoire has included the English-language game Kosher Land, produced in Crown Heights, Brooklyn, and based on the best-selling Milton Bradley game Candy Land, which for fifty years has been a best-selling first game for American children. It is possible that the makers of Handl Erlikh were attempting to follow in the footsteps of the successful Kosher Land game. (The description for Kosher Land reads: "Travel through Kosher Town past the Kiddush Ocean; fish for Matza balls; don't listen to the Latke Men Marching Band or you might get stuck in the honey! Make it all the way to your Kosher Home and you win!") As for the original Monopoly, it can be speculated that an adult Satmar once came across a group of girls playing it and was perturbed to see the children wasting their time, handling symbolic money (particularly on the Sabbath and holidays), and imbibing the materialistic values of that best-selling capitalist game. Hence, the idea for Handl Erlikh was born.

The Original Monopoly

In the original Monopoly each player starts with $1,500 of paper money. Most of the places on the board represent city streets, their names originating in Atlantic City, New Jersey, as well as railroads and utilities. The four corners of the board, which are specifically copyrighted by Parker Brothers, include "Go," "Go to Jail," "Jail," and "Free Parking." Each player, it will be recalled, in most instances collects $200 each time he or she passes "Go." One player acts as the "Bank," disbursing funds, collecting taxes, fines, and interest, and selling and auctioning the property. The game's equipment includes two piles of cards, known as "Chance" and "Community Chest"; a player who draws these cards is expected to follow the instructions, which usually involve either a penalty or additional earnings, such as "Go to Jail, Do Not Pass Go, Do Not Collect $200" or "Income Tax Refund, Collect $20." The object of the game is to become the wealthiest player through buying, renting, and selling property, including miniature houses and hotels. In the long version of the game, the winner must succeed in driving everyone else into bankruptcy. In the short version, the game ends when only one player goes bankrupt, and the richest one left is the winner.

The Hasidic Version

In the Hasidic version, the different agenda of the game is apparent almost immediately. Successful capitalist activity is not the goal here. Adherence to Torah and conformity to the norms of the community are. On the very cover of the game are inscribed twice, on both sides, the words in Yiddish: "The Torah is the greatest joy" (*Di Torah iz der bester glik*), and in the center the Hebrew verse from Proverbs 1:8: "Hear, my son, the instruction of thy father, and forsake not the teaching of thy mother," which in this context can be read as "Hear, my child."

To begin with, the paper money in Handl Erlikh is almost identical in size and color to that of the original Monopoly, but each denomination is inscribed with an appropriate Yiddish motto that would appear to negate any anxieties the players might have about money in general. This can be viewed as an important emotional safeguard in a community where it is estimated that anywhere from 30 to 50 percent of the population officially live below the U.S. federal poverty line and many are dependent upon government assistance. On

the $1 bill is written "Live piously [*handl erlikh*] and you will be successful."
"With trust in G——d all your worries will fall away," announces the $5 bill.
"Don't worry—have faith and be happy," proclaims the $10 bill. These say-
ings repeat themselves in the higher denominations until the $500 bill, which
reads: "Only with full faith and trust in G——d will your prayers be heard."
The money serves an important function. By noting the relative fines, penalties, and prizes written throughout the game, one may discern how far up or
down certain actions or places stand within the hierarchy of Satmar communal values.

The board itself is larger and contains more places than the original Monopoly. The property names are reminiscent of Jewish and Kabbalistic tradition,
and the cities invoke important Hasidic strongholds of the past and present.
Starting with the four corners, in place of "Go" is a grassy-green country scene
of a road with wagon wheel ruts in it, designated *onfang* (beginning). The picture could easily be that of Eastern European countryside seventy years ago.
Instead of "Jail" there is *tefiseh*, or prison, showing a photograph of a medieval
castle surrounded by a moat that would have struck fear into the hearts of the
players' Hungarian ancestors. On the fourth corner of the board is an illustration of fire and flame titled "Gehinnom," or the Jewish version of hell. According to Hasidic and Kabbalistic lore Gehinnom is not necessarily a permanent
resting place but a venue where sinning souls spend time in temporary repentance ("Just Visiting" is the equivalent message written on the "Jail" portion of
the original game). Finally, in place of "Free Parking" there is a vision of rush-
ing blue water and flowers titled "The Way to the Garden of Eden."

Of the place-names on the board, eight are of important towns or cities
for the contemporary Satmar world. Instead of "Park Place" or "New York
Avenue," they are, written in Yiddish letters, Williamsburg, Bais Rukhel—
the Satmar girl's school system—Boro Park, Monsey, Montreal, Antwerp,
London, and Manchester. The highest property values are for Williamsburg
itself, at $250, and the Bais Rukhel, at $450. (The same company that publishes
books for the Bais Rukhel school system incidentally publishes this game as
well.) Ten of the cities on the board are European Jewish and Hasidic centers
of ages past, most of their communities having been destroyed during World
War II. However, the founding members of the community, almost all of them
Holocaust survivors, obviously wish that these young American-born girls
will remember the names of those towns. They are Lizensk, Zanz, Koznitz,
Rimanov, Mezbuz, Berditchev, Pressburg, Kolib, Krakow, and Lublin. Entire
histories could be written about each of these towns and cities and the places
they hold in the Hasidic imagination.

As for other places on the board, there are three designated as "Yeshiva."
These display photographs of the community's academies for higher Torah
learning around the world. There are also several designated as *gescheftn*,

or stores—one for *shtreimels*, the distinctive fur hats worn by some male Hasidim including the Satmar, another for *esrogim*, and another for holy books. There are various sums offered as "prizes" if one lands in any of these places. Three spots on the board are called simply "Kollel," or the institution whereby Orthodox Jewish men study Talmud for a period of years after their marriage. "Torah is the best merchandise" claims one; "Happy are you, when you study Torah!" claims another.

Immediately one notices an incongruity here. Technically Satmar girls are not supposed to learn Torah, as teaching Torah to women is interpreted as being contrary to the strictest Jewish law. As we have seen, after they learn the basic Hebrew prayers, the Bais Rukhel school system, unlike other school systems for Orthodox girls such as Bais Ya'akov, goes to great lengths to provide the girls with only Yiddish text and workbooks so that they do not actually lay their eyes on any original Hebrew text. In addition, girls and women do not wear *shtreimels*, they are not responsible for buying or carrying *esrogim* for the Sukkot holiday, and they certainly do not spend time in yeshivas or kollels. Such places are strictly male preserves. While men who study in these places are the mates of first choice, as we shall see, the game does not describe the yeshiva or the kollel in reference to the young girls' potential husbands but in reference to the girls themselves. For them these ambitions truly are in the realm of fantasy. Perhaps as a corrective to this, there are eight spots titled *hakhnoses orkhim*, or the welcoming and feeding of guests, a communal and religious duty that does fall especially on the shoulders of women and girls. "Do a great mitzvah and take in a Jew immediately," they read.

In addition, there is a spot on the board that has no parallel in the original Monopoly. It is *mekhutz le-makhaneh*, or "outside the camp," a biblical term first encountered in the book of Exodus. This spot represents the powerful deterrent of communal sanction against anyone who deviates from its exacting lifestyle. "Distance yourself from evil! No one may be friends with you! Stay out for three turns!" is the lot of the unfortunate player who lands there.

There are also several spots where the player, on landing there, must choose cards corresponding to "Chance" and "Community Chest." These are orange *iberashung*, or "Surprise" cards, which speak of prizes for good deeds the player has done ("success is only through trust and faith" is written on each one), and *kheshbon-nefesh*, or "Repentance" cards, each of them describing a bad deed or action for which the player must seek forgiveness.

As in the original Monopoly, the players throw dice and advance with their tokens around the board. Certain advantages accrue if a player lands on "Kollel." There she must stay out of the game in order to *lernen fleysik* (learn diligently). However, she does receive a $30 living stipend for every turn she stays out. There is also monetary gain if a player lands on "The Way to the Garden of Eden"; the player receives a prize of $100. There is no financial penalty if a player lands on "Gehinnom"; however, she must stay out of the game for two turns and *tu teshuveh*, or repent.

Property acquisition is still important, as it is in the original game. However, while the title deeds as well as the miniature houses and hotels are identical to those of the English Monopoly, there are wide divergences in the rules. *Maaser gelt*, or tithing, is an important aspect of the game from the beginning to the end, reflecting its high value in the Hasidic and Orthodox Jewish communities. When the girls start, a *tsedokeh pushke*, or charity box, is designated, and it continually receives contributions. For example, at the beginning each player is instructed to contribute $200 to the charity box from the $2,000 originally granted from the "Bank." Every time someone passes "Go" (*onfang*), $25 of the total $250 she collects goes right into the *tsedokeh pushke*. Ten percent also goes in each time a player earns any money from prizes, sales, or rent of property. If she lands on "yeshiva," $20 goes to charity. Exhortations not to forget this duty are written several times in the game's Yiddish instructions. Should the charity box become empty at any point in the game, all the players are obliged to put $50 into it. Also, any player who runs out of money is allowed to take $50 out of it, thus making "bankruptcy" unlikely.

In addition to the charity box there is also a *gemilut khasadim* fund, where needy players may borrow up to $300. The rules specify that one cannot at any time borrow from the "Bank" but only from this special fund. Those who have borrowed must pay it back by contributing part of the funds they receive each time they pass "Go." Care must be taken not to forget what a player owes, and this information should be written down if necessary. The entire process is not dissimilar to the actual disbursement and donation of social welfare funds in the Hasidic community.

While the rules and the board itself are highly illustrative of community values, perhaps the most interesting and instructive part of the game is the texts on the "Surprise" and "Repentance" cards. These cover the gamut of the community's designated sins and good deeds, including Jewish observance, good manners (*midos tovos*), charity, helping parents, self-control, attitudes toward business and money, attitudes toward technology and the outside world, and, most of all, the importance of modest dress and behavior.

Directives on Jewish observance rank predictably high on the list. Proper blessings are important. "You forgot to say a *brokhe*. How can you eat that way? Pay a $20 penalty to the bank, and next time you'll know better," reads one "Repentance" card. "You made a *brokhe* without *yiras shomoyim* [fear of heaven]; go to hell and give $10 to charity." Judging by the financial prizes and penalties, honoring the Sabbath, with emphasis on female duties, and eating kosher food are the two most important religious directives. The latter is particularly strong because Satmar generally do not trust any meat or food that is not prepared by their own personnel. "You ate without definite *hekhsher* (kosher certification). Go to hell and pay a $500 penalty to the bank." "You baked challah for the holy Sabbath, and you 'took' it. You fulfilled the mitzvah of challah! You will have a pious Jewish home and you will be saved from many terrible things! You receive a house immediately." "You finished preparing for the Sabbath early! One gets the same joy out of the Sabbath as one puts into it! You've honored the Sabbath. You win $1,000 from the bank."

The *midos*, or forms of behavior and self-control that are covered so extensively in traditional Jewish texts, receive appropriately extensive coverage in the game. "You didn't listen to your mother and father! *Gevald!* The Torah tells you to listen to your parents! Go to hell and stay there for two turns; pay a $10 penalty to the bank," reads one "Repentance" card. Another reads, "You spoke with *derekh erets* (courtesy). A *kidush ha-shem!* (sanctification of G——d's name). Everyone will love you. You win $40 from the bank and go another turn." Likewise, eating nicely and slowly merits a reward, for "when a Jew eats the very table becomes an altar." Showing compassion for someone, which is the "sign of a Jew," earns $30. He who shows compassion [*rakhmonus*] to others will have compassion shown to him. Helping someone, which is also the sign of a Jew and good Jewish manners, merits the same sum. Telling the truth, the girls are told, is the greatest honor and saves the player from sin even when it shames her. Refraining from *loshn hara* ("evil speech" or "gossip") saves the player from hell for four turns.

Giving charity with a full heart, even to the point of having to "scrape it together" (*tzusamen genumen gelt af tsedokeh*) is considered a great mitzvah; the Holy One, Blessed be He, will always help the person who gives much charity, and thus the action merits $500 from the "bank." Not telling lies, not correcting someone who is wrong, keeping oneself from becoming angry, and banishing hatred of someone from one's heart all earn financial rewards, escapes from hell, or trips to the Garden of Eden. On the other hand shaming someone, which is the "same as killing" that person, earns a trip to prison.

A few of the good deeds described are not directly related to religious values, but nevertheless help to keep an orderly family life and to make bearable a home that might have as many as twelve children in it. "Don't quarrel with your sisters! Jewish children should not quarrel with one another!" is repeated twice. "You didn't clean up your room before going out to play! Who will clean it up? Your mother, maybe? Pay a $50 penalty to the bank." However, if one's room *is* tidy and clean, then "that's how a Jewish home should be": the player wins $40.

Not being jealous of those who may be richer than oneself is an important value in a community that is so financially poor and is so surrounded by the signs of conspicuous consumption. "Not running after money" and not becoming too absorbed in "business" earns a player a stay in the yeshiva, where she is advised to "repent and learn diligently" (*tu teshuve un lern flaysik!*) and earns support from the charity box for each turn that she stays out of the game. Once again, the occurrence of these directives is curious because in the real world only Satmar boys and men are given the opportunity to study in the yeshiva and to be supported by the community. More realistic are the admonishments against envy of others, which accrues the strictest of penalties. "You looked at what someone else had, and you coveted it!" (*gelust af dem*) proclaim not just one but two "Repentance" cards. "If you covet what someone else has, you'll lose what you have already! Your house is burned down and you'll have to pay dearly now—$600 to the bank."

One may derive certain hints about the business practices of the community by the warnings against making fun of a "goy" (a "desecration of G——d's name"), writing an uncovered check, and giving the bank a false name. In the original Yiddish these are *Aroys gegebn a tschek on a dekung! Batsol $20 shtrof farn bank*, and *Arayn gegebn in bank a falshn nomen! A khilul ha-shem! 3 geng gornisht koyfn*. We may well wonder why eight-year-old girls are expected to be familiar with such misdeeds. In any event, the penalties they carry are comparatively small.

While the above directives might be familiar or at least applicable to any fervently Orthodox Jew, Handl Erlikh is most instructive to the outsider when it deals with the extreme physical and cultural isolation and modesty that is demanded of Satmars. To exert such social control on children living in the middle of New York City is a tall order, and the emphasis the game puts on it is indicative of the challenge. However, the very fact that these acts are enumerated in the game are an indication that they are actually taking place.

"You looked at a television!" proclaims one "Repentance" card. "You made the very eyes in your head impure! That goes against the Jewish way! Go to hell and stay there three turns to overcome this great transgression. Repent!" This by itself might not cause surprise, since the evils of television watching are a matter of common concern even to the non-Orthodox. However, listening to the radio, reading a *treyfene* book, or speaking English among other Satmars are also forbidden and carry severe penalties. Listening to the radio makes the ears impure and earns a trip to hell. "Impurity! Impurity!" (*tameh! tameh!*) intones the writer of the game when speaking of reading non-Jewish books. This also earns a trip to hell and makes the giving of extra charity obligatory. Speaking English may be necessary when dealing with non-Yiddish speakers in business, but officially only the Yiddish language is acceptable. "Speaking Yiddish keeps you away from the goyim!" the girls are warned, and doing otherwise lands them "outside the camp."

Extreme anti-Zionism, which is so characteristic of the Satmar and which places them at such odds with the vast majority of the rest of the Jewish world, is also inculcated into the players. "You helped the Zionist state!" proclaims one card. "No good can come from ties to evil-doers, only misfortune. Repent!"

The penalty is to remain two turns in the yeshiva, receiving no stipend and paying extra charity to the charity box. The learning of modern Israeli Hebrew is a significant part of the curriculum of most Jewish day schools around the world, but for the Satmar it is a profanation of the Holy Tongue and an unacceptable recognition of the legitimacy of the State of Israel. "You spoke Hebrew [*ivris*], you Zionist!" admonishes another "Repentance" card. "For three turns you can't buy anything. Pay a $500 penalty to the bank." Here the prohibition anticipates the crime; the game is assuming that somewhere a Satmar child living in the United States might actually have picked up enough modern Hebrew to be able to speak it. Satmar living in Israel may avoid using modern Hebrew, but they are as fluent in it when necessary to speak to outsiders as the American Satmar are in English.

The most important theme in the game by far is the value of *tsnius*, or modesty in appearance and behavior, and it is here that the creator has gone to the greatest extremes and is most at variance with modern American culture. Out of sixty "Repentance" and "Surprise" cards on all sorts of subjects no fewer than sixteen are devoted exclusively to the subject of modesty. Five concern the distinctive dress the girls are supposed to wear, including the necessity of fortitude in the face of outsiders who may find their appearance strange. "You went out in a long dress," reads one. "When one goes about like the grandmothers of old, that's beautiful and clever and good, and one will be saved from many troubles. You are saved from the penalties of "prison" and "hell" for the next five turns." Similarly, "You weren't ashamed when someone laughed at your long dress. A sign of very good character [*zehr a gute mida*]. The next three turns you don't have to pay anyone anything, and no one can shame you. You win $150 from the bank and can go buy another long dress." Dark colors are the ideal. "Your clothes are too loud!" warns another card [*Di klayder zenen shrayedik*]. Modesty requires that you be less flashy. Pay a $10 penalty to the bank." Hair and makeup also come up for comment. Satmar and many other Hasidic girls generally wear their hair in two long braids. "You didn't undo your braids! Don't be ashamed in front of anyone. That's how a Jewish child should go about. From you will come pious Jewish generations and you will always be happy," the card proclaims. Becoming *tsufil zikh geputst*, which may be translated as making oneself excessively attractive, is a disgusting show of pride (*eklaftike gaveh!*). The girl must put herself "outside the camp" and stay there for two turns.

Even the most innocent pleasures are fraught with danger for the Satmar Hasidic girl. The players are warned against jumping rope in the street ("where is your sense of modesty?") or speaking too loudly in public, which is a desecration of G——d's name (a *khilul hashem*). A girl is not supposed to walk about in large groups, because "a good Jewish daughter is not noisy and does not call attention to herself." Indeed, in order to be saved from several transgressions she should not go out in the streets at all unless it is absolutely necessary. "The glory of the king's daughter is within the palace," the girls are warned, an oft-quoted saying from Psalms 45:13. Such a modest woman will help bring about again the Kingdom of David, and in the game a player earns herself a stay in the Garden of Eden for two turns.

In the realm of modesty, not surprisingly, the worst penalties accrue in misdeeds related to men; it is in this area that young girls must receive a most thorough training if they are to abide conscientiously by the community's concern that females are an ever-present temptation to the eyes and ears of males. "Jewish daughter! You danced where men could see you! The heavens cry! [*a himl geshrai!*] For this you'll burn in hell! Go to hell and stay there for four turns," reads one "Repentance" card. Singing, laughing, or speaking loudly within earshot of men are terrible transgressions that will send player either to hell or "outside the camp."

Imagination and Reality

The Handl Erlikh game as a whole obviously presents a rich field for interpretation, and many features about it are striking. These include the attitude toward Zionism and the Hebrew language, the poignancy of the preservation of the memories of lost East European towns as places on the board, the strong proscription against materialism, and most of all the social and religious control that the makers of the game are seeking to impose upon the young girls of the community. All this may constitute the vision of an ideal community that the makers of the game want these children to live in. However, in the real world and not the game world there are many pressures in the contemporary Satmar community that act to erode this idealized, insulated existence, for men as well as women.

The most important reality is the economics of having such large families. To an important extent, government aid provides a valuable cushion. Satmar, who were officially designated as a minority by the Department of Commerce after the 1984 presidential elections, have been adept at taking advantage of every possible public program that could help them and have also been adept at finding ways to reduce their income taxes. Medicaid, food stamps, public housing, and a host of other city, state, and federal aid programs support their population explosion (Hasidim refer to the government as "Uncle Shmuelik," or "Uncle Sam" in Yiddish). Still, this cannot provide for more than a subsistence economy, and the standard of living in the community has been growing higher. Since the 1960s it has become a norm that Satmar girls and married women who do not have children under the age of three must work outside the home to supplement the family income. Husbands, among whom

full-time Torah study is an ideal, cannot be and are not the sole breadwin-
ners, and women cannot possibly remain sequestered at home, their bodies
not seen and their voices not heard. While the conflict between maintaining
community values and obtaining economic security is sharp for both male and
female Satmars, it has been noted that the women, with their superior secular
education, better knowledge of the English language, and more conventional
appearance, have access to a wider range of jobs than the men do.[28] In fact,
in past years there has been a flourishing of business enterprise among the
Satmar in Williamsburg, and the women have been a large part of that flourishing. Perhaps one of the oldest and best-known Satmar businesses, 47th St.
Photo, employed hundreds of men and women (it was noted ironically during the years the store was open that the owners of and workers at one of the
biggest television retailers in the United States did not watch TV themselves
or own a set). One observer of the community notes that up to one-quarter of
the new stores and businesses advertised in the community's weekly Yiddish
newspaper *Der Yid* are owned and operated by women.[29] These include stores
that sell ladies' garments, wigs, hats, undergarments, handbags, children's and
infants' wear, shoes, fine jewelry—attractive jewelry and gold and silver are
very prized among the Satmar—home furnishings, crystal, china, and fine
linens. Some Satmar women have become exclusive agents for a number of
European and Far Eastern products, and they travel overseas at least twice a
year to handpick their imports.[30] Patrons from around the New York metropolitan area come to Williamsburg to shop, and Satmar men and women in all
their businesses must be prepared to deal with their non-Satmar customers in
a courteous manner.

Immersion in the business world also means moving beyond the world of
the Yiddish-language press, particularly *Der Yid*, which has been referred to
by its opponents as "the *Pravda* of the Satmar community."[31] In school all
their books are carefully censored, but once the Satmar are working they cannot be successful unless they partake of outside reading matter. Satmar mothers already read such publications as *Baby Care* and *Good Housekeeping*, and
many of the businesswomen will read the *New York Times*, the *Wall Street
Journal*, and other trade publications. They may aspire to live up to the standards of their grandmothers, but in the present day they are not prepared to
forgo things that will make their lives and those of their families healthier and
better.

Satmar cannot avoid extensive contact with the outside world when they
reach out as they to do obtain government aid, the best medical care, mental
health care, or services for their own disabled and handicapped children, for
whom they have been willing to go to the U.S. Supreme Court. One psycho-
therapist in contact with the community speaks of them as being "under siege."
"These people are geographically separated from the outside world but they

are still going to work, passing a newsstand, passing a movie, watching the street. No matter how much you close your eyes you are exposed to this secular materialistic world from which one would like to insulate oneself as much as possible. . . . There is social intercourse, whether you like it or not, between the traditional Jews and the outside world which is very hard to escape."[32]

Materialism, the craving for more and better consumer goods, and the urge for self-beautification remain strong among the women despite admonitions from teachers at the Bais Rukhel schools to hide their sexuality. In fact Satmar women, like Hasidic women in general, aspire to attractive, fashionable clothes and fine jewelry, which is considered especially important during the years of young adulthood. It has been observed that even women of the most extreme factions in Israel who shave their heads and wear black kerchiefs over them can be seen with glittering stud earrings, jeweled bracelets and brooches, and flowered dresses.[33] Women also put effort into decorating their homes and using the most up-to-date appliances. Says one contemporary Satmar woman, "Our parents and many of our older brothers and sisters came here from the concentration and DP camps with little more than the rags on their backs. Now after years of privation and hard work, we want to live like others and enjoy our homes."[34]

In general, Satmar community leaders may seek to insulate their young people from evil outside influences, but every day their dependence upon and interaction with the outside world grows greater. Heilman's observations of the Haredim in general are especially applicable to the Satmar: "In spite of their claims to be absolutely enclosed in the past, haredim were not. As an anthropologist, I should have known better. . . . In almost every place and situation I encountered, there was always a hint that the haredim were very much aware of and often touched by what went on beyond the borders of their world. . . . Word processing, car repairs, up to date political methods to achieve power, cellular phones, yeshivas with fax machines, and haredi confidence in modern medicine and technology. . . . These people were still around because they only appeared to belong to yesterday."[35]

The writers of Handl Erlikh may have imagined, through the game, an ideal community enclave where girls and women do not even venture out onto the street, their voices go unheard, they never interact with men, and the evils of the non-Jewish world are kept safely at bay. However, the fact that they used the original Monopoly as their model only goes to prove how far an important aspect of American culture has penetrated. By all reports the game continues to sell briskly, and Hasidic girls throughout New York are playing it. However, current conditions and economic realities favor Satmar girls and women moving ever further away from this idealized, sheltered existence that is envisioned for them. Thus the game may well become a preserve, if it is not already, where contemporary American Satmar girls in their few leisure hours can play at being their grandmothers, even as there is no hope that they will ever be exactly like them.

Acknowledgment

My thanks to Beatrice (Brukhe) Lang Caplan, who brought the Handl Erlikh game to our attention during Columbia's YIVO Yiddish-language program. The game can be purchased at several establishments in Brooklyn's Hasidic neighborhoods and is for sale at Eichler's Bookstore in Boro Park, Brooklyn.

Notes

1. See Samuel E. Heilman, *Defenders of the Faith: Inside Ultra-Orthodox Jewry* (New York: Schocken, 1992), p. 12, and Samuel C. Heilman and Menachem Friedman, "Religious Fundamentalism and Religious Jews: The Case of the Haredim," in Martin E. Marty and R. Scott Appleby, eds., *Fundamentalisms Observed* (Chicago: University of Chicago Press, 1994), p. 199.
2. The concept of an enclave culture is described in detail in Martin E. Marty and R. Scott Appleby, *Fundamentalisms Comprehended* (Chicago: University of Chicago Press, 2004), especially in Emmanuel Sivan's article, "The Enclave Culture," pp. 9–68. My thanks to Jonathan D. Sarna for bringing this concept and source to my attention.
3. Robert Eisenberg (a journalist for the *Village Voice*), *Boychiks in the Hood: Tales from the Hasidic Underground* (San Francisco: Harper, 1995), p. 10.
4. Much has been written about the animosity between the Satmar and other Jewish groups, in particular the Lubavitch Hasidim, and accounts of violence have appeared regularly over the years in New York area newspapers. For one of the best descriptions see Jerome R. Mintz, *Hasidic People: A Place in the New World* (Cambridge, Mass.: Harvard University Press, 1992), pp. 56–59, and chapters 14 and 15, pp. 154–188.
5. Mintz, p. 3.
6. Ibid., p. 4.
7. Ibid., p. 27.
8. On the relative survival of Satmar Jews and others living in Hungary and territory under control of Romania during World War II, see Mintz, p. 27; Israel Rubin, *Satmar: An Island in the City* (Chicago: Quadrangle Books, 1972), pp. 39–40; Eisenberg, p. 3.
9. Rubin, p. 40.
10. George Kranzler, *Hasidic Williamsburg: A Contemporary Hasidic Community* (Northvale, New Jersey: Jason Aronson, 1995), p. 227. George Kranzler began a longitudinal study of the Williamsburg Hasidic community in 1961 and produced three books on the subject.
11. Mintz, p. 34.
12. Quoted in Peter Applebome, "Our Towns," *New York Times*, June 20, 2004.

13. Kranzler, p. 173.
14. Marvin Schick, *A Census of Jewish Day Schools in the United States* (New York: Avi Chai Foundation, 2000), pp. 3, 7. Schick has also written extensively about the Satmar.
15. Kranzler, p. 170.
16. Ibid., pp. 19, 23–24.
17. According to Heilman, the Haredim in general refer to little children as the "anointed ones" or messiahs, most precious because they are still pure and free from sin; they are also "the human sanctuary, recipients of tradition and its carriers," p. 174.
18. Eisenberg, p. 24.
19. Rubin, p. 193.
20. For extensive discussion of the fervently Orthodox and in particular the Satmar attitudes toward Zionism and Messianism, see Heilman, pp. 29–39; Heilman and Friedman, p. 227; Mintz, pp. 36–39, 51–58, 85, 133–134; Kranzler, p. 4; Rubin, pp. 95, 172–176, 227; and Menachem Friedman, "The Haredim and the Holocaust," *Jerusalem Quarterly*, 53, Winter 1990 (cited in Heilman). One of Mintz's Satmar informants refers to the disillusion that surrounded Teitelbaum's death in 1979 and the belief that the Messiah would come (p. 85): "After the war people thought that the Messiah was coming. Because of the war experience, the horrors, the suffering, they expected the Messiah to appear. Then they began a new life, building, reconstructing. . . . The Messiah was going to come in the rebbe's lifetime."
21. Rubin, pp. 151–155.
22. Kranzler, pp. 57–59. According to one rabbinic injunction, teaching Torah to girls is conducive to *tiflut*, or moral deterioration.
23. According to Mintz, wives as well as husbands find "the change from Satmar to Lubavitch to be liberating." "At Satmar they don't believe a woman has to learn," says one informant. "There's basically what they learn in school and finish. Then it's into baking and cooking without learning. In Lubavitch a woman should know about Godly things. In Lubavitch they believe a person should learn more," p. 175. Mintz notes that a few of the ex-Satmars will still wear their *shtreimels* on the Sabbath and holidays, and they stand out among the more modern Lubavitch fedoras. Also, for a fascinating view into the girls of the Lubavitch Hasidic community and the life they have made for themselves, see Stephanie Wellen Levine, *Mystics, Mavericks, and Merrymakers: An Intimate Journey Among Hasidic Girls* (New York: New York University Press, 2003).
24. Kranzler, p. 70.
25. Ibid., p. 176.
26. See Rubin, pp. 154 and 259. In 1972 he observed, "The girls hold the key to Satmar's cultural outlook and their acculturation may necessitate radical changes," p. 199.
27. Monopoly, of course, reigns supreme among the board games. In addition to Orthodox Jews, board games in general and a Monopoly set in particular have become part of the hurricane survival kit for Floridian families who must be prepared to cope with extended power shortages during the hurricane season.

28. Kranzler, p. 59.
29. Kranzler, p. 92.
30. Ibid., pp. 45–48.
31. Mintz, p. 126.
32. Ibid., p. 235.
33. Heilman describes this vividly in his account of a Lag B'omer pilgrimage in Israel among Haredi Jews.
34. Kranzler, p. 48.
35. Heilman, p. 352.

Chapter 9   Jeffrey Shandler

Mediating Community
American Jewry and the New Media
of the Twentieth Century

In their 1998 book *Judaism Online: Confronting Sprituality on the Internet*, authors Susan Zakar and Dovid Kaufmann recount, through "conversation, journal entries, and actual e-mail dialogue," Zakar's spiritual journey. Her quest traversed fundamentalist Christianity, Conservative and Reform Judaism, "long stints of almost ignoring God, to, in the end, Orthodox Judaism." As *Judaism Online* reveals, the Internet served not merely as a vehicle for coauthoring the book but as an essential point of entry into the community of Orthodoxy for Zakar. This started with her online encounter with Kaufmann, a rabbi, "after she raised the question of women's role in Judaism on the Internet." Currently, the book's dust jacket reports, Zakar "is a familiar presence on the Internet, maintaining the world wide web pages for Jews for Judaism, Havienu L'Shalom, a 'Virtual Shul,' and local Jewish organizations. She is frequently called upon to offer online support and guidance to others who are in the process of converting [to Judaism] or becoming more observant. She and her husband now run a web-design business." Noting at one point that Zakar and her husband also met thanks to technology (as neighbors, her Apple II was interfering with his television reception), Kaufman remarks, "Divine Providence works even through computers!"[1]

Even as *Judaism Online* testifies to the extent to which computer technology, especially the Internet, has become an integral part of American Jewish life in recent times—much of what is described in the book would have been unimaginable before the 1990s—it is especially provocative in demonstrating how readily this new technology has been called upon to facilitate new forms of Jewish community. Beyond its ability to enable rapid communication across great distances, the Internet now provides simulated meeting places for Jews in Web-based Hebrew and Yiddish classes, virtual Passover seders, *havrutot* who study online, and Jewish matchmaking sites, among others.[2]

Implicit in these phenomena are daunting tests of conventional notions of Jewish communality, both local and international. To what extent can computers replicate the classroom, the synagogue, the theater, the rabbinical court, the summer camp, or the family table? What difference does actually (as opposed to virtually) "being there" make in Jewish study, worship, and ritual? On one hand, Internet connections offer the potential to bolster and extend a sense of community: helping people quickly convene a minyan or organize a meeting of a book discussion group, providing travelers with up-to-date information on Jewish religious and community life in unfamiliar locations, allowing school or summer camp alumni to stay in touch or locate old acquaintances, or enabling relatives who cannot attend family celebrations to participate in them vicariously from afar. On the other hand, the phenomenon of people engaged in Jewish group activities while sitting alone in front of their individual computer screens, often anonymous to the other members of the virtual community, might well be seen as a development that thwarts, rather than enhances, communality.[3]

In the same way that computer technology has revolutionized Jewish scholarship—most strikingly, by enabling the rapid searching and cross-referencing of traditional texts to an unprecedented degree—it is also transforming the nature of Jewish community life, even when it presents options that members of these communities elect not to pursue. This is a very new development; its consequences and implications are only beginning to unfold, and yet it already offers much to consider.[4]

By way of offering food for thought as to how this newest technological innovation is affecting American Jewish communities, I would like to consider here some precedent phenomena. This essay examines the role that ongoing encounters with new media of the past century have played in shaping notions of American Jewish community—that is, it considers what happens when an innovation in communications appears and members of the American Jewish community engage with it. The course of the twentieth century can be articulated as a series of engagements with new media: the advent of sound recordings and silent films at the turn of the century, followed by "talkies" and radio in the 1920s, television and audiotape recorders in the 1940s, videotaping and personal computers in the 1980s, among others. These encounters parallel a more familiar generational history of twentieth-century American Jewry, which is centered on Jewish immigrants arriving from Eastern Europe during the decades surrounding the turn of the century, followed by their children, grandchildren, and great-grandchildren. Moreover, these generational shifts often coincide with the advent of new media in significant ways: For example, the coming of age of the children of immigrants during the 1920s is concomitant with the advent of commercial radio and talking motion pictures; their children, American Jewish "baby boomers," grew up as television emerged as the nation's leading mass medium.

Silent Movies

Indeed, there is no more revealing example of the confluence of innovations in communications media and signal shifts in the American Jewish community than what took place at the turn of the twentieth century. As Jews from Eastern Europe arrived in larger numbers in the United States, along with many other immigrants from across the Atlantic, they encountered two new media, each with telling implications, which would endure well beyond the period of their advent.

First, consider the impact of silent films, which immigrants initially encountered in storefront nickelodeons in major American cities, especially New York, during the middle of the first decade of the twentieth century. This constituted one of the most important geographical coincidences in American Jewish life: At the turn of the century, New York's Lower East Side was simultaneously home to the world's largest, densest Jewish settlement and home to the greatest concentration of nickelodeons on the planet. It has been argued that this coincidence spawned a special relationship between Jews and movies. As moviegoing quickly expanded from a cheap amusement that largely attracted urban, working-class immigrants to an American national pastime, Jews became prominent leaders in a new entertainment industry as creators, distributors, and exhibitors. The cinema also emerged as an important new venue for presenting images of Jews, especially as immigrants, to the American public.[5]

Moreover, the activity of moviegoing helped to create a new kind of Jewish community. Along with live theater (itself a relatively new medium for most immigrant Jews from Eastern Europe) the cinema reconstituted Jews as an audience—a collective that attends works of drama, mediated as well as live, as a definitional act. The notion of a Jewish audience was a much a product of theater impresarios and film producers as it was a result of public behavior. Audience activity entails not only attending the theater or cinema but also discussing it; discussions include informal, spontaneous conversations in theater lobbies or over coffee after the performance as well as public discussions taking place in yet another medium, the press. Indeed, it is in the discussion that the Jewishness of moviegoing is defined, rather than in the content of films or the identity of filmmakers.[6]

Evidence of the powerfully contentious role of moviegoing for Jewish audiences can be seen in public discussion as early as the nickelodeon era. A telling case in point is a report in the Yiddish press of an impassioned audience debate in 1908 over a Jewish-owned theater screening the Edison Company's film *Cohen's Fire Sale*. Concerns over the image of Jews portrayed on the screen, freedom of expression (by audience members as well as filmmakers), and the challenge of how to respond to representations that one finds offensive—all familiar issues in public discussions of popular culture in the United States today—were already informing the experience of the Jewish moviegoing audience.[7]

Today, we can observe this audience in new contexts, including those attending the more than sixty Jewish film festivals now held annually in the United States. The fact that a sizable number of people attending these festivals analogize the experience to attending synagogue and explain that, for some of them, the Jewish film festival has replaced congregational worship testifies to larger shifts in notions of what, for some American Jews, constitutes Jewish cultural literacy and what now are the sites and practices of Jewish communion.[8]

Sound Recordings

In the 1890s, shortly before the advent of the nickelodeon, commercially produced sound recordings became readily available in the United States. Here, too, the coincidence of a new medium with a rapidly changing American demographic generated an important innovation, not only for Jews but for many of their fellow immigrants as well. In an effort to merchandise a comprehensive inventory of recorded sound, companies like Victor and Columbia began issuing series of recordings especially for different immigrant ethnic communities: Italian, Irish, Russian, Hungarian, as well as Jewish, among others.

These recordings—which included folk songs and instrumental music, sacred music, comic routines, national anthems—also created an immigrant audience, albeit one constituted differently from that of the movie house. Listening to sound recordings was—and, to some extent, still is—primarily a domestic experience, private rather than public. (This experience has grown more private, even as listening has beome more mobile, with headsets attached to portable devices, from the Walkman to the iPod.) The early inventories of commercial recordings configured the Jewish audience as one of a series of ethnic markets. They distinguished a certain repertoire and roster of artists as "Jewish," though this was (and still is) hardly a fixed, innate category. On old 78 rpm discs the same performers sometimes can be heard on recordings of Russian, Polish, or Hungarian music, and sometimes even the same instrumental musical numbers are listed in recording company catalogues as "Romanian" or "Gypsy" as well as "Jewish" pieces.[9]

At the same time, sound recordings have facilitated access to the music of discrete ethnic communities for an open market of listeners, crossing class lines—in particular, providing access to opera and classical music for people who could not afford to attend live performances—and ethnic boundaries. Thanks to sound recordings, one doesn't have to be Jewish or be anywhere near Jews to hear their liturgical chanting, dance music, folk tunes, or popular songs. (In the United States, sound recordings would have their greatest impact in facilitating access across racial lines, in particular, enabling African American music to reach national audiences during years of pervasive segregation.)

Of special interest in the case of American Jews is the role of sound recordings in transforming traditional notions of the cantor and his art. The flexibility of listening to recordings enabled anyone (including, of course, non-Jews) with access to a Victrola to hear a cantor sing at any time of the day or year, to listen repeatedly to a performance, to interrupt it (simply by lifting the needle), to comment about it (or anything else) as it was playing, or to play it alongside anything from Enrico Caruso to "Cohen on the Telephone." By separating their performance from its liturgical contexts, the act of listening to cantors on recordings transformed it into a distinct experience, which commodified and aestheticized *hazanut.*

Evidence of this transformation can be heard in the recordings themselves. Cantors often recorded liturgical passages with instrumental accompaniment that would never be heard when these were performed in Orthodox synagogues on the Sabbath or holidays. These selections were also transformed simply by excerpting them from the longer worship service (and they were often abridged as well, so as to fit within the confines of a single side of a ten-inch, 78 rpm disc, which lasts about three minutes). Cantors are usually heard on these recordings replacing names for God with substitute terms used when not addressing God in prayer—Adoshem, Elokeynu—thereby signaling to culturally literate listeners that what they hear is not worship, but something else. In addition, sound recordings enabled a number of women to perform *hazanut* publicly, which they could not do in Orthodox synagogues because of the traditional ban forbidding men to hear a female singing voice. During the first half of the past century several *khazntes* or "lady cantors," as they were then known, performed in live recital, on records, and even on radio—but not in synagogues.

Recordings were thus part of what ethnomusicologist Mark Slobin describes as the "cantorial craze" among American Jews, starting in the final decades of the nineteenth century. Cantors, he argues, played a key role "as a comforting transitional figure [for immigrants] as they oriented themselves in America."

Moreover, hiring a "star" cantor, usually someone "imported" from Europe, became a way that synagogues could "attract new worshippers and increase membership" as congregational life in the early twentieth century came to be concerned with "respectability" and "consumer satisfaction."[10] Recordings not only evince this development; they also helped facilitate the shift of the cantor's role from the traditional *shliah tsibur* to a celebrity artist—that is, someone who acted not merely as a community representative, facilitating engagement with God, but also as the center of attention, an end in himself.

The distribution of recordings also influenced live performance of *hazanut* in the United States. Cantorial tradition consists of dozens of different localized variants for the chanting of each prayer or sacred text. When recordings promoted certain cantors' performances, making them into widely familiar "standards," other variants, which weren't recorded, became more obscure as a result. Recordings also made some cantors into celebrities far beyond the scope of their congregations. The most famous cantors of the first half of the twentieth century, Yossele Rosenblatt and Moishe Oysher, became stars of stage and screen. Rosenblatt performed on the vaudeville stage and appeared as himself in the 1927 feature *The Jazz Singer* and in the 1934 film *Dream of My People* (which includes footage of the cantor's funeral in Jerusalem, where he died suddenly during the filming of this concert-cum-travelogue). Oysher starred in a series of Yiddish musical films made in the 1930s (*Dem khazns zindl, Der zingendiker shmid, Der vilner shtot-khazn*) and had his own radio program on WEVD.[11]

Indeed, thanks in considerable measure to sound recordings, cantors became popular dramatic figures in Yiddish- and English-language stage performances and films, where the cantor represents the Jewish people, not before God, but to American theater audiences. In some of these productions (most famously, the 1927 feature film *The Jazz Singer*) cantors became emblematic of the modern Jewish dilemma, torn between callings of traditional devotion and Jewish communal responsibility, on one hand, versus secular culture and the primacy of the individual, on the other hand. Watching these performances provided American Jews with a new kind of communal experience that both validated and problematized long-standing notions of the traditional Jewish community.

Broadcasting

Radio, and later television, would facilitate other new notions of community for Jews, in particular with the advent in the mid-1940s of ecumenical religious broadcasting. The first major, sustained use of radio by an American Jewish religious organization began in 1944 when the Conservative movement's Jewish Theological Seminary (JTS) initiated *The Eternal Light*, a half-hour program produced in conjunction with NBC. *The Eternal Light* continued to be heard on radio through the late 1980s; the series also appeared on NBC television beginning in 1952, lasting through late '80s as well. Thus, *The Eternal Light* constitutes the longest-running, regular presence of Jews as a religious community on American airwaves, with hundreds of broadcasting hours over the years.[12]

The Eternal Light epitomized American Judeo-Christian ecumenism of the early post–World War II era. Then, all three major commercial networks sponsored ecumenical broadcasts as part of their public service programming. On television *The Eternal Light* was aired on Sundays on a rotating basis with Protestant and Catholic programs. This was, in fact, one of the first and most popular enactments of this tripartite, Judeo-Christian vision of American religious pluralism of the period. Within this forum, *The Eternal Light* had, in fact, a double agenda: first, outreach to members of the Jewish community (especially the unaffiliated or geographically isolated); second, promoting understanding and tolerance of Jews among their gentile neighbors. In this latter respect, *The Eternal Light* resembled contemporary efforts by the Jewish Anti-Defamation League and other American Jewish organizations to combat antisemitism through public education.[13]

The earliest *Eternal Light* broadcasts were all original dramas. The first of these was a series on various synagogues of historical interest—beginning with "A Rhode Island Refuge," a play by Morton Wishengrad about the Touro Synagogue in Newport. This drama focused on the famous letter that George Washington wrote to this congregation in 1790, extolling the United States' commitment to religious toleration.[14] This debut broadcast typified *The Eternal Light*'s emphasis on demonstrating the compatibility of Jewish values with American values, and offering historical models for Jewish acceptance and integration into the American community at large. "A Rhode Island Refuge" also epitomized how *The Eternal Light* positioned Jews' role in the American public sphere as an ethical exemplar—a modern-day equivalent to serving as a "light unto the nations."

In its heyday, during the 1940s and '50s, *The Eternal Light* was heard on radio by some six million listeners across North America. Promotional literature for *The Eternal Light* vaunted this statistic to demonstrate the considerable scope of its ecumenical community of listeners (though small compared to the size of audiences for prime-time entertainment programming, this was a respectable number for a public service broadcast heard during the so-called "ghetto" of Sunday morning and afternoon). At the same time, of course, this number had special resonance for American Jews: Six million was both the estimated size of the North American Jewish community circa 1950 and the estimated number of European Jewish victims of Nazism during World War II.

The use of this statistic testifies to the double agenda that *The Eternal Light* had with regard to the American Jewry: on one hand, promoting its integration into an American ecumenical community that emphasized common ground among faiths and treated differences among them as adventitious; on the other hand, offering Jews a distinctive place within the virtual public sphere of American broadcasting. Although JTS was primarily concerned with addressing its non-Jewish audience, *The Eternal Light* also became a fixture of American Jewish life during the 1940s and '50s. Listener mail sent to the producers of the series suggests that quite a few American Jewish homes across America incorporated *The Eternal Light* into their Sunday routines. This behavior was both a private, idiosyncratic practice and part of a larger imagined community of simultaneous observance, centered around a shared text—similar, at least in some respects, to the Passover seder.

This widespread practice may have been responsive to another distinction of *The Eternal Light*: its aesthetic of decorous respectability. The series' producers used broadcasting to enable Jews to, in effect, pay a virtual Sunday social call on their non-Jewish neighbors and thus strove to portray Jews on their "best behavior." In this regard, *The Eternal Light* offered a striking alternative to the portrait that American Anglophone (as opposed to Yiddish) radio of the 1940s otherwise offered of Jews, typically as comic characters who spoke in a Yiddish-inflected dialect.[15] The broadcast of *The Eternal Light* was the one moment in the week when Jews appeared regularly, forthrightly, and with dignity as a religious community in the public forum of American broadcasting.

Comparison of *The Eternal Light* with the other most enduring public presence of Jews on the American airwaves in the middle decades of the twentieth century—the various incarnations of *The Goldbergs*—is telling. From the late 1920s to the mid-1950s, the Goldbergs were the most widely known American Jewish family, at one time or another heard on radio, seen on the vaudeville and Broadway stages, the subject of a Hollywood feature film and a newspaper comic strip, and, finally, seen on one of the very first television situation comedies. This multigenerational family was the brainchild of Gertrude Berg, who wrote, produced, and starred (as family matriarch Molly Goldberg) in all versions of *The Goldbergs*.[16]

In its radio incarnation *The Goldbergs* was a dialect comedy, signaling the characters' Jewishness through theatrical conventions of ethnically inflected speech (similar to the performance of Italian, Greek, Russian, African American, as well as other ethnic and racial identities in this sound-based medium). By contrast, the use of dialect was something *The Eternal Light* assiduously avoided; the intent of its producers was to ensure that the Jewish community not be perceived as ethnically distinct or in any way less than dignified. And yet the agendas of *The Eternal Light* and *The Goldbergs* were, in a sense, similar; like JTS, Gertrude Berg also sought to portray Jews as comfortably at home in America. Complementing *The Eternal Light*, which facilitated Jews' symbolic visits to their neighbors' homes, *The Goldbergs* provided virtual entry into a Jewish home for many gentile Americans who had limited or no such actual contact with Jews. Although her series dealt primarily with the challenges and comic mishaps of domestic family life, Berg did present occasional episodes on radio that portrayed major Jewish holidays and even directly addressed the issue of antisemitism in America. And, as their audience mail demonstrates, both *The Eternal Light* and *The Goldbergs* fostered special loyalties among Jewish audiences, who regarded these broadcasts as a source of communal pride.

Videotape

In the mid-1970s, a generation after television made its debut as a broadcast medium, the advent of videotape enabled a number of important innovations in Jewish communal activity to flourish around the TV set. In addition to its widespread use to document life-cycle events, celebrations, and travel, the amateur practice of videotaping figured strategically in the first, grassroots efforts (which were later professionalized) to record the testimonies of thousands of Holocaust survivors.[17] More than simply documenting these events and narratives, videotape has transformed their substance and significance. In particular, the medium has altered the nature of ritual experience, so that many Americans, Jews and non-Jews alike, have come to regard the making and viewing of video documentations as an essential component of rituals themselves. This has altered how many people understand what constitutes a ritual experience and what it means to be part of a community of ritual observers.

The most elaborate and provocative use of this communications medium by a Jewish community has been that of the Lubavitcher Hasidim (also known as Chabad). Radio, television, and video have all played a crucial role in creating Chabad's high public profile and in maintaining connections among the movement's widely dispersed following. Although Rabbi Menachem Mendel Schneerson, the last Lubavitcher Rebbe, almost never left New York City during his many years as the community's leader, he could then (and today, still can) be seen and heard via satellite broadcast or videotape by followers around the world.[18]

Unlike other Hasidim—who, at least officially, shun television—Lubavitcher Hasidim have embraced the medium, albeit on their own terms. They do so, in part, to demonstrate humankind's ability to use any God-given phenomenon—in this case, the science of broadcasting—to do good. Chabad's use of television also epitomizes its commitment to outreach to other Jews, encouraging them to become more observant of *mitsvot*, and—in the case of their annual telethons—to both Jews and non-Jews for financial support.

These telethons, produced annually since 1981 by the West Coast Chabad, based in Los Angeles, constitute extensive performances of cultural interface. They bring Hasidim together with Hollywood celebrities (actor Jon Voigt, for example, has been a regular guest on these telethons for years) and mingle testimonies from drug addicts and the homeless who have been helped by Lubavitch-run charities with performances by a variety of popular musicians from the Orthodox Jewish community. At once quintessentially American and distinctively Chabad in character, these telecasts celebrate the movement's sense of its compatibility with the modern world. The telethons position Lubavitcher Hasidim as living both distinctively and comfortably within the larger American community, while also presenting the boundaries of the Lubavitch community as welcomingly open to other American Jews.

Since the last Lubavitcher Rebbe's death in 1994, communications media have come to play increasingly powerful roles in shaping Chabad's sense of continuity, and this use of media has especially remarkable implications with regard to the controversial messianic movement within Chabad. During the years before his death, the Rebbe insisted with increasing fervor that the messianic age was imminent. Growing numbers of Lubavitcher Hasidim became convinced that their Rebbe was the Messiah. Then the Rebbe died, leaving this issue unresolved; he also left no heir, and so the future of his Hasidim, whose spiritual community had always been organized around the charismatic leadership of a rebbe, seemed very unclear.

Because many of the Lubavitcher Rebbe's public appearances had been filmed or videotaped since the mid-1970s, part of the legacy he left his followers is an enormous video inventory, and this, in turn, has enabled various new practices: For example, since shortly after the Rebbe's death, visitors to his gravesite in Queens can go to a house nearby to pray, wash their hands, have some refreshment—and watch videos of the Rebbe, which play there continuously. Those who went to see the Rebbe at his headquarters in Brooklyn on one of the many Sundays when he would hand each of hundreds of visitors a dollar bill (which was then meant to be given to charity) can relive their brief encounter with the Rebbe by purchasing a videotape of their visit. Footage of the Rebbe is also used to invoke his presence in a sizable inventory of telecasts and videos, including those created by followers who believe that the Rebbe is the Messiah and anxiously await his reappearance.

Such is the case in *International Demonstration to Greet Moshiach: Celebrating 46 Years of the Rebbe Melech Moshiach's Nesiyus*, a telecast produced by messianist Lubavitcher Hasidim and aired on 31 January 1996. In this broadcast, satellites and videotape enable a virtual gathering of believers around the world (the broadcast culminates with a split-screen, live simulcast of Hasidim located around the world—Russia, France, Israel, South Africa, and the United States—all singing "Yehi adoneynu," the signature chant of the Chabad messianists, in unison). And, through the juxtaposition of live broadcasting with vintage video and audio of the Rebbe, the telecast also facilitates the community's projection of the longed-for, redemptive return of their leader.

While the message of these messianic videos is controversial, they demonstrate the powerful ability of modern media to enable spiritual communion and even to serve as objects of devotion. In this case, satellites and videotape not only enable a virtual gathering of believers around the world but also facilitate the community's projection of the longed-for, redemptive return of their leader. At the same time, the facility with which video recordings of the Rebbe can be used and reused by his followers, suggests the possibility of the community's continuing with his virtual, rather than physical, presence as a source of inspiration.

·   ·   ·

There are other cases of American Jewish encounters with new media to consider, and each of the aforementioned examples can be examined in much greater depth; still, these demonstrate something of the range of responses that the advents of new media have prompted, especially when embraced as opportunities for enhancing or reconfiguring the community life of American Jews. To a great extent, each case reflects the particulars of social and historical context, of the medium in question, and of the Jewish community that elects to explore the possibilities of this new mode of communication. And yet there are some common attributes among these cases worth noting and bearing in mind for further study.

Each engagement with a new medium engenders a discussion, which, while itself new, raises certain common questions: How might this new medium work for the Jewish community? What might be "proper" Jewish responses to the opportunities that the medium offers and the challenges that it poses? Are Jews in accord with other Americans in their use of this medium, or are they finding their own distinctive ways of engaging with it? And, as the use of each new medium takes shape within Jewish communities, how do they deal with the unanticipated consequences that these innovations inevitably generate?

These recurrent discussions are in themselves as significant as whatever results from them. They extend the long-standing pattern of developing Jewish culture through the negotiation of Jewish precedents in relation to new cultural encounters. In other words, the very act of raising the question, Is there a Jewish way to listen to recordings, or to go to the movies, or to watch television? and of striving to respond to this question is, I argue, a Jewish act in itself—especially when it is undertaken as a communal discussion.

Notes

1. Susan M. Zakar and Dovid Y. B. Kaufmann, *Judaism Online: Confronting Spirituality on the Internet* (Northvale, New Jersey: Jason Aronson, 1998), dust jacket, p. 176.

2. Other popular guides to Jewish resources on the Internet include Irving Green, *Judaism on the Web* (New York: MIS Press, 1997); Diane Romm, *The Jewish Guide to the Internet*, 3rd ed. (Northvale, New Jersey: Jason Aronson, 2002).

3. On Jewish uses of computers and of the Internet, see also Jonathan Boyarin, "Jewish Geography Goes On-Line," *Jewish Folklore and Ethnology Review* 16, no. 1 (1994): 3–5; Lucia Ruedenberg, "Jewish Resources in Computer Networking," *Jewish Folklore and Ethnology Review* 16, no. 1 (1994): 12–18; Maury Sacks, "Computing Community at Purim," *Journal of American Folklore* 102, no. 405 (July–September 1989): 275–291.

4. See, e.g., Edward Portnoy, "Haredim and the Internet" (2004), http://modiya.nyu.edu/handle/1964/265 (accessed 25 December 2006).

5. On immigrant Jews and the nickelodeon, see also Andrew Heinze, *Adapting to Abundance: Jewish Immigrants, Mass Consumption, and the Search for American Identity* (New York: Columbia University Press, 1990), pp. 203–218; Judith Thissen, "Jewish Immigrant Audiences in New York City, 1905–1914," in *American Movie Audiences: From the Turn of the Century to the Early Sound Era*, ed. Melvyn Stokes and Richard Maltby (London: British Film Institute, 1999), pp. 15–28.

6. See "Entertaining 'Entertaining America,'" in J. Hoberman and Jeffrey Shandler, *Entertaining America: Jews, Movies, and Broadcasting* (Princeton: Princeton University Press, 2003), pp. 11–13.

7. See "Debating *Cohen's Fire Sale*," in Hoberman and Shandler, *Entertaining America*, pp. 32–33, which includes a translation of the original Yiddish article in question: Ephraim Koplan, "Jews Who Spit in Their Own Faces," *Yidishes Tageblat*, 1 September 1908.

8. On Jewish film festivals, see Mikel J. Koven, "'You Don't Have To Be Filmish': The Toronto Jewish Film Festival," *Ethnologies* 21, no. 1 (2003): pp. 115–132.

9. See Henry Sapoznik, *Klezmer! Jewish Music from Old World to Our World* (New York: Schirmer, 1999), chapter 3.

10. Mark Slobin, *Chosen Voices: The Story of the American Cantorate* (Urbana: University of Illinois Press, 2002 [1989]), pp. 52–54.

11. See J. Hoberman, *Bridge of Light: Yiddish Film Between Two Worlds* (New York: Schocken, 1991), pp. 257–274.

12. See Jeffrey Shandler and Elihu Katz, "Broadcasting American Judaism: The Radio and Television Department of the Jewish Theological Seminary," in *Tradition Renewed: A History of the Jewish Theological Seminary*, ed. Jack Wertheimer (New York: Jewish Theological Seminary, 1997), pp. 364–401.

13. See Stuart Svonkin, *Jews Against Prejudice: American Jews and the Intergroup Relations Movement from World War to Cold War* (New York: Columbia University Press, 1997).

14. Morton Wishengrad, "A Rhode Island Refuge," in *The Eternal Light* (New York: Crown, 1947), pp. 109–121.
15. See Henry Sapoznik, "Broadcast Ghetto: The Image of Jews on Mainstream American Radio," *Jewish Folklore and Ethnology Review* 16, no. 1 (1994): 37–39.
16. On *The Goldbergs*, see Joyce Antler, "'Yesterday's Woman,' Today's Moral Guide: Molly Goldberg as Jewish Mother," in *Key Texts in American Jewish Culture*, ed. Jack Kugelmass (New Brunswick, New Jersey: Rutgers University Press, 2003), pp. 129–146; Donald Weber, *Haunted in the New World: Jewish American Culture from Cahan to "The Goldbergs"* (Bloomington: Indiana University Press, 2005), chapter 6.
17. On the videotape testimony of Holocaust survivors, see, e.g., Oren Baruch Stier, "Framing the Witness: The Memorial Role of Holocaust Videotestimonies," in *Remembering for the Future: The Holocaust in an Age of Genocide*, ed. John K. Roth and Elisabeth Maxwell, vol. 3 (Basingstoke, Hampshire: Palgrave, 2001), pp. 189–204.
18. See Jeffrey Shander, "The Virtual Rebbe," in Hoberman and Shandler, *Entertaining America*, pp. 264–267.

III

Women as Agents of Communal Reconfiguration

Chapter 10

Karla Goldman

The Limits of Imagination
White Christian Civilization and the

Construction of American Jewish

Womanhood in the 1890s

In every activist generation Jewish women have struggled with the extent to which the inspiration for expanding their own public voices and roles has been drawn from non-Jewish American models. In 1838, the earliest American Jewish women activists, Rebecca Gratz and a group of other Jewish women in Philadelphia, created the first Jewish Sunday School. Since no English Jewish textbooks were available, they initially used Christian catechisms, with references to Jesus blacked out.[1] Today, Orthodox Jewish feminists draw language about the value of individual freedom and autonomy from a broader culture, which, in many ways, represents the antithesis of the values they hope to find and create within an observant Jewish community.[2] In a similar fashion, prosperous and acculturated American Jewish women of the 1890s sought to place themselves within a cultural order that was not their own. In order to make room for themselves, they adopted a discourse that not only subordinated Jewish women who were not like them but ultimately undermined their own assertions of inclusion.

Numerous generations of Jewish women activists have imagined and created new models of identity and activity for women that their own communities had hitherto been unable to provide. Turning to the broader culture to find appropriate frameworks of female respectability and activism, women in successive historical eras energized and redefined the contours of American Jewish life. Such change, however, did not come easily. In whatever era, redefining women's roles in meaningful ways constituted a strong challenge to the existing community. Imagining what American Jewish community could be if women were free to contribute fully proved to be challenging work. In addition to having to confront the limits placed upon them as women by both the Jewish community and American society, Jewish activists also found that the important but limited avenues being navigated by American women reformers could become unexpectedly treacherous for Jewish women trying to follow the same path. As different generations tested their ideas and hopes against Jewish and American realities, they explored the potential and limits of American Jewish possibility and identity.

One example of this ongoing exploration is exemplified in the efforts of a group of privileged American Jewish women at the end of the nineteenth century who grasped new public identities and in the process reinvented Jewish communal possibilities.[3] The pages of *The American Jewess*, a monthly periodical published between 1895 and 1899, offer a unique focus for exploring the implications and contradictions of this effort. The first English-language periodical directed specifically at Jewish women and edited by a woman, *The American Jewess* portrayed the intricate cultural negotiations at play in the attempts of American Jewish women to assert themselves both as Jews and as women. After a consideration of the historical context that led to the emergence of this new force in American Jewish life and the magazine that tried to represent it, this paper will examine *The American Jewess* in order to show how the promise of the moment was mediated and limited by the cultural forms and vocabulary of the time.

Emergence of the Jewess

To understand *The American Jewess*, we must consider the shifts in American Jewish women's communal identities that made its publication possible. Although nineteenth-century Jewish women had modeled their synagogue attendance on the patterns identified with female presence in Protestant churches, they had not joined in the great expansion of middle-class Protestant white women's activism that galvanized American society in the decades after the Civil War. Observers at the time and later historians have described how middle-class Protestant white women came to the fore in public life of the 1860s and 1870s, finding public voices within large-scale public movements. This emerging activism, however, did not find parallel expression among their middle-class Jewish contemporaries.[4]

Although Jewish women's public roles were also being redefined during this period, this did not translate into influential collective activism. There are a number of reasons for this. The broad nineteenth-century effort to create an increasingly formal worship atmosphere in American synagogues restrained much of the activities beyond the sanctuary that had shaped Jewish congregational life and actively engaged women during the antebellum period. Moreover, although women remained stalwart fund-raisers for their congregations and communities in the postwar decades, they lacked both the organizing energy and the expanding political voice that marked Protestant women's groups during this period. Much of this contrast may be traced to the causes that animated Protestant women during this period. Temperance work, carried out through the instrumentality of the Woman's Christian Temperance Union, and denominational missionary efforts to spread Christianity to all corners of the world drew hundreds of thousands of Christian women to organizational life. They represented the nineteenth century's largest grassroots movements and defined a prominent and influential public role for Christian women that involved them within their own local communities and far beyond.[5] Yet these particular causes had little relevance and appeal for Jewish women.

Nevertheless, by the late 1880s, the mass migration of Eastern European and Russian Jews sparked a clear shift in this pattern of Jewish women's inaction, culminating in the early 1890s. The arrival of what were often termed the immigrant "hordes" awakened a feeling among native or acculturated immigrant Jewish women in many cities that they should be addressing the pressing needs of their impoverished coreligionists, who lacked the education, culture, understanding, and resources to overcome the challenges of a hostile urban environment. The perceived needs of the Russian immigrants offered middle-class Jewish women a missionary cause to call their own.

Engagement in this work reflected contradictory impulses. Jewish women clearly felt a responsibility to respond to the needs of their coreligionists out of a sense of shared identity. At the same time, the available model of missionary uplift that they utilized in this work emphasized the vast social and cultural gulfs that lay between beneficiaries and benefactors. By drawing upon the models offered by benevolent and prosperous Protestant women, acculturated Jewish women were able both to address the needs of their own community and to highlight the great distance that separated them from the objects of their charity.[6]

The organized involvement of American Jewish women in immigrant relief work was inaugurated formally in 1888 when the rabbi of New York City's Temple Emanu-El mobilized the women of his congregation to form a Sisterhood of Personal Service. Similar groups to aid the needy and downtrodden through the uplifting force of personal contact and judiciously distributed clothing, food, fuel, and money were quickly formed in the city's other uptown affluent congregations. Similar efforts followed in other cities. The awakening of all this activity quickly shifted the way that many Jewish women came to think about their participation in and contribution to their communities.

Once organized to address the needs of immigrants, many of these groups took up causes that addressed the more general needs of their synagogues and communities.[7]

With the rise of many local activist women's groups, calls for a national organizing conference or organization among Jewish women soon followed. The Chicago World's Columbian Exposition of 1893 offered a timely opportunity to convert this thought into action. Encouraged to participate in the exposition by the Protestant women with whom they had worked within the Chicago Women's Club, a small group of elite women from Chicago's Jewish community were eager to complement the efforts of their male coreligionists, who were planning a Jewish Congress (with little female participation) for the world's fair. Through more than a year of planning the Chicago women established a network of contacts around the country to identify Jewish women who might be able to speak. Many were asked to address Jewish women's benevolent work and the needs of the immigrant communities; others were asked to reflect more generally upon the role of Jewish women. They were invited to Chicago for an unprecedented event, a Jewish Women's Congress, convened within the exposition's World Parliament of Religions in September 1893.[8]

It was a sensation.[9] All eyes seemed to be on Jewish women as they made this unprecedented foray into the world of public discourse. As Rosa Sonneschein later noted, "the American Jewess stepped out publicly into the intellectual arena, and was a marvelous surprise not only to those who knew her not, but also to her own people."[10] This first-ever national gathering of Jewish women featured an opening prayer delivered by a woman and a series of papers by women from all over the country reflecting on women's roles in philanthropy, education, religion, and work. The interest they aroused, the erudition they displayed, and the sense of purpose they conveyed marked the introduction of a powerful new force in American Jewish life. The Jewish Women's Congress quickly laid plans for creation of a National Council of Jewish Women (NCJW), the first national open-membership organization for American Jewish women. And so NCJW came into being, although without a specific agenda beyond bringing Jewish women together in order to harness their energies for the broad goals of self-education and philanthropy.[11]

Freed from the religious, cultural, and political constructs that had cut off or muted their collective and individual public voices, acculturated American Jewish women began to sense their ability to shape their own communities. *The American Jewess* magazine reveled in the promise of these new potentialities, and in the creativity and energy to be drawn from unleashing energies that had lacked communal channels for their expression. In addition to championing an expanded role for women in the synagogue, *The American Jewess* covered subjects ranging from practical benevolence, to household hints, to à la mode fashion, to the charms and danger of the bicycle.[12] The publication's sense of possibility was captured in its title. Though archaic to twenty-first-century ears, in the 1890s the phrase "American Jewess" described a new being, utterly unlike Jewish women in other regions and distinct from American women who were not Jewish. This new entity, this American Jewess, for the first time fully embraced the possibilities implicit in both the religious and the national aspects of a Jewish woman's identity. Thoroughly American and thoroughly Jewish, she need not experience these identities in contradiction to each other. Rather, she could feel fully at home in her overlapping worlds of American and Jewish culture. This was the audience envisioned by one of the publication's early male contributors when he argued that once the American Jewish woman understood her "exalted position" relative to her counterparts in other lands, she would "proudly proclaim, 'I am an American Jewess!' "[13]

Rosa Sonneschein, who created, oversaw, and edited the first volumes of *The American Jewess*, came to the United States from Hungary in the 1860s with her husband, Rabbi Solomon Sonneschein. For more than twenty years, she took a leading role in the St. Louis Jewish community where Solomon served as a rabbi. Discord with her husband, however, led to an 1893 divorce and her departure from St. Louis. Having written frequently for the Jewish press, she attended the Press Congress at Chicago's Columbian Exposition. The favorable notice she received for her participation in the congress apparently pushed her toward establishing *The American Jewess* magazine.[14] She drew her ultimate inspiration from the September 1893 Jewish Women's Congress, where, she later wrote, "then and there we conceived the impression that the time had come to establish a literary organ for the American Jewess, an organ which shall connect the sisters dwelling throughout . . . this blessed country, concentrate the work of scattered charitable institutions, and bring them to the notice of the various communities as an imposing and powerful unit."[15]

The American Jewess began publication in April 1895 full of lofty sentiments, eminent male and female contributors, and the intention of promoting Jewish women's "claim for religious and social equality." Sonneschein hoped the journal would establish Jewish women's credentials to join hands in the great "philanthropic endeavor of almost one million women to better the condition of sex, sect, and section."[16] In addition to its stated intentions, the magazine also set out on the complex task of fitting prosperous and acculturated Jewish women into prevailing modes of cultural discourse in a way that certified an expansion of their public roles and the assurance of their "womanliness."

Early issues of the magazine testified to the sense of possibility infusing both the efforts of the National Council of Jewish Women and, by extension, those of *The American Jewess* to assist and record NCJW's progress. A report in the June 1895 issue noted that "never before in the history of Judaism have its women more energetically devoted themselves to reviving the noblest elements of their ancestral faith. . . . Our women have suddenly sprung into prominence." NCJW officers reported enthusiastically that within one year of its founding the organization had already created thirteen local sections around the country and attracted 1,500 members. As study circles and philanthropic projects got underway, council organizers observed that "all over the country an active and increasing interest in our religion and its treasures has been aroused." The council had identified an avenue for its constituents to act in the world *as Jewish women*: "a desire to work has been awakened where before was only lethargy." The previous lack of activist frameworks for Jewish women, it was argued, had kept them out of public life, but, with the advent of the council, "energies only waiting for a channel into which to throw themselves have been properly directed." Council officers acknowledged that, beyond self-study, the goals of the council remained hazy; still, "the work accomplished during our first year was astonishing and but serves to show the power of energetic women working *together*."[17]

Before investigating the complications inherent in the efforts of Jewish women to find their way into a public world and public identities, it is important to note the enduring legacy of the enthusiastic moment that created both *The American Jewess* and the National Council of Jewish Women. The strongest and perhaps most influential arguments championed by Sonneschein within the pages of *The American Jewess* were those demanding synagogue membership and a role in synagogue governance for women, echoing similar calls from NCJW. With *The American Jewess* as her platform, however, Sonneschein became the first American Jewish woman to offer a strong and consistent critique of gender inequities in worship and synagogue leadership. She demanded that Jewish women "thirsting for the word of God" be allowed to "drink directly from the fountain of Religion." She advised the NCJW that they need "but knock at the doors of the congregations, and they will be speedily opened." She acknowledged that some congregations were perhaps "a little deaf from old age" and that "others may not want to hear; but knock, knock again," she admonished, "and the doors of the congregational council will be surely opened."[18] Response to this and other pressures led to a growing role for women in American acculturated synagogues in the 1890s and to a significant expansion in the possibilities and scope of American synagogues.[19]

Rightly then, participants in this movement took the emerging potential of their work quite seriously. Their efforts were bringing forth a new vision of Jewish communal endeavor. These possibilities were both facilitated and complicated by the adoption of American ideological currents that valorized women's benevolent work. In investing their work with millennial significance, some Jewish women activists sought to draw upon traditions that resonated within both Jewish and American (in this case Protestant) traditions. We can hear this in the words of Rebekah Kohut, the widow of a prominent rabbi in

New York, who came into her own as a public figure in the context of her work for NCJW. As president of the New York section, she reflected in 1896 on what the group had already accomplished and its future promise. "We know that we are sisters in a common religion," she advised her listeners; "it almost seems as if we could see the Temple of old take form again, and Judea's walls rise, for the glory of Israel has returned." Indeed, she suggested, "every Jewess," and especially every Council member, bore the duty of being "God's missionary. . . . Ours it is to be the saviors of our people."[20]

With her invocation of the rebuilt Temple in Jerusalem, Kohut's mention of the redemption promised by the potentiality of women's united drive was a particularly Jewish one. And yet it is here that the assertion of a new and powerful Jewish female identity became wrapped up with cultural assumptions that undermined these women's attempts to validate the Jewishness of their new roles. For in the broader discourse carried on beyond the pages of *The American Jewess*, the redemptive public emergence of white women in order to work for the betterment of the downtrodden and uncultured and extend missionary work to the unchurched was understood in strictly Christian millennial terms.

Prevailing cultural discourse identified white Christian Anglo-Saxon culture as the apex of human civilization and achievement. Thus, as radical as it may have been to demand a stronger voice for women within Judaism, the task of certifying the refined womanhood of middle-class acculturated American Jewish women may have been much more challenging. Indeed, much of the energy that informed the Jewish Women's Congress and the enthusiastic creation of the National Council of Jewish Women derived from the perceived need to create public roles for middle-class Jewish women that could establish their right to stand alongside their Protestant counterparts in the womanly work of tending to the needs of society. This desire, however, drew Jewish women into affirming a stratified social order in which their own respectability and acceptance came only at the expense of other dispossessed groups, including other Jewish women.

Joining a Mighty Wave of Civilization

These currents were apparent in the discussions at the 1893 Jewish Women's Congress, where speakers assailed themselves for having failed to live up to the standard of philanthropy set by Protestant women. Rebekah Kohut challenged the assemblage with an observation from Mrs. J. B. Lowell, "one of our most estimable women" and a leading practitioner of charity work among the urban poor. Kohut passed on a troubling question, which Lowell had addressed to her, to those at the congress: " 'Have you no missionaries, no King's Daughters [a large church-affiliated women's charity working to address the needs of recent immigrants] among your people? I visit your poor constantly, and have never yet met any of the better class Jewesses in the lower quarter of the city!' The dart," Mrs. Kohut reported, "went straight home. I knew too well the truth of her statement."[21]

Laura Jacobson of St. Louis suggested that in some ways Jewish women were "not on a level with our Christian sisters. . . . if you go into a Christian church upon a Sabbath morning . . . you will find many more than you find in attendance in a Jewish synagogue." Sonneschein herself pointed out that Jewish young women seemed to lack the "individual sense of responsibility for the performance of higher duties which is so commonly present in the case of their Christian sisters." In contrast to the practice of young Jewish women, "the young ladies among the Christian denominations are frequently found visiting the poor." Organizing themselves to bring aid and a refining influence to struggling immigrant Jews was seen as critical to establishing that Jewish women could be worthy and womanly instigators of societal uplift. As Flora Schwab of Cleveland observed, "Our Jewish council is the organization which will represent the modern Jewish women side by side with her non-Jewish sisters."[22]

The feeling expressed by these middle-class Jewish women that they could legitimate their claims to moral and spiritual equality by devoting themselves collectively to benevolence and self-education was confirmed when leaders of non-Jewish women's groups embraced them with sisterly feelings. Ellen M. Henrotin, president of the National Federation of Women's Clubs, addressed the NCJW at their first convention in 1896, telling them that "Jew and Gentile no longer exist. We stand hand to hand, heart to heart. . . . We ask no longer of any women, what do you believe, what is your sect, but . . . are you a clubable woman, are you willing to go work with us. And if she says yes, she is of us."[23] NCJW women loved the interest that those of other faiths took in their work and were proud that they were asked to participate as Jewish representatives in a variety of women's club settings. Sonneschein and her readers wanted to believe that their public work had become part of a broad white female middle-class movement that she described as "a mighty wave of civilization."[24]

This was clearly a "wave" that Sonneschein and her readers wanted to ride (one regular feature in the magazine was titled "In Woman's Wake"), but they also recognized that the undertow could be treacherous. Even the ways in which Christian women sometimes sought to include them could make *American Jewess* readers uneasy. A report on the convention of the Woman's Christian Temperance Union noted how "Miss Willard urged to admit as members to the W.C.T.U. Catholic as well as Jewish women." *The American Jewess* offered a restrained editorial response: "We can but hail with pleasure the spirit of tolerance and progress which prompted the adoption of this proposition, and regret that the name *Christian* indicates too narrow a sphere devoted to the interest of humanity."[25]

In the first issue of *The American Jewess* NCJW leaders informed readers that they hoped to emulate one aspect of Christian women's activism by entering "the missionary field. Our work," they carefully pointed out, "will be among the poor and indigent of our own faith." While affirming their high regard for Christian missionary work among "the savage and barbarous," they questioned why it was that "two hundred thousand dollars should be spent annually converting Jews." Although they emphasized their own social distance from the immigrant Jews that they hoped to serve, they found it offensive to suggest that any Jew should be treated as the spiritual equivalent of the savages and barbarians who were the proper objects of Christian missionizing.[26]

If Jewish women activists were uncomfortable with the notion of Christians doing missionary work among Jewish immigrants, they had no problem adopting models of Christian-identified charity for their own work among their coreligionists. The sisterhoods of personal service in different cities eagerly adopted the practice of "friendly visiting," an influential mode of charitable work that had emerged in the 1870s, which was frequently promoted in *The American Jewess*. It was thought that frequent friendly visits by cultured women to poor and/or immigrant families could induce moral uplift by imparting their own cultivated values to those deficient in basic virtues.[27] Adoption of this plan seemed to offer Jewish women the cultural validation of serving as exemplars of enlightened civilization. Yet the real problem with adopting this elaborately constructed cultural platform was that it was not really designed to be practiced by either Jews or Jewesses. American Christian missionaries, after all, regarded Jews as appropriate targets for missionizing, not as a group qualified to dispense cultural and religious enlightenment.

Historians are beginning to take a close look at the way that white middle-class Americans around the turn of the century talked about the development and nature of different societies across time and space in terms of their stage of "civilization."[28] As suggested in the reference to Christian missionary work above, the standard stages of cultural development were believed to be savagery, barbarism, and civilization. This model drew upon Darwin's theory of biological evolution to measure human progress along a scale of cultural evolution that advanced from a savage, nearly animalistic state of brutish, undifferentiated existence to life in a highly refined society where each type of person played a distinctive role in contributing to a harmonious whole. Among the most basic definitions of an advanced civilization were the distinctive roles and identities it assigned to men and to women. It was surely no coincidence that contemporary observers saw the cultural climb approaching its evolutionary peak among white Protestant nineteenth-century Anglos-Saxons. Female social reformers wielded this discourse of civilization to argue that it was the expression of white Anglo-Saxon Protestant women's moral force in the world that offered the best hope for the spread and advance of cultural progress.

This discourse of civilizational progress appears everywhere in late nineteenth-century thought. *American Jewess* contributor Israel Peres assumed his readers' familiarity with this worldview in his article "The Politico-Economic Status of Woman": "It must be taken for granted," he wrote, "that the great majority of readers are fairly conversant with the general geologic, economic and social laws which have nursed, sustained, and impelled man from his crude, brutal state to the point where he becomes the central figure of the highly complex social organism of to-day."[29] Historian Louise Newman argues that toward the end of the nineteenth century, "it became impossible to argue for a change in woman's sphere without first thinking the argument through in evolutionist terms." Kevin Gaines points out that this discourse was so pervasive that even the nation's African-American elite adopted the language of racial hierarchy (which relegated blacks to a lower rung) to talk about the aspirations of their own group.[30] Despite its noxious assumptions of white (Christian) racial and cultural superiority, the discourse of progressive civilization constituted late nineteenth-century American society's vocabulary for thinking about cultural values and social change. It is not surprising that this discourse staked out a healthy presence in the pages of *The American Jewess*.

Weighing Jewish Women on the Scale of Civilization

In a society where much attention was being paid to women's changing social and economic roles, the discourse of civilization was highly attuned to the treatment of women. The belief that "the civilizing status of a nation can best be judged by the social and civic position of its women" was so much of a given and a cliché in the late nineteenth century that it appeared in an *American Jewess* column as filler material next to: "Men should keep their eyes wide open before marriage and half shut afterward."[31] Dr. Adolph Moses's article in the inaugural issue, "The Position of Woman in America," offered a guide to using women as a gauge of civilization. He condemned both the "savage ancestors of modern nations" and "the savage Indian and Australian of to-day" for making woman into "a mere beast of burden, bought like any other chattel from her owner, her father. She was abused in every way, cruelly beaten, often starved, and not seldom killed by an enraged man-animal." Among savage peoples, woman was treated like an animal; among the barbarous, he noted, "woman was and is a slave."[32]

Moses exhibited no apparent self-consciousness that only a few decades earlier the United States had been home to a highly elaborated legal system of servitude that enslaved both women and men, suggesting that his moral outrage was largely reserved for white women. He noted the horror that Americans experienced when they traveled through Europe and saw women "with a heavy load of brick on their shoulders" or yoked to a plow. For Moses, the United States had made "a contribution of immeasurable value . . . towards the world's civilization." "If the American nation had done nothing else for progress of humanity," he wrote, "than to have at last redeemed woman from the state of legal, social and intellectual inferiority in which she had been kept from time immemorial, it would be entitled to rank among the great civilizing powers of the earth." America had "broken the fetters which the age of savagery had forged for her, which the age of barbarism had riveted upon her, with which even the most advanced nations continued to enchain her." As a result, "to-day the American woman has become the highest representative of womanhood." In the process of transforming the continent "from a habitation of howling savages into the seat of the utmost progressive civilization," America had created the sort of engaged woman that *The American Jewess* wanted to convince its readers that they were and could be: "She is enriching, ennobling and spiritualizing the life of the American nation."

More than this, Moses and other *American Jewess* contributors wielded the rhetoric of civilization in a way that allowed middle-class Jewish women to place themselves into the story of the development of white enlightened culture. Moses suggested that it had been the ancient Israelites who were the first to conceive of "the absolute equality of woman with man" and that this was a "cardinal conception of the great revolutionary heroes of humanity, the prophets of Israel." Moses acknowledged that these revolutionary Israelite ideas had been displaced by the influence of the more primitive cultures among which the Jews were forced to live, but he insisted that the core ideas "went from Zion and migrated from people to people, and from age to age," until finally "the American people" were able to carry "into practice the lofty ideals which the prophets and poets of Israel cherished regarding woman." Finally, a modern culture was able to institute the ancient "Jewish" ideal, "the dignity, the intellectual elevation, the social equality of woman."

Other writers also inserted Jewish civilization into their narratives of cultural progress. Ray Frank, the well-known female Jewish itinerant preacher of the 1890s, cited the words of Benjamin Disraeli when Disraeli responded to someone who questioned the appropriateness of his background for his role as a leader of Great Britain: "Yes, I am a Jew, but let me remind the honorable gentleman that when his ancestors were naked savages on the banks of the Thames, mine were princes in Solomon's temple."[33] But the popular discourse, to which *American Jewess* writers adopted their own story, was in its essence a narrative about Christianity's redemptive power to advance the course of civilization. Central to this view was the role of Jesus in freeing women from the rigid edicts and restrictions of Jewish law and tradition.

The story of civilization as it was told and used as a justifying basis for the work of women as missionaries, temperance activists, or benevolence workers was a story of Christian triumphalism. Louise Newman argues that Christian reformers were able to accept the suitability in this work of wealthy Jews who had a long enough background in the United States to have been able to benefit from its Christian civilizing influence.[34] Yet, as we have seen, as much as Jews might try to place themselves into this civilizing narrative, at critical points it was not going to be a good fit.

Male authors in *The American Jewess* were much more likely than female authors to delve into how the contemporary roles of women and of Jewish women specifically were shaped by the advance of civilization. The absence of extensive inquiry on the part of female authors may suggest their awareness of how problematic it could be to try to fit themselves onto this Christian scale. Sonneschein drew upon the tropes of civilizational discourse but in ways that were usually secondary to her main points. Their use, nonetheless, can still be disturbing to contemporary readers. The worst example appears in an editorial devoted ostensibly to condemning lynching. Sonneschein used the discourse's association of primitiveness with lack of control over one's passions to validate the racist rationale that lynching was a natural reaction by white men to the sexual violation of white women by black men: "the facts are that there are human beings of a low order, unable to restrain their brutal passion."[35]

By accepting a cultural scale that assigned black men to a "low order," Sonneschein was implicitly affirming the unquestioned place of her readers among the "higher" orders. Yet even as she utilized the civilizational rhetoric, Sonneschein understood that societal acceptance of Jewish women's civilized credentials was by no means secure. In noting that civilized societies had destroyed traditional prejudices against women, she implored: "now let us annihilate what prejudice still exists against the Jewess."[36] Examination of Sonneschein's magazine makes clear that even those Jewish women who felt they had achieved social acceptance from non-Jews still felt vulnerable in the face of common societal stereotypes assigned to Jewish women. These negative associations called into question the right of even the most cultured Jewish women to a secure claim at the top of the evolutionary cultural scale. American cultural representations of Jewish women highlighted their separation from and subordination to men within the context of the synagogue. These images connected Jewish women (more than Jewish men) to an exoticized Orient and its harems with their sexualized denizens who flouted the signal womanly values of purity, modesty, and refinement that defined civilized societies.

An article by Rabbi E. G. Hirsch suggested how in the popular mind these Eastern cultural defects became connected to contemporary American Jewish women: "Often is the Jewish woman held by prejudice to be under the spell of Eastern fancies. Under this mistaken judgment rests the ascription to her of a love for fineries, gems and loud colors."[37] *American Jewess* writers often fretted over behavior that might confirm these stereotypes. One columnist asserted that Jewish women who made a mockery of feminine virtues through their "forward, vulgar and pompous demeanor" only confirmed "those aspersions cast upon the entire race." Such trespasses, she pointed out, highlighted the Jewess's vulnerability. A "vulgar, undesirable upstart" who was a Christian would be dismissed as an insignificant individual. But should she be Jewish, then "with one full sweep all Jewesses are forthwith pronounced loud, common, obtrusive," undermining the accomplishments of the many "truly refined and cultivated women" who were "the true social saviors of our race." Sonneschein made a parallel observation on another occasion when she wrote that despite the "marvelous social and intellectual results" of NCJW's works, the whole was only as strong as its weakest member. "Biased as the world yet is," she pointed out, "the conduct of each individual reflects upon the whole community." As a result "the merits and defects of each section [would] reflect upon the Council at large."[38]

It was a delicate situation. Jewish women's claims upon civilization were so tenuous that they could be undermined by one mistake by the most marginal individual. In response, perhaps, to this challenge, the pages of *The American Jewess* offered a constant, though silent, dialogue with the civilizational discourse of cultural hierarchy. *The American Jewess*, which advertised itself as "the *only* illustrated Jewish monthly," in fact presented a veritable portrait gallery of contemporary Jewish women, offering "from time to time . . . such types of handsome American Jewesses, from the various sections of the country."[39] These portraits, most of which depicted officers of local NCJW sections across the country, were joined by occasional images bearing the caption "one of our celebrated co-religionists" and depicting prominent individuals, such as the actress Sarah Bernhardt.[40] Portraits of male contributors appeared, but the profusion of female portraits drawn from among the ranks of American Jewry's refined and respectable female elite seemed intended to challenge popular conceptions of what public Jews should look like. In this case they looked like genteel ladies.

These images stood in implicit dialogue with another common feature in the magazine, which depicted "primitive" cultures, in both articles and images. The contrast in these visuals highlighted a basic contrast between "higher" civilization, in which the differentiation between women and men was distinctive and pronounced, and "lower" civilizations, where little separated the male and the female.[41] Contemporary images from exotic lands ranging from Arcadia to Egypt to Africa (home to "the most primitive of women of today") presented figures portrayed either without the modesty of proper garments or with robes that hid the gendered shapes of their bodies. Men wore skirts; women had no discernible body shapes. Often there was little that distinguished males from females in depictions of family groups (paralleling the illustrations in an article about apes).[42]

The contrast with the images presented of more cultured women was obvious. A photo array of "some handsome types of American Jewesses" from Cleveland featured lacy necklines and elaborately styled hairdos.[43] The stark gap between high and low cultures was especially striking in illustrations that accompanied the magazine's fashion articles by "Madame La Mode." In these features, drawings of women adorned in the latest fashions featured pencil-thin, corseted waistlines that would put Barbie to shame. The exaggerated contours of these images left no doubt that cultured females looked nothing like their male counterparts.[44]

To complement these depictions, article after article reflected on the meaning of "womanliness" and of its heightened expression in Jewish women. Rabbi Henry Berkowitz offered a compelling list that included "gentleness, mildness, sympathy, tenderness, patience, confidence, devotion, trust and love." Pauline Wise summed up the womanly virtues more briefly as "beauty, grace and self-abnegation." Many authors fretted about the "mannishness" that threatened the emancipated women of the nineteenth century as they moved more often into the public sphere.[45] But readers were assured that Jewish women could approach their new roles in a way that emphasized their womanly grace. E. G. Hirsch attempted to leave no doubt that womanliness defined the essence of the modern Jewish woman: "In fact it is the ambition of the Jewess to be a woman so womanly as to exclude all qualifying adjectives." Lest someone suspect this reflected the surrounding culture rather than a Jewish religious upbringing, he clarified that "her Judaism inculcates and emphasizes this ambition."[46] These sorts of descriptions were reinforced by numerous short descriptions of prominent Jewish women, often accompanied by a portrait. Mrs. Oscar Straus, for instance, was described in a way suggesting that she was the product of generations of aristocratic breeding: the "refined elegance which surrounds Mrs. Straus in her home is but a fitting frame to a woman whose mobile face is a constant indicator of noble impulses."[47]

Ambivalent Benevolence

The womanliness of these cultured Jewesses was further elaborated by contrasts with one other group of women that appeared in the magazine. This contrast, however, was much more complicated than the one presented with primitive Africans or Australians. In the first three years or so of publication, recent Jewish immigrants from Russia were depicted almost exclusively as objects of charity for their more civilized sisters. The emphasis of these descriptions highlighted how a savage way of life could exist even in the most modern of American cities.

A description of the mothers of impoverished children who were able to attend a free kindergarten echoed portrayals of what were considered the most primitive cultures: "They know nothing outside of their own narrow sphere of existence. Life to them hardly means anything more than to eat, drink, sleep and drudge. They exercise but . . . the lower part of their nature." The purpose of such descriptions was to convey the certain "elevating refreshing effect" that "friendly, unrestrained intercourse with" their Americanized coreligionists could bring. Despite complete ignorance, among the immigrants, of nature, health, cleanliness, or how to care for children, contact with "their more fortunate sisters" could make the kindergarten "a training school for mothers; a place in which they will be quickened out of their dullness and apathy; where their dormant qualities will be awakened, and a love of the beautiful, the true and the good called into life."[48]

American Jewess descriptions of efforts to reach the Russian Jew echoed the approach of the Charity Organization movement that throughout the 1880s and 1890s sent volunteer female "friendly visitors" to impoverished urban immigrant families. These visits, it was argued, would impart the civilizing influence of refined American womanhood to those with no cultural resources of their own. An article about a Chicago maternity ward noted that patients who came from the population of Russian immigrants "who swarm and cluster together on the West Side of Chicago" found an "oasis" of "repose" and hope at the hospital. For a patient, her "first contact with refined and cultured women," and the "lessons of cleanliness" that she received, left "an imprint on the life of the heretofore ignorant, suspicious foreigner; who, from infancy steeped in the mire of misery and filth, now for the first time, beholds the glorious object-lesson of true charity. Thenceforth she regards herself linked to higher aspirations, which she begins to practice on her return to her own humble home."[49]

For middle-class acculturated Jewish women, bringing benevolence through "friendly visiting" to their immigrant coreligionists offered an opportunity to wield their moral force to bring their refining influence to the urban poor in a way that confirmed that they belonged to the nation's female elite. Yet their own religious identification with these women, who raised their children in "filth and squalor" while giving birth to another child every year, compromised their attempts to assert the essential purity and refinement of Jewish womanhood.[50] *The American Jewess* reflected this complex relationship, offering differing messages about the essential innate culture of the "American Jewess" and the difficult question of whether these lowly immigrant Jewesses would be able to traverse the hierarchy of cultures to join the ranks of their more cultured sisters.

The Limits and Possiblities of Imagination

The growing numbers of Russian Jewish women in the United States further complicated the efforts of those women represented by *The American Jewess* to navigate the tricky American shoals of culture and identity. Between religious restrictions within her own tradition, the prejudices that applied to Jews and to Jewish women particularly, the national politics of female emancipation and suffrage, the needs of Jewish men, and the expectations of Protestant women, the "American Jewess" had to work very hard to maintain her claims to cultural respectability. She also needed to sustain the momentum of energy and hopefulness that surrounded the early efforts at organizing American Jewish women as a moral and social force. This momentum, however, was drained by the difficulties encountered by the National Council of Jewish Women.

After its initial burst of energy, NCJW spent a critical period attempting to find its way and define its mission. In 1896, Sonneschein proposed that the organization adopt Zionism as its central concern (an idea that would meet with much success when Henrietta Szold made it the basis of Hadassah in 1912).[51] Although her own suggestion was not taken up, Sonneschein was pleased to report that NCJW's first national convention in 1896 unanimously determined upon a quest to uphold and preserve the traditional Jewish Sabbath (i.e., Saturday) in the United States. Sonneschein believed this great mission could sustain American Judaism and prove the worth of American Jewish womanhood. Unfortunately, the Sabbath had itself become a controversial issue among NCJW representatives. The founding officers of the organization came out of a Chicago radical Reform Jewish community that advocated transferring the celebration of Sabbath from the traditional Saturday to Sunday, the civil day of rest in the United States and the Christian Sabbath. Despite Sonneschein's optimism, heated confrontations over the Sabbath question at the 1896 convention suggested both that Sabbath observance could not provide a shared focus for effective activism and that the council would not be able to unify American Jewish women across religious differences.[52]

At first, Sonneschein insisted that if "as yet the Council has done nothing to immortalize itself," still, "even if the Council should never reach the goal of its ambition, it is surely ennobling and uplifting at least to strive and work for the realization of grand aims and objects." By January 1898, however, she was noting that fourteen months had passed since NCJW's "sacred declaration" about protecting the Sabbath, but "as yet not even the first official step has been taken to redeem the divine promise." As Sonneschein waited for action, her early positive evaluation of the ability of the council to attract five thousand members turned to a lament that no more were joining.[53]

Amidst NCJW's uncertainty and struggles with her own health, Sonneschein seemed to lose confidence in her ability to take on the Jewish world and champion the cause of Jewish women. Faced with business difficulties, she sold the magazine to a group that kept her on as chief correspondent but offered nothing to match Sonneschein's sharp editorial voice. Publishing stories and articles meant to be of interest to women as homemakers and mothers, the magazine no longer offered a vision of what Jewish women, and thus the Jewish community, could be. It lost its clear sense of purpose. When the magazine's last issue was published in August 1899, the publishers bemoaned the lack of support for the Jewish press among the American Jewish public (though they ironically noted that "the 'barbaric Russian' Jew" always seemed to have his Yiddish paper spread before him).[54]

And so, after some three thousand pages, *The American Jewess* reached the end of its brief run, with its initial blaze of enthusiasm and possibility burnt out. In the short term, proponents of what Jewish women could create had a difficult time standing up to challenges of finding their place within a cultural order that emphasized the tenuousness of their right to belong. Yet, in hindsight, the lessons of what American Jewish women were able to achieve in the last decade of the nineteenth century are clear. The expansion of women's activities in their synagogues and communities contributed to a rapid transformation of American synagogues, vastly expanding their congregational reach beyond the sanctuary. NCJW not only continued its own work, finding an effective and meaningful role in assisting single Jewish women immigrants as they disembarked and made their way into American life; it also provided a model to women of diverse Jewish backgrounds for all the American Jewish women's organizations that would follow.

The American Jewess, then, offers us a record of newly minted national Jewish activists taken up in a moment of power and possibility. By modeling their own public roles on those of prosperous Protestant women, the creators of the National Council of Jewish Women and *The American Jewess* hoped to find a comfortable place within a cultural milieu that itself offered only an ambivalent potential embrace to Jewish women and who they might become. Twenty-first-century hindsight allows us to recognize both the boldness of Rosa Sonneschein's desire to redefine American Jewish women and how the desire to challenge prevailing cultural restrictions was limited by the cramped imagination of the culture in which she wanted to claim a place. As much as the phrase "American Jewess" betokened a vision of new possibilities, of everything a Jewish woman might become in and offer to America, it also defined itself in opposition to what acculturated Jewish women had once been and what their less privileged sisters still were. Ultimately, their imagination of what Jewish women and Jewish community could be was limited by the cultural assumptions and vocabulary of the culture they hoped to join.

The American Jewess preserves the history of the complicated struggle to secure a place for Jewish women on the American spectrum of class, race, and gender. As it turned out, the future did not belong to the "Jewess." And yet, other strong American Jewish women would take up the challenge of finding a viable societal place from which they could add their voices to the creation of Jewish and American possibilities. Finding one's place in a society inflected by racism, religious prejudice, and sexism has never been and will never be easy, yet in their persistent struggle to master this complicated dance, American Jewish women have continued to define and transform the possibilities available to their communities and themselves.

Notes

1. Dianne Ashton, *Rebecca Gratz: Women and Judaism in Antebellum America* (Detroit: Wayne State University Press, 1977), pp. 152–153.
2. See *www.jofa.org*.
3. For the purpose of this paper, I was able to take advantage of (and was somewhat prompted by) the Jewish Women's Archive's project of assembling and digitizing the full run of *The American Jewess* for the purpose of creating an online searchable version. *The American Jewess* can be accessed at *www.jwa.org*. The project was funded by the Faith Breslaw Cummins Fund at the Jewish Women's Archive and the Fund for Jewish Cultural Preservation, sponsored by the National Foundation for Jewish Culture.
4. Karla Goldman, *Beyond the Synagogue Gallery: Finding a Place for Women in American Judaism* (Cambridge: Harvard University Press, 2000), pp. 137–150.
5. See Patricia R. Hill, *The World Their Household: The American Woman's Foreign Mission Movement and Cultural Transformation, 1870–1920* (Ann Arbor: University of Michigan Press, 1985); Peggy Pascoe, *Relations of Rescue: The Search for Female Moral Authority in the American West, 1874–1939* (New York: Oxford University Press, 1990); Anne Firor Scott, *Natural Allies: Women's Associations in American History* (Urbana: University of Illinois Press, 1992); and Ruth Bordin, *Women and Temperance: The Quest for Power and Liberty, 1873–1900* (Philadelphia: Temple University Press, 1984).
6. Paul Boyer, *Urban Masses and Moral Order in America, 1820–1920* (Cambridge: Harvard University Press, 1978), pp. 143–161.
7. Goldman, pp. 176–179; on sisterhoods of personal service, see especially Felicia Herman, "From Priestess to Hostess: Sisterhoods of Personal Service in New York City, 1887–1936," in *Women and American Judaism: Historical Perspectives*, ed. Pamela S. Nadell and Jonathan D. Sarna (Hanover, N.H.: Brandeis University Press, 2001), pp. 148–181.
8. On Jewish Women's Congress and its planning, see Faith Rogow, *Gone to Another Meeting: The National Council of Jewish Women, 1893–1993* (Tuscaloosa: University of Alabama Press, 1993), pp. 9–24; Deborah Grand Golomb, "The 1893 Congress of Jewish Women: Evolution or Revolution in American Jewish Women's History?" *American Jewish History* 70 (September 1980): 52–67.

9. "Congress of Jewish Women at Chicago," *American Israelite*, September 7, 1893.

10. "Salutatory," *The American Jewess* (hereinafter *AJ*), 1895. This article (no page number) appears bound with the sixth issue of the first volume of *The American Jewess* (September 1895), but it is possible that it originally appeared on one of the endpapers of the first issue (April 1895). The next page, also unnumbered, offers a "Prospectus" for the publication.

11. *Papers of the Jewish Women's Congress, Held at Chicago, September 4, 5, 6, and 7, 1893* (Philadelphia: Jewish Publication Society of America, 1894).

12. The most complete analysis of the content of *The American Jewess* can be found in Carole B. Balin, "Unraveling an American-Jewish Synthesis: Rosa Sonne-schein's *The American Jewess*, 1895–1899" (senior honors thesis, Wellesley College, 1986).

13. Rabbi L. Weiss, "The Jewess at Home and Abroad," *AJ* 1:3 (June 1895): 115.

14. Biographical information on Rosa Sonneschein can be found in David Loth, "*The American Jewess*," *Midstream: A Monthly Jewish Review* 31:2 (February 1985): 43–46; Jack Nusan Porter, "Rosa Sonnenschein [*sic*] and *The American Jewess*: The First Independent English Language Jewish Women's Journal in the United States," *American Jewish History* 68:1 (September 1978): 57–63; Jack Nusan Porter, "Rosa Sonneschein and *The American Jewess* Revisited: New Historical Information on an Early American Zionist and Jewish Feminist," *American Jewish Archives* 32:2 (November 1980): 125–131; Carole S. Kessner, "Rosa Sonne-schein: The Woman and Her Work," *Proceedings of the Tenth World Congress of Jewish Studies, Jerusalem, August 16–24, 1989*, division B, volume II (Jerusalem: The World Union of Jewish Studies, 1990), pp. 325–330; Benny Kraut, "A Unitarian Rabbi? The Case of Solomon H. Sonneschein," in *Jewish Apostasy in the Modern World*," ed. Todd M. Endelman (New York: Holmes & Meier, 1987), pp. 299–300.

15. "Salutatory."

16. "Salutatory," "Editor's Desk," *AJ* 1:1 (April 1895): 49.

17. "National Council of Jewish Women," 1:3 (June 1895): 129; Hannah G. Solomon, "Report of the National Council of Jewish Women," *AJ* 1:1 (April 1895): 27; Hannah G. Solomon and Sadie American, "National Council of Jewish Women," *AJ* 2:5 (February 1896): 278; "National Council of Jewish Women," *AJ* 2:1 (October 1895): 50.

18. "Editor's Desk," *AJ* 2:1 (October 1895): 63; "Editorial," *AJ* 4:3 (December 1896): 138. A few men rose up to decry the efforts of the National Council of Jewish Women and the editor of *The American Jewess*, questioning the need for a separate women's organization, but for the most part their arguments seemed petty and defensive, "Salutatory"; Israel Peres in *Reform Advocate*, January 2, 1897, pp. 323–325; Jacob Voorsanger in *Emanu-El*, Feburary 14, 1896, pp. 6–7; *Jewish Voice*, August 9, 1895. Jacob Voorsanger argued that now that Jewish women had been granted equality, "one-sex organizations" were "unnatural." The synagogue, he claimed, "has long since recognized the equal claim of the sexes." Although he acknowledged that "women can become no members in many Synagogues. . . . In aught else man and woman are equal. They have the same rights, privileges, and prerogatives." Ignoring the realities that women could take no part in the religious

service, that they were almost universally excluded from any role in synagogue governance (NCJW had begun to ask for the possibility of such representation, and *The American Jewess* had noted one instance where women were allowed to serve on the synagogue religious school committee), and certainly that no one had seriously considered the possibility that they might become rabbis, he asserted: "The congregational institutions do not deny women the right of participation. The Hebrew Union College admits women are on equal footing with men." The St. Louis *Jewish Voice* published an attack on Sonneschein for bearing a grudge against St. Louis and concluded by extrapolating on a traditional biblical commentary in a curious fashion: "Abraham saddled his ass for love's sake. Balaam saddled his ass for hatred's sake. Mrs. S. saddled her ass and we know the why and wherefore."

19. Goldman, pp. 179–185; David Kaufman, *Shul with a Pool: The "Synagogue-Center" in American Jewish History* (Hanover, N.H.: University Press of New England, 199), pp. 10–50.
20. "Report of the Convention 'Council of Jewish Women,' " *AJ* 4:3 (December 1896): 126.
21. Rebekah Kohut, in *Papers of the Jewish Women's Conference, Chicago, 1893* (Philadelphia: Jewish Publication Society, 1894), pp. 191–192. Kohut is most likely referring to Josephine Shaw Lowell, a founder and leader of the New York City Charity Organization Society, which was created in 1882. The New York society was part of a larger Charity Organization movement that began in the late 1870s. Boyer, pp. 143–146.
22. *Papers of the Jewish Women's Congress*, p. 120; "Editorial," *AJ* 2:11 (August 1896): 605–606; Schwab discussion, *Proceedings of the First Convention of the National Council of Jewish Women, New York, 1896* (Philadelphia, 1897), p. 115.
23. Ellen Henrotin, "Discussion," *Proceedings of the First Convention of the National Council of Jewish Women*, p. 28.
24. "Editor's Desk," *AJ* 1:1 (April 1895): 48.
25. "Searchlight on Woman," *AJ* 2:2 (November 1895): 101.
26. Hannah G. Solomon, "Report of the National Council of Jewish Women," *AJ* 1:1 (April 1895): 31.
27. Boyer, pp. 151–154.
28. See Gail Bederman, *Manliness & Civilization: A Cultural History of Gender and Race in the United States, 1880–1917* (Chicago: University of Chicago Press, 1995); Beryl Satter, *Each Mind a Kingdom: American Women, Sexual Purity and the New Thought Movement, 1875–1920* (Berkeley: University of California Press, 1999); Louise Michele Newman, *White Women's Rights: The Racial Origins of Feminism in the United States* (New York: Oxford University Press, 1999).
29. Israel H. Peres, "The Poltico-Economic Status of Woman," *AJ* 2:1 (October 1895): 23.
30. Newman, p. 39; Kevin K. Gaines, *Uplifting the Race: Black Leadership, Politics, and Culture in the Twentieth Century* (Chapel Hill: University of North Carolina Press, 1996), p. 35.
31. "Searchlight on Woman," *AJ* 2:2 (October 1895): 101.

32. Adolph Moses, "The Position of Woman in America," *AJ* 1:1 (April 1895): 15–20.

33. Ray Frank, "The Arch Enemy of the Jew," *AJ* 2:2 (November 1895): 74.

34. Newman, p. 11.

35. *AJ* 5:5 (August 1897): 236.

36. "Salutatory."

37. E. G. Hirsch, "The American Jewess," *AJ* 1:1: 11.

38. "Editor's Desk," *AJ* 2:3 (December 1896): 175.

39. "Publisher's Notes," *AJ* 1:6 (September 1895); "Editor's Desk," *AJ* 1:2 (May 1895): 101.

40. *AJ* 2:9 (June 1896): 454.

41. Newman, p. 39; Satter, p. 41.

42. *AJ* 2:10 (July 1896): 526, 528; 2:2 (November 1895): 78, 83, 85, 87; "The Ape Family," *AJ* 1:1 (April 1895): 43–46.

43. *AJ* (August 1896): 562. Another article offered portraits and descriptions of a number of young Jewish women under the title "Types of Californian Beauties," *AJ* 4:3 (December 1896): 116–120.

44. See, for example, *AJ* 2:10 (July 1896): 542, 544; 2:12 (September 1896): 640–641; 5:5 (August 1897): 228.

45. Henry Berkowitz, "Woman's Part in the Drama of Life," *AJ* 1:2 (May 1895): 65; Pauline S. Wise, "Successful Business Women," *AJ* 1:2 (May 1895): 68.

46. Emil G. Hirsch, "The American Jewess," *AJ* 1:1: 11.

47. *AJ* 1:3 (June 1895): 148.

48. Bertha Hirsch, "The Kindergarten for Mothers" *AJ* 2:7 (April 1896): 370–371.

49. "Michael Reese Hospital," *AJ* 2:1 (October 1895): 30–31; see also "In the World of Charity," *AJ* 1:4 (July 1895): 208.

50. "In the World of Charity," *AJ* 1:4 (July 1895): 208.

51. "The National Council of Jewish Women and Our Dream of Nationality," *AJ* 4:1 (October 1896): 28–32.

52. "Editorial," *AJ* 4:3 (December 1896): 138; Rogow, pp. 102–129.

53. "Editorial," *AJ* 4:5 (February 1897): 235–236; "Editorial," *AJ* 6:4 (January 1898): 191–192.

54. "Valedictory," *AJ* 9:5 (August 1899): 3.

"They Raised Beautiful Families"

Jewish Mothers' Child Rearing

and Community Building

According to many scholars of Jewish life, the Jewish family is an important lynchpin of Jewish identity, its quintessential social organization. Transmitting values that allowed Jews to survive the challenges of immigration, resettlement, and acculturation, the Jewish family seemed distinctive as a source of resilience, virtue, and cultural cohesiveness. Although scholars have also identified a darker side of Jewish family life, the survival of the Jewish community has been commonly linked to the strength and vitality of family life. "Given . . . the centrality of the community as distinct from the individual," David Hartman writes, "one can appreciate the role of the family within the Judaic tradition. The family is the social institution that brings the individual into the larger community . . . mediat[ing] the larger communal memories."[1]

Nearly two decades ago Paula Hyman set forth the importance of exploring "all of the ramifications of the interaction of family and community, of family and Jewish identity" to the "community of Jewish scholarship." Observing that "the contribution of the family . . . to the extraordinary social mobility of Jews in the modern period" had yet to be investigated, Hyman noted that

> family historians and sociologists have left to novelists such questions as to how the Jewish family selectively legitimated values from the larger society, how it perpetuated a measure of assertiveness among its women, how it secularized its values, and how it succeeded in sending forth its children to do battle in the world while keeping them closely attached.[2]

Hyman called for close scrutiny of economic and educational strategies used by Jewish families as well as greater attention to the "affective dimensions of Jewish family life." The questions that she set forth as a research agenda remain relevant today:

> Was the Jewish family able, for the most part, to serve as a buffer between its members and the demands of a new society while preparing its children for integration? If so, what were its special strengths? Are there similarities between Jewish and other immigrant families accommodating to new societies? Which immigrant settings were most conducive to the stability of the Jewish family? What has been the impact of migration upon the Jewish family and particularly upon intergenerational relations within the family circle?[3]

In this essay, I explore one body of evidence concerning the strategies of American Jewish families and their impact on American society and culture. I will look specifically at the American Jewish mother, a major character in the drama of Jewish family life, and her contributions to community life. Unfortunately, the caricature of the Jewish mother obscures her significant and varied contributions to family life and community building. Guilt-producing, nagging, and overprotective, this cardboard "Jewish mother" is continually depicted as a colossal, often malevolent figure, her negative imprint all over the lives of her children. Existing scholarship that touches on the Jewish mother generally focuses on Jewish sons' mother-blaming, although Jewish daughters have also scapegoated mothers; their attempts to connect with their Jewish mothers, as well as rebel against them, helped inaugurate and propel second-wave feminism.

Yet there is ample evidence that points, not to overprotection and "nagging" as parental strategies of Jewish family life, but to a style that privileged openness and flexibility, particularly on the part of Jewish mothers. Evidence provided in literary sources, historical and sociological reports, and behavioral and social science studies suggest that we must consider the Jewish mother as an important modernizing influence in her children's lives, encouraging their educational and professional goals, supporting personal and family choices, and nurturing spiritual and community involvements. While the extraordinarily upward mobility of second- and third-generation Jews in American life has been well noted (variously attributed to such factors as religious tradition and the penchant for education), these data suggest that family dynamics — especially, maternal strategies of child rearing — are contributing factors both to economic advancement and to the achievement of distinctive personal, communal, and civic goals. Historians and social scientists can profit by closely interrogating these maternal strategies. Mothers' communication of social attitudes, the creation of "family myths" and family stories, the use of incentives and discipline, direct teaching, role modeling, and social interactions have each played a role in transmitting values and visions of communal life to the next generation.[4]

Jewish women's deep philanthropic and community involvements are a matter of historical record. In the United States, even more than the Old World, Jewish women encountered enhanced opportunities to lead and shape charitable endeavors. As Hasia Diner has noted of women's benevolent work in the nineteenth century, "the mere fact of women's active public involvement" in philanthropy represented a "departure from the past."[5] By the end of the century, opportunities for such leadership had greatly expanded, as new associations of women, both secular and Jewish-sponsored, organized on behalf of reform causes to provide means of social betterment to those less fortunate. Jewish women participated in a veritable Jewish women's movement, visiting immigrant families, building settlement houses, creating such local and national organizations as the National Council of Jewish Women, Hadassah, and Sisterhoods of Personal Service. "Contrary to the popular view of American Jewish women as being narrowly focused upon family, home, and hearth," June Sochen noted in an early study of Jewish women's public lives, they were "among the first Americans who identified the social problems that needed solving in urban-industrial America; they raised money, attended meetings, and lectured on their cause with zeal and patience."[6] The voluntaristic concerns of Hadassah and NCJW moved outward as well, as these organizations worked to provide desperately needed services to European refugees and to the struggling population of the Yishuv.

From the maternalism of Jewish women involved in Progressive Era reform movements to the voluntarism of their midcentury successors, a concern for community well-being, local, national, and international, had become so characteristic of American Jewish women that observers considered it a gender-linked trait. Writing about Jewish suburban life in the 1950s, Rabbi Albert Gordon commented on Jewish women's distinctive attraction to community service. Gordon drew attention to Jewish mothers' community activism, reflected in their membership in Jewish organizations such as "Hadassah, the Women's Zionist Organization, Pioneer Women, Mizrachi, Women's Auxiliary of a hospital, O.R.T., or the Women's Division of Brandeis University, Federations or Jewish philanthropies" as well as secular organizations like "the League of Women Voters, the PTA (usually more than one) . . . the Garden Club . . . the Cub Scouts and the Brownies . . . the March of Dimes, Community Fund, Salvation Army, Muscular Dystrophy and/or any other organization that requires support."[7] Gordon commented as well on the vital role Jewish women played in religious life: "no synagogue in America could function well these days if it were not for the women who help to blueprint the program, agitate for its adoption and support it with their devoted efforts."[8] In their study of the Jews of a midwestern town dubbed "Lakeville," Marshall Sklare and Joseph Greenblum agreed that the differential response of men and women to organizational life was one of the outstanding features of "Jewish identity on the suburban frontier." Like Gordon, Sklare and Greenblum found the greater involvement of women in Jewish and communal organizational life to be so pronounced that they argued that "traditional sex roles have been . . . upset." Nothing less than a "sex gap" existed in suburbia, with Jewish women deeply involved in multiple organizations and Jewish men involved in comparatively few.[9] Jewish women's activism stretched beyond voluntary local organizational life to fuel many of the most important social movements of the twentieth century, including the antiwar movement of the 1950s, the civil rights movement of the 1960s, and second-wave feminism in the 1960s and early 1970s.[10]

While Jewish women's involvement in communal service and political life has been well documented, the question of how ideals of service and activism become ingrained in women's lives has been far less studied. One suggestive body of evidence about the transmission of communal values from mothers to daughters comes from memoirs and fiction. Women writing stories of immigrant families in both genres frequently referred to their mothers' helpful attitudes toward friends, family, neighbors, and coworkers, providing multiple examples of their community concerns. Immigrant writer Kate Simon, for example, describes her father's objections to her mother's neighborhood involvements in her memoir *Bronx Primitive*: "Why didn't my mother mind her own business," he said, "what the hell did these people, those foreign ignoramuses, mean to her. The answer was short and always the same, '*Es is doch a mench*,' yet these are human beings, the only religious training we ever had, perhaps quite enough."[11] In her autobiography, *I Belong to the Working Class*, social activist Rose Pastor Stokes praised her mother for her organizing work. "My mother never failed to agitate other workers," she boasted, "and exhort them to have courage and defy the masters; and she would always tell the story of her strike."[12]

In *Tell Me a Riddle*, writer Tillie Olsen creates a remarkable character, Eva, a mother and grandmother who had been a revolutionary during her girlhood in Russia, who is modeled after Olsen's mother. Eva spends a lifetime caring for her family, yet feels responsible for all the children of the world. As Eva lays dying, her children ask, "what did you learn with your living, Mother, and what do we need to know?" She gives the answer on her deathbed: "*Lift high banner of reason . . . / Justice Freedom Light / Humankind*."[13] Feminist author Kim Chernin was raised on stories of her mother's political involvements. Chernin recalls that "I sat at the edge of my seat. I held my breath. I didn't want to miss a word. Who ever heard of such a woman before? I wanted to be just like her. And I thought I could be. Her dedication. This struggle to make a better world for people. That interested me all the time I was in high school. I could not stand injustice."[14]

The link between motherhood and community care was a central theme in popular broadcast media as well as in literature. *The Goldbergs*, written and produced by Gertrude Berg, was on radio and television almost continuously from 1929 through the late 1950s, and remains the most ethnically Jewish of all sitcoms to this day. Berg played the central role of Molly Goldberg, a matriarch identified by her "mixing-in" and, as one critic wrote, the "prototype of the Jewish mother for the last twenty-five years."[15] Throughout the series, Molly Goldberg parents not only her own two children and assorted relatives but the entire neighborhood. "All the people in this house are like one big family," she tells the landlord of her Bronx tenement apartment as she schemes to prevent him from raising rents.[16] According to Berg, Molly is "constantly bringing people together, forcing them to realize what their role in life must be. In a sense, she transfigures and saves each character."[17] Molly's "mixing," which her husband, Jake, constantly opposes, is a regular feature of the series. To Molly, however, "not mixing, is not fixing."[18] Mixing is part of her faith in the overriding importance of love, which, in some early shows, is presented as connected to Molly's religious beliefs. In a 1943 Yom Kippur show, young Paul, the grandson of Molly's Uncle David, asks Molly if it's a sin not to love your parents. She replies that it's a sin not to love the whole world. "You must love and obey God but you have to love and obey Him by loving your neighbor." A neighbor, she continues, is "someone who lives with you in this world," anywhere.[19]

In a 1949 episode called "Rosie's Composition," Molly wonders whether she is a "bad mother" because she has spent too much time in the community. Her self-criticism is stimulated by the fact that her twelve-year-old daughter, Rosalie, has written an essay for a school assignment that Molly fears will criticize her. To become a "model of parenthood" so that Rosie will write a more favorable report, Molly tells her family to stop her if she gives one more "yoo-hoo. . . ." "Now," she says, "for my family and only for mine family." But when Molly stops talking to her neighbors, Rosalie criticizes her for lack of "proper community spirit." The message is clear: to be a "good"mother includes "mixing" with neighbors and living "in this world," not "living only for [the] family."[20]

Taking care of neighbors and fellow workers, promoting social justice, and solving community problems, popular-culture Jewish mothers like Molly Goldberg and the real mothers of writers like Rose Pastor Stokes, Kim Chernin, and Kate Simon helped to extend the meaning of "family" and "children" beyond biological definitions. Together with maternal modeling described in these sources, first-person oral history accounts provide valuable information on the values and strategies of Jewish mothers as seen from the perspective of mothers themselves.[21] One such study, the ambitious World of Our Mothers Project led by sociologist Rose Coser and a team of interviewers in the early 1980s, offers insights into the lessons immigrant mothers taught their children by virtue of their child-rearing strategies and the examples of their own behavior. The study suggests that rather than hovering over their children protectively, hindering their advancement in the world and their personal life choices, Jewish mothers nurtured their children's familial and professional accomplishments and provided formative visions of community. Mothers' flexible parenting styles, their concerns about neighbors and world events, and their deep investment in Jewish organizational life and the affairs of the Jewish people provided their offspring with valuable "social capital" plus the vision of what a "good life" might be. "Old World" in their heritage, these immigrant mothers acted as agents of modernity in the new communities they found and made in America.

The Coser Study: World of Our Mothers

"You gotta be a diplomat. A mother has to be everything," exclaimed Rose, a Jewish New Yorker who *was* everything—a union organizer, a PTA volunteer, a mother, an unofficial foster parent, and a daughter. Interviewed while in her eighties, Rose still practiced her special form of maternal diplomacy as a volunteer at the Jewish Workmen's Circle Home, where she cared for mothers who "worked their lifetime. They never had an education, they never had anything nice, like mink coats, but they raised beautiful families."[22] One of several dozen Jewish mothers interviewed by the researchers working on the World of Our Mothers project, Rose provided an immigrant eloquence to her discussion of Jewish family life.

Rose's voice and the scores of others captured in the ambitious oral history project are described in the book *Women of Courage: Jewish and Italian Immigrant Women in New York*, published after the death of principal researcher Rose Laub Coser and completed by one of her coresearchers, historian Laura Anker, along with sociologist Andrew Perrin.[23] The volume focuses on the experiences of 100 immigrant respondents (61 Jewish and 39 Italian) who were interviewed in 1983–4. All the Jewish respondents had immigrated from Eastern Europe (e.g., Russia, Poland, Austria, Hungary, Lithuania, Rumania) before 1927 when they were at least thirteen years old (most were between fourteen and nineteen) and had lived in the New York region.[24] The average age at the time of the interviews was sixty-seven.

The narrators at the time of the interview were not only mothers but often grandmothers, so answers were inevitably filtered through the memories and experiences of a lifetime. Some narrators were frail, forgetful, or inattentive (and interviewers' comment sheets noted such facts), but most responded to the full range of questions. These were elaborated according to a fixed schedule that probed a broad range of subjects—migration, marriage, home life, food, children, family size and sexuality, home economy, entrepreneurship, work outside the home, health, education, welfare, religion, politics, philanthropy, popular culture. All interviews took place face-to-face, usually in the subject's home.

Although the published book focuses primarily on the world of work, the original surveys, archived at the Henry A. Murray Research Archive at Harvard University, provide a wealth of additional information, especially about the family lives of the narrators, including rich material about the experience of Jewish motherhood and child rearing.[25] In this essay, I draw on themes about maternal ideas and behavior suggested in the archived data as well as on the published work.

The Jewish mothers in the study form a bridge between the worlds of their own European-born parents and those of their children, conceptualizing their relationship as children of Old World parents in terms entirely different from their expectations of their American-born children. Many of these mothers spoke to their children multiple times a week, if not daily. They were "disappointed when they don't call. You think they have no time to call. But, they are busy people and you have to understand." In defining good sons and daughters, they strongly objected to a child who "moves out of the house and forgets about you." Nevertheless they themselves had often moved out of the house—and off the continent—and complained that their parents asked too much of them, as they were expected to "write and also to send support."

As immigrants, these women created their own world out of the Old World they remembered and the New World they discovered. Child rearing for them was an experiment in modifying Jewish tradition and adopting American culture. As mothers and grandmothers, the women surveyed stressed that they hoped to raise "good Americans and good Jews." Happy to be part of their new country, they did not easily forget the past. But an attachment to Judaism required nurturing for many reasons, because America offered many temptations to forget heritage. Many lived in mixed immigrant neighborhoods, which posed special challenges. As Rose summarized, "You know we lived on Garden Street in the Bronx, it was a lot of Italian people but the Italian people are good families you know, they're very strict with their children so you could trust them. . . . We got along very nicely."

According to Coser, the main differences between Jewish and Italian mothers related to the ways they responded to socialization issues: Jews maintained "centrifugal" family structures, adopting to new surroundings by "orienting out of the family, aiming to assimilate to mainstream culture." Italians, on the other hand, were more "centripetal," forming more insular groups and attempting to maintain a more thoroughly Italian culture in the United States.[26] Aside from these binary patterns, many aspects of the home and work lives of the two groups of mothers ran parallel, according to the published report. Both groups of women participated in the labor force—usually doing factory work before marriage or participating in family businesses, doing homework, taking in boarders, and other sometimes irregular employment after marriage (over 65 percent of Jewish mothers and 85 percent of Italian mothers worked when their children were young or after they left home). In their record of employment and activism after marriage, these immigrant women "forged strategies of adaptation and resistance that stressed the goals of family advancement and community welfare over entirely individual needs."[27]

Coser's brief chapter on home life in *Women of Courage* focuses on the fact that the management of domestic life and child rearing were left almost completely to women; husbands were largely uninvolved and uninterested, with the wives receiving little appreciation for their labors and no opportunity to share stories and decisions. Whatever the complaints of the Jewish narrators, Italian mothers were even more frustrated. According to Coser, another major difference in domestic relations between Italians and Jews involved disciplinary methods, with 65 percent of Italian mothers, but only 25 percent of Jewish mothers, admitting to the use of corporal punishment (spanking).

The raw study data reveal many more significant aspects of Jewish child-rearing attitudes and strategies than those cited in the published work. It is clear, for example, that at home as well as at the workplace these Jewish mothers acted decisively to ensure the welfare and survival of their families and to allow their children maximum opportunities for enrichment. Education was an absolute priority for these mothers: "in the four years he went to City College," one mother typically remarked, "I didn't buy myself a dress." When the Jewish mothers were asked which kind of child they preferred—one who did well at school or one who helped at home—they overwhelmingly rated performing well in school much higher than good conduct at home. Another question asked whether a child should miss his exams to attend a grandparent's funeral; almost all mothers responded that the child should remain in school. As one mother put it: "Education is for the future and it gives them a broader outlook on life." "I always said to them, 'learn, learn, learn,'" replied another. With rare exceptions, the women agreed that because daughters' education was equally important as sons', parents should make the same sacrifices for them as for their male offspring. Because she had not had an education, one woman explained, "my ambition in life was to have my daughters educated."

The mothers' championship of education certainly paid off. Of the approximately seventy-five children of the Jewish mothers about whom information was collected, one-fifth had completed high school or less, with more than two-thirds completing college. The largest group of children had completed postgraduate or professional degrees: several had Ph.D.s and master's degrees; other children were doctors, lawyers, dentists, and nurses. Almost as many had careers that could be characterized as professional, although there were a handful of secretaries and businesspeople (insurance, office manager, controller, advertising). The most common occupation was teacher or professor; one was a dean, and another few worked in government or were engineers. Seventy-five percent of the female children, mostly born in the 1920s or 1930s, had occupations distributed in these general areas.

Also worthy of mention is the moderate and permissive attitude of these women toward child rearing. Mothers rather than fathers were the family disciplinarians, primarily because the fathers were rarely at home. Yet it is clear that mothers prized relationships based on mutuality rather than discipline. "Mothers have to be friends to their children. Not dictators," one woman explained. "The only way you can really hold onto your children is to let them go," suggested another. "Give them as much freedom as possible, as long as they don't abuse it," replied a third. When asked how they had been most helpful to their children, the mothers had a variety of responses: providing "proper morality" and financial assistance; taking care of children and listening to them; supporting their education; showing them how to "grow up to be good citizens"; acting as role models. Mothers seemed to pride themselves most when their children considered them to be "best friends."

These Jewish mothers distinguished between interfering in their children's lives and being asked for advice. Many noted that "they do what they want anyway. It would be a different life if children listened to parents." As immigrant parents, the mothers acknowledged that, not only did children have "their own brains," but often "more knowledge" besides. Mothers could give good advice, but it wouldn't necessarily help. "She had to see for herself," one mother remarked. "This I knew." For the majority of these mothers, persuasion was definitely a more effective strategy than coercion. "Demands on child are the wrong thing," said one mother. "Treat them like you want to be treated yourself," added another. "Stop hocking [nagging]," "don't lecture." In the words of another: "have the patience for your children. . . . Try and listen to them and understand them. What they feel [and] think." As one mother explained more fully:

> [A] mother should realize that her children are independent individuals, and they should realize that they have their moods and their problems which are different from the mother's—a different age of life and a different stage of life—we have different problems and to respect that. And not to put herself on a pedestal—"I'm the mother, you listen to me!" That is not the way to improve a situation, and it's the opposite! And a mother should feel, if she's sincere and unselfish, the children need her affection and her friendship. They need it. A lot of them are starved for a mother's love! . . . Giving love and tolerance . . . makes healthier people of your children. . . . They make mistakes and you are not to harp on it. None of us are angels—we commit mistakes, we make wrong, that's all part of a human being.

Could these mothers be considered worriers or overly protective? "Mothers always worry," one respondent commented, yet replies indicated that this group of mothers was not overanxious about their youngsters' well-being. When prompted, mothers did recall such concerns as children crossing streets, getting into car accidents, or returning home late at night, but they generally believed that their children were responsible and well behaved and would not get into trouble. "They were model children," was a typical sentiment. Because they trusted their community, neighbors, and friends, and the children's peers, mothers did not feel that they had to be especially vigilant on behalf of their children's safety.

Communal bonds were extremely important to these women. They belonged to a variety of school, civic, and community associations, creating deep networks of friendship and support outside the family. According to Coser, Jewish women respondents were not at all "homebound." Many went to meetings of the PTA, Hadassah, Pioneer Women, unions, the synagogue, or the Yiddish shul parents' group on a regular basis; they were "bustling with activities," both political and cultural. "We went to meetings, Broadway shows, restaurants, and concerts," reported one woman. "Went to shows, weddings, open meetings of the union, *shul* benefits with other people in the neighborhood," recalled another. Even as the women aged, patterns of communal and civic involvement continued. "My time is taken up by my work at the Home and at the union," one narrator reported. "I gotta work in the Thrift Shop for Hadassah, and give a day there. Tomorrow I work with the Golden Age Club 15."

Though many immigrant Jewish women from similar backgrounds became nonobservant, a surprisingly large number of respondents in the survey belonged to synagogues. When asked about the transmission of Jewish values across the generations, they reported great pride in raising their children as Jews. Most related that their grandchildren were also being raised Jewishly — attending Hebrew schools, observing holidays — and this filled them with satisfaction. Strong Jewish identification appeared especially in respondents' deep attachment to Israel. Having experienced antisemitism in their countries of origin and, for many, having lost relatives during the Holocaust, it was an "electrifying feeling" when Israel was created. More than one respondent reported that she had "danced in the streets" at the wonderful news.

These experiences deeply affected respondents' sensibilities as they raised their children in the United States and largely determined the nature of their communal involvements. Most of the organizations in which respondents participated had a strong Jewish (and, most frequently, a Zionist) component — Hadassah, Pioneer Women, ORT. Explaining why she participated in so many Jewish organizations, giving them financial contributions whenever she could, one woman responded, "It helps a Jewish organization to speak for us in numbers." Another volunteered for Hadassah, UJA (United Jewish Appeal), and

222 • Women as Agents

other organizations, giving money as well to her sisterhood and the temple, "to help the Jews. Because I was Jewish and it was my place." "Hadassah is us," a mother of two daughters and a son, all of them college graduates, responded. It " builds Homeland." At the time of their interviews, many of these immigrant mothers often had decades-long relationships with Hadassah and their temple sisterhoods, even after they had moved to senior citizen homes or other retirement communities. One woman, the mother of a daughter who was a bookkeeper, another who was a nurse, and a son who was an office manager, continued to work for Hadassah "because I got a Jewish heart. I always feel I have to do something." It was important to volunteer, even if her job was only to serve coffee, "because I'm a Jewish woman and there is Jewish people. I have to do it." One member of Pioneer Women explained that she had joined the organization "to help people here [and] in Israel"; another member preferred to emphasize the benefits of belonging to a women's Zionist association: "Men didn't have the right to tell us what to do."

For a mother of three who came to the United States in 1921, when she was nineteen, World War II was a defining experience in her community involvements. During the war, this mother served as a canteen worker in her local hospital and became involved with the Red Cross as chairman of production and head of fund drives. Because of her Red Cross connections, she then chaired a local Blood Drive for Israel. This worked turned out to have ecumenical consequences when she asked her Red Cross cochair, a non-Jewish woman and a good friend, to cochair the blood drive. The friend's priest "blessed the work" they were doing and expressed how proud he was of his parishioner, offering to give "blood for Israel" if they needed him. This mother continued her hospital volunteer work for some forty years, and continued her strong Jewish involvements as well. "They used to call me the girl who couldn't say 'no,'" she remarked, recalling that she had been a member of "every organization in existence. Hadassah, Ort, B'nai Brith, the synagogue sisterhood" because "they deserved to be . . . supported." "In numbers there is strength," she believed. "As a Jewish woman, I wanted to be part of the organizations."

The experience of antisemitism was another motivating force. "When I applied for a job with the Telephone Company," recounted one mother about an incident that had happened nearly thirty years before, "I went in and made an application. I had very nice handwriting and I made a nice appearance. . . . I was well-dressed, and I filled out an application. And the woman told me . . . 'Better look for something else. I don't think there'll be anything available.' " This respondent, the mother of a daughter who was a teacher and a physician son, became active in Hadassah, ORT, B'nai Brith, the Zionist Organization of America, her local synagogue, the sisterhood of another synagogue, and other organizations that promoted interest in Israel. "I'm helping the world," she believed.

Interviewers attempted to elicit how specific experiences of the Holocaust and antisemitism had affected the way these immigrant women raised their children. They also asked respondents what they did "at home" to emphasize Jewish history, culture, and "problems." Some respondents could not provide specific answers to these probes — "we discussed it and he used to listen, and that's it," says one mother. But she reported that she was very happy that her son said his prayers. "And when he says he is going to temple, I say he is doing a good thing."

Others spoke eloquently about the motives of their child rearing. One woman who had lost her sisters and other relatives in the Holocaust explained how the tragedies of World War II influenced the kinds of values she taught her children: "I tried to make them realize that the world is small and it can reach anybody and that they should be good people. They should be good Jews. And they should be good to each other and to the whole . . . everybody around them. Not to mistreat anybody."

This respondent, who worked first as a dressmaker and then went into business with a cousin at a corset shop, raised a daughter who became a teacher and two sons who worked in advertising. She was a life member of Pioneer Women — "a very important place for me" — but contributed to a variety of other Jewish organizations: B'nai Brith, Hadassah, ORT, UJA. Another respondent, the mother of a physicist son and a daughter who was a nurse, became interested in Judaism only after her kids were born. At home, she would "lecture to them" and call their attention to "Jewishness and Jewish problems." As for her grandchildren, "I'm always telling them about it." This woman, who was "always an Executive Officer" in the many groups she belonged to, spent most of her time working for Hadassah and local Jewish centers because "they were concerned about the plight of the Jews not only here in the United States but all over the world."

A mother whose daughter had lost her job because of antisemitism felt that the "killing of Jews in World War II" had definitely affected the way she raised her children. Born in Austria in 1896, the mother of three children, including a daughter who became a high school teacher and another who was a postal clerk, she sent her children to Hebrew school, which she felt "brought Jewish life to them" to encourage their Jewish connections. For the same reason, another mother took her children every Saturday to the library "to read about Jewish history and culture." A mother of two sons, one a university professor and the other a public school administrator, remarked that both she and her husband tried to teach their children to be "good Jews." She believed that a "good Jewish woman" was not only a "good housewife" but also someone who "tries to teach the children the right way, love they neighbor as you love thyself." To teach her children about Jewish history and culture, she made sure they "read up on it" and understood what the Jewish experience "was all about." But just as importantly, "we lived it." That her grandchildren, too, went to Hebrew school was a source of great satisfaction.

Another mother explained how she encouraged her son to "continue his Hebrew education from Talmud Torah to High School." She also sent him to Jewish religious camps and "kept talking and discussing with him Judaism, what Judaism stands for," trying "to put a love into him for Jewish life." When later she complained that he was giving too much money to UJA and he couldn't afford it, her son replied that "they give blood" while he was only "giving money." The mother, who was involved with the Histradut Ivrit, the Jewish Theological Seminary ("Because it has to do with Hebrew"), and the sisterhood, because it meant supporting the synagogue, concluded that "the way I raised him made him feel that he has to help Jews."

When asked what she did at home to teach about Jewish history and problems, another mother responded, "Everything." They "told stories," went to talmud torah services on the Sabbath," and she encouraged her children's religious education. This respondent, who came to the United States in 1920, when she was sixteen, "because the Cossaks were coming," had three children, all college graduates, including a daughter who worked for Social Security. World War II had made her more aware of antisemitism in the United States, which she believed remained a potent force as her children set out on their own lives—her son-in-law, in fact, had experienced antisemitism in the workplace. Through night school, this mother had become involved in Zionism, and now, about eighty years old, she was still involved.

For one mother, the growth of the dark forces of fascism became the "stunning" force that affected her mothering. She recounts that when, in 1933, she gave birth to her son, an only child, "I noticed the newspapers mentioned the fact that Hitlersim came into power and what they're doing in Germany. I felt, 'My God, what have I brought a child into the world for?' And it was revolting to me. And, that was my answer, getting into, fighting for, Zionism. I am of Jewish extraction and my son is, and I feel that he's entitled to live in a righteous world." Although she did not bring up her son in a "religious" manner, she tried to teach him about Jewish values, especially by teaching him Yiddish. She didn't get far, because she felt it "doesn't work too well . . . with your mother as teacher." But her son became "a very good human being," an "ardent" member of his temple, deeply involved in UJA—perhaps, his mother speculated, because "he's seen me work in Hadassah and work hard on it."

Some mothers in the group had been involved with radical secular groups, not Jewish ones, exposing their children to these currents. One respondent who had been a Communist Party member recalled that she and her husband never had to worry about their daughters when they went to meetings or rallies after school, because "they were always with me." At night, neighbors who "admired us because we were people who were doing something" watched out for her children. Even the prostitutes would say, "Don't bother these kids, they're Communist kids!" Thus "the neighborhood protected them, protected us all because the Communist Party was doing good work at that time" and "they respected us." Her daughters joined political organizations as they were growing up—from the Young Pioneers to the Young Communist League—and eventually the Communist Party. Their own children became professionals—mainly professors and doctors—but maintained the family's political radicalism, which made the narrator especially proud, as she was of the family's closeness: "We always visited together . . . all our lives, always together." A lesson she tried to impart to her grandchildren and, now, great-grandchildren was one that she had taught her daughters as well: "that it's important to do things for people, to belong to the progressive places where you can really help people out—to work for the future." Though this narrator did not organize for Jewish groups, her background as a Jew in Russia had taught her the lesson that became a guide to her lifelong activism: "I learned all the hard things—what Jews go through . . . and that was my beginning."

While narrators revealed that they took pride in their own achievements as workers, citizens, volunteers, and community activists, for most success in parenting loomed largest as they looked back on their lifetime in America. Although being a mother was hard—especially the responsibility "to make sure to bring up as good a human being as possible"—the Jewish mothers in the survey believed that the rewards were well worth the effort. While often they had to put their own dreams on hold as they promoted the goals of their offspring, overall they expressed deep satisfaction with their child rearing, remarking on their children's success as family members, in their work and professional lives, and as citizens and community members. "They participate in the community," one respondent acknowledged with pride. "And they teach their children the right way to live . . . they work for Israel, they buy bonds, they sell bonds, and that's all you want from your children." A few expressed regret that they had not passed on adequate Jewish and/or religious education while others felt that "you don't have to be religious to be a Jew. . . . Just practice. Be a good person. . . . That's all." But other mothers found satisfaction in the religious and moral values they had instilled and in their offspring's deep commitments to the Jewish community. Some acknowledged that Jewish solidarity needed to incorporate broad ethical imperatives. As one mother put it, the definition of a "good Jew" was that of a "good person. If he is a Jew, he should relate to his Jewishness and he should be a good Jew. But he has got to be good."

As Coser explained it, Jewish women's social activities incorporated a "moral value," a "sense of social obligation." Survey mothers spoke specifically of their efforts to transmit such values, and husbands also recognized them as part of family ethics. As one narrator reported: "[W]hen I started to go out like this, [my husband] came and he hears me once holding a speech and he said, 'If you can talk like this you have no right to sit at home. You should be doing something for people.' And he made me do it. He made me go."[28]

. . .

The attitudes of Italian mothers that emerge from the survey offer similarities as well as contrasts with those of Jewish mothers. Jewish mothers' emphasis on mutuality and friendship and their recognition of offspring as "independent individuals" were not common among their Italian counterparts. For the latter, the concept of respect was central. Many respondents complained that children in America were less respectful than young people in Italy—they did not listen, went with bad company, and disobeyed orders. Worried about too much freedom, the Italian mothers placed primary importance on parental control: they wanted their children to listen to them, not argue with their rules, and keep them informed about what they did outside the house. These mothers expected that if they had done a good job in raising their children, the latter would naturally show respect for parents, teachers, their culture, and religion. Respect was not antagonistic with being American; rather, it would help children become successful while maintaining traditional values.

Jewish mothers also worried less about the freedom available to their children than did Italian mothers, and they referred to themselves more as their children's friends than as disciplinarians. For the Jewish mothers, openness to and sacrifice for education played the largest role in future dreams of success, while many Italian mothers expressed regret at lack of educational opportunities, achievement, and sacrifices. The Jewish mothers firmly believed that family resources should be stretched to send both daughters and sons to college. The response that men's and women's education should be valued equally was significant among these mothers.

Differences also related to communal involvement. According to Coser, one out of three Jewish respondents (22 out of 69 or 32 percent) compared to only 1 out of 31 Italian narrators reported that they regularly went to meetings.[29] There may not have been a "clear dichotomy" among these groups regarding social relationships, but Coser and her coauthors note that Jewish women's multiple contacts with the outside world provided important "social capital" for their families.[30]

Differences between Italians and Jews regarding education, achievement, and communal and family values have been noted before, and it may be useful to report the perspectives of earlier commentators. In a 1958 article, Fred L. Strodtbeck compares Jewish and Italian attitudes toward achievement, noting important differences in views on family and community life that agree with Coser's interpretation. "*La famiglia* in the Southern Italian culture was an inclusive social world," Strodtbeck writes. "Everyone outside the family was viewed with suspicion." While the Jewish family was also close-knit, "it was the entire Jewish *shtetl* community rather than the family which was considered the inclusive social unit and world," Strodbeck says. "All Jews were considered to be bound to each other."[31] For Strodtbeck and these early commentators, Jewish mobility "in all probability" had been facilitated by the successful transformation of this complex of behaviors in the New World: Jews leveraged "old-culture" attitudes like respect for learning and responsibility for the community into modes of positive achievement. In contrast to Italians' inward-looking "familism," Jews' loyalty to a larger collectivity ensured that, in Strodtbeck's view, Jews would become more like the "U.S. achiever"— the successful scientist, executive or professional Protestant whose hard work could guarantee success and the rational control of the universe.[32]

In the Coser study, Jewish mothers showed great interest not only in economic achievement but also in world affairs, often discussing them with their husbands. While Italian women were often frustrated and resentful about their husbands' narrow interests, Jewish women and their husbands loved to talk "politics, politics," as one woman put it, especially world events. As Coser and her coauthors explained, "their concerns about those who were left behind in dangerous or otherwise unpleasant situations provided the stuff of which cohesion is made."[33]

Communal ties facilitated mothers' economic contributions to family well-being. Fully 88 percent of Jewish women in the Coser survey had worked before marriage. The social relationships they forged in the workplace became a significant part of their ethnic identity and helped them extend their networks outward.[34] These women took back to their homes and to their families the broader sense of solidarity they had discovered on their jobs. About one-third of Jewish women continued to work when their children were young, with community support helping to provide child care; nearly two-thirds worked outside the home when their children were grown. The "extended bonds of mutuality" that immigrant women nurtured in their communities were important elements in the continuum these Jewish women created between family, work, and neighborhood over the course of their lives. The ties of friendship and social interaction forged through participation in Jewish and secular organizations—such as Hadassah, Ort, Pioneer Women, B'nai Brith, the PTAs of public and religious schools, even the Communist Party—also proved to be vital components of Jewish women's communal networks.

.　.　.

The snapshots of immigrant Jewish mothers' attitudes and behavior presented here indicate coherent and consistent parenting strategies. Although they pressured children to achieve and expected to enjoy close intergenerational bonds, Jewish mothers fostered generally tolerant and permissive child-rearing attitudes, which in turn encouraged an unusual degree of independence on the part of children. Overall, the cultural mores of Jewish mothers generated optimistic hopes and dreams for the future and a set of positive standards for children and for parent-child interactions. The transmission of values through deliberate teachings, the encouragement of connections to Jewish religious schools, traditions, and customs, and role modeling through their own behavior at home and in the community at large helped shaped children's attitudes, ambitions, and ethical standards. Constructed in the less hospitable environment of European shtetls, cities, and villages, these parenting strategies changed and flourished in the American setting, adapting in profound ways to the new context.

The data suggest three characteristic clusters of parenting behavior on the part of these immigrant Jewish mothers. First, the mothers established high expectations for their children's futures, placing a significant premium on education. They encouraged learning and achievement, citing a desire for their children to attend college and often to obtain further training; success meant that their offspring would take their places in the larger world, joining communities of professionals and other workers who would serve still other communities of clients. These hopes and expectations were placed on daughters as well as sons. At the same time, these mothers placed a high value on their children's overall well-being, worrying about social adjustment and other indicators of emotional happiness.

Second, the mothers tolerated a wide range of acceptable behavior and demonstrated moderate and flexible methods of discipline; punitive strategies were generally absent. Interaction with children, and usually with spouses, appeared democratic and flexible. Respect and obedience were expected but were not considered automatic responses to parental authority, which they felt needed to be fair and earned.

Third, as the dominant figures in all aspects of child rearing, bearing responsibility for socializing the child as well as for caring for its physical and emotional needs, mothers served an important role as keepers of morality. Their own experience in the workforce, which frequently continued throughout the life cycle, their involvement in community life, and their interest in the broad issues of local and world politics introduced their offspring to ways of thinking and acting that moved beyond the household. "Extended bonds of mutuality," which immigrant mothers nurtured in their neighborhoods, provided important networks of support and modeled communal interaction.

The experience of antisemitism at home and in the world, especially the tragic events of the Holocaust, deepened these mothers' commitment to Jewish communal life as well as their conviction that the way they raised their children had consequences beyond individual and family success. Many became active in Jewish and Zionist causes after the birth of their children, acknowledging that they, and eventually their offspring, needed to "help people" and play a role in creating a more "righteous" world. "The Jewish mother was very forceful in what she wants to do," declared one respondent. "We want the best for our children, and we must be forceful to assert ourselves." Whether encouraging their children's educational achievements, friendships, and social activities or working in the clothing bazaars and fund drives of Hadassah, Pioneer Women and the many other organizations to which these women belonged, often for thirty-five, forty, and even fifty years, they asserted themselves as mothers and expressed and modeled the behaviors and values they cared about.

By sustaining Jewish families, modeling attitudes of civic involvement, and encouraging achievement, Jewish mothers contributed immeasurably to Jewish and American community life. Their characteristic parenting styles—a relative absence of coercion and punitive enforcement, a reliance on self-control and confidence that children would make proper choices, and, finally, a hopeful vision of life and the sense that their children would enjoy success if they worked hard and respected moral principles—were the foundations of modernization and the building blocks of community. Mothers' focus on educational attainment and social well-being fostered an openness to learning, enabling Jewish offspring not only to become successful as individuals but also to participate in larger communities in their workplaces and in local, philanthropic, or government organizations. Their interest in passing on Jewish values, culture, and history to the next generation through religious or secular Jewish schooling, trips to the library, reading and discussions with children, and their own involvement in Jewish and secular community organizations suggests that mothers recognized and acted upon the importance of their own teaching functions in the family.

Undergirding the Jewish mother's actions and beliefs lay her own vision of the future, which shaped the ways in which her children grew and learned. Instilling communal values, stimulating behavioral styles that focused on independence and autonomy, and providing a supportive and nurturant atmosphere that was comparatively open and permissive, Jewish mothers enabled their children to develop as modern, successful, achieving, and caring citizens. Cognitively, affectively, emotionally, motivationally, and attitudinally, Jewish mothers showed their children the way to the future. In so doing, they effectively built the "villages" that in their turn would help to raise the next generations.

Acknowledgment

This article is an expanded version of material that appears in the author's *You Never Call! You Never Write! A History of the Jewish Mother* (New York: Oxford University Press, 2007).

Notes

1. David Hartman, foreword, in Norman Linzer, *The Jewish Family: Authority and Tradition in Modern Perspective* (New York: Human Science Press, 1984), p. 11.
2. Paula E. Hyman, "Afterword," in Hyman and Steven M. Cohen, eds., *The Jewish Family: Myth and Reality* (New York: Holmes and Meier, 1986), pp. 232–233.
3. Ibid.
4. On the role of parents as educators, see Seymour Sarason, *And What Do You Mean by Learning?* (Portsmouth, N.H.: Heinemann, 2004), pp. 43, 53.
5. Hasia R. Diner, *A Time for Gathering: The Second Migration, 1820–1880* (Baltimore: Johns Hopkins University Press, 1992), pp. 103–104.
6. June Sochen, *Consecrate Every Day: The Public Lives of Jewish American Women, 1880–1980* (Albany: State University of New York Press, 1981), pp. 2–3.
7. Albert I. Gordon, *Jews in Suburbia* (Boston: Beacon Press, 1959), pp. 60–62.
8. Ibid, p. 63.
9. Marshall Sklare and Joseph Greenblum, *Jewish Identity on the Suburban Frontier: A Study of Group Survival in the Open Society* (Chicago: University of Chicago Press, 1967, 1979), p. 256.
10. See, for example, Debra L. Shultz, *Going South: Jewish Women in the Civil Rights Movement* (New York: New York University Press, 2001); Joyce Antler, *The Journey Home: How Jewish Women Shaped Modern America* (New York: Schocken Books, 1997), and *Jewish Women and the Feminist Revolution*, online exhibit of the Jewish Women's Archive, *jwa.org* (2005).
11. Kate Simon, *Bronx Primitive* (New York: Harper & Row, 1982), p. 52.
12. Herbert Shapiro and David L. Sterling, *I Belong to the Working Class: The Unfinished Autobiography of Rose Pastor Stokes* (Athens: University of Georgia Press, 1992), p. 23.
13. Tillie Olsen, *Tell Me a Riddle* (New York: Delta, 1989).
14. Kim Chernin, *In My Mother's House* (New York: Harper's, 1983), p. 45.
15. Charles Angoff, "'The Goldbergs' and Jewish Humor," *Congress Weekly* 18 (March 5, 1951), 13. On Molly Goldberg, see Antler, *The Journey Home*, pp. 235–238, and Antler, *You Never Call! You Never Write! A History of the Jewish Mother*, ch. 2 (New York: Oxford University Press, 2007).
16. "The Rent Strike," Sept. 5, 1949. *Goldberg* episodes may be screened at the Museum of Radio and Television in New York and Los Angeles, at the National Jewish Archive of Broadcasting at the Jewish Museum in New York, and at the Radio and Television Archive at the University of California at Los Angeles.
17. Donald Weber, "Popular Culture and Middle-Class Imagination: The Figure of Gertrude Berg in Radio and Television, 1930–1962," 1993, unpublished paper, p. 36. Also see Weber, *Haunted in the New World: Jewish American Culture from Cahan to the Goldbergs* (Bloomington: Indiana University Press, 2005), ch. 6.
18. *The Goldbergs*, April 3, 1950.
19. *The Goldbergs*, October 22, 1943, Yom Kippur show.
20. "Rosie's Composition," October 10, 1949, University of California at Los Angeles Film Archive.

21. I would like to thank Alexis Antracoli, Denise Damico, and Jessica Lepler for assistance in processing data from the Coser study.

22. This research used the World of Our Mothers Study of Jewish and Italian Immigrant Women data set (made accessible in 2001, original paper records and audiotapes). These data were collected by Rose Laub Coser and are available through the Henry A. Murray Research Archive of the Institute for Quantitative Social Science at Harvard University, Cambridge, Massachusetts (Producer and Distributor). All quotations without endnote references are from anonymous coded interview respondents in this study.

23. Rose Laub Coser, Laura S. Anker, and Andrew J. Perrin, *Women of Courage: Jewish and Italian Immigrant Women in New York* (Westport, Conn.: Greenwood Press, 1999). The research team consisted of Coser, Anker, and two other sociologists, Kathy Dalhman and Gladys Rothbell. Prof. Rothbell designed and administered the study's methodology.

24. Some interviews were conducted in Florida and California, where subjects had moved from the New York region.

25. World of Our Mothers Study of Jewish and Italian Immigrant Women, Henry A. Murray Research Archive.

26. On p. 4 of *Women of Courage*, Coser et al. refer to Italian families as "centrifugal" and Jewish families as "centripetal," but they explain in fuller detail that the Italian family is "centripetal" and the Jewish family "centrifugal" on pages 40, 43.

27. Ibid., p. 144.

28. Ibid., p. 43.

29. Ibid.

30. Ibid., p. 46.

31. Fred L. Strodtbeck, "Family Interaction, Values, and Achievement," in Marshall Sklare, ed., *The Jews: Social Patterns of an American Group* (New York: The Free Press, 1958), p. 151. For a more contemporary view of Italian immigrant women, see Jennifer Gugliemo, "Negotiating Gender, Race and Coalition: Italian Women and Working Politics in New York City, 1880 to 1945," Ph.D. dissertation, University of Minnesota, 2004.

32. Ibid., p. 155. On the many works on Jews and economic advancement, see, for example, Leonard Dinnerstein, "Education and the Advancement of American Jews," in Bernard J. Weiss, ed., *American Education and the European Immigrant, 1840–1940* (Urbana: University of Chicago Press, 1982), pp. 44–60, and in the same volume, Selma Berrol, "Public Schools and Immigrants: The New York City Experience," pp. 31–43, and Salvatore J. LaGumina, "American Education and the Italian Immigrant Response," pp. 61–77.

33. Coser, Anker, and Perrin, *Women of Courage*, pp. 64–65.

34. Ibid., p. 129.

Feminism and the American Jewish Community

Feminist movements have always imagined utopian communities. Feminism, after all, called for equal rights for women in societies in which women were legally subordinated and lacked both social status and power. Envisioning a society in which women were equal required imagining a situation that had not ever existed. As the struggle for equal civic rights ground its way slowly through the nineteenth century, some feminists dreamed of liberating women from the burden of housekeeping responsibilities, of enabling free love, and even of establishing all-female communities.[1] In the twentieth century control of one's reproduction, through contraception and abortion, and ultimately control over one's body, became the most prominent utopian demands of the women's movement in America.

Utopianism occurs only when its proponents are single-minded and see little possibility of quickly achieving piecemeal solutions to pragmatic issues that demand attention. Jewish feminism has always faced both competing identity claims and opportunities for limited change. I am defining Jewish feminism as various movements of Jewish women who have endorsed feminist goals and seen themselves at the same time as fully a part of the "Jewish community." For them, feminism provides a lens to analyze the problems of that community and to develop solutions to those problems. For those individual feminists who were also Jewish but found the community so mired in patriarchal assumptions and so resistant to change that they felt alienated from it, the Jewish community did not assert competing claims to their feminism. They chose to take advantage of the postemancipation modern option of a secular, rather than a Jewish, identity and to dismiss Jewish communal concerns as irrelevant. The Jewish feminists I am addressing asserted that both their Jewishness and their feminism were essential to their identity. As the feminist theologian Judith Plaskow, who described her 1990 book *Standing Again at Sinai* as "a theology of community," wrote of her own commitment to a whole Jewish/feminist identity, "sundering Judaism and feminism would mean sundering my being."[2] That statement, however, does not exhaust the ongoing debates, often within each individual Jewish feminist, as to how to reconcile compelling feminist critiques of Judaism with an essentialist commitment to one's Jewishness and to the Jewish people.

The pragmatic nature of Jewish women's and Jewish communal needs have also diminished the utopian element of Jewish feminism. The Polish Jewish Feminist Organization of the 1920s, the Yiddisher Froyen Organizatsie, for example, fully embraced and articulated feminist goals of equality, including female suffrage in the *kehile*, but chose not to place those goals at the top of its agenda. Instead, it focused on providing vocational education, day care, and political and cultural education to the needy masses of Jewish women in Poland. The German Jüdischer Frauenbund, founded in 1904, called for female leaders to have a say in communal matters and for women to be granted the right to vote in the *gemeinde*, but their form of feminism was rooted in philanthropic care for impoverished Jewish women and children and focused on the issue of what was then called white slavery.[3] In the United States the National Council of Jewish Women (NCJW) similarly sought recognition in communal allocation of funds and came to articulate feminist goals particularly after World War I, but its primary concern was to meet the needs of disadvantaged women and children.[4] Although all these organizations had (or in the case of the NCJW still has) a strong feminist consciousness, for the most part they framed their work in the language of domestic or social feminism, rather than in the language of equal rights. They also recognized as most compelling the general issues that mobilized the Jewish community of their time: poverty, Zionism, and antisemitism. Similarly, contemporary Jewish feminists in America participate actively in communal discussions about Jewish continuity and the situation of Israel.

Despite, or perhaps because of, their commitment to the Jewish community, Jewish feminists articulated strong criticism of the nature of Jewish communal institutions and of religious tradition. In contemporary times, dissent is often understood as weakening the Jewish community, which many claim requires unity to survive. Yet the attack on Jewish feminists has been relatively muted, in part because Jewish feminists criticized from within, even if not as quietly as communal leaders may have preferred, and because feminism brought some disaffected and alienated Jews back into the community. As Lewis Coser demonstrated in his now classic work, *The Functions of Social Conflict*,[5] conflict can serve to reinforce group cohesion and stability and clarify social boundaries. American Jewish feminism reinforced the cohesion of the majority of

American Jews who defined their Jewishness in terms of their liberal social agenda; feminism was part of that agenda. It also sharpened the line between Orthodox Judaism and the Reform, Conservative, and Reconstructionist movements and shifted the social boundaries within Orthodoxy.

American Jewish feminism that developed as "second wave" feminism exploded in the United States in the late sixties and early seventies addressed the Jewish community largely in terms of rights and only secondarily in terms of a new vision of community. The demand for equal access, the extension to women of rights accorded to men, has been largely successful in terms of the synagogue; much of the "equal access" agenda has been met in the course of the past thirty years. The more amorphous questions connected with envisioning a community different from what was inherited remain in the realm of theory.

The demand for equal access did, of course, envision a changed community in that power would no longer be wielded by men alone. Jacqueline Levine, a vice president of the Council of Jewish Federations and Welfare Funds and one of the highest-ranking women in Jewish communal life — the token woman, as she described her position — eloquently raised the issue at the annual meeting of the 1972 Council of Jewish Federations. "We are asking that our talents of maintaining Jewish communal life through the centuries . . . not be set aside any longer on the grounds of a pre-fabricated sexual role difference," she proclaimed. "We are asking, in short, to be treated only as human beings, so that we may be . . . participants in the exciting challenge of creating a new and open and total Jewish community."[6] The 1976 feminist book *The Jewish Woman: New Perspectives*, which grew out of the 1973 New York Conference on the Jewish Woman, included an article surveying the underrepresentation of women in communal organizations and suggesting strategies for change.[7]

In its early years in the 1970s *Lilith*, then the only self-declared Jewish feminist magazine, also devoted several articles to the absence of women in leadership positions in the organized Jewish community.[8] In a major survey of the Jewish community a decade later, *Lilith* provided a number of assessments. Jacqueline Levine stressed progress, especially in the volunteer realm, but noted that there were only four women on the UJA's (United Jewish Appeal) national board.[9] Rela (Geffen) Monson, who commented that there were sweeping changes in the federation world, acknowledged that the women who functioned in the federations were chosen because of their husbands' status and that the women who served on boards of national Jewish organization were "window dressing."[10] The article noted the continued salary gap between women and men as well as the fact that there were no female directors of Jewish Community Relations Councils in big cities. Naomi Levine, formerly one of the highest-ranking women in Jewish communal life who had resigned her position at the American Jewish Congress to become a vice president at New

York University, concluded in the same issue, "I have not seen any real progress in the top category in the past ten years. In fact, we're worse off today than ten years ago."[11] All the critics of the communal system noted that the persistence of women's auxiliaries, such as the Women's Division of the UJA, was a sign of women's lack of power, an issue that the article on Jewish communal institutions in *The Jewish Woman* had seen as disputed among feminists.

The lead author of the 1985 *Lilith* survey, Aviva Cantor, offered the most radical critique: "The time has come to acknowledge that not only can the system not be changed from within but it is not worth salvaging and changing." Instead, she argued, American Jews should fashion a completely different system, egalitarian, democratic, and open to people with ideas (and, by implication, not just money).[12] This radical critique of the Jewish community never became a major tenet of Jewish feminists, in part because they lacked resources for organizing, in part because when they did organize, Jewish feminists focused on issues of women's role in the synagogue, in part perhaps because most Jewish feminists shared Naomi Levine's pessimism and recognized that opportunities for ambitious women were more plentiful in the larger society than in the Jewish communal organizations. Although there are more women in positions of Jewish communal leadership than three decades ago, women have not attained parity in the Jewish communal world.

Feminist pressure and funding has recently raised the previously dormant issue to prominence. In February 2004, the United Jewish Communities (UJC), the umbrella organization of the federation world, announced an initiative to "seek increased participation by females in its new Mandel Executive Development Program." That announcement derived from a report on the status of women, titled "Creating Gender Equity and Organizational Effectiveness in the Jewish Federation System," a joint venture of the UJC and the organization Advancing Women Professionals and the Jewish Community (AWP). Spearheaded by AWP's founding president, Shifra Bronznick, the report examined gender issues within Jewish communal institutions and led to a public affirmation by the president of the UJC that "bridg[ing] the gender gap and expand[ing] opportunities for women who want to advance in federations" was a goal of his organization.[13]

Still, the impact of Jewish feminism on communal life in the past thirty years can be measured primarily by changes in the synagogue and in religious education and by changes in the topics of discussion within the Jewish community and its institutions. It's important to recognize that Jewish feminism was immeasurably facilitated by the pervasiveness of feminist discourse in American society in the 1970s, especially in the liberal circles to which many Jews have gravitated. The fact that other American religious groups confronted feminist challenges also "normalized" the issues that feminists were raising in various Jewish denominations.

The most obvious change in the Jewish community that has resulted from feminist pressure is the opening up to women of roles of religious leadership that had been reserved for men. In Conservative, Reconstructionist, and Reform synagogues the rabbi now may be a woman. The first woman rabbi in America was ordained by the Reform movement in 1972, before feminist pressure was mobilized. The Reconstructionists followed suit in 1974, and the first Conservative woman rabbi was ordained in 1985.[14] There were in spring 2004 almost 700 women rabbis in the United States. Hebrew Union College (HUC) had ordained 417 since 1972 (and 8 more in Israel since 1992), the Jewish Theological Seminary 138, and the Reconstructionist Rabbinical College 118 since 1974. Interestingly, women entered the cantorate later than the rabbinate, even in the Reform movement, which had no halakhic obstacles to contend with. Since 1975 HUC had invested 161 female cantors, who constituted about 40 percent of the total, while the 87 women of the Conservative Cantors' Assembly comprised almost 20 percent of its 500 members.[15] Within the Reform movement there have also been many uncertified female cantorial soloists—Debbie Friedman being the best known. Perhaps because the cantor is seen as subordinate to the rabbi, there appears to be less communal resistance to having a female cantor than a female rabbi.[16] Women have also assumed active, participatory roles in non-Orthodox synagogue ritual, including chanting from, and being called to, the Torah in Conservative services. With bat mitzvah for a daughter as expected as bar mitzvah for a son and the gap between the Jewish education of males and females narrowing over time, the linkage between synagogue skills and gender has been severed. The category of the learned within the Jewish community has also expanded; the inclusion of women necessitates rethinking the very definition of status and authority within the community.

Although women are not permitted to be rabbis in any of the streams of American Orthodoxy, feminism has made its mark on Orthodoxy in America. Most Orthodox women claim not to be feminists, but feminism has changed the experience of all women in the Orthodox community.[17] Young Orthodox women simply take for granted the new conditions that older feminists have struggled to achieve. Feminists have pushed the halakhic envelope in terms of ritual, establishing women's *tefillah* (prayer) groups, beginning in the late 1970s. In 1984 five rabbis from Yeshiva University issued a one-page responsum banning women's tefillah groups, women's *hakafot* on Simhat Torah, and women's Megillah readings on Purim.[18] Their authority intimidated many Orthodox communal rabbis. Subsequent articles by Herschel Schachter, one of the RIETS Five, as they came to be known, personally vilified the women who led the informal network of prayer groups. Despite the hostility that women participating in women's prayer groups encountered, they persevered. A 1988 *psak* by the Va'ad Harabonim of Queens reiterated that women's tefillah groups were against Jewish law, and yet women's prayer groups continue to exist. It is estimated that there are about seven hundred such groups worldwide, with the vast majority located in the United States.[19] That fact suggests a weakening of the unquestioned authority of some Orthodox rabbis. Women who affirm their loyalty to halakha have asserted their own reading of halakhic texts.

Orthodox feminist parents, female and male, and their rabbinic supporters have also found ways to ritually celebrate a girl's becoming a bat mitzvah. Although most such ceremonies do not include reading from the Torah or chanting the haftarah, when the ritual is held in a woman's tefillah group, the bat mitzvah girl does have those opportunities. Again feminism has raised questions of what constitutes a davening community and of how a community bound by halakha should deal with issues that affect the status of half its members.

The self-empowerment of Orthodox feminists is most visible in JOFA, the Jewish Orthodox Feminist Alliance. Founded in 1997, in the wake of the first (of now five) international biannual conferences that regularly draw two thousand participants, JOFA advocates "meaningful participation and equality for women in family life, synagogues, houses of learning and Jewish communal organizations to the full extent possible within halakha."[20] It maintains a website and publishes a newsletter, the *JOFA Journal* (established in 1998). While it always defers to rabbinic authority, JOFA has identified sympathetic rabbinic voices and also ensures that the issue of the *agunah*, the chained wife unable to secure a *get*, a Jewish divorce, remains high on the agenda of the Orthodox community. The *JOFA Journal* regularly reports on matters pertaining to the situation of *agunot*.[21] The JOFA website not only includes references to articles about agunot; it also provides links to advocacy groups worldwide.

The significance of feminism to the Orthodox community can be measured by the fact that in the past twenty-five to thirty years—and especially recently—articles about Jewish feminism have proliferated in Orthodox journals. This phenomenon reflects the reality that feminist issues, which most American Jews see as resolved (or irrelevant), remain unresolved within Orthodoxy, and feminist Orthodox women and their male allies are aware of the significance of those issues. Writers for the journal *Tradition*, which represents centrist Orthodoxy, continue to wrestle with the ability of halakha to respond to pragmatic issues, such as the *aguna*, as well as with such philosophical questions as egalitarianism.[22] Agudath Israel's *The Jewish Observer*, and the Orthodox Union's *Jewish Action*, on the Right, continue to publish articles suggesting the danger that feminism poses to Orthodoxy.[23] Those articles, when they do not demonize feminists, dismiss them, in one example, as having fallen prey to the American sin of self-indulgence, as they evaluate mitzvot by the criterion of personal fulfillment and defy the difficult aspects of obedience to God's will.[24] But *Jewish Action* has occasionally acknowledged that feminists raise important questions that cannot simply be dismissed and has published a few women reflecting on their pain at their exclusion from ritual and study and their delight when they have the opportunity to learn within an Orthodox context.[25] Orthodox writers, such as Tamar Ross and Joel Wolowelsky, have also discussed questions of Orthodoxy and feminism in general Jewish journals such as *Judaism*.[26] Self-defined Orthodox Jewish feminists thus challenge the Orthodox Jewish community, as JOFA puts it, not only to define its norms but also to "respect and protect the rights of those who may be affected by the definitions or left out of those definitions. Perhaps the Orthodox community has a larger struggle because the norms are more limited and more defined."[27]

The most significant influence of feminism on the lives of Orthodox girls has been in the realm of education. Although many Orthodox educators would deny that the changes in the education of girls are responses to the feminist challenge, in the decades since the emergence of feminist voices the education of girls has been enhanced in Orthodox schools. In fact, in a recent study in which forty modern Orthodox women and twelve men participated in in-depth interviews about Jewish feminism, all cited as areas of change related to feminism "high level Jewish education for women."[28] To be sure, girls are not educated to the same extent as boys in the study of Talmud, but the study of Talmud is now an integral part of girls' education at least in modern Orthodox institutions. When they graduate from Orthodox high school, girls are expected to study at a "*mikhlala*" or "*midrasha*," the parallel institution to a male *yeshiva*, in Israel. Institutions like Drisha in New York City have pioneered in advanced education in classical Jewish texts for female students. Founded in 1979, Drisha describes itself as a "forum for empowering Jewish women to be Jewish scholars and educators." It notes today that "the long-term impact of Drisha on the world-wide community is reflected in the informed voice and active leadership of the women who have graduated from Drisha and now serve as scholars, educators, and role models in every sphere."[29] Some current Drisha students have even indicated their interest in becoming rabbis.[30]

The contemporary American Orthodox concern for providing a significant Jewish education for girls is analogous to the Orthodox response in Poland to the challenge not of feminism per se but of secular education. When Agudath Israel, in 1919, adopted Sarah Schenirer's Beis Yaakov schools to provide a supplementary Jewish education for girls attending secular public or private schools, and when the Chofetz Chaim the previous year endorsed teaching Tanach and rabbinic ethics (but not Talmud) to girls because of the conditions of the time, that is, the strong lure of assimilation, they were engaging in innovation for the sake of defending Jewish tradition from competing claims.[31] Introducing enriched Jewish education for girls in Orthodox institutions in contemporary America is a similarly defensive measure to reinforce the loyalty of Orthodox girls and women and to counter the feminist message that traditional Judaism is irredeemably patriarchal. Yet, however defensive the move, the inclusion of women among the learned challenges the presumption that religious authority resides among men alone. Orthodox Jewish feminists have at least raised the question of whether and when women will be rabbis or *poskot* (decisors) recognized within the Orthodox community.[32] As Blu Greenberg has phrased it in a recent *JOFA Journal*, "*To'anot, yo'atzot, madrichot ruchaniot*, congregational interns, *shul* presidents, torah *layners*, executive directors, day school principals, *mashgichot, gabbaiot*, scholars-in-residence, contributors to halachic journals, megillah chanters, tefillah organizers, ketubah readers—titles we never imagined, words that did not appear in our lexicon barely a decade ago. . . . Taken together, the new titles and positions for women constitute a fundamental redefinition of women's roles in traditional Judaism."[33]

Feminism has led to changes in Jewish liturgy and hence in the Jewish davening community. Indeed, what siddur Jews use often defines their community. Within non-Orthodox Jewish religious movements and prayer groups, in fact, the impact of feminism has been most apparent in pointing to the inadequacy of traditional liturgy. Feminist discussions of God-language and the metaphors of prayer struck a responsive chord, especially in the Reform and Reconstructionist movements, but also among those spiritual seekers who have been labeled as following the amorphous movement of New Age Judaism. By focusing on the pervasiveness of the masculine imagery for God in traditional liturgy, feminists opened a broad discussion of the language of prayer precisely when many laypeople and religious leaders in the liberal movements were thinking about revising their *siddurim* so that they might better reflect the worldview of those who used them.[34] Most significant was the exchange in the pages of *Tikkun* magazine between Marcia Falk, indubitably the most important creator of feminist liturgy, and Lawrence Hoffman, the preeminent scholar and designer of Reform liturgy.[35] Initial liturgical changes ranged from eliminating the morning blessing "Who Hast Not Made Me a Woman" to introducing the matriarchs, sometimes only as an option, into the *amida*, the core of the service. Virtually all the changes have been located in the English translation of the liturgy; the Hebrew most often remains untouched. The mainstreaming of feminist ideas is reflected in the teaming up of Conservative liturgist Jules Harlow, the editor of the movement's prayer books, with feminist activist Tamara Cohen to produce a guide to Jewish prayer under the auspices of the Hadassah organization.[36]

More radical feminist critiques for revisioning God have yet to make their way into nationwide *siddurim*, though feminist groups have incorporated them in their own prayer books and local congregations have included them in their self-designed prayer books.[37] The synergy of feminism and "New Age"

Judaism, however, has fueled experiments with creative worship that have gradually been mainstreamed into Reform and Reconstructionist services. What I am suggesting here is that feminism, in conjunction with the spiritual quest that American Jews have shared with other Americans in the past generation, has fostered receptivity to new forms of Jewish religious expression, thus changing the public face of American Judaism as expressed within the Jewish community.

In addition to liturgical change, feminists have introduced new rituals that have brought women into communally performed events in which they were previously either absent or marginal. In doing so, they have sensitized Jewish men as well as women to the erasure of women from the Jewish narrative and have developed a model of a more inclusive community.[38] As in the case with liturgical innovations, information about the new rituals initially passed through personal contacts and publicity in feminist publications. Leaders and educators within the Conservative, Reconstructionist, and Reform movements, however, began disseminating information about the innovations as well as new feminist midrashim by the 1980s. The Conservative-sponsored *Melton Journal*, the *Reconstructionist*, and the *Journal of Reform Judaism* have all participated in "normalizing" ritual change and feminist approaches to interpretation within their movements, as have *Tikkun* and *Hadassah* magazines. The Reconstructionists have also established a women's center called Kolot at the Reconstructionist Rabbinical College that fosters women's spirituality and creativity, while the Jewish Theological Seminary now has a Women's Studies Program to promote the study of women in Judaism and in Jewish history.

The most significant new feminist ritual that has become a fixture in American Judaism is the baby naming for a newborn girl. Traditionally, the birth of a daughter was barely noted in ritual terms; the father would be called to the Torah and name his daughter virtually in passing. Neither mother nor baby was present. In the early 1970s feminist parents developed a variety of ceremonies that celebrated the birth of a daughter in a communal setting, though originally not in the synagogue. As early as 1977, Ezrat Nashim, a small Jewish feminist group, privately published a collection of such ceremonies under the title *Blessing the Birth of a Daughter: Jewish Naming Ceremonies for Girls*.[39] Orthodox feminists discovered and revived the Sephardic ritual of *Seder Zeved Ha-bat*, a home ritual that celebrated the birth of a daughter. So widespread was the feeling among Jews of the inequity in the way boys and girls were welcomed into the Jewish community that these ceremonies, lay inspired and lay led, became so popular that rabbis soon began to perform synagogue naming-rituals that included mother and baby and more of a communal celebration than simply a father's aliyah had previously demonstrated. A communal "new tradition" that extended to Jews who would not have described themselves as feminist was created in less than a generation.

Similarly, the feminist symbolic placement of Miriam on the seder table, with a cup of water dedicated in her honor, has been mainstreamed into a statement of women's mythic and real roles in Jewish history. Within major American Jewish denominations, the recognition of the justice of women's call for equality led to overt references to women's roles in the Exodus story. In 1982 the Conservative movement's Rabbinical Assembly, for example, published a new Haggadah, *The Feast of Freedom,* edited by Rachel Anne Rabinowicz, that highlighted women's roles by adding midrashic narrative to the basic text. As in the case with liturgical change, the synergy of feminism and New Age Judaism facilitated the acceptance of new rituals.[40]

These new rituals expanded the community rather than dividing it. That is, they added women to a communal celebration; they did not segregate them. Even the women's seder, which does temporarily divide women from the larger community as it focuses on women's responses to the main themes of the Passover holiday, is celebrated in addition to the inclusive family or communal seder, not instead of it. Nor does it exclude men from participating. One of the most popular rituals that Jewish feminists have created, the women's seder—Ma'yan's in New York City alone annually attracted eight hundred participants—apparently serves to enlarge the community, bringing women who have felt alienated from traditional Judaism (because of its perceived gender discrimination) into the Jewish community. Through random conversations with young Jewish women who have become newly involved in Jewish public activity, I have repeatedly heard of how Jewish feminist rituals and celebrations, and particularly the women's seder, have drawn them into the Jewish community. Feminist ritual legitimates, in a Jewish framework, their experiences as women. When they have the option to be an equal part of an inclusive community, feminists, like most women, choose not to be apart from, but rather a part of, a mixed-gender collectivity.

Feminist rituals, like the celebration of Rosh Hodesh, the new moon, attract a small following, as do rituals marking of the onset of menarche or its cessation, "crone" rituals, which celebrate a woman's aging into wisdom, or creative all-women prayer services. These rituals are meaningful to their participants and often provide secular feminists with an opportunity to experience Jewish ritual in a positive context, but they remain too separatist for most mainstream venues because they focus exclusively on women's experience. They do model, however, a vision of the celebration of Jewish rituals designed for various subsets of the community.

The emergence of feminist scholars has also transformed the way in which American Jews understand their history and community. Most of the research on Jewish women and on women and gender in Judaism has been pursued by scholars, both female and male, who define themselves as feminists. From Daniel Boyarin's feminist reading of Talmudic texts to Ada Rapoport-Albert's investigations of women in both Hasidism and Sabbateanism, from Chava Weissler's exploration of women's spirituality in seventeenth- and eighteenth-century Europe to Marion Kaplan's placement of women at the center of the creation of the German-Jewish middle class, from Rachel Adler's Jewish feminist theology to Tamar Ross's interrogation of feminism's challenge to Orthodoxy, feminist scholars have reconfigured the definitions of such basic Jewish categories as law, interpretation of Torah, and spirituality; and such fundamental themes of Jewish history as acculturation and the nature of the community.[41] They are participants in a scholarly discourse on gender that has enlivened the academy. It would be misguided to dismiss the significance of the proliferation of Jewish Women's Studies in the academic world. In the first place, the majority of young American Jews attend college, and those who sample Judaic studies courses are likely to find more references to women and gender than would have been conceivable a generation ago. Second, Jewish scholarship that focuses on women and gender remains in demand. Third, Jewish women scholars are frequent lecturers at events sponsored by communal institutions like synagogues, Jewish Community Centers, and Hadassah groups. Their very presence as learned authorities, as well as their topics, popularizes their scholarship.

To measure the influence of feminism on the American Jewish community, it is necessary, however, to go beyond the issues I have discussed: the expansion of women's roles in the synagogue, the emergence of female spiritual leaders, the enrichment of women's Jewish education, the creation and adoption of new rituals, and the flourishing of Jewish scholarship on women and gender. These are important results of Jewish feminism. There have been other changes, though, in the conceptualization and organization of community to which Jewish feminism has contributed.

Although Jewish feminists have sought a place at the communal table, they also have recognized the importance of the small groupings that facilitate self-empowerment. Influenced by the general feminist goal of creating a woman's consciousness that both identifies and transcends difference, Jewish feminists have asserted the need for an inclusive Jewish community that would not be limited to synagogue affiliation or participation in the federation world. Their own experience of marginalization within the organized Jewish community and in Jewish ritual has sensitized them to other marginalized groups in American Jewry. Through feminism many lesbians, for example, found a way to assert their presence within the Jewish community and to highlight a tradition of secular Jewish culture and political activism. The journal *Bridges*, for example, subtitled *A Journal for Jewish Feminists and Our Friends*, stated in its first issue in 1990:

> The editors bring . . . a commitment that combines the traditional Jewish values of justice and repair of the world with insights honed by the feminist, lesbian

and gay movements. . . . We are especially committed to integrating analyses of class and race into Jewish-feminist thought and to being a specifically Jewish participant in the multi-ethnic feminist movement. We will work . . . to . . . publish material which recognizes and honors difference.[42]

In addition to political issues, *Bridges* also focuses on the presentation of Jewish culture by women—poetry, fiction, and the visual arts. Because of the aversion of many lesbian feminists to much of Jewish religious tradition, they have also been active promoters of phenomena that recall the secular culture of Eastern Europe, such as klezmer music and Yiddish.[43] Two lesbian feminist anthologies, *Nice Jewish Girls* and *The Tribe of Dina*, and Rebecca Alpert's later book, *Like Bread on the Seder Plate*, were also influential because of their emphasis on the political and the secular and their efforts to include marginalized groups.[44] The feminist emphasis on the celebration of difference often directly states that the mainstream Jewish community's stress on unity has led to the erasure of those who present an image at odds with the dominant ideal: independent women, homosexuals, Sephardim, working-class Jews, singles. The Jewish feminist movement's vision of a diverse Jewish community, and its success in achieving the expansion of women's roles and the recognition of women's claims to redress of grievances (even within many segments of the Orthodox community), have paved the way for homosexuals to press their claims, with feminist support, in a parallel way.

Jewish feminism has always recognized the centrality of community. As Judith Plaskow has written,

> The conviction that personhood is shaped, nourished and sustained in community is a central assumption that Judaism and feminism share. For the Jew, for the feminist, for the Jewish feminist, the individual is not an isolated unit who attains humanity through independence from others or who must contract for social relations. Rather, to be a person is to find oneself from the beginning in community—or as is often the case in the modern world, in multiple communities. To develop as a person is to acquire a sense of self in relation to others and to critically appropriate a series of communal heritages.[45]

Plaskow's words assert the constructed nature of community but also acknowledge the centrality of community, with its inherited traditions, for the Jewish feminist. Jewish feminists not only participate in multiple communities; they also define the Jewish community itself as heterogeneous and diversified. They do not seek a unified Jewish community, but rather an inclusive one that accords women equality and power, even while recognizing that various elements of the community will continue, on the basis of halakha, to deny women equal rights defined, as most feminists would, as gender-neutral.

In the past three decades Jewish feminists have asserted that women must be regarded not as passive members of the community, subordinated to those who make the decisions, but as full participants in communal discourse and in the decision-making process itself. That is, feminists have argued that women cannot simply join a community whose structure, values, and policies have already been formulated; rather, the inclusion of women must lead to a fundamental rethinking of the structure, values, and policies of the Jewish community. As Rachel Adler has argued, the Jewish community must create a new *nomos* or law, a new universe of meaning, values, and stories to infuse our life. To create such a nomos, and "remove the stigma from gender difference, we would have to identify unstated standards that assume maleness is normative and replace them with norms that reflect gendered existences. Narratives of women's subjective experiences will be useful sources for such new norms."[46] Such a far-reaching transformation has not occurred, but there has been some recognition in Jewish communal discussions that pluralism, and perhaps even dissent, may be good for the Jews.

Jewish feminists have also reassessed their view of women's organizations within the Jewish community. Volunteer organizations, in particular, were seen as resistant to feminism and deemed slow to assert women's rights.[47] That evaluation has changed for a number of reasons. Jewish feminist scholarship has amply documented the important role that groups like Hadassah and the National Council of Jewish Women have played not only in philanthropy but also in providing a voice for women in Jewish and American politics.[48] The growing acceptance of feminist perspectives by the National Council of Jewish Women, and by Hadassah, has narrowed the gap between feminist activists and the volunteer Jewish women's organizations. NCJW does not use the term feminist in its mission statement, but its goals are feminist. It presents itself as "a volunteer organization that has been at the forefront of social change for over a century. Inspired by Jewish values, NCJW courageously takes a progressive stance on issues such as child welfare, women's rights, and reproductive freedom." It has updated the social feminist program that led it to take political stands on issues relating to women and children as early as the first decade of the twentieth century. The organization has also founded the B.A.-granting Women and Gender Studies Program at Tel Aviv University.[49]

In its mission statement, which stresses its "Jewish and Zionist education programs," Hadassah includes as one of its goals "advocating for issues of importance to women." By 1987 it had published *Bat Kol*, a Jewish education guide for women. Focusing on the status of women in Jewish law and encouraging a variety of women's voices to be heard, it proclaimed that its publication "honors Hadassah women's public voice and pays homage to fifteen years of proud achievement for the Jewish women's movement."[50] Today it runs educational programs for young adults and women, provides information on health for women, maintains a Legislative Action Center, and has raised the feminist issue of violence against women. Through the Hadassah Foundation it funds programs in Israel and the United States that are specifically feminist in orientation—for the economic empowerment of low-income women, for a women's cultural center, and for a rape crisis and domestic violence center, all in Israel, and for the creation of a self-esteem guide for girls, a Rosh Hodesh program held at Kolot to strengthen the self-esteem and Jewish identity of adolescents, and a musical by a prominent young Jewish woman composer. Hadassah is also the cosponsor of the Hadassah-Brandeis Institute, founded in 1997, that cosponsors the English-language feminist Israeli journal *Nashim* and seeks to develop "fresh ways of thinking about Jews and gender worldwide by producing and promoting scholarly research and artistic projects."[51] While continuing its commitment to Zionism and health care in Israel, its foundational raison d'être, Hadassah, which was lukewarm to Jewish feminism in the 1970s, has incorporated feminist concerns into its very mission.

Women's auxiliaries still engender dispute, because they are perceived as offering women honorific positions without real power and as preventing women from assuming leadership positions within the Jewish communal structure. The Women's Division of Federation has always been acknowledged as a way to squeeze "plus giving" from the American Jewish family, not as a means of meeting the needs of women. But an argument can be made that some women's auxiliaries in communal organizations promote a feminist agenda. The American Jewish Congress, which includes the advancement of women's equality in its mission statement, disbanded its women's division in the early 1980s and integrated women into the general institution. After a few years it reconstituted the division as the Commission for Women's Equality precisely to advocate women's issues that had lost their organized voice. The Commission for Women's Equality seeks to eliminate sex-based discrimination, support reproductive freedom, promote pay equity, encourage responsiveness to health issues, and end violence against women, and it addresses issues of women in Jewish communal life.[52]

I introduced this paper with the comment that Jewish feminism did not indulge in utopian dreams, because its adherents were not prepared to separate themselves from the Jewish communal enterprise and because they anticipated that they could transform the Jewish community in incremental steps. Yet perhaps the imagined community of Jewish feminism was utopian. In a 1980 symposium in *Lilith* titled "How to Get What We Want by the Year 2000," one participant stated confidently that in 2000 "the concept of equal opportunity for both sexes will have been mainstreamed."[53] Another envisioned a "strong, independent national Jewish feminist organization" that would provide a support system for feminists, cooperate with the woman's movement in secular society, cooperate with feminists of other faith groups, and provide a "Jewish" home for Jewish feminists who will not join existing institutions.[54] And the most radical of all called for a separate women's community—with women's synagogues and a Torah written by women. She concluded, "In my ideal future there are no rabbis or Federations. We as Jews will be an ethnic, cultural, and spiritual group within a non-threatening feminist society."[55] It is questionable whether the basic communal change that most Jewish feminists desired—the recognition of difference without the imposition of a hierarchy—has been attained. As Judith Plaskow has noted, the "hierarchical understanding of difference is perhaps the most significant barrier to the feminist reconceptualization of Jewish community."[56] Rachel Adler underscored this point in her own formulation: "difference itself needs to be redefined as *variation* rather than *deviation*."[57] Future scholars and communal activists will evaluate the success of feminism in creating a community that values difference, rather than just tolerating it.

Notes

1. See, for example, Charlotte Perkins Gilman, *Herland* (London: Women's Press, 1979), reprint of 1915 original.
2. Judith Plaskow, *Standing Again at Sinai: Judaism from a Feminist Perspective* (San Francisco: Harper and Row, 1990), pp. v, xi.
3. Marion Kaplan, *The Jewish Feminist Movement in Germany: The Campaigns of the Jüdischer Frauenbund, 1904–1938* (Westport, Conn.: Greenwood Press, 1979); Paula E. Hyman, *Gender and Assimilation in Modern Jewish History: The Roles and Representation of Women* (Seattle: University of Washington Press, 1995), p. 164; and Hyman, "The Jewish Body Politic: Gendered Politics in the Early Twentieth Century," *Nashim* 2 (1999), pp. 37–51.
4. Faith Rogow, *Gone to Another Meeting: The National Council of Jewish Women, 1893–1993* (Tuscaloosa: University of Alabama Press, 1993).
5. Lewis Coser, *The Functions of Social Conflict* (Glencoe, Ill.: The Free Press, 1956).
6. *Response* 18 (Summer 1973), p. 65. See also Sylvia Barack Fishman, *A Breath of Life: Feminism in the American Jewish Community* (New York: The Free Press, 1993), pp. 217–29.
7. Stephen [*sic*] M. Cohen, Susan Dessel, and Michael Pelavin, "The Changing (?) Role of Women in Jewish Communal Affairs: A Look into the UJA," in *The Jewish Woman: New Perspectives*, ed. Elizabeth Koltun (New York: Schocken Books, 1976), pp. 193–201.
8. Amy Stone, "The Locked Cabinet," *Lilith* (Winter 1976/77), pp. 17–21; Stone, "The Jewish Establishment Is Not an Equal Opportunity Employer," *Lilith* 4 (Fall/Winter 1977/79), pp. 25–26.
9. *Lilith* 14 (Fall/Winter 1985/86), p. 9.
10. Ibid., p. 7.
11. Ibid., p. 8. In a 1980 article, Anne G. Wolfe, of the American Jewish Committee, had come to a similar conclusion. Quoted in "How to Get What We Want by the Year 2000," *Lilith* 7 (1980), p. 19.

12. Ibid., p. 13.

13. Announcement from UJC, New York, Feb. 20, 2004, Chicago Jewish Community Online, http:www.juf.org/news_public_affairs/article?key=4941.

14. On the struggle of women in the Reform movement in America to be accepted into the rabbinate, see Pamela Nadell, *Women Who Would Be Rabbis: A History of Women's Ordination, 1889–1985* (Boston: Beacon Press, 1998). On the ordination of women at the Jewish Theological Seminary (JTS), see Beth Wenger, "The Politics of Women's Ordination: Jewish Law, Institutional Power, and the Debate Over Women in the Rabbinate," in *Tradition Renewed: A History of the Jewish Theological Seminary of America*, ed. Jack Wertheimer (New York: Jewish Theological Seminary, 1997), volume 2, pp. 483–523.

15. Hebrew Union College website, www.huc.edu, front page; conversations with representatives of the Rabbinical Assembly, the Rabbinical School of JTS, and with Cantor Steven Stein, president of the Cantors' Assembly, Feb. 19–Feb. 26, 2004. Information from Barbara Hirsh, Dean of Administration, Reconstructionist Rabbinical College, Feb. 23, 2004.

16. Sylvia Barack Fishman, "The Impact of Feminism on American Jewish Life," *American Jewish Yearbook* 89 (1989), p. 50.

17. Sylvia Barack Fishman, "Comparative Reflections on Modern Orthodoxy and Women's Issues, *The Edah Journal* 1:2, Sivan 5761 (2001), pp. 2–3. The most important work on feminism and Orthodoxy globally is Tamar Ross, *Expanding the Palace of Torah: Orthodoxy and Feminism in a Postmodern Age* (Waltham, Mass.: Brandeis University Press, and Hanover, N.H.: University Press of New England, 2004).

18. See Rivka Haut, "Women's Prayer Groups and the Orthodox Synagogue," in *Daughters of the King: Women and the Synagogue*, ed. Susan Grossman and Rivka Haut (Philadelphia: Jewish Publication Society, 1992), pp. 135–57.

19. Laura Shaw Frank, "Women's Tefillah Groups Grow and Face New Challenges," *JOFA Journal*, Fall 1998.

20. JOFA website, www.jofa.org.

21. See, for example, Sharon Shenhav, "Pursuing Justice: Notes from an Agunah Activist," *JOFA Journal* 4:4 (Winter 2004–Tevet 5764), p. 5.

22. See, for example, Marc D. Stern, "On Egalitarianism and Halakha," *Tradition* 36:2 (2002), pp. 1–30.

23. See, for example, Levi Reisman, "Feminism: A Force That Will Split Orthodoxy?" *The Jewish Observer* 31:5 (1998), pp. 37–47.

24. Emanuel Feldman, "Orthodox Feminism and Feminist Orthodoxy," *Jewish Action* 60:2 (Winter 5760/1999), pp. 12–17.

25. See Adam Mintz, "Toward a Constructive Dialogue," *Jewish Action* 60:2, pp. 10–11; Batya Gold (pseudonym), "Dancing on the Edge," ibid., pp. 19–21; Chana Henkin, "Yoatzot and Halachah: Fortifying Tradition Through Innovation," ibid., pp. 17–18; and Esther Shkop, "Women and Learning: A Personal Retrospective," *Jewish Action* 61:4 (Summer 5761/2001), pp. 18–24.

26. See Tamar Ross, "Can the Demand for Change in the Status of Women Be Halachically Legitimated," *Judaism* 42:4 (1993), pp. 478–91; Joel Wolowelsky, "Feminism and Orthodox Judaism," *Judaism* 47:4 (1998), pp. 499–507.

27. www.jofa.org, page named "community challenges."

28. Sylvia Barack Fishman, *Changing Minds: Feminism in Contemporary Orthodox Jewish Life* (New York: The American Jewish Committee, 2000), p. 74.

29. For information on Drisha see www.drisha.org.

30. Personal communication from Rachel Gordan, who interviewed students at Drisha in fall 2003, December 2003.

31. On Schenirer and Beis Yaakov, see Deborah Weissman, "Bais Yaakov: A Historical Model for Jewish Feminists," in *The Jewish Woman*, pp. 139–48. For the Chofetz Chaim's *psak*, see *Liqutei Halakha* (New York, 1959) in reference to Sota 20a, pp. 21–22.

32. See, for one example, Blu Greenberg, "Orthodox Feminism and the Next Century," *Shma*, 2000.

33. Blu Greenberg, "Orthodox Women and Leadership: The Journey Continues," *JOFA Journal* 4:4 (Winter 2004–Tevet 5764), p. 1.

34. See Marcia Falk, "Notes on Composing New Blessings: Toward a Feminist-Jewish Reconstruction of Prayer," *Journal of Feminist Studies in Religion* 3 (Spring 1987), pp. 39–53, and Falk, *The Book of Blessings: New Jewish Prayers for Daily Life, The Sabbath, and the New Moon Festival* (Boston: Beacon Press, 1999); Ellen Umansky, "(Re)Imaging the Divine," *Response* 13 (Fall/Winter 1982), pp. 110–19, and "Charting Our Future: Liberal Judaism in the Twenty-First Century," *CCAR Yearbook* 100 (1991), pp. 63–69; Judith Plaskow, "Language, God, and Liturgy: A Feminist Perspective," *Response* 44 (Spring 1983), pp. 3–14, and Plaskow, *Standing Again at Sinai*, pp. 134–46.

35. Marcia Falk, "Toward a Feminist Jewish Reconstruction of Monotheism," *Tikkun* 4:4 (July/August 1989), pp. 53–56, and Lawrence A. Hoffman, "A Response to Marcia Falk," in ibid., pp. 56–57.

36. Jules Harlow with Tamara Cohen, *Pray Tell: A Hadassah Guide to Jewish Prayer* (Woodstock, Vt.: Jewish Lights Publishing, 2003).

37. The *siddurim* include the Reform *Gates of Prayer: The New Union Prayer Book* (New York: Central Conference of American Rabbis, 1975) and *Gates of Prayer for Shabbat: A Gender Sensitive Prayerbook*, ed. Chaim Stern (New York: Central Conference of American Rabbis, 1992); the Reconstructionist *Kol HaNeshama* (Wyncote, Pa., 1989); and the Conservative *Sim Shalom: A Prayerbook for Shabbat, Festivals and Weekdays*, ed. Jules Harlow (New York: Rabbinical Assembly, United Synagogue of America, 1985).

38. For an overview of feminist ritual, see Shulamit Magnus, "Reinventing Miriam's Well: Feminist Jewish Ceremonials, in *The Uses of Tradition: Jewish Continuity in the Modern Era*, Jack Wertheimer, ed. (New York and Jerusalem: Jewish Theological Seminary of America, 1992, distributed by Harvard University Press), pp. 331–47; Rebecca T. Alpert, "Our Lives Are the Text: Exploring Jewish Women's Rituals," *Bridges* 2:1 (Spring 1991–5751), pp. 66–80; Susan Weidman Schneider, *Jewish and Female: Choices and Changes in Our Lives Today* (New York: Simon and Shuster, 1984); Penina Adelman, *Miriam's Well: Rituals for Jewish Women Around the Year* (New York: Biblio Press, 1986). For a more traditional perspective, see Tamar Frankiel, *Voice of Sarah: Feminist Spirituality and Traditional Judaism* (San Francisco: HarperSanFrancisco, 1990).

39. *Blessing the Birth of a Daughter: Jewish Naming Ceremonies for Girls*, ed. Toby Fishbein Reifman with Ezrat Nashim, 1977.

40. Rebecca Albert made the same point in her article "Our Lives Are the Text."

41. Daniel Boyarin, *Carnal Israel: Reading Sex in Talmudic Culture* (Berkeley and Los Angeles: University of California Press, 1993) and *Unheroic Conduct: The Rise of Heterosexuality and the Invention of the Jewish Man* (Berkeley: University of California Press, 1997); Ada Rapoport-Albert, " On Women in Hasidism: S. A. Horodecky and the Maid of Ludmir Tradition," in *Jewish History: Essays in Honour of Chimen Abramsky*, ed. Ada Rapoport-Albert and Steven J. Zipperstein (London: Halban, 1988), pp. 491–525; Chava Weissler, *Voices of the Matriarchs* (Boston: Beacon Press, 1998); Marion Kaplan, *The Making of the Jewish Middle Class: Women, Family, and Identity in Imperial Germany* (Oxford and New York: Oxford University Press, 1991); Rachel Adler, *Engendering Judaism: An Inclusive Theology and Ethics* (Philadelphia: Jewish Publication Society, 1998); Ross, *Expanding the Palace*.

42. *Bridges* 1:1 (Spring 1990), p. 3. The issue included, as one of the main articles, Faith Rogow, "The Rise of Jewish Lesbian Feminism," pp. 67–79.

43. As demonstrated at the 1995 Conference on Women and Yiddish, convened in New York and sponsored by the National Council of Jewish Women New York Section and the Jewish Women's Resource Center, lesbian feminists identify with Yiddish as the secular language of Jews and as a woman's language, without, however, making a sustained effort to learn Yiddish. See, in particular, the critical remarks of Sharon Kleinbaum, "Jewish Feminism, Secularism, and Religious Identity," in Conference Proceedings, *Di froyen: Women and Yiddish. Tribute to the Past, Directions for the Future* (New York: National Council of Jewish Women New York Section and Jewish Women's Research Center, 1997), pp. 89–90.

44. *Nice Jewish Girls: A Lesbian Anthology*, ed. Evelyn Torton Beck (Watertown, Mass: Persephone Press, 1982); *The Tribe of Dina*, ed. Melanie Kaye/Kantrowitz and Irena Klepfisz (Vermont: Sinister Wisdom Books, 1986); Rebecca T. Alpert, *Like Bread on the Seder Plate: Jewish Lesbians and the Transformation of Tradition* (New York: Columbia University Press, 1997).

45. Plaskow, *Standing Again at Sinai*, pp. 76–77.

46. Adler, *Engendering Judaism*, p. 40.

47. *Lilith* 5 (1978), pp.16–22: articles by Paula Hyman, Pearl Water, Betty Lieberman, and Aviva Cantor.

48. Rogow, *Gone to Another Meeting*; Hyman, *Gender and Assimilation*, pp. 163–65; and Paula Hyman, "The Jewish Body Politic: Gendered Politics in the Early Twentieth Century," *Nashim* 2 (1999), pp. 37–51.

49. NCJW website, www.ncjw.org.

50. *Bat Kol* (Fall 1987), p. 5.

51. www.Hadassah.org (see under advocacy).

52. Conversation with Mark Stern of the Commission for Women's Equality, American Jewish Congress, Feb. 19, 2004; americanjewishcongress.org, Commission for Women's Equality, see under advocacy and action.

53. Rela Geffen Monson, *Lilith* 7 (1980), p. 18.

54. Annette Daum, ibid., p. 20.

55. Jane Litman, ibid., p. 22.
56. Plaskow, *Standing Again at Sinai*, p. 7.
57. Adler, *Engendering Judaism*, p. 40. The emphasis is hers.

IV

Community and Culture

Rereading the Americanization Narratives of Antin, Zangwill, and Cahan

Imagining and Unimagining the Jewish Community

Prologue

On February 1, 2003, the NASA Space Shuttle *Columbia*, after a successful mission in space, burst into flame and exploded when it reentered Earth's atmosphere, killing its entire crew, including Israeli astronaut Col. Ilan Ramon, a payload specialist who took part in the mission. At the official, military memorial ceremony held for the fallen crew, the first to speak was a Jewish U.S. Navy chaplain, whose remarks included lines, in Hebrew, from Haim Nahman Bialik's poem *"Aharei moti"* (After my Death). Making the very first gesture of America's collective mourning allude specifically to Ilan Ramon's sacrifice bespoke the nation's greathearted generosity. It also aptly evoked the Jewish American ethos; for the American rabbi spoke not on behalf of America's Jews but in the name of his country — *including* its Jews.

He thus bore out, in a particularly moving way, the idea that it is in the common realm of American civic and political life, more so than in their particular Jewish backyard, that Jews have chosen to imbue their world with common strivings, civic participation, and expressions of symbolic loyalty and unity. Their position as part of the American community is maintained by virtue of their place in the American public square. It is *by being Jews* in that square —

speaking Bialik to the rest of America—that they realize the dual ambition of sharing in a common polity while upholding their individuality. That is the unique characteristic of American Jewry among other modern diaspora Jewries, who have invested far more than American Jews have in constructing a unified community around a central representative board and/or a chief rabbi. The Jewish community in America has proven relatively weak in the realm of internal organizational or cross-denominational unity, but relatively more attuned to the possibilities of community that they share with their fellow countrymen and women. Three hundred and fifty years of Jewish history in America have made it possible for the United States to be officially represented by a military chaplain who knows Bialik. The questions to be raised in this paper draw upon this exceptional virtue of the American diaspora and compare it with U.S. Jewry's posture on its own internal sense of communal collectivity.

. . .

The concept of the "imagined community," as suggested by Benedict Anderson and amplified by the work of Ernest Gellner and E. J. Hobsbawm, has been used in critically deconstructing the social formation of nations as symbolic collectives.[1] When, out of disparate social classes and distinctive localized subcultures, there emerges a sense that, despite their disjunctive histories, these various social groups constitute one nation, endowed with a singular national "character" and national history, we are directed by the "imagined community" thesis to pay particularly close attention to the active, directive role played by political and cultural elites, institutions, and external factors in giving rise to this new social entity. "Community" here denotes a set of social relationships, arrangements, and obligations, while the adjective "imagined" refers to the awareness and articulation of these bonds and, more particularly, to their ideological justification.

The concept of the nation as an "imagined community" is, moreover, closely associated with two further, intertwined concepts—collective amnesia and collective memory—that relate, respectively, to the erasure or devolution of social boundaries and formerly separate histories and to the reinforcement of a symbolic notion of a seamless, shared past.[2] Both are equally essential steps in the social construction of new communities that are meant to supersede their constituent subgroups. Moreover, the new "imagined" community becomes invested with significance and symbolic authority precisely because there is (as Hobsbawm put it) an "emotional void left by the retreat or disintegration, or the unavailability of *real* human communities."[3] Both processes—the disintegration or forgetting and the new construction or "imagining"—can readily be discerned in the formation of American society, both at the national level and in the formation of agglomerated American ethnic groups.[4] While various groups and institutions are actively engaged in this sorting-out process, among the most influential and articulate contributors to this enterprise are intellectuals, writers, and journalists.

Dealing retrospectively with the ways in which Jewish community life in America has been *imagined* by intellectuals and writers is not the same as examining the historical reality of Jewish communal experience in its various forms. In the word "imagined" we signal our wish to find notional projections or representations of the concept of community, as these might have been ideologically or culturally articulated. In this paper I analyze three seminal Americanization narratives by early twentieth-century Jewish writers from the standpoint of their imaginative treatment of a Jewish collectivity and its capability of maintaining bonds of relation and obligation.

The texts in question are Israel Zangwill's play *The Melting Pot* (1908), Mary Antin's memoir, *The Promised Land* (1912), and Abraham Cahan's novel *The Rise of David Levinsky* (1917). They represent the earliest significant projections of the East European Jewish immigrant onto the new literature of social complexity that was emerging on the early twentieth-century American scene. As such, these works played a central role in reformatting the Jewish American narrative. Their *"un-imagining*," or sublimation, of the Jewish community contributed some share toward the reconstructed image of the Jew as an American—not just as a citizen, but as a participant in the emerging, larger American collective.

This new construction depended upon the device of portraying the Jew as an individual personality, beset by inner conflicts, possessed of personal merits and talents as well as faults and failures, rather than as a "racial" or religious "type." Indeed, in these narratives we find a number of different Jewish characters, rather than one archetypical figure, lending credence to the claim of the Jew to social and psychological individuality. By placing individual consciousness rather than tribal solidarity at the center of the reader's perspective, these texts not only recast the new immigrant—the "ghetto Jew"—as an American urban character; they also portray the Jewish "ghetto" itself as a subjective contrivance—an imagined community, if you will—more than an expression of some innate, reified, or lasting Jewish group distinctiveness.

Now, the mere absence of a collective dimension or perspective in a literary work, in itself, is unremarkable and might pass without further comment, given that modern literature, by and large, is structured around the individual imagination, not a collective. Much of the modern literary idiom, particularly in Western culture, is given over to the quest for self-transformation and self-realization. Among other themes, the modern cultural imagination turned upon the dissonance between social status and inner feeling, setting up a pejorative code of resistance to the sham world of conformity to communal proprieties and regularities. For many Jewish writers working within this aesthetic discourse, this transformative quest and critical point of view were almost inseparable from the tension between *staying* behind in the world of the Jewish ghetto and *leaving* it behind. Because modern Jewish writers and artists first emerged as minority-group figures within the wider cultural scene, they leaned heavily on the polarity between "them and us," formulating for Jewish art and culture—and for themselves personally—a posture of uneasy mediation between their two worlds.

There is no question that literature serves autonomous, aesthetic purposes, quite apart from recording or representing reality. That is patently the case not only for works of fiction like *David Levinsky* or dramas like *The Melting Pot* but also for self-narrations like Mary Antin's memoir. Ostensibly a work of factual documentation, *The Promised Land* was laboriously and painstakingly crafted for literary effect,[5] and is replete with musings, flights of fancy, and self-reflection. These narratives possess no less integrity, in themselves, simply because they fail to incorporate either realistic data or imaginative thinking with regard to the organized American Jewish community.

For all that, partial exceptions to the priority of aesthetics over documentary and social considerations in literature are works that are intended as political statements. These *are* framed with society in mind and necessarily point beyond the individual character. Drama, poetry, and prose fiction inspired by Marxism, for example, aim to project an image of the collective, working-class "masses."

It is, therefore, relevant that the texts that I have selected are consciously political in intent. Israel Zangwill was deeply involved in Jewish national affairs and in particular was active in the fight against immigration restriction, both in England and the United States. Indeed, *The Melting Pot* was dedicated to Theodore Roosevelt because of the stand he took against the immigration restrictionists.[6] Likewise, Mary Antin, who became Zangwill's protégée in the years before she published her memoir, went on the lecture circuit to promote the cause of free immigration and corresponded on the subject with leading intellectual and political figures, including Theodore Roosevelt.[7] Antin then wrote and published a strongly pro-immigration political tract, *They Who Knock at Our Gates* (1914). Zangwill's play and Antin's memoir explicitly support a positive ideal of America as a potential, supernational human community.

"Although I have written a genuine personal memoir," Mary Antin explained, "I believe that its chief interest lies in the fact that it is illustrative of scores of unwritten lives." It is here that she makes her social and political program explicit, in terms that virtually encapsulate Zangwill's *Melting Pot* theory of the great synthesis:

> We are the strands of the cable that binds the Old World to the New. As the ships that brought us link the shores of Europe and America, so our lives span the bit-

ter sea of racial differences and misunderstandings. Before we came, the New
World knew not the Old; but since we have begun to come, the Young World has
taken the Old by the hand, and the two are learning to march side by side, seeking a common destiny.[8]

The texts in question, therefore, are not simply "individualistic" on aesthetic or literary-paradigmatic grounds; rather, they deploy the individual perspective as a strategy by which to probe the moral, metaphysical, and political
dimensions of America, taking the individual immigrant to be the emblematic
site of an encounter between the new self and the new society. All three texts
deal with the "rediscovery of America" by the Jewish immigrant "self."

Indeed, for David Quixano, immigrant hero of *The Melting Pot*, his own
particular encounter with the New World is not enough. His intention to com-
pose the music that might capture America's essence represents a higher act of
discovery. In pursuit of this goal, David is constantly reliving his own American epiphany:

> Oh, I love going to Ellis Island to watch the ships coming in from Europe, and
> to think that all those weary, sea-tossed wanderers are feeling what *I* felt when
> America first stretched out her great mother-hand to *me!*[9]

Primarily involved with understanding "America," the texts project an
amalgam of values that create and sustain American society at large. Thus,
while at the simplest level they define character (at the moral and intellectual levels) as what is at stake, at the political level of discourse they delin-
eate an ideal social community. It is here that they fit most closely within the
Anderson-Hobsbawm meaning of the phrase "imagined community," for it is
here that they extend to "America"—an abstract entity—a coherence of values and qualities that the immigrant Jew encounters as a new point of view.

Indeed, of all the constructions of "imagined community," who fits the paradigm better than the newcomer whose role in the national discourse cannot
but be "imagined" from scratch, lacking as she or he does any actual history in common with the national community? Mary Antin defined herself as
"the youngest of America's children and into my hands is given all her priceless heritage."[10] Zangwill, of course, was an outsider per se: an English Jew
who frequented the literary scene on both sides of the Atlantic.[11] Abe Cahan,
author of short stories and novels in English for an American audience, was
also a pioneer editor of the Yiddish ethnic press, with intellectual roots in the
world of Marx, Tolstoy, and Russian radicalism—living, as John Higham put
it, "between three cultures."[12]

In those chaotic if heady days of the great immigration, it was too early
to make the conceptual leap between the immigrant ghetto-community of
the present and the as yet unimagined Jewish community of the future. Yet,

even then, there were forms of communal life to be observed and portrayed, and these texts do appear to privilege one type of projected community over another. To be specific: two main (and somewhat competing) versions of "community" would be fostered in American Jewry in the succeeding decades. The first, a "civic," participatory model, is the community embodied by the voluntary infrastructure of fraternal societies, synagogues, charitable organizations, welfare boards, defense agencies, and seminaries. A good deal of this infrastructure was already established in American Jewish life by the time our texts were composed. The second type of Jewish community, a version familiar to us from literary works, memoirs, and identity surveys, is the private, emotive model, wherein an ethnic *Gemeinschaft* of family, intimacy, and heritage (into which one grows rather than voluntarily joins) is seen to operate within and alongside the *Gesellschaft* of America at large. It would appear that our texts project and reinforce this second type of Jewish community, but play down the first (civic) model.

One would never know, for example, from Mary Antin's memoir of immigrant life in Boston that here the first citywide Jewish philanthropic federation had been established. The only social work mission that we hear about in *The Promised Land* is a Christian mission, the Morgan Chapel.[13] One might also never have guessed that the New York Jewry Cahan depicted in *David Levinsky* was going through an ambitious and controversial experiment in communal governance, called the Kehilla, or that the author was an active opponent of the campaign to establish an American Jewish congress.[14] And one would never know that in 1906 Israel Zangwill was intimately involved with Jacob Schiff in trying to set up an intercommunal mechanism for organizing Jewish immigration from Russia to the American West (the "Galveston Project").[15] These texts make "bad"—unreliable—history, in this regard.

In *The Melting Pot*, the Quixano family home is situated not on the generically Jewish Lower East Side, with its plethora of Jewish agencies and organizations, but on Staten Island, which, as Zangwill is careful to inform us, is "the non-Jewish borough of New York." At the nearby settlement house, therefore, Vera (the progressive daughter of the benighted, judeophobic Russian aristocracy) works with "Dutchmen and Greeks, Poles and Norwegians, Welsh and Armenians"—but no Jews—and has, not surprisingly, never encountered the concept of "Shabbos."[16] When David does venture over to the "People's Alliance" in the "Jewish quarter," he goes (as in his visits to Ellis Island) in search of inspirational material for the American symphony that he is composing:

There I saw the Jewish children—a thousand of 'em—saluting the flag. . . . But just fancy it, uncle. The Stars and Stripes unfurled, and a thousand childish voices, piping and foreign, fresh from the lands of oppression, hailing its fluttering folds. . . . Uncle, all those little Jews will grow up Americans![17]

But, whereas notional projections of a "civic" type of Jewish community are all but absent, we do see in these narratives the idea of the Jewish individual whose inner world is formed around an involuntary, emotive core: a symbolic, other self that supplies the traction against which the protagonists must contend. These texts frame the question of the Jewish American's personality as one of perennial inner struggle between the competing impulses of assimilation and ethnic self-affirmation.[18] They portray this tension as one that pertains to individual personalities—quite in keeping with the individualizing program of these narratives—though it would be fair to say that the reader is asked to extrapolate from the particular case to the general.

It is significant, too, that the chief protagonists in these narratives are presented to the reader as "orphans in history," either literally or metaphorically so. Zangwill's David is a "pogrom orphan," having seen his parents and younger siblings massacred in the infamous Kishinev pogrom of 1903. Cahan's David Levinsky, bereft of his father as a small child, then suffers the loss of his mother, bludgeoned to death by Russian hoodlums. He is left all alone in the world. Mary Antin, while not an orphan in the literal sense, consciously sets out to write her memoir as an act of giving birth to herself, the butterfly writing the autobiography of a caterpillar, thus setting aside the centrality of her biological parents—the maturing young woman becoming, as it were, her own progenitor. Her other, former self is "just as much out of the way as if I were dead."[19] Her self-portrait, set against the backdrop of immigrant America, tells the story of an adolescent's coming-of-age as an actual rebirth, the gaining of a new sensibility of, and openness to, the world's wonder, a triumph of the transcendent will over narrowness of circumstance:

> The endless ages have indeed throbbed through my blood, but a new rhythm dances in my veins. My spirit is not tied to the monumental past . . . No! It is not I that belong to the past, but the past that belongs to me. . . . Mine is the whole majestic past, and mine is the shining future."[20]

Antin refers just once to the "Jewish community," but only in a speculative and rather loosely defined sense. She imagines her older sister, Frieda, vicariously reaping the rewards of Mary's precocious celebrity as a local schoolgirl poet:

> For the girls, the foreman, the boss, all talked about Mary Antin, whose poems were printed in an American newspaper. Wherever she went . . . she was sure to hear her sister's name. For with characteristic loyalty, the whole Jewish community claimed kinship with me, simply because I was a Jew; and they made much of my small triumphs and pointed to me with pride, just as they always do when a Jew distinguishes himself in any worthy way.[21]

Any notion of community betokened by these remarks is clearly the reflection of a defensive need to project a positive image for the sake of the non-Jews outside, rather than an expression of inherent cultural, moral, or religious bonds. Certainly, these are ties that do not bind Mary herself, even if they may be relevant to Frieda, whose life is encompassed by the Jewish ghetto. Indeed, it is fair to say that Antin has portrayed her Jewish experience, in both Russia and Boston, as a ghetto.

Elsewhere, Antin allows that Jewishness may be a rooted quality that is subconsciously maintained, but she is unable to define or imagine what form it should take:

Perhaps [my grandchildren] may have to testify that the faith of Israel is a heritage that no heir in the direct line has the power to alienate from his successors. Even I . . . think it doubtful if the conversion of the Jew to any alien belief or disbelief is ever thoroughly accomplished. What positive affirmation of the persistence of Judaism in the blood of my descendants may have to make, I may not be present to hear.[22]

Abraham Cahan's character, David Levinsky, the self-alienated figure, is similarly detached from any positive form of community. As shop boss, he plays a role in creating a society of *landslayt* (fellow townsmen) among his workers—the "Levinsky Antomir Benevolent Society"—which makes it simpler for him to reinforce his employees' dependency on him and avoid the unionization of his shop. Much later, Levinsky rubs shoulders with wealthy German American Jews and, "though an atheist," joins one of their synagogues "chiefly because it is a fashionable synagogue," a place for "currying favor."[23] Such signs of a debased "solidarity," striking at the core collective values formulated by Jewish tradition, indicate that, in the capitalist American city, "community" becomes a commodity, at best, and a tool of exploitation, at worst. In making this point, Cahan was hewing closely to the line on urban, capitalist morals adumbrated in the works of two of his literary heroes: Theodore Dreiser's *Sister Carrie* (1900) and Nikolai Gogol's *Tales of St. Petersburg* (1842). Gogol's Petersburg, it has been remarked, was "a world deprived of grace, where only human greed and vanity can thrive"[24]—a fair approximation of the way Cahan portrayed David Levinsky's world. The story line in *David Levinsky* gives us precisely the opposite of what may be observed about "imagined communities": rather than superseding the divisive boundaries of class with a homogeneous image of a society endowed with a collective consciousness, Cahan "unimagines" Jewish society by presenting us with a map to its internal dissolution.

Israel Zangwill's *Melting Pot* gives us another sort of unraveling in the case of *his* David: David, the psalmist of a new, universal religion; David, the idealistic Russian Jewish immigrant, creating his "Sinfonia Americana"; David, who is (like Zangwill himself) torn between his ancestral heritage and the religion of the future (the "God of our children," as he puts it).[25] David ultimately inscribes the synthesis between the two in his own soul through his love for Vera, daughter of the butcher of Kishinev, who is, like David, an acolyte of the new, humanistic faith. They are both, therefore, "of the same religion," as Zangwill apparently wished to argue.[26] Zangwill is at pains, therefore, to distinguish David religiously from a Judaism of "pots and pans and plates and knives." The family's Irish maid, Kathleen, is quick to note that, in terms of actual practice, there is little to connect David to his pious grandmother, just as the reader will be certain to note that David's spiritual vision is set apart from the mere secularism of the run-of-the-mill Jewish immigrants—"clothiers and pawnbrokers and Vaudeville actors"—who were perfectly willing to put "mate and butther" on one plate together. "The most was that some wouldn't ate the bacon," jibes Kathleen, "onless 'twas killed *kosher.*"[27]

The narrowness of "community" bothered Zangwill. A decade after writing *The Melting Pot*, under the impact of the Great War and the drive for national self-determination that featured so prominently in that war, he noted approvingly that "thinkers whose thought . . . embraces mankind must needs grow restive under [the] apotheosis of family feeling."[28] Zangwill's case for a benevolent, multinational and multiracial society of the future, under the aegis and tutelage of expansive great powers (such as the United States, France, and Great Britain), rested upon the detaching of nationality—which he is reluctantly willing to grant as a principle of political sensibility—from the chauvinistic constraints of tribal community:

> If we are now to be penned within "the principle of nationalities," let us at least insist that they shall only be individual expressions of the universal, friendly, Intensive Imperialisms. For here, in a word, is the problem and the ideal—how to maintain the virtues of tribalism without losing the wider vision; how to preserve the brotherhood of Israel without losing the brotherhood of man; how to secure that, though there *shall* be both Jew and Greek, there shall yet be neither.[29]

· · ·

Of the three texts in question, Cahan's novel comes closest to expounding a theory of community, in that *David Levinsky* is a fully realized political novel that articulates a critique of contemporary bourgeois society. It therefore points toward an *alternative* human community. It is, indeed, in this negative, backhanded fashion that literature sometimes contributes most clearly toward "imagining" society.

Cahan believed strongly that worthwhile literature fulfilled a political function, insofar as realistic fiction is capable of supporting a discourse of ideas relevant to social issues. For Cahan, realistic fiction and political ideas were

two sides of a coin. His literary models, in both Russian and American literature, understood literature to serve a social function. With Tolstoy, Dreiser,
and William Dean Howells, Cahan believed that fine literature, to be socially
meaningful and "true" (as opposed to the "lies" of cheap romantic fiction),
ought to make its point through a realistic aesthetic, but not through heavy-
handed propaganda. True art could strive to walk hand in hand with an overt,
ideational orientation.[30]

There was, of course, some irony, if not a deep, inner contradiction, in the
attempt by a socialist to write a novel, as the novel has been widely conceived
as *the* bourgeois art form. With its concern for plot (social order), character
(inner sensibility), and the resolution of dilemmas and conflicts (gesture vs.
affect), and with its ultimate appeal to the aroused sentiment of the reader,
the novel's discursive strategies could easily subvert the author's own social or
political intent. Cahan, parenthetically, showed in David Levinsky's divided
inner world how much he (Cahan) understood the entrapment of consciousness by this sort of contradiction. The politics of *David Levinsky*, then, are
certainly not incidental, but were deliberately intended to show through the
novel's conventional literary form.

In that light, it is revealing of the primacy Cahan attached to his public role
in politics and journalism—that is, his most community-oriented functions—
that after writing *The Rise of David Levinsky* he discontinued his literary
career, devoting himself over the rest of his life exclusively to publishing the
Forverts and to politics. Thus, Cahan ultimately chose to "do" rather than to
"imagine." Of him it might surely be said—as Susanne Klingenstein observed
about another contemporary figure, Joel Spingarn, who, like Cahan, finally
chose the civic realm over the intellectual and aesthetic one:

> [His] "political sense"—his view that only "the sense of relation to a civitas"
> could be the source of an individual's identity—and his "aesthetic sense," which
> perceived . . . in a great work of art "a vision of reality," were equally strong and
> theoretically irreconcilable. The first thrust him into life and connected him
> with the community, while the second isolated him.[31]

In *David Levinsky*, Cahan wielded the Marxist argument of alienation,
but he did so through a psychological drama of one man's increasing self-
estrangement rather than through a crudely drawn anticapitalistic cartoon. The
character of David Levinsky is desperately eager, from his impoverished and
orphaned youth, to achieve a spiritual bond, a sense of communion with those
around him, but he is increasingly frustrated in this quest as utilitarian considerations become uppermost in his mind. True comradeship, community, and
love elude him because his "rise"—spurred ever onward by the exigencies of
survival in a materialistic world—is conditioned upon his embrace of a self-
centered view of life. The women he loves are portrayed as givers, involved

with others, endowed with powers of empathy, and in possession of core ethical principles; they are, therefore, ineluctably beyond his reach.

. . .

Thus, the politics of our three texts tend to articulate, either by negative or by positive reference, a credo of community as something transcending narrow self-interest and partaking of a humanistic ethic. Within this overarching concept, these Jewish intellectuals portray the immigrant Jew as a solo performer. To understand why it was that these texts posit an individualistic role for Jews, while simultaneously promulgating "imagined communities" in which Jews ought to be able to participate as full-fledged members, we need to address the two constructs—individual and community—in tandem, as, I believe, our authors intended.

In order to partake of the ideal community-in-formation, it is necessary for the individual to perform an act of self-transformation, to move from the level of mere self-gratification to the socially meaningful level of community participation. Mary Antin, for example, is aware that there must be a trade-off if the new, "imagined" American community is to have a chance at all. Describing her father's insistence on his children's Americanization, at the cost of their separation from the parochial Jewish enclave, and at considerable cost to her mother's religious sensibilities, she observes:

> The price that all of us paid for this disorganization of our family life has been levied on every immigrant Jewish household. . . . Nothing more pitiful could be written in the annals of the Jews; nothing more inevitable; nothing more hopeful. Hopeful, yes; alike for the Jew and for the country that has given him shelter. For Israel is not the only party that has put up a forfeit in this contest. The nations may well sit by and watch the struggle, for humanity has a stake in it.[32]

Ultimately, the aim of Antin's memoir is not narcissistic but social: "But hark to the clamor of the city all about! This is my latest home, and it invites me to a glad new life."[33]

This stress on the place of the individual in the larger scheme of things receives expression, as well, in the final passages of *David Levinsky*, where Cahan leads his character through an extended assessment of his accomplishments in life, and where Levinsky compares himself disparagingly with his fellow Russian Jewish immigrants. Their successes, he argues, are more important than his because they have given something *of themselves* to the national community:

> [I]t is often pointed out that the man who has built the greatest sky-scrapers in the country, including the Woolworth Building, is a Russian Jew who came here as a penniless boy. I cannot boast such distinction, but then I have helped build

up one of the great industries of the United States, and this also is something to be proud of. But I should readily change places with the Russian Jew . . . who is the greatest physiologist in the New World, or with the Russian Jew who holds the foremost place among American songwriters and whose soulful compositions are sung in almost every English-speaking house in the world.[34]

In its original context, this passage extols the superior virtues of artistic and intellectual accomplishment, to which mere business acumen cannot really compare. In rereading it in light of the present discussion, however, it is the litany of individual excellence that turns this passage into a commentary on self and community. Levinsky feels himself to be a failure, if not a fraud, *not* because he holds himself aloof from his fellow Jews—he clearly does identify with them—but because he has squandered his individuality, his innate yearnings, while they have fulfilled theirs, consecrating them to the greater good. His rejection of the idea of marrying an otherwise suitable non-Jewish woman, and his support of Jewish charities and synagogues—the bread and butter of the civic type of Jewish community—are, therefore, mere window dressing on an empty house.

It is no accident that our narratives assign a good deal of significance to the emotive feelings that tie one Jew to another. It is precisely the penchant of Jews to club together separately on the basis of local affinity, sentiment, or an aggrieved sense of the Jewish plight that is highlighted in these texts. Our authors thereby relegate the Jews, as a group, and the ties that bind them, including religion, to the private zone of the emotions, while reserving truly significant notions of community to the much wider societal realm, within which Jews, too, are called upon to play a role.

What Zangwill, Antin, and Cahan share, ultimately, is a profoundly political understanding of the nature of "community," very much along the lines suggested by the Anderson-Gellner-Hobsbawm theory of the national community. Though they might find in Jewry a platform, they sought a *community* elsewhere. A community worthy of the name, they seem to argue, endows the individual with worth in consequence of that person's participation in the common quest for the greater good. They thus construe it to mean the coming together of people who are willing to make some sacrifice of themselves, to demand something of others, and to entertain some notion of common governance. From small-town American models to the traditional Jewish *kehilla*, to the European Union of our own day, the community in this public, political sense requires that a common good be recognized as a worthy aspiration above all private and sectoral goals. The common good embodies the values and rules that will enable individuals and subgroups to "do their own thing" while participating in the larger social contract. This is what enables a community to conduct a town meeting, or to elect a town council, and to support both instrumental and symbolic activities that are seen as beneficial to all.

Simply put, our authors doubted that the Jews of America could, qua Jews, claim a credible or adequate communal ethos or social contract, regardless of how much kinship, solidarity, or sentiment they might display, prompted either by the pressure of antisemitism or by the benign pride of success. Yet they also believed (or hoped) that *as Americans*, Jews were being offered an opportunity to belong to a political community, as they had so egregiously not belonged in Russia. In this same vein, it is worth noting that the projected American civic community is depicted in all three texts as an urban society, thus conflating city (with its heterogeneity and modernism), *citoyen*, American, and Jew; whereas the provincial Jewries of the "old world," the sites of our protagonists' lingering Jewish memories, where Jews experienced *Gemeinschaft*—Antin's Polotzk, Cahan's Antomir, or Kishinev in *The Melting Pot*—are also where Jews suffered from repression, pogroms, poverty, and a stunted existence. The contrast between real historical community and imagined ideal community could hardly be more striking.

Our authors' dismissal of the Jews' capacity to construct a social contract around their own public square cannot be taken lightly by the contemporary historian, despite their books' aforesaid unreliability as social documents. These imaginative works do coincide with historical reality in two respects. First, their intuition was not essentially wrong insofar as American Jewish politics are concerned; second, their posture toward organized Jewry was not idiosyncratic but rather typical of Jewish intellectuals and writers, and this itself has had concrete and lasting implications for the processes of community construction in American Jewry.

That they were fairly correct in guessing that Jews in America were best defined as a subgroup or, indeed, a multitude of subgroups within the wider sociopolitical framework, rather than a full-fledged community with its own, self-conceived commonality of purpose, is borne out by the history of American Jewry in the early to mid–twentieth century. The period from *The Melting Pot* to *David Levinsky* coincides with the period from the founding of the New York Kehilla to that of the American Jewish Congress, two crucial attempts to create a public realm, a *farhesia*, for the American Jewish community. Both attempts failed dismally.

Just a few years later, at the 1920 London Zionist Conference, Louis D. Brandeis—arguably the political leader of greatest stature to appear on the American Jewish scene, then or since—turned down the chance to head the World Zionist Organization.[35] Despite the strong position he took on the need for a structured and democratized Jewish community, it was the American public square that mattered to him most. He thereby affirmed in practice what Zangwill, Antin, and Cahan had maintained hypothetically.

Later still, as we move into the era of Nazi Germany and the Holocaust, American Jewish leaders proved capable of forming tactical, temporary, and partial coalitions, but (as every historian who examined this period has found) could not adhere to a unified notion of communal governance.[36]

As for our authors' typicality, it must be admitted that the distance that Jewish intellectuals have maintained from corporate expressions of Jewry, whether construed as organized religion or organized communal welfare, possesses a strong and long-established pedigree in the history of modern Jewish culture. It is ultimately traceable to the rift that appeared during the Enlightenment period between the forces of reform and innovation within the Jewish cultural elite, on the one hand, and the adherents and practitioners of pragmatic survival and stasis, on the other. This breach was never healed, and in consequence modern intellectual figures searching to renew a life of ideas within Jewish society had little use for the existing Jewish communal milieu. We find such figures, rather, in the forefront of groups championing an alternative community of their own. The imagination of the intellectual Jew is often more an antidote to community than a devising tool of community.

American Jews have at their disposal an array of communal institutions but are at a cultural disadvantage when it comes to "imagining" an American Jewish community as a religious or ethnic polity. Perhaps that is why Hana Wirth-Nesher and Michael Kramer, in their introduction to Jewish American literature, found it most appropriate to point out that Jews in America have produced disparate *literatures* (plural), rather than a literature (singular).[37] Cultures nurtured by nationalist movements (as Anderson, Hobsbawm, and others argue) are relatively rich in terms of a collectivist imagination. By contrast, American Jewry is typically well endowed with individualistic motifs. Except by recourse to the formulaic slogans of the professional Jewish communal services or the emotive, personalized idiom of subjective ethnic feeling, there is a relative dearth of collectivist Jewish vocabulary. Seldom does the American Jewish narrative extend beyond an aggregate of individual success stories; rarely does it point beyond the intimate tensions between parents and children, men and women, love and distance.

It is symptomatic, for example, that the United Jewish Communities concept has not overcome the trend toward privatization in philanthropy; rather, the UJC appears to suffer from a fundamental lack of vision and clarity about its mission. It is not surprising, either, that Arnold Eisen and Steven M. Cohen's study of Jewish identification among adult American Jews found that they focused, above all, on the personal, privatized realm.[38] Some of the most compelling and validating images we have of Jewish community life, relating to notions of individual fulfillment within a group context, come out of the work done by anthropologists on microcommunities—such as Barbara Myerhoff's classic study of the elders of the Aliyah Center in Los Angeles, or Jack Kugelmass's eloquent portrait of an isolated Jewish enclave in the South Bronx. They reveal to us a vocabulary of vitality, intimacy, and commitment from which an "imagined" community might yet derive sustenance.[39]

This luxuriant activism at the subcommunal level is not an essentially new feature on the American Jewish scene, which was always characterized by diverse needs and views. Diversity has undeniably enriched the lives not just of individuals but also of the subgroups that they formed. Jews have fashioned communi*ties*—plural—in place of community (singular), and these smaller communities have possessed a great deal of esprit and grassroots nourishment. Pluralism and diversity have, indeed, been the hallmarks of American Jewry's history and its self-image. Where once there were "Germans" and "Russians," Yiddishists, Hebraists, a panoply of hometown *landsmanshaftn*, and an entire world of sectarian socialism, now there are Jewish subcommunities founded on an identity politics of gender, sexual orientation, generation, liberalism, neoconservatism—and even highly specialized, "virtual" Internet communities.[40]

Respect for diversity is a cornerstone for a free society, as Mary Antin argued, and American culture is peculiarly dependent on a pluralized social interaction, as Zangwill suggested. Yet, were one to ask whether the pluralistic rhetoric of Jewish diversity is also the rhetoric of Jewish "community" on any wider plane beyond that of one's own denomination, faction, minyan, or school of thought, one would be very hard pressed to find the point of congruence. As the proponents of the "imagined community" theory have argued, internal diversity in a social system is a historical fact of life; diversity as such is no bar to the emergence of an overarching symbolic identity. But the sine qua non in the process of community formation is the predominance of collective commitment over sectoral and private self-definitions.

I do not commend the early Americanization narratives of Zangwill, Antin, and Cahan to our attention in this respect because they offer a more accessible communal definition of American Jewry—they do not. I suggest, rather, that they serve as foundational texts for that individualistic, present-tense Jewishness that has comprised the core of the Jewish American imagination. Zangwill's play expressed it quite succinctly, one hundred years ago: "Each generation," David Quixano proclaims, "must live and die for its own dream." To this, his beloved Vera replies: "Yes, David, yes. You are the prophet of the living present."[41]

But I also suggest that anyone who would "imagine" a more robust, more structured, or more democratically united American Jewish communal ideology should consider well the ideals embedded in these texts: that an essential attribute of community must be a readiness to sacrifice something for others for the sake of a common goal, and that the essential responsibility involved in community is, not the identity-politics commitment to "being," but the civic willingness for "doing."

And perhaps we might also view these texts as cautionary tales; for, as intimated earlier, when the life of the Jewish "street" is sentimental, parochial, "virtual," or bent on private goals of self-realization, rather than collectivist and public-regarding, some of the most talented and spirited minds in American Jewry will surely be tempted to imagine community elsewhere.

Notes

1. Benedict Anderson, *Imagined Communities: Reflections on the Origin and Spread of Nationalism* (London: Verso, 1983); Ernest Gellner, *Nations and Nationalism* (Oxford: B. Blackwell, 1983); E. J. Hobsbawm, *Nations and Nationalism Since 1780: Programme, Myth, Reality* (Cambridge: Cambridge University Press, 1990).

2. The importance of "collective amnesia" is an insight that goes as far back as Ernest Renan's conceptual essay *Qu'est que c'est une nation?* (Paris: Sorbonne, 1882). His oft-cited phrase appears on pp. 7–8: "L'oubli et je dirai même l'erreur historique, sont un facteur essential de la formation d'une nation et c'est ainsi que le progrès des etudes historiques est souvent pour la nationalité un danger."

3. Hobsbawm, *Nations and Nationalism*, p. 46.

4. See Jonathan D. Sarna's insightful essay on ethnicization, "From Immigrants to Ethnics," *Ethnicity*, vol. 5 (1978), pp. 370–378.

5. The memoir was first published in installments in the *Atlantic Monthly*, for which Antin laboriously edited the manuscript, and then extensively reedited for the book version. See her correspondence with Ellery Sedgwick in 1911 in Evelyn Salz (ed.), *Selected Letters of Mary Antin* (Syracuse: Syracuse University Press, 2000), pp. 51–66.

6. Zangwill, a prominent Zionist and subsequently a leading Territorialist, wrote his earlier novel, *Children of the Ghetto* (1892), against the backdrop of the anti-immigration campaign in England. As one observer has noted, "Its impact may have influenced attitudes in favour of immigrants," and in particular may have resulted in Conservative MPs dropping plans for anti-immigration legislation at that point. See Cecil Bloom, "The Politics of Immigration, 1881–1905," *Jewish Historical Studies: Transactions of the Jewish Historical Society of England*, vol. 33 (1992–1994), p. 199.

7. Salz (ed.), *Selected Letters of Mary Antin*, pp. 72–73, 75, 151–152.

8. Mary Antin, *The Promised Land* (London: William Heinemann, 1912), introduction, p. xiii.

9. Israel Zangwill, *The Melting Pot: A Drama in Four Acts*, in *The Works of Israel Zangwill* (London: The Globe Publishing Co., 1925), vol. 12, pp. 30–31.

10. Antin, *Promised Land*, p. 364.

11. See Zangwill's speech and the remarks in his honor at the "Zangwill Night" at the New York "Judæans" Society, recorded in *The Judæans*, vol. 1 (New York: The Judæans Society, 1899).

12. John Higham, "Abraham Cahan: Novelist Between Three Cultures," chap. 5 in

Higham's *Send These to Me: Jews and Other Immigrants in Urban America* (New York: Atheneum, 1975), pp. 88–101.

13. Antin, *Promised Land*, pp. 266–270; Daniel J. Elazar, *Community and Polity: The Organizational Dynamics of American Jewry* (Philadelphia: Jewish Publication Society, 1995), p. 209.

14. See Arthur A. Goren, *New York Jews and the Quest for Community* (New York: Columbia University Press, 1970).

15. See Zosa Szajkowski, "The Impact of the Russian Revolution of 1905 on American Jewish Life," *YIVO Annual*, vol. 17 (1978), pp. 95–102.

16. Zangwill, *Melting Pot*, pp. 1, 11, 30.

17. Ibid., pp. 52–53.

18. It is by no means unique that an "imagined community" is constituted within this kind of dialectical self-image, so that duality as such becomes an integral part of its sense of self. For a clear parallel see the case of Russia in Orlando Figes, *Natasha's Dance: A Cultural History of Russia* (London: Penguin, 2002).

19. Antin, *Promised Land*, introduction, p. xi.

20. Ibid., p. 364.

21. Ibid., p. 253.

22. Ibid., p. 249.

23. *The Rise of David Levinsky* (New York: Peter Smith, 1951 [1917]), pp. 378, 528.

24. Figes, *Natasha's Dance*, p. 160. It is perhaps worth noting that Dreiser's London publisher, William Heinemann, was also the publisher of Zangwill's and Antin's books, and that Cahan was dubbed "the American Zangwill"—another of the several coincidences linking our three authors.

25. Zangwill, *Melting Pot*, p. 98. On Zangwill's views and their expression in *The Melting Pot*, see Joseph H. Udelson, *Dreamer of the Ghetto: The Life and Works of Israel Zangwill* (Tuscaloosa: University of Alabama Press, 1990), chap. 9; cf. Neil Larry Shumsky, "Zangwill's 'The Melting Pot': Ethnic Tensions on Stage," *American Quarterly*, vol. 27, no. 1 (March 1975), pp. 38–39.

26. Udelson, *Dreamer of the Ghetto*, p. 197, citing a letter from Zangwill to Stephen S. Wise dated 26 October 1909: "My hero and heroine *are* of the same religion."

27. Zangwill, *Melting Pot*, pp. 3, 6, 24.

28. Israel Zangwill, *The Principle of Nationalities: Conway Memorial Lecture* (London: Watts and Co., 1917), p. 16.

29. Ibid., p. 89.

30. See Abraham Cahan's comments on realism in art and literature in his memoir, *Bleter fun mayn lebn* (New York: "Forverts" Association: 1926), vol. 2, pp. 421–423; cf. Ronald Sanders, *The Downtown Jews: Portraits of an Immigrant Generation* (New York: Harper and Row, 1969), pp. 181–185, 202. On William Dean Howells's views, as expounded in his novel *The Rise of Silas Lapham*, which was in many ways a model for Cahan's book, see the introductory remarks by Robert Lee Hough to the Bantam Books edition (New York, 1967), p. vii. Hough quotes Howells's objections to the kind of romantic fiction that is interested above all in achieving a titillating effect: "Romantic novels hurt because they are not true—not because they are malevolent, but because they are idle lies about human nature and the social fabric, which it behooves us to know and to understand, that we may

270 • Community and Culture

deal justly with ourselves and one another." (The cited passage is from William Dean Howells, *Criticism and Fiction, and Other Essays*, ed. Clara Marburg Kirk and Rudolf Kirk [New York: New York University Press, 1959].)

31. Susanne Klingenstein, *Jews in the American Academy* (New Haven: Yale University Press, 1991), pp. 108–109. The phrases in quotation marks are cited from Marshall van Deusen, *J. E. Spingarn* (New York: Twayne, 1971), p. 109.

32. Antin, *Promised Land*, p. 248.

33. Ibid., p. 364.

34. *David Levinsky*, p. 529.

35. See Ben Halpern, *A Clash of Heroes: Brandeis, Weizmann, and American Zionism* (New York: Oxford University Press, 1987), pp. 213–214, 216–218. "He [Brandeis] explained at length . . . that retiring from the Court might undermine his argument that Zionist and American loyalties were compatible" (p. 217).

36. Henry L. Feingold, *The Politics of Rescue* (New York: Walden Press, 1970); idem, *The Jewish People in America: A Time for Searching; Entering the Mainstream, 1920–1945* (Baltimore and London: Johns Hopkins University Press, 1992), chaps. 6–8; David Wyman, *The Abandonment of the Jews* (New York: Pantheon, 1984); Aaron Berman, *Nazism, the Jews, and American Zionism* (Detroit: Wayne State University Press, 1990); Gulie Ne'eman Arad, *America, Its Jews, and the Rise of Nazism* (Bloomington: Indiana University Press, 2000).

37. Michael P. Kramer and Hana Wirth-Nesher (eds.), *The Cambridge Companion to Jewish American Literature* (Cambridge: Cambridge University Press, 2003), p. 4.

38. Arnold Eisen and Steven M. Cohen, *The Jew Within: Self, Family, and Community in America* (Bloomington: Indiana University Press, 2000). See also Samuel C. Heilman, "Holding Firmly with an Open Hand," in Jack Wertheimer (ed.), *Jews in the Center: Conservative Synagogues and Their Members* (New Brunswick: Rutgers University Press, 2000), pp. 105–140, 180–192.

39. Barbara Myerhoff, *Number Our Days* (New York: E. P. Dutton, 1979); Jack Kugelmass, *Miracle of Intervale Avenue* (New York: Schocken, 1986).

40. Other signs of a weak overall communal consciousness may be sought in the political sphere. Since the 1980s, American Jewry has taken several steps away from the consensual ethos that held sway during the postwar decades. The erstwhile liberal political hegemony among American Jews has devolved into a fraught debate over basic civic and political values and options in the American polity. Whether liberal or conservative, Jews today are less inclined to view politics as a reinforcement of ethno-communal consensus. See, e.g., Steven M. Cohen and Charles S. Liebman, "American Jewish Liberalism: Unraveling the Strands," *Public Opinion Quarterly*, vol. 61 (1997), pp. 405–430.

41. Zangwill, *Melting Pot*, p. 147.

Chapter 14

David E. Fishman

From Yiddishism to American Judaism

The Impact of American Yiddish

Schools on Their Students

Shortly before World War I, immigrant intellectuals from Eastern Europe began to establish Yiddish-language supplementary schools in America. These schools were generally referred to as secular Yiddish schools, a term that clearly distinguished them from the other, more common, forms of Jewish education in America—the Hebrew school and the religious school. During the interwar years, American Yiddish schools grew in number and enrollment, and were organized in four distinct systems, under the auspices of sponsoring organizations with different ideological orientation: the Jewish National Workers' Farband (Labor Zionist), the Sholem Aleichem Folk Institute (nonpartisan Yiddishist), the Workmen's Circle (Socialist), and the International Workers' Order (Communist).[1]

At their peak, in 1934, some twenty thousand Jewish children were enrolled in Yiddish secular schools in the United States, and constituted 10% of American Jewish children receiving a Jewish education.[2] These were neighborhood institutions, averaging sixty children and two teachers per school. They most commonly met three days per week, for a total of six hours of instruction. (There were also a significant number of five- and six-day-a-week schools, which provided more than ten weekly hours of instruction.) The Yiddish school system consisted overwhelmingly of elementary schools and provided five years of instruction to children aged eight to thirteen, although there were a handful of *mitlshuln* for teenagers. In addition, each sponsoring organization conducted summer camps associated with the schools.[3]

The Yiddish schools were usually located in rented space in densely Jewish urban neighborhoods. In addition to providing instruction for children, they served as community centers for parents and other adults, conducting lectures, reading clubs, and holiday celebrations during evening hours.[4]

All four school systems mentioned above taught Yiddish language and literature, which were considered the core subjects in their curriculum, and utilized Yiddish as their language of instruction for other subjects. They were, broadly speaking, the educational expression of the Yiddishist movement in America. The schools defined themselves as secular and freethinking, but they differed widely on the degree to which they incorporated aspects of the Jewish religious heritage (such as the Bible and religious holidays) into their curriculum. They openly differed in their political ideologies (Zionism vs. democratic socialism vs. communism), and their attitude toward Hebrew depended on the position they took vis-à-vis the Jewish religious heritage and the Zionist enterprise.

Elsewhere, I have explored the main ideological and educational conundrum that confronted the Yiddish schools: the issue of secularism and religion, as it was addressed in their programmatic statements, textbooks, and educational practice between 1910 and 1948.[5] In this study, I would like to consider the question of their social impact and outcomes. What was the nature of the Jewish identity of the students who attended these schools? To what degree were Yiddish schools successful (or not) in transmitting Yiddish culture and Jewish commitments to their graduates? What Jewish affiliations and commitments did former students retain later on as adults?

A popular conception (or misconception) concerning the secular Yiddish schools in America is that they were politically radical, internationalist, and antireligious. Historians of the Jewish community in America have paid very little attention to the Yiddish schools, on the assumption that they were marginal to the perpetuation of Jewish communal life and, if anything, facilitated the absorption of young Jews into American secular liberalism. I believe that the essay that follows will demonstrate that this was not the case.

This essay reviews critically several surveys and interview-studies conducted among students and graduates of American Yiddish schools between 1930 and 1960. Most were conducted by Leibush Lehrer (1887–1964), the director of the Sholem Aleichem Folk Institute, who was a trained social psychologist and secretary of YIVO's research division for psychology and pedagogy.[6] One important study was conducted by Nathan Goldberg (1903–1979), a sociologist associated with YIVO and later a professor at Yeshiva University.[7] Together, these materials enable us to paint a portrait of the youngsters who attended Yiddish secular schools, including their Jewish attachments, and to follow their Jewish development years later, in adulthood.

The focus of our consideration will be the students who attended Yiddish schools in the 1930s, when these schools were at their peak.

Lehrer's Studies in the 1930s: American and Yiddish

The youngsters who attended Yiddish schools were overwhelmingly the American-born children of immigrants, who were bilingual in English and Yiddish. In a survey of 85 students, age twelve to seventeen, who attended a Yiddish *mitlshul* (middle and high school) in New York in 1930, Lehrer asked students what language their parents spoke to them, and what language they spoke to their parents. Most of the students reported that their parents spoke to them in Yiddish *only* (60%). A significant minority reported that their parents spoke to them in both Yiddish *and* English (40%), but none (0%) reported that their parents spoke to them in English only. These responses tell us not only that the parents were immigrants but that all the children/students heard Yiddish at home. Yiddish was not a foreign language that they needed to learn from the beginning. In fact, when asked what language they spoke to their parents, most students responded that they spoke to their parents in both Yiddish *and* English (65%). Very few spoke to their parents in English only (6%), and a noticeable minority (29%) spoke to their parents in Yiddish only.

All the students of the Yiddish *mitlshul* attended public school. The questionnaire, which was filled out anonymously, asked the students what grades they received at school for "English" over the past three report cards. The average grade was 83. Thus, the students' overall aptitude in English was good. They were not childhood immigrants fresh off the boat from Europe, with faulty English. Nor could they have been. The questionnaire was administered in 1930, six years after the end of mass migration to the United States.[8]

A year later, in 1931, Lehrer conducted an interview-study with 53 young men and women, between the ages of fourteen and twenty-four, who had either studied in Yiddish schools or attended summer camps associated with the Yiddish school systems. The respondents were an elite group, with regard to their level of contact or involvement with these institutions: they had spent an average of more than seven years in Yiddish schools and/or camps, an extensive period of time. Most of them were beyond the age of Yiddish schooling and were entering young adulthood. The interviews were conducted by young, American-born questioners and not by Lehrer himself, in order to increase trust and candor in the interviews.

The interviewees expressed a strong interest in Jewish affairs. Of the 53 participants, 49 (92%) reported that they read books and news items about Jews and Jewish problems. Forty of them (75%) reported that they were interested in the movements that guided and influenced Jewish life. But the respondents did not lead a sheltered or insulated Jewish life. Forty-seven out of 53 (88%) reported that they belonged to clubs or organizations that were not related to Jewish affairs.

When it came to the respondents' use of and attachment to Yiddish, the figures were quite strong. A majority, 32 out of 53 (60%), reported that they read books in Yiddish during their free time. An even larger majority reported that they attended Yiddish theater—46 out of 53 (85%) (35 respondents mentioned attending Maurice Schwartz's Yiddish Art Theatre by name). Lehrer noted that the reading of Yiddish newspapers fared very poorly among his respondents, but he did not provide any numbers for this question or explore why there was such a large disparity between the respondents' reading of Yiddish books and Yiddish newspapers. Sixty-five percent (34 out of 53) stated that they would be interested in joining a club dedicated to Yiddish culture.

It is fair to conclude from these figures that the Yiddish schools were at that point, in 1931, quite successful at producing young people who were interested in Jewish affairs, fluent in Yiddish, partook of Yiddish books and theater, and were interested in Yiddish culture. Or, to be more precise, the schools generated such attachments and interests among those young people who attended Yiddish schools and/or camps for an extended number of years.

Lehrer noted, however, that there were significant differentials between the responses given by young women and young men to the questions about the use of and attachment to Yiddish. Thus, 85% of the young women responded that they read Yiddish books in their free time, whereas only 45% of the young men did. Ninety-five percent of the young women were interested in joining a Yiddish culture club, whereas only 45% of the young men were. Seventy-five percent of the young women believed that Yiddish had a future in America, whereas only 49% of the young men felt the same. Lehrer concluded that the Yiddish schools were more successful in imparting their values to their female students. He suggested that this gender gap was caused by differences in the adolescent development of boys and girls. Girls matured earlier and therefore developed an earlier interest in "serious matters," which included Yiddish culture. Particularly in America, he noted, teenage boys focused almost exclusively on recreation and sports.

On the affective level, the respondents felt emotionally attached to their schools and to the Jewish people at large. Forty-six out the 53 interviewees (88%) stated that the Yiddish schools and camps were an important factor in their life. In anecdotal responses, the youngsters stated that "I now understand who we are," "I've drawn closer to the Jewish people," and "we've mastered Yiddish."[9]

The topic of the loyalty of graduates of the Yiddish schools to the schools and their values preoccupied Lehrer considerably and became the focus of a study conducted in two waves—in 1935 and 1939. In both cases, he administered a brief anonymous questionnaire to graduates of Yiddish schools between the ages of sixteen and twenty-four, the vast majority of whom had also attended or completed a Yiddish *mitlshul*. As in the previous study, the respondents were a group with many years of contact with and involvement in these institutions. (In both waves of the study, 85% of the respondents had attended the Sholem Aleichem or Workmen's Circle schools.) When asked whether they would send their children to Yiddish schools, 57 of the 64 respondents answered in the affirmative in 1935 (89%), and 61 of 64 answered in the affirmative in 1939 (95%).

Lehrer asked the respondents how many teachers they had had in their Yiddish schools over the years and how many of those teachers elicited feelings of respect from them now, in retrospect. He found that the majority of teachers were recalled with respect: 329 out of a total of 651 teachers in 1935 (51%), and 462 out of 741 teachers (65%) in 1939. In the context of widespread dissatisfaction with Hebrew schools and their teachers among Hebrew school students and graduates, Lehrer took these results as indicators of relative success. He attributed the growth of respect for former teachers between 1935 and 1939 not to improvements among the teachers but to a changed mood among the students. With Nazism on the rise, European Jewry in greater peril, and war imminent, the students' attachment to the Yiddish schools and their teachers grew.[10]

But there were some shortcomings to Lehrer's studies in the 1930s. First, the samples were rather skewed. His 1931 interviews were conducted at Camp Boiberik of the Sholem Aleichem Folk Institute, and the majority of the young men and women who were questioned had attended Sholem Aleichem schools. This left open the question whether the same level of Jewish and Yiddish attachments would be found among the students of the Farband, Workmen's Circle, and IWO (Communist) schools. In addition, the range of questions asked was rather limited. No questions were asked on Jewish holiday observance or membership in Jewish organizations. There were also no attitudinal questions about the Jewish religion, antisemitism, European Jewry, Palestine, and Zionism. Lehrer did, however, convincingly demonstrate that young people attending Yiddish schools were truly bicultural, American and Yiddish. They participated in and felt an attachment to Yiddish culture.

The 1934 Goldberg Study: The Range in Jewish Attitudes

To a certain extent, the flaws in Lehrer's studies were corrected by a study conducted by Nathan Goldberg in 1934—the only study to compare students in all four Yiddish school systems with regard to their Jewish attitudes and (to a lesser extent) behaviors. Goldberg distributed a questionnaire among 261 youngsters, age twelve to nineteen, who were enrolled in the Yiddish *mitlshuls* associated with the five Yiddish schools systems that existed at that time: 78 students from the Workmen's Circle, 69 from the IWO, 68 from Sholem

Word/Term	WC	SA	Farband	IWO
Rabbi	7.7%	8.8%	0%	81.2%
Purim	3.8%	1.5%	0%	76.8%
Matzah	6.4%	8.8%	0%	43.5%
Shabbes	2.6%	1.5%	0%	33.3%

Source: N. Goldberg, "Natsionaler bavustzayn fun hi-geboyrene yidishe kinder," *Kultur un dertsiung,* January 1939, p. 10.

Aleichem, 30 from Yidishe Arbeter Shuln, and 16 (a very small sample) from the Farband. (The fifth Yiddish school system, the Yidishe Arbeter Shuln headed by Yankev Levine, was ideologically perched in between the Socialist Workmen's Circle and the Communist IWO. These schools subsequently merged into the Workmen's Circle schools.)

The questionnaire was written in Yiddish and was distributed at school.

Goldberg measured the students' attitudes toward Jewish concepts in an original manner: he gave them a list of words/terms and asked them to erase those which elicited unpleasant feelings or memories.

Regarding words related to antisemitism, there were no differences between the responses given by the students in the different Yiddish school systems. The words "pogrom," "blood libel," and "antisemite" were erased (as eliciting unpleasant feelings) by more than 85% of students in all the Yiddish school systems. But when it came to Jewish religious terms, there was a high percentage of negative attitudes among the students of the IWO schools—and among those students only. (The percentages given in the table above are of students crossing out the word.)

Thus youngsters in the socialist-oriented Workmen's Circle schools displayed no anti-religious or anti-rabbinic animus. On the contrary, the Jewish religious taboo on pork resonated with most of them. The word "khazir" (pig, pork) elicited a negative emotional response from 59% of the students in the Workmen's Circles schools, 56.3% in the Farband students, and 38.2% of the Sholem Aleichem students. These figures are surprisingly high, considering that the Workmen's Circle and Sholem Aleichem schools in the mid-1930s were secularist, and kashrut was not kept, taught, or encouraged in them. But the word "khazir" elicited very low negatives from the IWO students—only 8.7% crossed out the word. This was not a coincidence. Jewish agricultural colonies in the Soviet Union, which were celebrated in the IWO schools, were famed for breeding pigs and took pride in this fact.

There were also sharp differences in students' reaction to words related to Zionism and the land of Israel: 85.5% of IWO students responded negatively to the word "Zionism," while only 32.1% of the Workmen's Circle students did. The latter figure indicates that most youngsters in the Workmen's Circle schools were not "anti-Zionist" in this basic, emotional sense. Even the word "Palestine" elicited a negative response from most (53.6%) of the IWO students, but only 7.7% of Workmen's Circle students responded negatively to it. (In both cases, the percentage of negatives from Sholem Aleichem students was lower than those from the Workmen's Circle students.) On the other hand, the word "Arab" elicited a negative response from more than two-thirds of the Farband students (68.8%) and from nearly half of the Workmen's Circle students (43.6%), but only 7.2% of the IWO students responded negatively.

Goldberg demonstrated that the Jewish attitudes of IWO students were significantly different from those of the students in the other types of Yiddish schools. The students in the IWO schools were indeed anti-religious and anti-Zionist. The others were not. The differences between the responses given by the students in the Socialist Workmen's Circle and the Communist IWO schools were quite dramatic, across the board.[11]

The Goldberg Study: Students' Connection to Yiddish Literature, Jewish History

Since the one Jewish value clearly shared by all Yiddish schools was Yiddish, Goldberg attempted to measure the *degree* of English-Yiddish biculturalism among the students—both in their everyday lives and in their consciousness. He did this by asking students to list books they had recently read, writers they enjoyed, and heroes/freedom fighters they admired. The questionnaire did *not* specify that students should list any particular kind of books and writers (Yiddish or English) or freedom fighters (Jewish, American, or Socialist). "Jewish" responses were suggested only subliminally, by virtue of the fact that the questionnaire was written in Yiddish and administered in the Yiddish school. Goldberg wished to ascertain the degree to which such open-ended questions would, in fact, elicit "Jewish" responses.

When students were asked to list books that they had read during the past year, 22.5% of the responses given were titles of Yiddish books. There was considerable divergence between the students of the different school systems. Among the Sholem Aleichem school students, 42% of the responses were titles of Yiddish books, but in the IWO schools only 4% of the titles given were those of Yiddish books. The Workmen's Circle students hovered around the overall average—22% of the books they indicated as having read during the past year were Yiddish books. These responses seem to indicate that the Sholem Aleichem schools were the most successful in developing Yiddish reading habits among their students. This corresponds to Lehrer's finding in his 1931 study, which was conducted mainly among Sholem Aleichem school students, in which 60% of the respondents claimed to read Yiddish books in their spare time.

Students were asked to list their favorite writers. This was a question about affective attachment to literature, not about reading habits. Students could list as many writers' names as they wished. Among the students of the Sholem Aleichem, Workmen's Circle, and Farband schools, 55% of the responses given were of Yiddish writers. This indicates a high level of emotional attachment to Yiddish literature, given that the respondents were high school students who read English authors for both school and leisure/enjoyment. The response among students of the IWO schools was lower. Only 35% of the names they entered as their favorite writers were those of Yiddish writers. Nonetheless, the much higher rate of Yiddish answers given by IWO students to the latter question (on favorite writers) compared to the former question (on books recently read) indicates that students, across the board, felt a strong emotional attachment to Yiddish literature.

The Farband, Sholem Aleichem, and Workmen's Circle students generally admired the same Yiddish writers: Sholem Aleichem (mentioned by more than 60% of the students in all three school systems) and I. L. Peretz (who ranked second in number of mentions by students of both the Workmen's Circle and Sholem Aleichem schools, and was first in the Farband schools). There were some variations: Sholem Asch was much more popular among students of the Farband schools than elsewhere, presumably because his novels on Jewish martyrdom and piety (*Kiddush hashem, Shloyme Nogid*) were studied there. And Avrom Reisen enjoyed more popularity among Workmen's Circle students than elsewhere, probably owing to his poems and short stories on Jewish poverty and workers' struggles, which were part of the curriculum.

The students of the IWO schools who had beloved Yiddish writers gave entirely different names. Most popular was the labor poet Morris Vinchevsky, mentioned by 34.8% of the students. The second most popular Yiddish author was humorist and feuilletonist Moishe Nadir, a long-standing writer in the Communist *Morgn Freiheit*, with 29%.[12]

Students were asked to list the names of freedom fighters. Overall, 24.5% of the responses mentioned the names of Jewish freedom fighters. Here the dividing line was between the Farband and Sholem Aleichem schools, on the one end, and the Workmen's Circle and IWO schools on the other. Among the students of the Farband and Sholem Aleichem schools, half of the responses given were those of Jewish freedom fighters. In the Workmen's Circle schools, only 25% of the responses were of Jewish freedom fighters, and in the IWO schools—only 4%. Thus Jewish historical consciousness was strongest or sharpest among students of the Farband and Sholem Aleichem schools. It seems that in the Workmen's Circle schools students were more attached to Yiddish literature than to Jewish history.

The most popular Jewish freedom fighter was Moses, mentioned by 68.8% of the students in the Farband schools, 57.4% of the students in the Sholem Aleichem schools, 32.1% of the students in the Workmen's Circle schools, and 5.8% of the students in the IWO schools. A similar downward progression occurred with the second most mentioned hero: The Maccabees. They were mentioned by 32.4% in the Sholem Aleichem schools, 31.2% in the Farband schools, 7.7% in the Workmen's Circle schools, and 0% in the IWO schools.

Interestingly enough, modern figures, such as Theodor Herzl and Vladimir Medem (of the Bund), received very few mentions. This seems to indicate that Yiddish schools paid much more attention to ancient Jewish history than to modern times. It also suggests that the curriculum of the Farband and Workmen's Circle schools was not as partisan or "politicized" as one might expect. Farband school students rarely mentioned Herzl as one of their heroes, and Workmen's Circle students rarely mentioned Medem.

The students' differing political orientations were reflected in the names they submitted of general, non-Jewish freedom fighters or heroes. The most popular hero among IWO students was Lenin (98.6%); among Workmen's Circle students, Karl Marx (47.4%), and among Farband and Sholem Aleichem students, George Washington (62.5% and 55.9% respectively).

Students were asked to list three holidays, without any specification that they be Jewish holidays. In the Farband, Sholem Aleichem, and Workmen's Circle schools, the overwhelming majority of mentions (ranging between 88.9% and 94.4%) were of Jewish holidays. Very few "votes" (mentions) were given to civil or other holidays. The Yiddish word *yontev* was associated with Jewish holidays. By far the most popularly mentioned holiday was Passover, mentioned by 95% of the students from these three school systems. Purim was a distant second, mentioned by 47.4%, and Chanukah third, mentioned by 33.8%. By contrast, Rosh Hashanah, which was not observed in the Yiddish schools because of its religious character, was mentioned by only 25% of the students.

In the IWO schools, the situation was very different: only 4.5% of the total holiday mentions went to Jewish holidays; 93% of the students mentioned May 1, and 65% mentioned November 7 (the day of the Bolshevik revolution).[13]

Goldberg's study indicated that the students of the IWO schools had a much weaker attachment to Jewish history, holidays, and Yiddish culture than the students from the other Yiddish school systems. On the other hand, it indicated that the students of the three other Yiddish schools felt a strong attachment to Yiddish culture, Jewish history, and Jewish holidays.

Lehrer's Retrospective Study of 1959

Lehrer conducted his most ambitious and most interesting survey toward the end of his career, in 1959. It was a retrospective survey of adults between the ages of thirty and forty who had attended Yiddish schools and the Yiddish camp Boiberik. In other words, the target population of the study had attended Yiddish schools and/or camp fifteen to thirty years earlier, between 1929 and 1944. The target population was thus very close to the group he had queried in his 1931 interview study—people who had been youngsters in the 1930s. The objective of the 1959 survey was to gauge the Jewish identity of these former students and campers as adults, many years *after* their exposure to Yiddish educational institutions. The intervening years had witnessed the dramatic decline of Yiddish in America, the Holocaust, and the establishment of the State of Israel. The central question was thus whether former students' Jewish identities had weakened, intensified, or remained unaltered in the years since their Yiddish education.[14]

Lehrer sent a questionnaire consisting of thirty-two questions to 425 men and women, among which 173 responded, a 40% response rate.

Surprisingly, 30% of those who responded defined themselves as "religious," some of them using terms such as "half religious" and "religious and secular," wheras 70% defined themselves as "secular." (Some of the latter used the terms "atheist" and "agnostic.") The fact that 30% of the respondents defined themselves as religious raises questions about how, when, and why, after being educated in avowedly secular Jewish institutions, they adopted a religious Jewish self-definition. The survey did not provide answers. But the fluidity of movement from secular Jewish education to a religious self-identification suggests not only that the education they received was not anti-religious, but also that their secular Jewish identity could transform itself into a religious identity with relative ease as the respondents matured in the 1940s and 1950s.

Only 4 of the 173 respondents were intermarried, fewer than 2.5%. This was lower than the presumed national average of 5% in 1959. And only 10 of the 173 (6%) disagreed with the statement "Jews in America should remain a distinct group, alongside other religious and cultural groups." One hundred thirty-one of the respondents (76%) reported that they observed Jewish holidays (35 observed "all" and 96 observed "some").[15]

Unfortunately, Lehrer removed the self-defined "religious" 30% of the respondents from his further analysis. He was interested in probing the Jewish identity of self-defined secular Jews who had been educated in secular Jewish schools. Seen from this perspective, the 30% were beyond his purview. (Perhaps they could even be considered "dropouts" or "failures" of the secular Yiddish schools.)

Lehrer's findings concerning the remaining 122 respondents were quite illuminating. First, let us describe the population: 81 (68%) had attended Sholem Aleichem schools, and 34 (28%) had attended other types of Yiddish schools. (The remaining 6% had either attended Hebrew school or received no Jewish schooling at all.) The average length of study in the Yiddish schools among the respondents was seven years. Lehrer gave some general information about the responding sample: 70% were college graduates, and another 10% had doctoral degrees. The most popular occupations among them were as housewives, schoolteachers, businessmen, attorneys, and executives.

The overwhelming majority of respondents had a positive Jewish identity. When asked "What do you feel about the opinion that Jews should continue to exist as a distinct group, among other religious and cultural groups in America," 109 responded that they agreed (89%). When asked if they had Jewish objects or books on Jewish subjects in their home, 118 out of 122 (95%) responded in the affirmative.

Interesting responses were given to the following question: "What, if anything, do you think being Jewish requires, other than being born into a Jewish family?"[16] Seventy-four (61%) responded "to identify as a Jew," and 73 answered "to know Jewish history and culture." A much lower figure, only 42 (34.5%), answered "to engage in Jewish activity or behavior." (Lehrer grouped the responses into these general categories.) Thus, for the respondents, Jewishness was more a matter of subjective feeling, awareness, and knowledge than of behavior or action.

Nonetheless, this population did exhibit a number of Jewish behaviors and activities. As noted above, the overwhelming majority observed Jewish holidays. The most popular holidays celebrated by the self-defined secular respondents were Chanukah, Passover, Rosh Hashanah, and Yom Kippur. This list is interesting, because, whereas Chanukah and Passover were universally celebrated in Yiddish schools, Rosh Hashanah and Yom Kippur were not. The Workmen's Circle and Sholem Aleichem schools in the 1930s did not mark Rosh Hashanah and Yom Kippur, which they considered to be "religious" holidays. The respondents' celebration of the High Holidays was another instance of their joining the Jewish mainstream of the 1950s, and traversing the border between "secular" and "religious."

Lehrer was struck by the fact that the boundary between religious identity and secular identity was not firm in his respondents' minds, despite the fact that they had attended avowedly secular Jewish schools. From his East European Jewish perspective, there were startling inconsistencies in the anecdotal comments offered by respondents: "I am a secular Jew, I observe only Rosh Hashanah and Yom Kippur"; "I am a secular member of a Conservative synagogue"; "I am Orthodox, but not religious"; "I am secular. I keep only Rosh Hashanah, Yom Kippur and Passover. I observe them in an Orthodox manner." The clear ideological division between secular and religious, common among East European Jews, had fallen by the wayside.

The overwhelming majority of these 122 respondents—87%—reported that they gave to Jewish philanthropies. The most common Jewish charities among the respondents were the United Jewish Appeal (90), the Federation of

Jewish Philanthropies (27), and the Jewish National Fund (12). Sixty-six of the respondents (54%) reported that they belonged to Jewish organizations, and 56 reported that they did not (46%). The most common memberships listed by respondents were the Sholem Aleichem Folk Institute (18), YIVO (11), the Workmens' Circle (11), Bnai Brith (10), and synagogues/temples (6).

The figures on philanthropy and membership in organizations are further indication of the process of "Jewish mainstreaming" among the graduates of the Yiddish schools. Many more of them gave to the United Jewish Appeal (90) than belonged to Yiddish-related organizations (44—the sum total for membership in the Sholem Aleichem Institute, YIVO, Workmen's Circle, and other organizations).

Of these 122 respondents, 75 had school-age children. Within this sub-group, 61 gave their children a Jewish education (81%), while 14 did not (19%). Among those who indicated the type of Jewish school that their children attended, the breakdown was as follows: Yiddish schools, 27; congregational/religious schools, 27; 7 other respondents who gave their children a Jewish education did not specify the type of school they attended. Thus, half of the self-professed "secular" respondents who provided information on this question sent their children to religious schools. It is interesting to note that when asked whether they were satisfied or dissatisfied with the type of Jewish school their children attended, only 7 respondents (out of the 61) reported that they were dissatisfied. In other words, a large majority of those who sent their children to religious or congregational schools were satisfied with them. The boundary between "secular" and "religious" Jewish identity was apparently traversed with ease.

It is telling that Lehrer did not ask any questions in his 1959 questionnaire about the reading of Yiddish books, attending Yiddish theater, or speaking Yiddish. Presumably, Lehrer knew full well that the response levels to these questions would be extremely low, and he considered it unnecessary to inquire. The only Yiddish indicators measured in 1959 were the ones mentioned above: approximately a third of respondents belonged to organizations that supported Yiddish culture (44 responses, with some multiple answers), and 40% of the respondents with school-age children sent them to Yiddish secular schools (27 out of 75).

If one extrapolates from the 122 secular respondents to the entire sample of 173, one reaches the following conclusions: Several decades after leaving the Yiddish school, most of the graduates of such schools had not retained Yiddish as an active language, or an association with Yiddish cultural organizations. On the other hand, most of them observed Jewish holidays, including religious ones such as Yom Kippur, most of them sent their children to congregational Hebrew schools, and 30% professed a "religious" Jewish self-identity.

Lehrer also conducted personal interviews with 42 of the respondents who defined themselves as "secular," and who lived in the Greater New York area. The interviews lasted between two and three hours, and were conducted in Lehrer's home, in order to create an informal atmosphere of ease and trust. Since the vast majority of interviewees had been students in Sholem Aleichem schools, they knew Lehrer personally from their childhood and teenage years. The interviews were conducted in the form of an informal conversation among friends.

First, Lehrer asked his interviewees questions about their years in the Yiddish schools. What were the most important qualities of their Yiddish school-teachers? Twenty-five of the 42 interviewees considered the teachers' love of the Jewish people, and their love of the children, to have been their most important trait. As one interviewee put it, the outstanding teachers were "those who were able to create the atmosphere of a family at school." This familial, communal aspect of the Yiddish school was again highlighted when interviewees were asked what aspect of the school left the strongest impact on them. The largest number, 20 interviewees, responded that the co-curricular activities—singing, dancing, holiday celebrations, and the staging of school plays—left the strongest impact. The second most popular response was that the friendships created at the Yiddish school left the strongest impression (16 responses). Subject matter taught, "Jewish history, stories and literature," was third (14 responses).

Lehrer then turned to his population of 42 "secular" interviewees with questions about their Jewish behavior. All 42 celebrated Jewish holidays; 26 of the 42 stated that they celebrated Jewish holidays more intensely than their parents had, and noted that their parents had either not celebrated Jewish holidays at all or had celebrated them in a minimal way. It is safe to conclude that the interviewees' Yiddish school years had a strong impact on this intergenerational shift in behavior.

With regard to kashrut, Lehrer found the opposite trend. Many of the interviewees noted that their parents did not eat certain non-kosher foods, such as pork. Even parents who were described by their children as secular or anti-religious did not eat pork. But none of the interviewees themselves observed any aspect of kashrut. Even those with the most positive, enthusiastic attitude toward the Jewish religion did not distinguish between permitted and forbidden foods. One may conclude that this disinterest in kashrut was the legacy of the secular Yiddish schools, where kashrut was not taught or observed in any way.

Two questions addressed the issue of boundaries between Jews and non-Jews. Thirty-five of the 42 interviewees strongly opposed intermarriage. The same proportion reacted with strongly negative responses when asked about Jews sending Christmas greetings to Jewish friends and acquaintances: 35 found such behavior to be "disgusting," "horrible," and so forth.

Conclusion: The Law of Unintended Consequences

Leaving aside the IWO schools, the Yiddish schools in America set for themselves two basics goals: to produce American Jews who (a) would be fluent Yiddish speakers and active Yiddish readers, and (b) would have a strong emotional attachment to the Jewish people, their history and culture. During the 1930s, it appears that the schools were reasonably successful on both counts. But in the long term, Yiddish language retention among their graduates proved to be very weak. By the 1950s, very few of them were reading Yiddish books, or speaking Yiddish at home or with friends—so few that Lehrer did not bother to ask, or did not want to know the answer to this question.

On the other hand, the schools succeeded extraordinarily in their second goal of instilling a strong sense of Jewish community and solidarity among their students and graduates. But this success, ironically, led many of the graduates to leave secular Yiddishism behind and join the mainstream institutions that expressed Jewish communal cohesiveness and solidarity in the postwar years—Jewish philanthropies and the synagogue. Among many Yiddish school graduates, religion became the haven for their Jewish ethnicity, to use Will Herberg's formulation, which was written, not coincidentally, in the 1950s.[17]

Thus, the Yiddish schools did not, in most cases, lead their graduates out of Jewish communal life to a de-ethnified liberalism or radicalism, but led them into the religious and philanthropic forms of Jewish communal life. Whether the schools' founders would have been happy with such an outcome, or have comprehended how it could have come to pass, is another matter.

Notes

1. For overviews on Yiddish schools in America, see F. Gelibeter et al. (eds.), *Shul almanakh: di yidishe moderne shul oyf der velt*, Philadelphia, School Committee of the Workmen's Circle, 1935; Shmuel Niger, *In kamf far a nayer dertsiung: di arbeter-ring shuln—zeyer opshtam, antviklung, vuks, un itstiker tsushtand*, New York, Educational Committee of the Workmen's Circle, 1940; Y. Kh. Pomerants et al. (eds.), *Shul pinkes*, Chicago, Sholem Aleichem Folk Institute, 1948. In English, see Zalman Yefriokin, "Yiddish Secular Schools in the United States," in *The Jewish People—Past and Present*, vol. 2, New York, CYCO, 1948, pp. 144–150; Melech Epstein, "The Yiddish School Movement," *Contemporary Jewish Record*, vol. 6, no. 3 (June 1943), pp. 261–272; Sandra Parker, "An Educational Assessment of the Yiddish Secular School Movements in the United States," in Joshua A. Fishman (ed.), *Never Say Die! A Thousand Years of Yiddish in Jewish Life and Letters*, The Hague: Mouton, 1981, pp. 495–513.

2. *Shul almanakh*, pp. 353, 356; Israel S. Chipkin, *Twenty-Five Years of Jewish Education in the United States*, New York, Jewish Education Association of New York, 1937, pp. 37, 117. The figure of 20,000 students is also given by both Epstein and Yefroikin (see note 1), writing in the 1940s.
3. *Shul almanakh*, pp. 57, 139.
4. On the latter, see N. Chanin, "Kultur tetikayt in un arum di shuln," *Kultur un dertsiung*, April 1944, pp. 6–7.
5. "Yiddish Schools in America and the Problem of Secular Jewish Identity," in Zvi Gitelman (ed.), *Secular Dimensions of Jewish Identity* (forthcoming).
6. Lehrer received an M.A. in psychology from Clark College in 1917. For a detailed biography, see *Leksikon fun der nayer yidisher literatur*, vol. 5, New York, Congress for Jewish Culture, 1963, pp. 235–239.
7. Goldberg attended the University of Pittsburgh, where he received his B.A. in 1928 and an M.A. in sociology in 1930. I fondly recall studying sociology with Goldberg as an undergraduate.
8. Leibush Lehrer, "Der aynflus fun yidish afn English fun undzere kinder," *Di Tsukunft*, August 1930, pp. 571–574; reprinted in Lehrer's collection of essays, *Fun dor tsu dor*, New York: Farlag Matones, 1959, pp. 11–19.
9. Leibush Lehrer, "Tsvey yidishe doyres in amerike," *Di Tsukunft*, September 1931, pp. 593–599; reprinted in *Fun dor tsu dor*, pp. 20–35.
10. Leibush Lehrer, "Shtimungen bay undzer yugnt," *Yorbukh fun Amopteyl*, vol. 2, New York, American Branch of Yiddish Scientific Institute, 1939, pp. 133–146.
11. N. Goldberg, "Natsionaler bavustzayn fun hi-geboyrene yidishe kinder," *Kultur un dertsiung*, January 1939, pp. 10–11. Yudl Mark wrote a scathing (and to my mind unfair) review of this study in *Kultur un dertsiung*, March 1939, pp. 7–9. In the review, Mark noted that the investigation had been conducted in 1934.
12. N. Goldberg, "Natsionaler bavustzayn fun hi-geboyrene yidishe kinder," *Kultur un dertsiung*, November 1938, pp. 13–17.
13. N. Goldberg, "Natsionaler bavustzayn fun hi-geboyrene yidishe kinder," *Kultur un lebn*, December 1938, pp. 17–18.
14. L. Lehrer, "Di yidishkeyt fun tsveytn dor veltlekhe," *Yivo Bleter*, vol. 42 (1962), pp. 67–80; reprinted in Lehrer's volume *In gayst fun traditsye*, Tel Aviv, I. Peretz, 1966, pp. 275–291.
15. The latter figure is contained in the typescript version of the study as it was read at the annual YIVO conference in January 1960; YIVO archives, Leibush Lehrer collection, RG 507, file 150, "Geleyent oyf der 34ster konferents fun yivo, dem 30stn yanuar, 1960," 16 pp. (The published version of the study contains a typographical error.)
16. The original questionnaire is contained in YIVO Archives, RG 507, file 137.
17. Will Herberg, *Protestant-Catholic-Jew: An Essay in American Religious Sociology*, Garden City, N.Y., Doubleday, 1955.

Chapter 15

Hana Wirth-Nesher

The Accented Imagination
Speaking and Writing Jewish America

One of the continuous features of Jewish life in the diaspora, from ancient to modern times, has been negotiating more than one language.[1] This multilingual dimension of Jewish civilization does not mean that Jews were equally competent in more than one language, but it does mean that their collective identity, regardless of the language and culture of the place they inhabited, encompassed the Hebrew language as sound and, through its alphabet, also as sight. In the Eastern European Jewish world, the origin of the majority of North America's Jews, to be Jewish meant familiarity with *loshn-koydesh* (Hebrew and Aramaic) for prayer, study, and self-governance; Yiddish for domestic, social, and communal exchanges; and the language of their Gentile neighbors for commercial, social, and public interaction beyond their own community. The contemporary Jewish American community, in most cases several generations removed from immigration, may seem to be equally far removed from this multilingual legacy. According to Cynthia Ozick, "Since the coming forth from Egypt five millennia ago, mine is the first generation to think and speak and write wholly in English."[2] But I would argue that, in America, language has continued to be a key factor in how Jews imagine their community, even as they revise the significance of these languages to reflect historical change. One of the most intriguing sites of this multilingual awareness is Jewish American literature, from Abraham Cahan in the late nineteenth century to the most recent work of Philip Roth, Grace Paley, Jonathan Safran Foer, Allegra Goodman, and Aryeh Lev Stollman, to name only a few.

Just as in Eastern Europe Yiddish was associated with speech and Hebrew with textuality, so too in America. On the one hand, Hebrew letters serve as icons of Jewishness, whether on gold necklaces, beaded bracelets, tee shirts, sepia photographs of shop signs on the Lower East Side, or on ritual items at home encompassing the traditional mezuzah and the framed *ketuba*, where the Hebrew calligraphy and its illuminations may upstage the content. Furthermore, a common way of signaling Jewishness is to write English (Roman) letters so that they resemble Hebrew, as in recent posters for the Broadway revival of *Fiddler on the Roof.* In the visual arts, Ben Shahn's striking *Alphabet of Creation* or *Monumental Alphabet* underscore the iconic power of the letters themselves, as does his arrangement of HALLELUJAH in English and in Hebrew. Hebrew print also acts as a Jewish identifying mark on the cover of Jewish American magazines and journals, from *Hadassah Magazine* to *Tikkun* and *Prooftexts.*

On the other hand, so-called Jewish speech seems to bear traces of Yiddish, even if the speakers don't understand a word of it. The Jewish voice as comic, irreverent, and vulgar has been a marker of Jewish popular culture since early stand-up in clubs and on television, and the list of such accented speakers includes Molly Goldberg, Mickey Katz, and Sid Caesar, and more recently Mel Brooks, Woody Allen, Jackie Mason, and Fran Drescher in *The Nanny.* In the recent film *The Fockers*, Barbara Streisand instructs her son's Gentile in-laws on how to pronounce Jewish sounds when they fail to say "L'Chaim." "Ch, ch," she says, "it's like when you get popcorn stuck in your throat."

Jewish American literature has registered the community's engagement with both the sight and sound of languages other than English from the end of the nineteenth century to the present. I would like to highlight this feature of Jewish writing in English, by focusing on a few works that demonstrate how writers have been captivated by the Jewish voice and the Jewish letter.

In a recent interview, when asked to describe his childhood in Newark, Philip Roth made the following observation: "Contrary to some stereotypical misunderstanding, there is no New Jersey accent."[3] This remark is clearly intended to distinguish his speech and his writing from that of Jews in America who do have an accent, undoubtedly across the Hudson in New York. Only three pages into his novel *The Plot Against America*, he characterizes his Newark neighborhood also by its "American English that sounded more like the language spoken in Altoona or Binghamton than like the dialects famously spoken across the Hudson by our Jewish counterparts in the five boroughs."[4] What Roth means to redress in this linguistic disavowal is the "stereotypical misunderstanding" among readers who would place him in the same category with New York Jews, such as Alfred Kazin and Delmore Schwartz, or maybe even Mel Brooks. These are Jewish writers, Roth seems to be claiming; they have that Jewish accent. But do not be mistaken—a writer from New Jersey is an American; he does not bear the marks of Jewish accent in his speech. This disclaimer about his own voice, unsolicited by any question about language, and minutes from the start of a six-hour video interview, signals his desire to be read as accent-free, as American as Henry James, for whom speech markers were the domain of vulgar dialect writers like Twain. The real American, for James and for Philip Roth, who sees himself as his literary descendant, doesn't speak or write with an accent.[5] And certainly not with a New York accent, which for Roth is synonymous with a Jewish voice.

This "anxiety of accent" among Jewish American writers goes back a long way and is most forcefully articulated in Abraham Cahan's *The Rise of David Levinsky* (1917) where Levinsky is obsessed with performing English well enough not to be detected as a Jew. Although his struggle with the pronunciation of English consonants leads to some harsh words about his adoptive tongue—"English is the language of a people afflicted with defective organs of speech" (precisely the verdict that German linguists had rendered about Jews in the nineteenth century)[6]—this is an obvious camouflage for the self-loathing that locates those defective organs in his own body: "That I was not born in America was something like a physical defect which, alas! No surgeon in the world was capable of removing" (291). Levinsky is tormented by every aspect of his Jewish voice—its volume, tone, and sheer garrulousness, and his unbridled gesticulation—all of which seem to him congenital: "It seemed to me that people who were born to speak this language [English] were of a superior race" (139). *The Rise of David Levinsky* is one long, excruciating struggle to shake off his accent, along with pangs of remorse at abandoning what it represents.

If accent is the mark of personal history on the body in that it restricts what the mouth and lips can produce, then writing, as a disembodied form of communication, has always held out the promise of attaining an American voice for Jewish immigrant writers. Yet the anxiety of accent felt by immigrant writers was so great that it often permeated the very pages that bypassed speech. Again and again, pronunciation and diction, the acquisition of English, took over as theme, or served as climactic moments in their stories. In Anzia Yezierska's *Bread Givers*, true love comes to the heroine Sara Smolensky in a *Pygmalion*-like moment in which her husband-to-be places his hand on her throbbing throat to prod her larynx into making proper American sounds.[7] In *The Rise of David Levinsky*, erotic tension between David and his lover Dora revolves around correcting each other's pronunciation. And in Mary Antin's autobiography, *The Promised Land*, her gradual Americanization is measured by her conquest of the "dreadful English *th*" or the equally troublesome *w* in the word "water." Antin is so embarrassed by her accented English that, in her account of an episode a short time after her immigration when she mispronounces the word "swim" as "shwimmen," she introduces third-person narration so as to disassociate herself from a girl who mangles English. Eventually, she will admit somewhat wistfully, "At least I learned to dream in English without an accent."[8] The fact that she could write in English without fear of betraying an accent did not free her to abandon this painful subject in her prose. If accent was all that was left of her Jewishness, abandoning it altogether would have seemed like another kind of betrayal.[9]

But these are all immigrant writers, and it should not surprise us that speech impediment born of late arrival would shadow their lives and their writing careers. Most of these writers came to America at a time when nativist Americans were experiencing their own anxiety of accent; namely, they feared that their native language might not survive its mutilation in the mouths of hordes of foreigners. Diction manuals addressed to native Americans were designed to fortify their speech against contamination from accents. As one author of such a handbook observed, "It is undeniable that we get our strongest impressions of a person from the way he speaks, that therefore a handicap of prejudice must pursue through life those who discount themselves by vulgar accents" (Clara Rogers, *English Diction*, 1915).[10] Among the many exercises for proper diction were sentences such as "The Jew jumped from the barge and joined Jonah," or "She showed the jewels to the Jew." A useful word, it seems, for practicing pronunciation of both *u* and *zh* sounds was the word "usurer." In such a linguistic climate, Jewish immigrants, including the writers among them, recognized that an accent was a liability in their fierce drive to become Americanized. But why would Philip Roth, two generations removed from immigration and several years into the twenty-first century, insist that he comes from an accent-free zone? His anxiety stems from the specific connotations of Yiddish-inflected speech and from the perceptions of Yiddish American culture by the children and grandchildren of these immigrants.

For college-educated native-born Jewish Americans, Yiddish has often signaled the vulgarity of popular culture—of dialect humor, borscht belt standup, "Yinglish."[11] The central role that this mass entertainment has played in the forging of American culture, particularly on stage and screen, has been documented, from Al Jolsen and Fannie Brice to the Marx Brothers, from Rogers and Hammerstein to Mel Brooks. Although the most gifted and original Jewish American writers, such as Henry Roth, Delmore Schwartz, Saul Bellow, Cynthia Ozick, Grace Paley, and Philip Roth, have been inspired by Jewish speech as it developed in the dense neighborhoods of working-class Jews clambering up the social ladder, their immersion in English literature and their literary ambitions in that language have kept Yiddish at a distance from their writing. Undoubtedly, the attitude toward Yiddish on the part of American authors who could understand the language well enough to appreciate its literature, such as Saul Bellow, Cynthia Ozick, and Isaac Rosenfeld (all of whom were also translators from Yiddish at some stage of their careers), has differed markedly from the attitude of those writers like Philip Roth, who knows no Yiddish whatsoever; yet they all strive, in their literature, to ensure their literary descent from James, no matter how circuitous. In other words, as audacious or subversive as their English prose might be, their ultimate concern as artists has been the quality of that English prose. Given the provocative and transgressive themes and language of Henry Roth and Philip Roth, it might seem paradoxical that they would fear the vulgarity of Yiddish leaving its mark on their English page. Yet each, in his own way, has harnessed the perceived coarseness of Yiddish (regardless of his own proficiency or ignorance of the language) for elaborate wordplay or self-conscious performance of that language.[12]

I do not mean to give the impression that Yiddish has meant the same thing to Jewish American writers regardless of their own personal history or poetics, namely brash humor. On the contrary: the lyrical and nuanced Yiddish "translated" into English in *Call It Sleep* dramatizes the chasm between the verbal richness within the community and the garbled and deficient speech of these same characters in English; the cliché-ridden English of lower-middle-class Jewish immigrants in Delmore Schwartz's "America! America!" marks their linguistic limits, but it is more revealing about the artistic pretensions, social snobbery, and self-derision of their children; the Yiddish lullaby that ruptures the English text in Ozick's *The Shawl* acts as a touchstone of Jewish authenticity in a work in which the recoil from Yiddish resulting from social snobbery is shared by contemporary Jewish American readers and their counterparts in prewar Warsaw.[13] In other words, whatever Yiddish may signal when viewed from *within* the Jewish community, or when heard by characters who have some knowledge of the language, there are many moments in Jewish American fiction when that accent is heard by "native" ears, that is, when the Jewish writer imagines how these sounds might be heard by American readers. "Tanks so viel," blurts out Genya Schearl to the police officer who has found her son, erstwhile silver-tongued mother in Yiddish humiliated by her fractured English. Culture wars among Yiddishists in postwar New York in Ozick's "Envy—or, Yiddish in America" suddenly pale when Edelstein's telltale accent unleashes an antisemitic diatribe by a southern evangelist: "You talk with a kike accent. You kike. You Yid."[14] Ozick's Ruth Puttermesser (like Ozick herself) recalls endless diction lessons to eliminate the dentalization that would mark them as New York Jews. It is not surprising then that the last line of *Portnoy's Complaint*, "so, vee may perhaps to begin, yes?" merges the Viennese German of psychoanalysis with Yiddish-inflected stand-up comedy. German and Yiddish being too close for Jewish comfort and psychoanalysis signaling both social snobbery and a threat to Gentile civility,[15] the accented speech of the Jewish analyst can stand in for the accented writing of the Jewish American novelist.

Jewish American literature has always aimed at a double audience, at the general and the Jewish reader. Although the children and grandchildren of immigrants do not convey the embarrassment of an Antin or a David Levinsky, whose mortification at not being able to pass linguistically can even make the reader cringe, their self-consciousness about how Yiddish-inflected speech might be perceived by other Americans persists in their writing. Given the association of Yiddish with vulgar or popular culture, the occasional Yiddish reference may serve either to challenge that notion or to anticipate, and thereby thwart, a belittling response to the work. Each artistic strategy of bringing Yiddish into the work seems to be saying, This isn't what you think, this is *literature.*

The turning point for the representation of Yiddish in Jewish American literature was the Holocaust. Concurrent with the titillating stand-up mode of Yiddishism that would persist into the latter half of the twentieth century, a new testimonial and elegiac tone began to emerge. Undoubtedly the most provocative use of Yiddish-inflected speech as a vehicle for Holocaust testimony is Vladek's monologue in Art Spiegelman's *Maus*, where two clashing modes of representation disorient and disturb readers. On the one hand, realistic portrayal is abandoned when Jews in Nazi Europe are depicted as mice in cartoon images of the Holocaust; on the other hand, realism is meticulously observed in the speech representation of Spiegelman's father, Vladek, whose story is transcribed as heavily accented English: "And every day we prayed. I was very religious and it wasn't *else* to do."[16] By drawing Jews as despised animals, Spiegelman literalizes Nazi rhetoric of dehumanization; by painstakingly transcribing their speech into writing, Spiegelman restores their humanity, drawing the reader's attention to the human voice of the victims, to the familiar sound of the survivor in America English. The vehicle for remembering this story, Spiegelman insists, should not bypass the living and speaking body of the survivor; it should not be "corrected" into standard English that would erase the speaker. What the reader sees on the page, and then hears in his own mind, is not the language (or languages) of the annihilated Jewish prewar world, not Yiddish itself, but the accent that testifies both to that lost world and to the efforts of survivors to renew their lives in America.[17]

Maus does not offer an elegy to the language that has been erased, but neither does it depict Yiddish-inflected speech as a handicap to be overcome or as ethnic comic relief, as was frequently the case with portrayal of immigrant speech in the decades before the war. It insists on not severing the tale from the teller, on preserving the voice of the survivor on the American landscape, a voice unashamedly, even heroically, accented. A sobering experience for the Jewish American reader shaped by S. J. Perelman or Leo Rosten,[18] *Maus* requires a new kind of reading and listening, where Yiddish-inflected speech does not automatically elicit laughter. Not only has Spiegelman subverted the American genre par excellence, the comic strip, but he has also subverted a Jewish American convention of speech performance. In short, *Maus* draws on popular culture, from both mainstream American and Jewish arenas, in order to restore psychological complexity to Jewish immigrants whose accented speech had been reduced to mass entertainment. In a chilling turnabout, Spiegelman gives us the *visual* image of Jews as defective through the eyes of antisemitic Europe, where their pronunciation of German had been used as conclusive evidence of their defective speech organs, while simultaneously recording one of the most poignant sounds of postwar Jewish life, the voice of the survivor refugee in English.

As the intonation of Vladek's generation disappears, Yiddish as a spoken language in literature and art disappears as well. What remains in popular culture is a series of performances: in festivals, classrooms, summer camps, and drama.[19] The language recedes but does not disappear from contemporary literature. Rather, it undergoes a transformation from the inflected speech of survivors in narratives about their lives to the disembodied, speechless spirit of the language, now a sign of holiness and martyrdom. A language that had traditionally been the conduit of everyday social interaction is reified out of the worldly, becomes pure spirit. Jacqueline Osherow's poem "Ch'vil Schreiben a Poem auf Yiddish" treats Yiddish as the language of martyrs and hence purified by fire.

> I want to write a poem in Yiddish
> And not any poem, but the poem
> I am longing to write,
> A poem so Yiddish, it would not
> Be possible to translate.[20]

According to Osherow, "it's not the sort of poem / that relies on such trivialities, as / for example, my knowing how to speak / its language—though, who knows? / Maybe I understand it perfectly; maybe, in Yiddish, things aren't clearer / than the mumbling of rain on cast off leaves. . . ." Osherow's poem "exists in no realm at all / unless the dead still manage to dream dreams" (a reference to Jacob Glatstein's poem "Without Jews"). In other words, devoid of speakers, Yiddish has become an icon, a language without speakers and speech, and therefore without content, without accent, without sound. Her English poem can only gesture toward an untranslatable and unutterable poem, akin to the ineffable Hebrew name of God. In Osherow's imagination, Yiddish is a signifier of longing for an unattainable purity, the longing itself expressed in the phonetic twilight zone of transliteration—where the sound of Yiddish transcribed into the Roman alphabet of English is alien to both languages. "Ch'vil Schreiben a Poem auf Yiddish" is a paradoxical title—written by an admitted non–Yiddish speaker, it requires an English reader to mouth the words of a language that has become tragically disembodied, and through the enunciation of Yiddish sounds made possible by romanization, Osherow breathes life into a dead language. In this poem, the merger of Yiddish sound and English art takes the place of Hebrew prayer. This radical transformation of *loshen-koydesh*, which reverses the roles of Yiddish and Hebrew, undermines the divinity that is inseparable from Hebrew. "It's even a question whether God himself can make out the text of my Yiddish poem." His omniscience and omnipotence called into question by the Holocaust, "God" himself is not righteous enough to read this ineffable Yiddish poem. The title of the poem encapsulates the tragic irony of the fate of Yiddish, for Osherow has translated *spoken* Yiddish by her use of "ch'vil," rather than "Ikh vil," thereby affirming Yiddish as the language of lost speakers and accentuating its difference from German, which is evident in the spelling of "Schreiben." The literary endeavor of writing a poem is conveyed in the Germanic "Schreiben," but the essence of the poem that cannot be expressed in writing is the speech community of "Ch'vil," the colloquial contraction being the last trace of that community that the American poet desires to memorialize, "Ch'vil—I want."

Although the representation of Yiddish in Jewish American literature has changed considerably from the beginning to the end of the twentieth century, in part as the experience of immigration receded and in part as the language became a metonym for the world destroyed in the Shoah, Hebrew (to be more exact, *loshen-koydesh*) has served continuously as holy tongue, making its appearance intermittently in Jewish American literary works. This continuity of Hebrew in the literature corresponds to the American Jewish community's shared experience of Hebrew as a unifying principle, regardless of degree of knowledge. Whereas Yiddish has been an ethnic marker for American Jews, the sign of their Jewishness, Hebrew has always been a religious marker, the sign of their Judaism. This difference is highlighted even in Yiddish writing where the orthographic difference between the languages calls attention to itself on the page.[21] Yiddish literature written in America bears this same marker, so that when Yekl in Abraham Cahan's novella grieves for his dead father, he recalls the old man's voice reciting the first words of the Kiddush, and the Hebrew prayer is conspicuous by its nonvocalized density. When such liturgical fragments are translated into English the effect is not as striking, but when they are transliterated, Hebrew does appear as strange and foreign, and this effect is multiplied many times over when Hebrew typeface materializes alongside Roman type.

As an ancestral rather than a familial language of immigrants, and as a religious as well as ethnic signifier (indicating the resistance of Jewish civilization to separation of religion and ethnicity), Hebrew has been a continuous presence in English Jewish American writing, not as inflected speech, but rather as pronunciation in Judaic rituals or ceremonies. Among the most frequent intercalations of Hebrew into English are the first few lines of the Kaddish and excerpts from the Passover Haggadah.[22] Apart from the poems entitled "Kaddish" by Charles Reznikoff and Allen Ginsberg, the lines themselves appear in works by Max Apple, E. M. Broner, Johanna Kaplan, Tony Kushner, Philip Roth, James McBride, Robin Hirsch, and Art Spiegelman, to list only a few. Jewish American literature has tended to treat the Kaddish as a signifier of the "essence" of Judaism or Jewishness, as a ritual untouched by the processes of assimilation or accommodation. In his usual acerbic manner, Philip Roth captures the attenuated Jewishness that Kaddish recognition implies in *The Human Stain*, a novel that dramatizes identity politics manifested in debates around essential or performed models of identity formation. At the funeral of a black American Gentile who had successfully passed as a Jew, Nathan Zuckerman becomes aware of the man's son Mark,

> with the book in his hand and the yarmulke on his head . . . chanting in a soft and tear-filled voice the familiar Hebrew prayer.
> *Yisgadal, v'yiskadash . . .*
> Most people in America, including myself and probably Mark's siblings, don't know what these words mean, but nearly everyone recognizes the sobering message they bring: a Jew is dead. Another Jew is dead. As though death were not a consequence of life but a consequence of having been a Jew."[23]

In this scene, the attenuation if not disappearance altogether of some stable Jewish identity in America is conveyed not only by that minimal rite, the Kaddish, but also by the fact that, in this case, what does it mean to say that "another Jew is dead"?

I would like to suggest that the persistence of the Kaddish, particularly in recent decades despite its much debated and overdetermined role in Jewish practice, can be attributed to several factors related to the American Jewish experience: (1) that funerals continue to be one of the few Jewish rites that American Jews are exposed to with some regularity (and are regularly depicted in Jewish American literature); (2) that a linguistic marker of difference (beyond religious difference) enables Jewish Americans to situate themselves on the multicultural map now that race and ethnicity have been redefined so that Jews are in the category of white Europeans which reflects neither their history nor their contemporary sense of themselves;[24] (3) that post-Holocaust consciousness looms so large in contemporary Jewish identity, turning the Kaddish into a public declaration of loss that denotes both personal mourning and communal elegy; (4) that American Jews need to mark the difference between the modern Hebrew of the State of Israel and the Hebrew of Jewish communal life in the diaspora. In Leon Wieseltier's recent book *Kaddish*, a contemplation and inquiry into the evolution and meaning of this prayer during his year of mourning for his father, he recalls being moved by the sight of two brothers struggling with the transliterated prayer, uttering sounds that made no sense to them yet displaying "so much fidelity, so much humility, in their gibberish."[25] Stubborn and touching insistence on mouthing what is incomprehensible and in some cases even unpronounceable is an intriguing, recurring motif in Jewish American writing. The fact that most of it is in Aramaic may also be reassuring in that the sounds are familiar, but there is no expectation that it could be readily comprehensible as might be the case if it were entirely in Hebrew. Therefore, its ritualistic and incantatory features satisfy both spiritual and communal needs.

If the Holocaust radically transformed the way in which Yiddish is manifested in a substantial portion of Jewish American writing, then the State of Israel has had a similar effect on the manifestation of Hebrew. Israel has complicated the linguistic space in which American Jews have found themselves. If, in their imagined community as Jews, Israel is their ancestral homeland, then Hebrew is their home language. But with the exception of some minimal Hebrew School education aimed at a Bar or Bat Mitzvah, and familiarity with a few liturgical texts, the majority of American Jews find Hebrew to be foreign and difficult to acquire—both in speech and in literacy. Indeed, even the alphabet is formidable. In Robert Alter's words, they are "strange forbidding square letters, against the grain of all European systems, from right to left."[26] What I am suggesting is that, in the United States, the letters have become powerful emblems of a religious identity, which is not the equivalent of familiar signs from an ethnic homeland.

This magnetic force of Hebrew as a sign of collective origins as well as its foreignness have been articulated by American Jewish writers throughout the twentieth century. "How difficult for me is Hebrew," wrote the poet Charles Reznikoff in 1927, "even the Hebrew for *mother*, for *bread*, for *sun* is foreign. . . . I have learnt the Hebrew blessing before eating bread / is there no blessing before reading Hebrew?"[27]

After the Holocaust, for many Jewish American writers Hebrew letters became icons of Jewish religious and cultural tenacity. Karl Shapiro's 1958 poem titled "The Alphabet" begins with "The letters of the Jews as strict as flames / Or little terrible flowers lean / Stubbornly upwards through the perfect ages, / Singing through solid stone the sacred names." When Linda Pastan observes, in her poem "Passover" (1971), that only on the night of the seder "far beyond the lights of Jersey / Jerusalem still beckons us in tongues," she does not mean Jerusalem as the capital of the modern state of Israel.[28] It is one thing to have a mystical, spiritual alphabet that is invoked on ceremonial occasions and rites of passage; it is another matter altogether not to comprehend the language of what is the Jewish homeland, to lack the linguistic ability to experience life "at home." This is exacerbated for writers, whose artistic medium and source of pride is their skillful use of language.

The paradox of a language of "home" that is also a source of profound alienation is registered in many works of Jewish American writers. I believe that this accounts for statements such as Leslie Fiedler's that "I feel myself more hopelessly a foreigner in Jerusalem than in Rome. . . . Israel remains for me, even when I walk its streets, somehow an abstraction."[29] For the secular Jew and writer, even Catholic Rome, Jerusalem's antithesis, is more familiar than the central site of Judaism. His surprise and disappointment at feeling a foreigner "even when I walk its streets" betrays his belief that it is the mundane social world, the earthly Jerusalem of the modern city, where he most expected to feel at home. Yet ironically Israel remains an abstraction for him *because* he walks the streets, not "even when" he walks them, for the Hebrew that is spoken on those streets is foreign. The social texture that is material for writers such as Fiedler (as in his remarkable story "The Last Jew in America") is inextricable from the language of its speakers. "The only place that I did not excel [as a child] was Hebrew School," admits Philip Roth. Alexander Portnoy's impotence in Tel Aviv, ultimately, is the analogue of Philip Roth's impotence in a Hebrew environment. Why else would Portnoy report that the Tel Aviv hotel clerk "speaks English as though he were Ronald Coleman"?[30] Back in 1959, the first sign of Eli the Fanatic's breakdown, according to his monolingual neighbors, is his substituting "shalom" for "hello." As soon as Hebrew is no longer confined to the synagogue and it encroaches on everyday life, it is a sign of that counterlife where it *is* the language of the street, namely Israel. The expectation that a Jew should know it, the resulting sense of inadequacy and unease from not knowing it—this is one of the major reasons for the sparse depiction of Israel in Jewish American writing, and the reclamation of Hebrew as a holy tongue rather than secular tongue.

Saul Bellow's major foray into Israel in his book journal *To Jerusalem and Back* reveals the same self-consciousness about negotiating languages. Polyglot Bellow repeatedly imparts to the reader the language of his conversations as if to testify to their authenticity in a land where the author cannot converse in the native tongue. When the old barber at the King David Hotel strikes up a conversation with Bellow, he writes, "We are speaking Spanish—Ladino rather." He makes a point of noting that Chaim Gouri "knows no English" and so "we have been speaking French more or less correctly, in high gear." Taking a walk with the poet Harold Schimmel in the Old City, he prefaces his account of their afternoon with "He has learned Hebrew well enough to write in the language." Even while luxuriating in the company of Teddy Kollek, whose reminiscences he finds riveting, he remarks that "he is fluent in English and speaks it with a slightly British accent."[31] All these seemingly irrelevant observations, which at face value add nothing to the chronicle of his impressions of Jerusalem, are indicators that his linguistic antennae are actively at work in a place where mainstream society is beyond his ken, where the Israeli equivalent of Augie March is completely inaccessible to him.

By underscoring the purely religious aspect of Hebrew, American Jews have reclaimed its role in diasporic Jewish civilization. Recently Jamaica Kincaid wryly recalled that when she landed at Ben Gurion airport for the first time and encountered a barrage of Hebrew lettering on the billboards and advertisement posters, she thought, "And what prayer is this?" Although the spirituality of Hebrew, its status as holy, has been inscribed into Jewish American literature from the outset, in recent years it has played an ever greater part in these writings. No artistic device illustrates this more sharply than reproducing Hebrew typeface on the page, an act that trails with it the unique attributes of the Hebrew alphabet in Jewish textuality—meaning attributed to individual letters and prohibitions about both writing and uttering God's name. Ozick clears space on the page for HaShem in *The Puttermesser Papers*, although the initiated reader knows that this is not what her character must have actually pronounced in order to breathe life into her female golem; it is the substitute for the sacred tetragrammaton that Ozick will not deface by reproducing on the page.[32] Thane Rosenbaum reproduces the entire Kaddish in *Second Hand Smoke*, and Myla Goldberg and Nicole Krauss both reproduce God's ineffable name in Hebrew in their novels *The Bee Season* and *The History of Love*.[33]

In 2002, two extraordinary Jewish American novels appeared with strikingly similar titles: *The Illuminated Soul* by Aryeh Lev Stollman and *Everything Is Illuminated* by Jonathan Safran Foer.[34] Virtuoso performances by young writers several generations removed from immigration to North America, each of these novels articulates Jewish American literature's fascination with the "foreign" languages of its origin, experienced as pronunciation, accent, and script, and when read alongside each other they demonstrate two dramatically different expressions of Jewish communal identity in their relation to languages other than English.

One of Foer's narrators, a Ukrainian tour guide specializing in taking American Jews on heritage tours to the sites from which their families originated, speaks in a hilarious and inventive accent, marked by wildly inappropriate usage and scrambled syntax. Another of the book's narrators, the Jewish American character who is a stand-in for Foer, writes English prose that does not bear any trace of his immigrant ancestors. Among its many achievements, Foer's novel reverses one trajectory in Jewish American writing from the work of immigrants to the present, namely the preoccupation with Yiddish-inflected English that an author or character either attempts to overcome or exploits for its inventive wordplay. One of the oddest features of *Everything Is Illuminated* is the recognition that times have changed dramatically if the Jewish character in search of his Yiddish roots in Eastern Europe writes without a trace of accent, and the character with the Eastern European inflection is the Gentile.

Among recent fictional works to draw inspiration from Hebrew is Aryeh Lev Stollman's *The Far Euphrates*, a bildungsroman that begins and ends with Hebrew letters.[35] As a native Canadian who has lived in the United States for many years, Stollman can serve as an exemplary North American writer. The

work opens with one of Aryeh Alexander's earliest childhood memories—
being taught two alphabets while still in kindergarten:

> My mother baked me sugar cookies in the shapes of those transmuting and
> buoyant letters that drifted down to us from the seafaring Phoenicians. And
> my father had started reading Genesis with me, slowly, in its original tongue,
> where the dotted vowels clustered like bees around the honeyed consonants.
> We read each sentence carefully, first in Hebrew, then in English, and finally in
> German. (2)

From the earliest days of his childhood, Alex is surrounded by languages,
living and dead, European and Semitic, sacred and secular. "My father was
determined that I learn as many languages as possible. Moses had spoken all
seventy known in his time, and my father had resolved that I start out in life
with at least three" (3). Choosing Genesis as his son's first reading lesson, the
rabbi asserts the primacy of the Hebrew text and the secondary status of the
translations into English, Alex's native language, and then German, the language of the rabbi's childhood, of Nazi Germany from which he fled to North
America, and of the approach to Jewish textuality that marks his own and
his father's research, *Wissenschaft des Judentums*. But the rabbi also reads
Grimm's Fairy Tales to his son with the translation process in reverse. "He
first said each sentence in the original German and then he translated it into
English. Finally, he translated it again, into Hebrew" (3). In either case, English is a stopping place between Hebrew and German, Hebrew as an ancestral, primordial language and German as a primal language of childhood for
the rabbi.

As a result, German and Hebrew both function as markers of a home language that requires translation into English, yet each also needs to be translated into the other. German and Hebrew are conveyed to Alex in letters as well
as speech, first with the honeyed consonants of Hebrew on his mother's sugar
cookies and eventually with his grandfather's travel book, whose Gothic script
is an enigma that he learns to decipher and rewrite into modern German script
"until [he becomes] accustomed to the old lettering" (151). German, therefore,
is home to the extent that it is the tongue of his patrimony, the language of his
father's childhood and grandfather's scholarship. The choice of Genesis for
his Hebrew initiation and *Grimm's Fairy Tales* for his German study would
seem to be their role as primal narratives, each conveying a romantic *"Volk"*
essence, yet each also a contested site with traces of precursors that undermine naïve ideas about origins and cultural authenticity. The sugary Hebrew
letters have drifted "down to us from the seafaring Phoenicians," and the fairy
tales—*"ekht Deutsch"* according to the Brothers Grimm in their campaign to
fortify German national identity in the face of French incursion—were never
transcriptions of oral storytelling by German folk, but rather a composite of

ancient Persian tales accessed through both Italian and French folklorists. The power of both of these texts, Stollman suggests, has more to do with the yearning for homes, linguistic and otherwise, than with the scholarly assertion of national or ethnic origins.

Pronouncing the letters of alphabets other than the Roman script that marks English plays an even greater role in Stollman's most recent novel, *The Illuminated Soul*, in which a man named Joseph Ivri (his very name meaning "Hebrew") recounts the events of a special summer in his youth when he volunteered to serve as *baal koreh* for his congregation. Cautioned by his mother that "the words of the Torah are not to be taken lightly. . . . That's why we have to be careful not to mispronounce them, because then they become distorted and false" (31), Joseph evaluates each of his performances: "I caught the one pronunciation error I had made in the densely syntactic word *v'ho'safsuf*— 'and the mixed multitude' — and corrected it. . . . I was very relieved" (168). One day that summer an elegant, mysterious woman by the name of Eva Higashi arrives in their town. She is in possession of two manuscript treasures that she smuggled out of Prague: *Clouds of Glory*, the unfinished scholarly work of her father, who was murdered by the Nazis, and *The Augsburg Miscellany*, a priceless medieval illuminated manuscript that she hid from the Nazis. Because she is his family's boarder, Joseph is privileged to see several pages of the illuminated manuscript during the time that he is rehearsing his readings from the Torah scroll, also a manuscript on parchment.

The Illuminated Soul invites the reader to consider the affinity between an illuminated manuscript and an illuminated soul and the role of writing, letters, and textuality in the life of the spirit. When Eva interrupts Joseph as he practices the weekly Torah portion, he explains the difficulty of his task: "You have to be able to read it without seeing the vowels" (81). "Yes, yes," concurs Eva, "the vowels are very important. The solid consonants are like our material bodies and the invisible vowels are like our souls that make our bodies come to life." The widow of a Japanese man who saved her life during the war, Eva's name signifies origins: Eva being the Romanized, Anglicized version of Chava, Eve, and Higashi the Japanese word for the East. Twice in this novel letters from Eastern alphabets that signify beginnings emerge between the Roman type: the Hebrew letter א and the Japanese glyph for East, which is the sun rising behind a tree: 東. The aleph represents the enlarged and illuminated letter of the author of the *Augsburg Miscellany*, Alexander of Augsburg, a transliteration of his Greek name into Hebrew, a letter "drawn large, almost a quarter of the page, transfigured into a strange bird, its two eagle-clawed feet on the ground, its upper extremities, gilded wings, folded forward, protecting itself." Eva suggests that this letter represents "the Divine Presence, the Holy Shekhinah, or the wings of eagles which will carry God's people back to Jerusalem when the Messiah comes" (110). Joseph is awed by the illuminations of the scribe/artist of the *Miscellany*, particularly by those for Psalm 104. Only with the help of a microscope can Joseph discern "shimmering beneath the surface of a lapis lazuli sea . . . pale sapphire forms of fish—all kinds—and dolphins." Although this undoubtedly refers to the line "O Lord, how manifold are thy works, So is this great and wide sea wherein are things innumerable, both small and great beasts" (1.25), it is important to note that this Psalm opens with an image of God as himself illuminated, wrapped in light, "Oteh or."

In *The Illuminated Soul*, the concept of illumination encompasses light in the sense that God is the source of all illumination, visual art illustrating the words on the parchment, and the manuscript itself with its elaborate calligraphy in which the letters are illuminated, and illuminating. What I want to suggest is that Stollman reaches beyond the Western alphabet in his novel to demonstrate that Roman phonetic script is not universal. On one hand, the Hebrew א, like the other letters of the Hebrew alphabet but to a greater degree, is itself a signifier of meaning, not merely a phonetic sign. By reproducing this letter here and on the book jacket, Stollman reminds his readers of the materiality of the signifier in Jewish tradition (not only in Kabbalah, to which he is also gesturing), of the holiness that inheres in the letters themselves. On the other hand, by reproducing the Japanese pictogram, he is demonstrating that there are other ancient civilizations with nonphonetic script, whose concept of textuality differs from that of the West (but is not identical with that of Judaism). The only English monolingual speaker in this book is Rabbi Kremlach's parrot Nebuchadnezzar, whose mindless repetition of English words and whose biblical namesake make him an emblem of exile, a parody of he who cannot sing his songs in a strange land. Spiritual nourishment in *The Illuminated Soul* comes from looking home to the East—to Jerusalem, to other ancient civilizations, and to the rising sun. Intellectual nourishment comes from the West, as Eva's father's biblical scholarship is grounded in *Wissenschaft des Judentums*. As the one who alludes to the Shekhinah, Eva is herself a mysterious presence whose name, Higashi, is both the rising sun in Japanese and nearly a homonym for the Hebrew "I served" or "offered" sustenance. As original mother, Eve serves Joseph her treasured manuscripts, and after she retreats, he falters in his Torah reading so that "all the letters and words just lay there in a jumble. They were all indistinguishable to me. . . . I could not remember what the letters represented to me. " At that point, his own mother, Adele Ivri, "fed me the words of the Torah, one by one," until "the holy letters began to swim back into view, reasserting themselves on the pale parchment of the open scroll" (270).

At the end of *The Far Euphrates* at his father's funeral, Alex also returns to the Hebrew letters that his father taught him when he was a child, this time the letters merging with the souls of his loved ones, living and dead. "When I said the prayers at the graveside, I spoke in the language of earliest times. I said all the words, with their constellations of letters that had once combined themselves this way and that in myriad forms to create all of our souls and to create this world, which is our home" (206). In both of these novels by a young writer several generations removed from pronunciation of English as a matter of social acceptance, pronunciation of Hebrew letters in prayer is an affirmation of love, for his father and for the very fact of creation itself. Stollman's Judaic and Hebraic learning leaves its imprint on his English prose.

In this very brief survey of the way that Hebrew and Yiddish have figured in the imagination of Jewish American writers, I want to emphasize that the presence of these languages has played, and continues to play, a major role in American Jewry's sense of community. In Allegra Goodman's novel *Paradise Park*, published one year before *Everything Is Illuminated* and *The Illuminated Soul*, a young Jewish American woman on a sojourn in Jerusalem poses a question that captures the spirit of one kind of newly emerging Jewish American literature: "I lift up my voice in the wilderness, eyes to the hills . . . and dance on the sand a song of praise with words I don't understand. What can you do with just an alphabet?"[36] A great deal, it appears. Insofar as literature is spun out of desire and memory, longing and forgetting, Jewish American writers have made great contributions to American literature, dreaming "their dreams in English phrases," in Mary Antin's terms, and imagining their worlds "with just an alphabet." One sign of this literature, I would contend, is that it is not exclusively English. It never has been. It has always borne the traces of that other script and those other sounds, and contemporary Jewish American literature is no exception. When Henry James first heard the speakers of this new American Jewish community, he dubbed their spoken English, reluctantly, "the accent of the future." He has been proven right to the extent that American Jewish writing has become mainstream American writing, and many Yiddish words and phrases have become American English. But in their imagination, the writers of this community have always heard, and recorded, the accents of the past.

Notes

1. Seminal works on the multilingualism of Jewish literature are Baal-Makhshoves [Israel Isidor Elyashev], "Tsvey shprakhen: eyn eyntsiker literature," in *Petrograder Tageblatt*, Petrograd, 1918. Reprinted in *Geklibene verk* (New York: Cyco-Bicher Farlag, 1953). In English, "One Literature in Two Languages," trans. Hana Wirth-Nesher, in *What Is Jewish Literature?* (Philadelphia: Jewish Publication Society, 1994); and Shmuel Niger, *Bilingualism in the History of Jewish Literature*, trans. Joshua A. Fogel (New York: University Press of America, 1941).
2. Cynthia Ozick, "Preface," in *Bloodshed and Other Novellas* (New York: Knopf, 1976), 9.

3. *Words and Images: The Jerusalem Literary Project*, ed. Eleonora Lev and Natan Beyrak, 2002. In an interview in 1966, Roth made a somewhat similar remark: "Oh, very little Yiddish was spoken. . . . What I heard, however, wasn't always English at the other extreme. I heard a *kind* of English that I think was spoken by second-generation people in what was essentially a very tightly enclosed Jewish neighborhodd in Newark." See transcription of National Educational Television interview with Jerre Magione, in George Searles, *Conversations with Philip Roth* (Jackson: University of Mississippi, 1992), 3.

4. Philip Roth, *The Plot Against America* (London: Jonathan Cape, 2004), 4.

5. For the importance of Henry James in the literary geneaology of Jewish American writers, particularly Roth, see Jonathan Freedman, *The Temple of Culture: Assimilation and Anti-Semitism in Literary Anglo-America* (Oxford: Oxford University Press, 2000), and Malkiel Kaisy, "Passionate Correctors: The Rise of Modern Textuality and the Impression of the Jewish Man," chapter of unpublished doctoral dissertation, Tel Aviv University.

6. Abraham Cahan, *The Rise of David Levinsky* (New York: Penguin, 1993 [orig. publication Harper & Brothers, 1917]), 130. For Gentile attitudes toward Jewish speech, see Sander Gilman, *The Jew's Body* (New York: Routledge, 1991).

7. Anzia Yezierska, *Bread Givers* (New York: Persea Books, 1952 [orig. publication 1925]).

8. Mary Antin, *The Promised Land* (New York: Penguin, 1997 [orig. publication 1912]).

9. For a fuller treatment of Antin's linguistic passing see *Call It English: The Languages of Jewish American Literature* (Princeton: Princeton University Press, 2006). Parts of this essay are abbreviated versions of longer discussions in this book.

10. Clara Katherine Rogers, *English Diction* (Boston, 1915), 21.

11. See Donald Weber, "Accents of the Future: Jewish American Popular Culture," in *The Cambridge Companion to Jewish American Literature*, ed. Michael Kramer and Hana Wirth-Nesher (Cambridge: Cambridge University Press, 2003); Weber, *Haunted in the New World: Jewish American Culture from Cahan to the Goldbergs* (Bloomington: Indiana University Press, 2005); and Gavin Jones, *Strange Talk: The Politics of Dialect Literature in Gilded Age America* (Berkeley: University of California, 1999). See also Jeffrey Shandler, *Adventures in Yiddishland: Postvernacular Language and Culture* (Berkeley: University of California Press, 2006).

12. For how Henry Roth expresses this in *Call It Sleep*, see my essay on multilingual Jewish writing in *The Cambridge Companion*.

13. Cynthia Ozick, *The Shawl* (New York: Random House, 1990); Henry Roth, *Call It Sleep* (New York: Farrar Straus & Giroux, 1991 [orig. publication 1934]); Delmore Schwartz, *In Dreams Begin Responsibilities* (New York: New Directions, 1948).

14. Cynthia Ozick, *The Pagan Rabbi and Other Stories* (New York: Vintage, 1971), 100.

15. For discussions of the significance of the affinity between German and Yiddish, see Ruth Wisse's analysis of Kafka's poetics in *The Modern Jewish Canon: A Journey Through Language and Culture* (Chicago: University of Chicago Press,

2000), and Sander Gilman's *Jewish Self-Hatred: Anti-Semitism and the Hidden Language of the Jews* (Baltimore: Johns Hopkins University Press, 1986).

16. Art Spiegelman, *Maus: A Survivor's Tale* (New York: Pantheon, 1986), 54.

17. For multilingual strategies in *Maus*, see Alan Rosen's essay "The Language of Survival: English as Metaphor in Spiegelman's *Maus*," *Prooftexts* 15 (1995).

18. Leo Rosten, *The Joys of Yiddish* (New York: Simon and Schuster, 1968).

19. For the performativity of contemporary Yiddish in America see Shandler, *Adventures in Yiddishland*.

20. Jacqueline Osherow, *Dead Men's Praise* (New York: Grove, 1999).

21. See the "Introspectivism—*In Zikh*" Manifesto of 1919 by Glatstein, Leyeles, and Minkov, in *American Yiddish Poetry*, ed. Benjamin and Barbara Harshav (Berkeley: University of California Press, 1986).

22. For a fuller discussion of this subject, see my essay "Magnified and Sanctified: Liturgy in Contemporary Jewish American Literature," in *Ideology and Identity in American and Israeli Jewish Literature*, ed. Emily Budick (Albany: SUNY Press, 2001).

23. Philip Roth, *The Human Stain* (Boston: Houghton Mifflin, 2000), 313–314.

24. David Hollinger, *Post-ethnic America* (New York: Basic Books, 1995).

25. Leon Wieseltier, *Kaddish* (New York: Knopf, 1998), 18.

26. Robert Alter, *Necessary Angels: Tradition and Modernity in Kafka, Benjamin, and Scholem* (Cambridge: Harvard University Press, 1991), 27.

27. Charles Reznikoff, "Poems 1918–1975," in *The Complete Poems of Charles Reznikoff* (Santa Barbara: Black Sparrow Press, 1977).

28. Karl Shapiro, "The Alphabet," in *Poems of a Jew* (New York: Random House, 1958), 3; Linda Pastan, "Passover," in *A Perfect Circle of Sun* (Chicago: The Swallow Press, 1971).

29. Leslie Fiedler, *To the Gentiles* (New York: Stein and Day, 1972).

30. Philip Roth, *Portnoy's Complaint* (New York: Random House, 1967), 254.

31. Saul Bellow, *To Jerusalem and Back* (New York: Viking, 1976), 30, 50.

32. Cynthia Ozick, *Puttermesser Papers: A Novel* (New York: Knopf, 1997), 40.

33. Thane Rosenbaum, *Second Hand Smoke* (New York: St. Martin's, 1999); Myla Goldberg, *The Bee Season* (New York: Random House, 2000); Nicole Krauss, *The History of Love* (New York: Penguin, 2005).

34. Jonathan Safran Foer, *Everything Is Illuminated* (New York: Harper Collins, 2002), and Aryeh Lev Stollman, *The Illuminated Soul* (New York: Riverhead, 2002).

35. Aryeh Lev Stollman, *The Far Euphrates* (New York: Riverhead, 1997).

36. Allegra Goodman, *Paradise Park* (New York: Dial), 2001.

Chapter 16   Arnold Eisen

American Jewish Thought
and the Imagination of
American Jewish Community

Robert Bellah observed more than twenty years ago in *Habits of the Heart* that the "first language" spoken by Americans of this generation where moral, political, and social matters are concerned is highly individualist, while America's more communal "second language"—derived from biblical and republican traditions—is spoken far less often and less well.[1] Surprisingly enough, that insight also applies to much of late twentieth-century American Jewish religious thought. A great deal of attention has been devoted to subjects such as the Holocaust, the impact of feminism, the authority of halakhah, and the attractions of spirituality. Relatively few pages, however, have been devoted to the imagination of contemporary diaspora community—this despite the fact that Jewish tradition is full to overflowing with reflections on this matter, and despite the formidable challenges posed to the maintenance and transmission of Jewish tradition in this country by American individualism, voluntarism, and mobility. Jewish organizations and institutions have devoted countless resources to shoring up group boundaries, membership, and cohesion in the face of these challenges. Leading Jewish religious thinkers in America have rarely followed suit. Sophisticated normative reflection on what Jewish community requires and provides has been episodic at best.

My purpose in this paper is therefore twofold. First, I want to analyze the most important writings about community by the two American Jewish thinkers whose work on the issue was most sustained and profound: Rabbis Mordecai M. Kaplan and Joseph Dov Halevi Soloveitchik. The reimagining of Jewish community in America was of course *a* major focus, perhaps *the* major focus, of Kaplan's lifelong project of Reconstruction, first spelled out in (wonderfully rich) detail in his magnum opus, *Judaism as a Civilization*. Soloveitchik— the most influential modern Orthodox thinker in America during the latter part of the twentieth century—addressed the matter in several key essays; his notion of the "covenantal faith community," I shall argue, offers a useful supplement and corrective to Kaplan's ethnic/cultural definition of Jewishness and his highly institutional understanding of community. My second purpose in this essay is to take note of several other images or accounts of Jewish community—including reasons, motivations, and sources of authority for such community—that are plainly exhibited in the classical texts of Jewish tradition and the varieties of Jewish history but either absent or understated in the writings of Kaplan and Soloveitchik alike. Setting these elements side by side with recent findings concerning American Jewish attitudes and behaviors should, I believe, point up the limits of either an ethnic/cultural or a "covenantal faith" conception of what Jewish commnity has been and could be. In conclusion I will suggest several implications for the imagination and building of Jewish community in America today; in this section of the paper I will join Kaplan and Soloveitchik in speaking normatively about what Jewish communal life in America could and should comprise.

Two Views of Jewish Community

Kaplan begins his masterpiece, *Judaism as a Civilization* (1934), with an elegantly simple account of how Jews came to be faced with the crisis that he proposes to resolve. For centuries, even millennia, Jews were kept apart from Gentiles' society and culture by external political and economic circumstances on the one hand and by their own religious beliefs and practices on the other. The circumstances changed drastically with the onset of modernity. The traditional religious beliefs and practices were no longer operative. Jews had to respond to these challenges with radical transformations of their own. Something had to be found to replace religion as the bearer or purpose and meaning of Jewish existence. Kaplan aims in the book to supply it.

Religion (or rather its liabilities) is thus crucial to Kaplan's analysis from the outset, the survival factor for Jews and Judaism over which Jews can exercise a measure of control and therefore the focus of his discussion in the opening chapter (indeed throughout the book). The key to Kaplan's plan for revitalizing his community is the transformation of Judaism from a religious tradition to a civilization. If faith in God and God's rewards in this world and the next had played the major role in maintaining Jewish distinctiveness in the past, "the present crisis in Judaism" could be addressed only through provision of a functional substitute for the claim to supernatural providence and revelation.

If day-to-day meaning had been provided in the form of a unique and all-embracing regimen of activities commanded or sanctioned by God and God's earthly representatives, it too would have to be offered in another form. In short, the promise of *salvation*—eternal life in a world to come—would have to be matched by a different sort of salvation: fulfillment in this world. Such was Kaplan's proposal for a new secret of Jewish survival, the new basis of Jews' "faith in the worthwhileness of being a Jew."[2]

Kaplan puts the matter with characteristic directness: in the modern world "the aura of divine election has departed from his people . . . the Jew is maladjusted morally and spiritually as a result of losing the traditional conception of salvation." A new purpose in life had to be evolved, and "that purpose will have to constitute his salvation."[3] Kaplan would provide it by defining Judaism as *civilization* rather than religion. The individual Jew would be wrapped up in a distinctive set of practices—to be understood as "folkways" rather than revealed commandments—so all-embracing that they made Jewish "otherness" "intuitive." Jews would naturally, unthinkingly, turn to their own civilization in pursuit of self-fulfillment. Judaism as civilization is defined as "that nexus of a history, literature, language, social organization, folk sanctions, standards of conduct, social and spiritual ideals, esthetic values, which in their totality form a civilization."[4] Kaplan presents the plan not only as sensible and straightforward but as inevitable—if Jews wish to survive. All other options, he declares, have utterly failed in any case.

One tends to read Kaplan's book as one of supreme and overweening confidence. The doctor confronts the illness without blinking, prescribes stern medicine, and begins to deliver it to the patient. But Kaplan's diaries from the years leading up to the writing of his great book do not betray any such confidence,[5] and I think a careful reading of the published work supports that view. For one thing, the secret to Jewish survival over nearly three millennia was by Kaplan's own account no longer available. "The only way in which the Jew believed it was possible for him to achieve salvation was by remaining loyal to his people, for it was only by sharing their lives in this world that he was certain to share their life in the next world."[6] Whether or not we agree with Kaplan that this survival factor was the most important, it seems reasonable to agree that it mattered a great deal; further, even if we do not believe as Kaplan did that "all Jews had but one conception of salvation,"[7] it is difficult to deny that the "plausibility structure" consisting of Jewish neighborhoods, Jewish schools, Jewish courts, a Jewish calendar, Jewish friends, Jewish rituals, and so on—all this in a context of Gentile hostility and difference—was undergirded by belief in an exclusive covenant with God that crucially altered Jewish fate in *both* worlds, this one and the one to come. Loss of belief in privileged Jewish access to eternal life might well play a role in the difficulty of sustaining Jewish community in twentieth-century America. If so, Kaplan is right that "some new purpose in life as a Jew" will have to substitute for those elements of purpose in which Jews once believed but can believe no more.[8] But can such a purpose in fact be found? Before suggesting one, he offers a masterful survey of the constraints to which he feels all modern Jews, himself included, must submit: modern social, economic, and political conditions, as well as such "ideological" forces as scientific and historical consciousness. In this respect, though not others, Kaplan's masterpiece reads remarkably like Yehezkel Kaufman's *Golah-ve-nekhar* (Exile and Estrangement), which he read in 1930.[9] Both analysts argued that supernatural religion had kept Jews Jewish for a very long time—and that it could do so no longer.

Nor could Kaplan be content with minor adjustment of the tradition to suit the Jews' new circumstances. History had changed too radically for that—and the tradition was too permeated with outmoded supernaturalism to be of much use. In *Judaism as a Civilization*, Kaplan not only criticizes all the religious forms of Judaism thus far developed to meet the challenge: Reform, Orthodox, and Conservative. He also decisively denies the ability of premodern Jewish texts to provide Jews with ultimate meaning on anything like their own terms. Biblical and rabbinic sources on community, as on all other topics, are subjected to "functional interpretation,"[10] a method renamed and reconfigured in *The Meaning of God in Modern Jewish Religion* (1937) as "revaluation." As opposed to previous commentators, who (beginning with the rabbis) tended in his account to read their own beliefs and customs into earlier sources—a method Kaplan calls "transvaluation"—his own method, "revaluation," begins with recognition of "the chasm between the traditional and the modern world-view."[11] The point of "revaluation" is "disengaging from the traditional content those elements in it which answer permanent postulates of human nature, and in integrating them into our own ideology."[12] These can then be translated into contemporary terms, in the service of present needs.

Note that Kaplan frames "the traditional content" of Judaism in the singular, just as he assumes that all Jews held one belief concerning the world to come. He also trusts his own ability, thanks to science (a tool the ancestors of course lacked), to discern the "permanent postulates of human nature" underlying the ancestors' beliefs and practices. Because the ancestors were not modern and the faith was permeated with "supernaturalism" and "other-worldliness," only *reformulated* notions of creativity, freedom, covenant, and so forth can prove useful to him and his readers. Kaplan pejoratively names the past stages of Jewish history as "henotheistic," "theocratic," and "other-worldly." None can offer a reliable or useful guide for modern belief or practice. Traditional sources in his view cannot in themselves provide content or authority for contemporary thinking about community—or anything else. They can fortify contemporary hopes and aspirations only by rooting modern Jews in their collective past. "The advantage of utilizing traditional concepts is [only] that they carry with them the accumulated momentum and emotional drive of man's previous efforts to attain greater spiritual power."¹³ It is clear that Jews get no special purchase on truth or goodness or God through attachment to their classical sources. They gain only "momentum and emotional drive," the same as any other group.

In *The Meaning of God*, published three years after *Judaism as a Civilization*, Kaplan makes significant (and at times brilliant) use of biblical and rabbinic sources, suitably "revaluated." The book reconstructs the Jewish ritual calendar in a fashion that logically inverts the classical Reform abandonment of ritual observance. Where the latter argued, in effect, that the eternal substance of Judaism was ethical monotheism, and that individual rituals should therefore be retained only if they (like some Sabbath observances) advanced the mission of refining ethical monotheism and spreading it to all mankind, and should be abandoned if they (like dietary laws) got in the way of that mission, Kaplan takes Jewish civilization as a whole to be a treasure in need of safeguarding, and Jewish folkways as a principal tool in its survival. If a ritual no longer resonates with contemporary meaning, one should not abandon that ritual but fill it with new meaning. He aims, as we would say today, at a *community of practice*. Jews are defined, united, and inspired by what they *do together*. They share a community of experience. *Judaism as a Civilization* abounds in the imagination of things for Jews to do in groups: from folk pageants to philanthropy, from language classes to recreation. However, for all the attention to "folkways" in the book, Kaplan's imagining of the collective Jewish future cannot make good use of the rabbis or the Bible—indeed, of the whole of premodern Jewish tradition. His notion of Jewish community is, to that degree, denied a crucial resource. The tradition cannot form the basis of what we would call a Jewish *narrative community* without substantial reformulation.

No less striking is the fact that *Judaism as a Civilization* says virtually nothing about the shape of Jewish communities in the premodern past, or about the communities of Eastern Europe from which Kaplan's own family, like the families of many of his readers, recently emigrated.¹⁴ Kaplan does not make room for his own institutional innovations by citing the diversity of communal models adopted by Jews over the centuries, or the persistence of tension between "religious" and "secular" leaders across these variations, or the perennial balancing act among local, regional, and worldwide Jewish needs. There is no appeal to the semiautonomous kehillah as warrant for Kaplan's argument on behalf of its reconstruction in a different form in the United States. Yiddish culture too is barely discussed despite the fact that its secular character might have provided Kaplan with useful precedent, as it surely did with inspiration. Kaplan is virtually silent on all these points. In sum: the lack of a complex account of Jewish history, which might have enriched contemporary planning with a repertoire of varied possibility, is matched by the lack of a complex notion of tradition, which might have furnished Jewish imaginations with images of self and community drawn from halakhah and aggadah; philosophy and kabbalah; Hasidim and Mitnagdim. The value of the latter resource will become apparent when we turn to Soloveitchik.

Before doing so, however, I want to note two dilemmas that surface clearly in Kaplan's analysis and that continue to confront Jews seeking to conceive or build Jewish community in America. Both dilemmas render Kaplan—along with many others who share his project—less than sanguine about their chances for success. One, recognized episodically by Kaplan, is that the call for a "maximalist Judaism" comes down in the end (and long before the end) to "a maximum program of Jewishness compatible with one's abilities and circumstances."[15] On the one hand, Kaplan states in the authoritative voice of social science, "a civilization demands that the foundations of personality in the child be laid with the material which the civilization itself supplies."[16] This is certainly Kaplan's aim in outlining a Jewish culture that includes language, history, attachment to a homeland, mores and folkways, and a communal structure far more encompassing than the synagogue.[17] On the other hand, Kaplan recognizes that he can hope at best for American Jews to live in two civilizations, and he acknowledges that Jews in America can never "live Judaism" as their primary civilization, as they could in Palestine, or even as a "co-ordinate" civilization as they might in a situation of true cultural autonomy. Judaism in America can survive only as a "subordinate civilization." Since the civilization that can satisfy the primary interests of the Jew must necessarily be the civilization of the country he lives in, the American Jew will be first and foremost an American, and only secondarily a Jew.[18] The two sides of the identity-hyphen, we might say, are not and cannot be equal.

Kaplan rebels against this realization. He denies that Jews have any option for fulfillment ("salvation") in Gentile America. Non-Jewish Americans turn to Christianity for their ultimate purpose in life. American civil religion is as yet unequipped to provide it. Kaplan set to work on remedying that problem too, attempting to assist in the creation of an American civil religion to serve the spiritual need of all the nation's hyphenated citizens. In the meantime Jews had no choice but to turn to Judaism for "moral and spiritual security." All the Jew asked, he says with no little pathos, is that Gentiles "not monopolize his life [so] as to leave no room in it for the Jewish civilization."[19] Kaplan, we observe, is driven back upon an updated and more benign version of the survival factor he identified as so crucial to the premodern Jewish past: Gentile hostility and rejection. But he cannot and does not want to rely on its continuation. His hopes for America, maintained in this book and others despite a trenchant critique of American political and economic institutions, and full appreciation of antisemitism, convinced him that Jews would soon have to *choose* Judaism. It would not be forced upon them by Gentile rejection. He worried that, absent supernatural faith, and despite the allure of reconstructed beliefs and folkways, Jews might not make that choice in significant numbers for the community and its civilization to survive. Maximalist Judaism in most cases might well not amount to much.

A related dilemma is front and center in the chapter "Jewish Communal Organization," where Kaplan repeatedly worries that the *voluntarist* character of Jewish life—which he of course embraces—might militate against or even preclude fulfillment of his hopes for the rebirth of Jewish community. Early in the chapter, Kaplan criticizes his mentor Ahad Ha'am for not taking sufficient account of the "progressive self-assertion of the individual which may almost be formulated into a law of human history."[20] Individuals in the twentieth century will have to choose whether or not to devote resources and energy to the Jewish community, and will not give their loyalty to the Jewish group unless it gives them back what they need and want from it. "Salvation presupposes a community which treats the individual as so organic a part of itself that in promoting his life it is aware that it promotes its own."[21] The most reasonable thing for Jews to do, given their circumstances, is to construct such a community. But for this to happen, the community has to accept responsibility for the welfare of the individual. "It must come to the assistance of the Jew: first, by obtaining for him a place in the sun; secondly, by helping him make his social and economic adjustments; thirdly, by imparting to him cultural values and habits which can make his life significant."[22] Kaplan is emphatic on this point. "It is just as essential for the community to accept responsibility for the welfare of the individual, as for the individual to be responsible, to the extent of his ability, for the welfare of the community."[23] "The economic security of every Jew" is the responsibility of the community.[24] And again: "Without that concrete service which the community rendered to every Jew, rich or poor, learned or ignorant, Judaism would long ago have disappeared." The premodern community helped Jews achieve their share in the world to come. Today the community has to help Jews gain salvation in *this* world.[25] If it does not, Jewish individuals will have no cause to give the community their allegiance, or even their attention.

Voluntarism—the fact of Jewish choice where Judaism is concerned—then becomes Kaplan's strongest argument on behalf of an all-embracing kehillah. The congregational synagogue is "only a recently evolved form of social organization," and one that Jews have come upon "absent-mindedly, as it were, in their attempt to adjust themselves to the new social and political conditions resulting from the emancipation." It cannot do the job required. For the congregation was "set up as something apart from other Jewish interests," both material and spiritual. What is more, it "lacks the element of socialized authority," the "involuntarism characteristic of national life," which Kaplan knew he had somehow to reconstruct if Jewish community was to be revived in America. Jewish life requires a "civic type of organization." Jews have to learn once more to be "communally minded."[26] Kaplan quotes at length the plan for the stillborn New York Kehillah earlier in the century;[27] in the absence of that sort of all-embracing community, it might be possible to "re-form the community idea in its original scope and vigor" with a structure of local federations of philanthropies. "The Jewish federations . . . furnish the initial framework for the type of communal structure which Jewish life calls for, provided, of course, they be enlarged in scope and transformed in purpose."[28] Kaplan neither lays out that scope nor details that purpose (though he does call for representation on federations' governing bodies of the "interests and point of view of the contributors" and not only of the agencies that are the beneficiaries of the welfare funds). The key, he concludes, is not the specifics of organizational machinery but the vision—which he has provided—"of an integrated Jewry."[29]

Kaplan alternately reverts to and retreats from the underlying problem of voluntarism time and again in this chapter. The Jewish community as presently organized around synagogues lacks "the element of socialized authority." Jews, he laments, have embraced voluntarism with a vengeance. Kaplan claims weakly that "the normal individual does not want to be a law unto himself" but then returns from descriptive to prescriptive voice: "If Jewish nationhood is to work in the diaspora, its principal manifestation must be this very element of involuntarism characteristic of national life."[30] His vivid imagination cannot but rub up against the limits of what one can expect from Jews in present circumstances, and cannot but take on the task of persuading Jews to "live Jewish civilization" and see themselves as members of the Jewish community. As a result, Kaplan's work—like so much of modern Jewish thought—is strongest when it comes to picturing *private* observance, voluntarily assumed and performed in the precincts of home and synagogue. The chapters on Jewish milieu and Jewish folkways are richly detailed. Kaplan is much weaker when it comes to the imagination of the Jewish *public sphere*—and weakest of all, perhaps, when it comes to the motives that will elicit or impel Jewish behaviors that can no longer be compelled.

The success of Jewish communities thus depends (according to Kaplan's analysis) upon a combination of continued Gentile hostility, vestigial Jewish tendencies toward "aggregation," and—Kaplan's contribution—the creation of a "way of life" so all-embracing that the choice for Jewishness becomes "intuitive," a natural outgrowth of inescapable "otherness." Given a profound and beautiful array of meaningful Jewish practices and a set of Jewish communal institutions that answer the Jews' every material and spiritual need—this in a situation of Gentile nonacceptance—why would Jews *not* choose Judaism? The construction and maintenance of that Jewish way of life, however, of course depends on thousands of individual choices that will likely not be forthcoming in the absence of the reality that they are meant to create. Kaplan's theory of Jewish community is caught in a truly vicious circle.

He never really escaped from it, though he tried mightily (and inventively) in subsequent works to do so. *The Future of the American Jew*, published in the wake of World War II, reiterates much of the analysis and prescription offered in *Judaism as a Civilization*. Jews still need one another despite the assimilatory forces of modernity "because of the failure of democratic nationalism to live up to its promise of economic and social equality . . . Jews are still regarded as an alien group in the United States." That situation, along with "the still surviving residue of the past tendencies on the part of the Jews to pool their common interests," will have to be sufficient to bring Jews together.[31] They can do little to get the larger world to care for them as fully as it does for non-Jews, Kaplan writes resignedly. But Jews can "so re-organize their communal life" that Jewish individuals will be confident that the Jewish community cares about them. They will do so if that community is so organized as to "overcome those political, social and economic disadvantages from which [the Jew] suffers."

Kaplan offers somewhat more detail about what this community should look like. He continues to believe that attachment to Gentile America will come as a matter of course despite the vestiges of antisemitism and the horrors of recent Jewish history, while allegiance to the Jewish community is by contrast in doubt, and must be won. Kaplan therefore decries once again the reliance upon synagogues as the major institution of Jewish life and calls for a "structural pattern . . . determined by regional propinquity rather than by interest in particular objectives." In other words, all the organizations in a given locality should collaborate so as to elicit Jewish energies and tap new resources—and all must be animated by concern with Judaism conceived as holistic civilization. The Jewish Family Service, for example, must be "dominated by the purpose of conserving Judaism, [or] it will become a strong factor for liquidating it."[32] Kaplan urges better training of Jewish communal professionals; greater attention to the Jewish arts and the Jewish calendar as means of unifying Jews; and an organized community open to all Jews regardless of "how they conceive the form or content of [Jewish] life." Synagogues, community centers, and schools are given pride of place in his exposition, but among the functions of an "organic Jewish community" he lists as well the maintenance of vital statistics, the compilation of relevant information concerning all aspects of Jewish life, and collaboration with non-Jewish groups as well as with world Jewry.[33] The focus throughout is heavily institutional. Subsequent chapters deal primarily with Jewish education, though they also address "the status of the woman in Jewish law" and the need for "a new understanding of Jewish religion."

I have devoted so much attention to Kaplan's ideas and dilemmas because no American Jewish thinker has ever laid out the former in comparable detail, or articulated the latter with such precision. Kaplan's major contribution to contemporary thinking about community was threefold: (1) the blueprint (first laid out in *Judaism as a Civilization* and expanded most fruitfully in *Meaning of God*) for creation of a *community of practice*, not only through religio-cultural rituals at home and in synagogue but through an all-embracing multiplicity of "folk arts" and daily activities; (2) the outline of a *worldview and shared set of values*, the result of a civilization far broader and more pervasive than religion alone ever could be in the modern world; and (3) the outline (presented in his magnum opus and expanded in *Future of the American Jew*) for an *organized institutional community* that would serve not only the spiritual but the material needs of the Jews who considered themselves its members. Kaplan emphasized repeatedly that the organized community had to "care for" individual Jews in tangible ways if they were to concern themselves with it—or with Judaism. No less important, he insisted—as in the critique of the Jewish Family Service—that Jewish institutions had to be animated by the values of Jewish civilization and organized so as to serve these values. Kaplan sadly never quite spelled out how this was to be accomplished.

Beyond these three contributions, Kaplan usefully and forcefully restated—in refined and updated, sober yet hopeful, form—the three postulates of modern Jewish community-building first laid out in Moses Mendelssohn's *Jerusalem* (likely the source where Kaplan learned them). In Kaplan's thought, as in Mendelssohn's, these postulates as it were comprise the frame in which any diaspora Jewish public sphere can be imagined.[34]

(a) Jewish community must be *voluntarist*. Jews must be persuaded to choose it, attracted by its moral and religious teachings, its narratives and ceremonies, and the goods of community itself.

(b) Jewish community will claim only *part* of the individual's collective loyalties and comprise only part of a hyphenated self. Consciousness, time, and resources will be shared. Jews must learn to live in two civilizations if they are to live Jewishly at all.

(c) Jewish community will require *pluralistic acceptance of and respect for difference* on the part of the Gentile society as well as on the part of Jews.

These conceptual achievements are of major importance, I believe; one cannot proceed to imagine Jewish community in America without them. But neither are they sufficient. One gains additional insight into what is needed—and the resources available to meet that need—when one turns to the very different diagnosis and prescription for what ails American Jews offered by Soloveitchik.

. . .

The major factor making Soloveitchik so useful in the imagination of community might well be the "transvaluation" evident on almost every page of his work. "The Rav," that is, speaks *only* normatively about Jewish community and everything else, rather than historically or sociologically (though he does make reference to history and sociology). He also speaks in the name of Jewish tradition, often in the form of commentary on or analysis of classical texts. Indeed Soloveitchik's preferred mode is the construction of dichotomous ideal types—Adam I versus Adam II in *The Lonely Man of Faith*, "homo cognitivus" versus "homo religiosus" in *Halakhic Man*, "fate" versus "destiny" in *Kol Dodi Dofek*. Soloveitchik's exposition of these types, however unsatisfactory, generally proves the vessel for a far more complex account of Jewish community than one might expect. I will examine each of these major essays, as well as a later address titled "The Jewish Community," in search of elements in the imagination of Jewish collective life that Kaplan rejected or missed.

Consider first the earliest of Soloveitchik's major essays, *Halakhaic Man*, published in Hebrew in 1944.[35] Its rationale and program for Jewish community are straightforward. Jews are commanded by Torah to transform the world in accordance with divine command. The point of the law is to impose divine order on the reality that God's creation left in need of our completion. Halakhic Jews engage in what Max Weber called "inner-worldly asceticism": directing their wills, marshaling their intellect, to the reshaping of the world.

Community in this imagining is a doubly religious imperative. It is required, first of all, by God's instructions—the mitzvot—which presume that Jews and other human beings are by nature social beings, and reflect the fact that God seems to care about human institutions and practices as much as or more than about what transpires in human hearts. Concern for institutions takes up the bulk of biblical and rabbinic instruction in God's name. No less important, community is required in Soloveitchik's account because God's ambitions for human subjects must overcome, or make positive use of, God's palpable distance from our world. Divine *tzimtzum* makes human effort both possible and necessary. God has left the work to us, and—not always being as available as we would like for either consolation or consultation—God has made it harder for us to speak directly about God to one another. This in turn makes the experience of shared action, and the shared reality created by that action, all the more important as a source of human meaning. Put another way: we cannot speak to one another about God, Soloveitchik argues, but we can, we *must*, speak to one another about what God wants us to do together.

The shared language of halakhah, then, both concerns community and creates it.[36] Jews come together in order to undertake their divinely ordained common project, and only by so doing can they come together as Jews at all. This common labor, Soloveitchik writes in the second part of *Halakhic Man*, becomes the vehicle of personal repentance or *teshuvah*: the creation by the Jewish individual, under God's direction, of a new self, joined by covenant to other such selves as well as to God. The work Jews do at God's command, collectively and individuallly, constitutes what the political philosopher Robert

Paul Wolff called a "community of labor," in which not only the product of the work but also the collective effort to bring it into being is a source of satisfaction, self-fulfillment, and group identity.[37] In Soloveitchik's vision, this community of labor is most palpable among the elite of halakhic theorists, whose job it is to discern underlying principles and apply them to new circumstances. But—as in Kaplan—it extends to all the Jews who join in the actions mandated by their commitment.

Soloveitchik's conception of the grounds and motivations for Jews' collective labors is enriched by his conceptualization of two covenants in *Kol Dodi Dofek* (1956).[38] Jews are bound up in a covenant of *fate*, willingly or against their will, before they undertake participation in the covenant of *destiny*. Egypt comes before Sinai; shared circumstances, shared suffering, and "the awareness of shared responsibility and liability" all *precede* "a deliberate and conscious existence that the people has chosen out of its own free will and in which it finds the full realization of its historical being." "Camp" comes before "congregation." The former results from fear and the need for self-defense; the latter is "created as a result of the longing for the realization of an exalted ethical idea and . . . nurtured by the sentiment of love."[39]

The power of Soloveitchik's analysis, as I have already noted, rests to a large degree in its refusal to take explicit account of what American Jews are likely to believe—sociology, as it were. He rather joins the Torah, "written" and "oral," in addressing Jews normatively with demands that apply, in the first instance, to Jews alone. But in this case Soloveitchik joins Kaplan (who of course also spoke normatively about community) in presuming something about contemporary Jews that may well be sociologically accurate: namely that they will join Jewish community because they suffer from and recognize a common fate, or at least a common predicament; this perceived situation allows for no other outcome (Kaplan might say no other *reasonable* outcome). The difference between the two thinkers is that Soloveitchik offers his account of the two covenants in an essay that contrasts God's apparent absence from the stage of history during the Holocaust with God's apparent renewed presence on that stage in the birth and defense of the State of Israel. Kaplan pays remarkably little attention to the Holocaust in his many writings. More important, he cannot ascribe any historical event to the actions of a God involved in history, because he believes there is no such God. Talk of divine providence is ruled out as a vestige of "supernaturalism." For Soloveitchik providence is utterly crucial. God is apparently "absent" during the years of Hitler's triumph, but "knocks on the door of the beloved" once more (hence the title of the essay, taken from the Song of Songs) when the UN votes for partition in 1947 or Israel's army triumphs in 1948.

Soloveitchik's summons to mutual responsibility among Jews, especially where the State of Israel is concerned—for all that it depends on these controversial assertions about God's "presence" or "absence"—is at one with central tropes of Jewish tradition as well as with what is arguably the single most powerful trope of contemporary Jewish civil religion, best expounded by Elie Wiesel and Emil Fackenheim: "Am Yisrael Chai." The Jewish people lives. It must and will go on living. This is the so-called "614th commandment" famously articulated by Fackenheim: not to grant Hitler posthumous victories. Jews who do not believe in God are obligated in his account of "the commanding voice of Auschwitz" to believe in—and assist in the survival of—the Jewish people.[40] *Am Yisrael Chai* is the credo of their religion—because, Soloveitchik insists, "*od avinu chai*": Our Father still lives. In sum: Jews come together in community because they must; even if they cannot agree about the *purpose* of their collective existence, they can have no doubt about its *inevitability*.

A third crucial element in Soloveitchik's imagining of Jewish community is the depiction of human existence that drives the embrace of communal bonds: especially the fact of human beings' fundamental *aloneness*, set forth lyrically in *Lonely Man of Faith* (originally published in 1965). The historical isolation of the Jewish people mirrors that of the individual Jew, the latter nowhere more vivid than in the story of the wrestler-ancestor after whom Jews are named. Both mirror the loneliness of every person of faith in every monotheistic tradition. No human being can satisfactorily communicate his or her deepest thoughts and feelings about God—and, one suspects, not only about God. In the modern world and the modern self—both devoted to the pursuit of "majesty" and control at the expense of covenantal relationship with God or human fellows—the loneliness of any person of faith is still more acute, and that of the members of Israel's minority faith community still more so. We have already noted Soloveitchik's conviction that human beings require the shared, public, objective space of commanded activity afforded Jews in the halakhah. In *Lonely Man of Faith* the emotional aspect of this need is further highlighted.[41] Ritual, as Durkheim and many others have argued, takes us out of our individual selves and into a larger consciousness, that of our group. It then returns us to our selves enlarged and ennobled. For Soloveitchik, halakhah does this in both its ritual and its legal mode, thereby answering—with community—the Jews' individual human need as much as it answers a divine summons. Indeed, the latter is given with the former in mind.

A great deal of Soloveitchik's essay is given over to ideal-typical distinction between "Adam I" and "Adam II" communities. The former, as in much Enlightenment social contract theory, is utilitarian, founded on the rational recognition of individuals that Robinson Crusoe–like existence deprives them of much they need and want. Hence they band together in a "natural community" founded on division of labor, the better to satisfy individual desires and to triumph collectively over hostile forces. "The two are better than one," says the Book of Ecclesiaster, "because they have a good reward for their labor."[42]

By contrast, "redemptive" or "covenantal community" demands mastery of self rather than of other; its foundation is a lonely self in search of identity. God's declaration in Genesis that "it is not good for man to be alone" is taken "in ontological terms, with emphasis upon 'to be.'" Fulfilled existence requires a relation with God as well as with a human partner. The Adam II community is one of "three participants: 'I, thou and He,' the H in whom all being is rooted."[43] Only this community, in which human beings "meet God . . . as a comrade and fellow member," affords us the chance to communicate, indeed to commune with, and to enjoy the genuine friendship of others, as Adam did in marriage to Eve.[44] Human beings meet only in the depths, Soloveitchik seems to argue, because only in the depths do they attain true being. What they attain there cannot be discussed. But as opposed to surface Adam I conversation about common projects, Adam II silence offers "communication" founded on common, unspoken relation to the third partner in the community, God. The covenantal community has the added advantage that it extends across time and space. "Countless 'thou' generations . . . advance toward [the member of this community] from all sides and engage him in the great colloquy in which God Himself participates with love and joy."[45]

There is something distinctively modern—indeed, American—in this appeal to the individual self to join in community in pursuit of its own highest self-interest (even if this same appeal may be present, albeit implicitly, in biblical and rabbinic sources as well). One sees the same invocation of self-fulfillment in Abraham Joshua Heschel.[46] It is of course evident in Reform thinkers such as Borowitz, for whom, unlike Soloveitchik, "autonomy" is a norm that cannot be violated, and a good that cannot be overturned.[47] We have already marked this feature in Kaplan. It arguably exists in non-American Jewish thinkers such as Samson Raphael Hirsch as well (and of course in numerous non-Jewish thinkers in the modern period). The difference in Soloveitchik's case is not only the unequivocal subordination of human fulfillment to convenantal obligation but also—far more strikingly—the passion, the angst, the exhibition of a self in turmoil. *Lonely Man of Faith* owes much of its persuasive power to its articulation of existential pain and its promise that Jewish community offers the best (perhaps the *only*) remedy for it.

The essay only gains in credibility when Solovietchik declares, Freud-like, and in the manner of existentialism, that the "cure" can never be entirely satisfactory. Personal unhappiness is built into the human condition. We never become unified selves, Soloveitchik warns. We shall always remain divided between Adam I and Adam II urges.[48] Nor can we escape our loneliness, for what is deepest in us cannot be communicated to others. But like the first covenantal community described in Genesis, the marriage between Adam and Eve, covenantal community through Torah offers Jews as much togetherness as any group of human beings can possibly know. Love between husband and wife, the most basic of communities, in fact grows according to Soloveitchik's ideal account into (and out of!) the loving attachments of family and community. Love depends upon depths of relation that are shared. A community of Torah must be animated, at least in some measure, by love.

A still more recent address on the subject, "The Community" (delivered in 1976 and published two years later), stresses empathy with the other's suffering and recognition of the other's "ontological worth" as the means for overcoming the "alienation" and loneliness of a world dominated by Adam I concerns. "To recognize a person . . . is an act of identifying him existentially . . . [and] to affirm that he is irreplaceable." Recognition then entails responsibility. "Recognition is identical with commitment."[49] The echoes of Buber and Levinas are apparent (though Soloveitchik may of course have drawn not on them but on common philosophical sources such as Hegel,[50] if not on sources more ancient still). Soloveitchik's sources are of less concern to me than the nature of his claim (articulated beautifully in Charles Taylor's account of the self, avowedly derived from Hegel).[51] Community does not merely serve the highest self-interest of the self, by leading to the self's fulfillment, but provides the recognition without which the self cannot come to be. It is thus of "ontological" importance. Soloveitchik also names two other sorts of community in the essay: the *community of prayer*, which joins us in the suffering of our fellows and the plea for its relief as well as the work needed to accomplish what we pray for;[52] and the *narrative community* (he does not use the term) created by stories that "form the foundations of Jewish morality" and "precipitate the reexperiences of events which transpired millennia ago." The past has not vanished if we so retell it. Nor is participation in that past oppressive. "It is a privilege and a pleasure to belong to such a prayerful, charitable, teaching community, which feels the breath of eternity."[53]

The question arising from this portrayal of covenantal communty for the imagination and building of community among American Jews in the twenty-first century would seem to be whether Soloveitchik's vision can reach out beyond the Orthodox community for which he wrote most of his work to include at least the Conservative, Reform, and Reconstrucionist Jews (or the elite among them) who might likewise be responsive to Soloveitchik's emphasis upon mitzvah, covenant, and halakhah, let alone to include those who reject God and/or halakhah. Is there a way to embrace in a normative vision of "involuntarism" even the Reform (and secular) worlds that Soloveitchik derided (in apt parallel to Kaplan's derision of Reform, Orthodoxy, and other versions of Conservative Judaism)? Soloveitchik, like Kaplan, believed that Jews *must* embrace some normative vision, whether it be ethno-cultural or "covenantal." He also seems to have believed (again like Kaplan) that a substantial minority of Jews (if not more) would be willing to make this attempt. The key task identified by both thinkers, then, is to provide convincing accounts and images of what it might be to live as a member of a contemporary American Jewish community, taking full account of the hyphens marking Jewish identity today. Both seek to provide convincing reasons why Jews should aspire to be the sort of human beings whom they describe. That task becomes all the more difficult if one grants Soloveitchik's conclusion in *Lonely Man of Faith*—suggested by Kaplan in his more pessimistic moments but never stated as such—that at some point Jewish commitments cannot be satisfactorily explained to "Adam I" (i.e., American) culture—including the elements of that culture residing along with "Adam II" (i.e., Jewish faith) inside the Jewish self. Modernity in general, and the twentieth century in particular, has marginalized Adam II commitments and accorded Adam I overweening dominance—nowhere more than in America.[54] Adam II must "withdraw"—without explaining satisfactorily why he/she has done so. The obstacles facing the maintenance of distinctive Jewish communities are clearly immense.

Soloveitchik's contribution to the imagination of such community in these circumstances includes at least four crucial elements. (1) His *theory of the self* resonates with a great deal of influential modern thought, and his picture of the conflicting forces driving Jewish individuals in the current historical situation is marvelously nuanced. (2) The *covenants of fate and destiny* have become basic building blocks of contemporary Jewish thought. Jews are driven to mutual responsibility against their will, and impelled to it by shared purpose. (3) The *communities of Adam I and II* are likewise influential formulations. Jews are brought to community in pursuit of their highest ends—whether these be Adam I commitments or Adam II relations with the personal God. (4) Finally, Jews build and inhabit communities because they subscribe to a common story about themselves. Conversely, the Jews not attracted to Jewish community, or actually repelled by it, reject that story as mythological. They reject common Jewish "fate" as well as the leading formulations of Jewish "destiny," have other notions of the Highest or of what it demands from them, and may well cleave to a very different notion of self than the one that Soloveitchik puts forward.

There is another possibility, however. Jews resistant to the claims of Jewish community may simply not be attracted by either of the two regnant accounts we have examined thus far, which I (with obvious oversimplification) have labeled the "ethno-cultural" and the "covenantal/faith" communities. Soloveitchik and Kaplan, taken individually and even together, do not exhaust the images and accounts of what Jewish communal identity might mean and entail. Judaism has arguably never attracted Jewish loyalties with only one or two such accounts, whether the stated reward for community was "salvation" in this world or the next. There is no reason that statements of Jewish tradition or community should do so today. What might a more diverse set of accounts and images of Jewish community include?

The Reimagining of Jewish Community

One invaluable source for locating such accounts and images will not be drawn on here: Jewish history. The variegated shapes that Jewish community assumed in the past provide both precedent and possibility for what can be conceived and constructed today. Given its varieties and scope, I cannot even begin to perform the task of mining that history here. Suffice it to say that Jewish historiography over the past two generations has greatly enriched our knowledge about how Jews over the past two millennia, in communities around the world, variously organized and understood themselves. The use of this resource for theological ends—that is, for normative visions of Jewish community informed by the Jewish people's age-old conversation with God and one another—has barely begun.[55]

I will undertake an easier task: the suggestion of several images and accounts of community that come readily to mind but are either absent from, or insufficiently developed in, the writings of Kaplan and Soloveitchik. I will then juxtapose these with findings (primarily those reported in *The Jew Within*) concerning American Jewish attitudes and behaviors where community is concerned.[56] My aim, I repeat, is neither to exhaust the imaginative possibilities of normative statements about community nor to convey a subtle sociological picture of American Jews. I want only to indicate several additional imaginative possibilities and suggest why they might "speak to" contemporary American Jews.

One image that comes immediately to mind is that of the *community of Israel gathered at Sinai*. American Jews have seen this image portrayed countless times: whether in films such as *The Ten Commandments*, or in the graphics of numerous Passover haggadahs and other ritual objects, or on stained glass windows in their synagogues. They have heard the story of Sinai told on innumerable occasions and have conjured it in song, stood to attention at its recital, transmitted it to their children. Indeed the Torah, which they continue to read at home or in synagogue or in the classroom, seems to address readers who, by virtue of telling and attending to the story of Sinai, come to identify with the group who according to its story were vouchsafed at Sinai a unique relation to the God of all the earth. The Torah's readers are called upon to mark their own membership by a set of distinctive practices. The text in effect continues to address the Jews among its readers as follows: This is the way Jews have walked, since Sinai; this is the way you, who likewise were at Sinai, should walk in the presence of God or approach the presence of God or conceive the presence of God; this path leads away from and back to the precious experience at Sinai described here, and enables you to share in that experience. Sinai is the origin-point of the story that members of Jewish communities tell each other about these things, and in this walking and this telling, this halakhah and this aggadah, they are constituted again and again as a Jewish community.

The image of Israel at Sinai is fundamental, in differing ways of course, to Kaplan and Soloveitchik alike, though as we have noted Kaplan cannot make overmuch use of it, because he sees the need to proclaim his disbelief that there ever was an event at Sinai such as the one described in the Torah and pours scorn on anyone who believes in a God remotely like the one Israel is said to have encountered there. Standing with the Jewish people at Sinai for Kaplan means "living" the Jewish civilization that the Jewish people (according to its story) began there. I wonder, though, if one might find a middle ground between the two thinkers—or an expansive space beyond them—by forgoing their shared insistence upon one and only one legitimate view of God and covenantal obligation. A broader notion of Sinai might then embrace a wider variety of Jews than either "folkways" or "halakhah" can command. We know, for example, that the word "tradition" offers wide appeal to contemporary American Jews.[57] So—albeit to a lesser extent and in a more complicated fashion—does the word "mitzvah."[58] Many American Jews who chafe at *mitzvah* in the sense of commandment nonetheless feel an imperative to mitzvah in the senses of good deed, instruction, and obligation. Half of those surveyed for *The Jew Within* rejected the idea that Jews have obligations to fellow Jews over and above those owed to humanity in general.[59] They rejected the proposition that Jews are duty bound to be more ethical than the next person. But they took pride in the perception that Jews do so, overwhelmingly value their heritage, and accept some responsibility to know and transmit that heritage. They did not entirely rebel at the expectation that they live up to a higher-than-average standard of ethical attainment and social justice, in keeping with the perceived traditions of their ancestors, so long as they were not coerced into doing so. Nor, as we will see in a moment, did they reject ritual out of hand in the manner of their Reform or assimilationist ancestors. Half declared belief in God essential for being a good Jew.[60]

In short: the notion of belonging to a people marked and constituted by the distinctions set forth at Sinai still resonates widely. Not for nothing is the best-known statement of Jewish feminist theology titled *Standing Again at Sinai*.[61] Plaskow begins with the exclusion of women from direct participation in the covenant expressed in Moses' injunction to the Israelites "not to go near a woman" (Exodus 19:15) in preparation for the holy encounter. Jewish women insist on the fact of their membership in this covenant throughout the ages, an undeniable feature of their experience whatever Jewish authorities (or the text of Exodus 19) might say. The image of Sinai clearly resonates powerfully in Plaskow's and other recent accounts of Jewish community. Sinai is a place where many Jews of many varieties long to stand.

Note too, however—as the biblical text does repeatedly—that the community of Israel is united before, during, and after the events at Sinai by its recognition of *the authority of its leader, Moses.* They are bound together by their absolute dependence upon his prophetic mediation of God's word. The reader today still comes to identify with Moses, as he or she follows the Israelites' journey out of Egypt and through the wilderness. Moses is very much what Buber called a "living center" in the strictest sense of the term: a teacher, a prophet, a priest, a model, a rebbe. American Jewish community by and large lacks such figures. Only members of the Orthodox world—and particularly the Hasidic world—still possess such a potent and visible living center for their Jewish communities. Lubavitcher Hasidim, dependent upon the leadership of the late Menachem Schneerson, have refused to replace him or even, in many cases, to acknowledge his death. The majority of American Jews not only lack any such charismatic authority; they would likely be suspicious of any candidate who came forward to claim it. The sense of community afforded by shared allegiance to charismatic leadership is unavailable to them. Heschel, nurtured in a Hasidic world, clearly recognized the need for role models. One learns to be pious by watching those who already are. In the absence of exemplars of piety who could be imitated up close by American Jews, Heschel arguably projected proper behavior onto a large public stage, modeling it for all to see through his social activism.[62] Elie Wiesel too, at the height of his popularity, might have been accorded the right to speak on their behalf by a broad cross section of American Jewry. But even that recognition was granted implicitly, in a fashion that cannot be documented. Soloveitchik and Kaplan both served as authoritative leaders in their own communities but not beyond them. American Jewry lacks such leadership at present, and is not likely to allow the lack to be filled.

The mention of Wiesel calls to mind a third image of Jewish collectivity, one that exercises great power in our time: Auschwitz, the concentration camp, the Jew behind barbed wire marked out for annihilation. The image as we have seen is central to Soloveitchik and marginal to Kaplan; its impact is, I think, far more complex than either could have imagined. It is not clear that the appeal to a "common fate" (Soloveitchik) or even to shared difficult circumstances (Kaplan) can serve as an effective rhetorical strategy for attracting Jews to Jewish community when the threat to Jews is not palpable or there is no perceived escape from whatever threat is acknowledged to exist. Holocaust memory, we have learned, is awesomely complex. On the one hand, the imperative to "remember" seems widely accepted among Jews (and many Gentiles) today, as close to a universal sense or urge among Jews as any known to me. On the other hand, the "moderately affiliated" Jews interviewed for *The Jew Within*, when they spoke about the Holocaust, overwhelmingly told a universal story of human evil and divine inaction rather than a particularly Jewish story of antisemitism. Their perceived obligation to the six million does not entail responsibility for carrying on the tradition, the identity, that Hitler sought to destroy. Fackenheim's theology, if I am correct, has had limited success in this respect. In traditional Jewish terms, one might say that Jews are obedient to the command to remember, *zakhor,* but not to the command to observe, *shamor.* One is tempted to say that the obligation to remember is readily accepted, in part, because the object of memory is by definition distant rather than near at hand, past rather than present.

There is one exception to that rule, however: the perceived obligation to ensure the survival of the State of Israel—Soloveitchik's focus in *Kol Dodi Dofek* and Fackenheim's in *To Mend the World* (1982). The *State of Israel* is of course the other dominant image of Jewish community that exercises contemporary American Jewish imaginations. It does so, I think, in several principal forms: the utopian socialist kibbutz, peopled by strong, healthy Jews working the soil; Jerusalem (the sacred, "eternal capital"); Tel Aviv (the modern secular city, built by Jews from nothing on the sand); the West Bank settlement, militant and defiant. One cannot permit Amalek to kill Jews again with impunity, according to widespread American Jewish conviction; one can and must affirm life against death by building the state, making the desert bloom, ingathering exiles, promoting high-tech development. Yet here too one is struck with how complex these images are with respect to the building of Jewish community in America. For one thing, there is the variety of forms mentioned above. Identification with the image Jerusalem likely serves different purposes and responds to different longings than exultation in the nightlife of Tel Aviv. What is more, the American Jews held rapt by images of Israel work hard to keep Israel at a safe distance. Fewer than 30 percent of the respondents to the survey reported in *The Jew Within* professed to be very attached to Israel; only about 40 percent of American Jews have even been there;[63] Israel's marginal place in American Jewish literature, thought, liturgy, education, and even philanthropy have often been remarked. Time will tell whether renewed threats to Israel's existence, or renewed antisemitism in Europe and elsewhere, will foster a heightened sense of community based upon shared suffering—or whether it will cause more Jews, convinced that that suffering is escapable, to seek their place outside the "covenant of fate" and find their meaning elsewhere.[64] In the meantime, prevailing images of community in America offer a countermodel to the sort of Jewish community perceived as Israeli: voluntarist rather than coerced, inidividualist rather than collectivist, pluralist rather than hostage to Orthodoxy, accepted rather than rejected by Gentile neighbors.

The Torah, like many subsequent texts, traces the origin of the Israelites/ Jews not to inescapable enemies or charismatic leadership or any other feature of shared history but rather to *nature,* to *family.* The children of Israel descend from one ancestor. Were it not for the abrupt transition from the stories of

Genesis, which remain as it were within the family of siblings and cousins, to the stories of Exodus, which play out on a national and world scene, the reader would more easily remember that Moses, son of Amram, son of Kehat, son of Levi, son of Jacob, is only four generations removed from the man whose name all Israelites bear and six removed from Abraham, who received the divine promises that he, Moses, is helping fulfill. The Jewish nation is imagined by the rabbis *as the extension of a human family that God takes as His own*. This is another key building block of the Jewish communal imagination strangely underdeveloped by Kaplan and Soloveitchik alike. Neither makes obligations to extended family as important as obligations to God and the covenant or the Jewish people and its civilization. Contemporary American Jews arguably build community, in large part, because the ties of extended family must not be allowed to weaken.

Many Jewish texts, moreover, do a persuasive job *of linking these ties of family, and so of intergenerational community, to one's own highest and deepest self-interest.* The Torah portion chronicling Sarah's death is called "hayyei Sarah"—the life, or lives, of Sarah—and the one chronicling Jacob's death is titled "Va-yehi," "and he lived," for the same reason that the story of Jacob and Esau is introduced as "toldot Yitzhak"—Isaac's story, or generations; and that of Joseph is introduced as "toldot Ya'akov," Jacob's story. The logic is clear: the story of any one person continues those which preceded it, and continues in those which follow, especially if the line is one of family. The meaning of any life cannot possibly be known at an individual's death. Each of us depends on those who follow to take the story forward. We need to trust that those who follow will take up the work that we have left incomplete. Individual Israelites/Jews depend not merely on their biological family to perform this task but on the community, their people, all of whom are children of Israel. Identification with the community carries with it a palpable sort of this-wordly immortality: agency transmitted over the course of many generations. Purposes not of one's own making can be appropriated in one's own lifetime, and can survive one's death. This is a good well worth having, given the brevity of life. It is a powerful image and motivation for community.

One can usefully read both Kaplan and Soloveitchik, I think, as struggling to regain something of the primordial power of this tribal loyalty. Recall Kaplan's quest for identification so "intuitive," for "otherness" so taken for granted, that "unlikeness" (the myriad expressions of Jewish distinctiveness) will take care of itself. Kaplan clearly has in mind, but does not quote, Ahad Ha'am's famous remark that he can no more ask why he should remain a Jew than wonder "why I remain my father's son."[65] Soloveitchik tries through multiple typologies to position the Jews uniquely on the spectrum of human achievement, and to reinforce that position by appeal to unique fate and unique destiny as well as unique obligations and opportunities. Paradoxically, the Jews surveyed in *The*

Jew Within gave voice to an inherited sense of tribal loyalty at the very same moment as they insisted upon complete autonomy when it comes to the choice for or against Jewish commitment.[66] "A Jew is a Jew is a Jew," they believed; given that a Jew is defined as one who converts to the religion or is born the child of one Jewish parent (it does not matter which), one's descendants cannot *not* be Jewish, by definition, unless someone along the line converts to another religious tradition. Neither behavior nor belief renders any Jew more Jewish than any other. It comes down, in the end, to blood—though most would have recoiled from that term, were it proposed to them.

The Jews interviewed and surveyed for the book rebelled against suggestions that someone else could ever be a better Jew than they were—even as they embraced the image of Jews as extended *mishpokhe*, aunts and uncles and cousins who have the right to make demands (or at least to voice expectations), inflict guilt, demand attention, even ask for money—because they speak the same language, share the same history, laugh at the same jokes, enjoy the same ethnic cuisine, celebrate (or knowingly violate) the same holidays. More immediately, American Jews credit grandparents with being the role models who, remembered much later in life, inspired their own Jewish commitments. They find more meaning in the performance of rituals at home with children and grandchildren than in any other Jewish activity. Jewish communities, it seems, could induce greater loyalty among Jews—both locally and worldwide—by taking steps to build on this sense of extended family, whether through adoptive grandparents to replace the real ones far away (or Jewishly disinterested) or the strengthening of family ties across continents.

Thus far I have followed Soloveitchik's lead in presenting the elements of community in entirely positive terms. The Torah, followed by the rabbis, acts otherwise. It takes care to chart *complex family* dynamics, and still more harsh *communal dynamics*, in which conflict and discord are ever present. Identification with the Israelites by later generations of Jews is accomplished in part thanks to the sarcasm of "Were there not enough graves in Egypt, so that you had to bring us to the wilderness to die?"—a fount of Jewish humor, and so of Jewish solidarity, ever since. Readers from the rabbis to Bialik have bent over backward to excuse the faults of the wilderness generation depicted in the Torah. Contemporary Jews do too—identifying with what the Israelites were up against because of their less-than-pleasant dealing with other members of their own Jewish communities (and with God), and perhaps anxious to excuse their own failures in these relationships. Paradoxically, I believe, the image of Israelites squabbling with one another—and banding together in rebellion against God—continues to be a powerful incentive to community. The family, after all, is the one group that cannot throw one out for being disagreeable or contentious.

But the biblical text goes still further. The Israelite community is united, as it were, not only by its divisions, but by its actual *sin* and *guilt*. The Torah pictures a group bound by shared responsibility for complaint and disobedience. The spies and Korah represent the culmination of behavior that reaches an earlier climax with the Golden Calf. Mendelssohn, following previous Jewish thinkers, pointed to the *theological* necessity of this story. Jews had to know that they could sin grievously against God and still be forgiven. This is the heart of prophetic visions of covenant and redemption. Its *sociological* indispensability is no less evident. Jews need assurance that "a Jew who sins is still a Jew." One is not expelled over minor infractions, or even major ones. Return to the fold is easy. Modern-day marranos no less than those of Spain and Portugal will be welcomed back with open arms. Freud supplied a *psychological* account of these same dynamics. The Israelites' collective guilt for their collective sin is in fact, if we take his approach, the most significant tie that binds them. (The Torah suggests as much time and again.) Guilt is an essential building block of community.

A great deal of what drives contemporary American Jews both to practice Judaism and to abandon it, to participate in the community and to flee it, might well be guilt for felt sins of omission and commission: whether for what Jews failed to do during the Holocaust, for survival when others did not survive, for failure to emigrate to Israel or do enough on its behalf, all this in addition to the usual (and universal) guilt toward parents and grandparents, in part because of the traditions altered or abandoned. Jews, one might say, are those who share such sins, need forgiveness for them, repeat the sins over and over again, confirm each other's confidence that God forgives them nonetheless, and alternately demand, provide, and deny forgiveness to one another. Jewish communities, perhaps, provide the structures in which this process is undertaken by Jews, time and again, together. It is not clear what course community building should take in response to these dynamics, particularly given the fact that the latter are usually unspoken and unconscious. But the existence of the dynamics seems incontestable.

I conclude this nonexhaustive survey of images with that of the Israelites gathered in the Temple at Shavuot in order to express the sentiment on which a great deal of communal life depends: *gratitude*. For contemporary American Jews the gratitude is both collective—for life after the Holocaust, for the rebirth of Israel, for the successes of America, for the meaning that comes from tradition—and individual: for the birth of children, recovery from illness, guidance when it is most needed, the succor of companionship, all of which are bound up by ritual and experience with Jewish traditions and communities. Kaplan well understood that voluntarist ties depend for their survival upon an exchange of gifts, and so upon thanksgiving. Members of Jewish communities become and remain members because they experience belonging as a gift—a privilege, as Kaplan put it, rather than a burden. Jewish teachers and leaders struggle mightily to create and reinforce this sense. At times the reward highlighted is one of meaning, acknowledged in Sabbath morning services when Jews crowd to kiss the Torah as it parades by, or sing "Hashiveinu" with great feeling as the Torah is returned to the ark. "Return us to You and we shall return. Renew our days as of old." At other moments gratitude flows from the simple facts of togetherness, release from loneliness, shared pain, or mutual recognition. Soloveitchik was alert to this. But Kaplan was on the mark in suggesting as well, I think, that the claim of community will be credible only if it offers tangible "social and economic security" to those who have nowhere else to turn. Jews who are not confident that they will be taken care of when in need may experience their purported community as something less than real—and perhaps even a sham. If on the other hand they perceive membership in it as a gift, material and spiritual, one for which they are profoundly grateful, they are more likely to be prepared to give of themselves in return. It is not clear, of course, how the community could afford the burden of offering this care, even if it could get far more Jews to share in its provision. But the importance of the element of gratitude seems indisputable, one insufficiently addressed by American Jewish religious thinkers and insufficiently nurtured by communal institutions as they currently operate.

Conclusion

One could carry on this exercise with many other biblical and postbiblical texts—not for the purpose of arriving at an agreed-upon set of elements, putatively basic or essential to the imagination of community, but precisely in order to show that a *multiplicity of elements* appear and disappear as one moves through the library of tradition, assume centrality or fade into the background. My own list would "privilege" images of Jews living alongside and among Gentiles without sacrifice of authenticity; it would omit images that presume the Jewish need to separate decisively from Gentiles because of alleged ontological differences between the two. One turns with profit to multiple images and accounts of community, in multiple texts written in multiple diasporas across the centuries as well as in the Land of Israel during various periods. No less, one turns to historical sources and accounts for examples of how Jewish communities have been constituted and what they have meant to their members. It seems a truism to suggest in our day that only multiple imaginative entry-points to Jewish community will do, given the variety of Jews who today must be persuaded to walk through these doors again and again.

It seems clear to me as well that given the unbridgeable differences dividing Jews from one another at present, one must increasingly look at membership in the Jewish people in terms of an *array of intersecting face-to-face communities* rather than as a homogenous entity with local chapters. This is particularly the case in America. It also seems clear that *face-to-face communities* alone can provide the sense of meaning and the experience of connection needed to sustain loyalty to the Jewish community as a whole or to the still more abstract and less visible notion of an "American Jewish community." Loyalty to the Jewish people as a whole springs from experiences with local exemplars rather than the other way around. This may become all the more true as Jews on the global level are beset by lethal enemies, by antisemitism from left and right, and by unsettling moral quandaries.[67]

I have tried, with the help of Kaplan and Soloveitchik, to indicate some of the images and accounts of community that may prove most useful in attracting American Jews to join Jewish communities—and so attach themselves to the Jewish people as a whole—despite these and other obstacles. Communities of practice and of narrative require appropriate institutional structures and adequate normative grounding. Shared and commanded public activity needs to be rooted in some sense of covenant: whether of fate, destiny, or loving partnership. Existential aloneness and material suffering must both be eased. Recognition must be reciprocated and suffering shared. "Standing again at Sinai" involves forceful leadership, common action in the face of perceived common enemies, ties of family, and the conviction that one's own highest self-interest demands attachment to others who will carry on one's story and one's work. Guilt and sin must both be accepted. Gratitude must be forthcoming. And, if all that is not a difficult enough set of prescriptions, Jewish community must share the selves it joins together with other communities of which they are a part, other nations, other families—and must grant these partners legitimacy. The list of requirements is long, and the obstacles to achieving it—given voluntarism, fragmented selves, and pluralism—are well known. Kaplan's pessimism at times seems prescient indeed.

This is not the place for evaluating the chances for success of his or any such program, or even for suggesting how one might measure success in terms other than sheer numbers of Jewish names appearing on organizational membership charts. It may be appropriate, however, to conclude these reflections with the observation that both Soloveitchik and Kaplan highlighted one prerequisite for Jewish community that usually does not appear on Jewish organizational reports or vision statements of communal agencies: prayer, the sense of standing in the presence of God. Soloveitchik argued that Jews are and must be a "prayer community," standing before God so as to stand with one another, and then completing the work of prayer by working together to see their prayers fulfilled.[68] Kaplan, in an ingenious rationale for the holiday of Shmini Atzeret, described public prayer (which of course did not mean addressing a personal God who hears petition) as the prelude to transforming our selves, our communities, and our world.[69] Prayer in these senses, according to both accounts, links ultimate beliefs concerning reality and meaning to daily activity in the world.

I say this not to urge Jews to pray as much as to urge them to engage in the activities and reflections that prayer, as Kaplan and Soloveitchik differently conceived it, entails. Prayer requires (and, in a way, constitutes) collective normative discourse about the transcendent ends that our membership in the community should serve. Why put attention to transcendent ends forward as a desideratum, given the resolutely secular character of so many American Jews? For two reasons. First, if American Jews are to choose one side of their hyphenated identifies over the other as the locus of greatest meaning; if they are to pay the price in distinctiveness that comes of marked and consequential affiliation; if they are to marry Jews in greater numbers, raise their children as Jews, educate themselves as Jews—the community has to make its case for all this extremely compelling, and has to do so again and again, at various stages of life. Ethnic attachment does not enjoy the weight possessed by religion in American culture (not to speak of the Constitutional protections), though it also, of course, does not arouse the hostility that religion induces in many Jews. Jewish federations, like Zionists, in fact couched their claim to unite and speak for Jews as a whole on the notion that religion is a particular loyalty, further subdivided into the various denominations, while ethnicity is by definition universal, all-inclusive.

Second, I am not convinced that the alleged division of our community into religious and secular is inevitable, or even that it is persuasive to the bulk of American Jews. The amount of common ground shared by Kaplan and Soloveitchik despite real and significant theological differences is likely exceeded by American Jewish "laypeople" who are *not* theologians and so less committed to marking intracommunal divisions. Nor is God an alien subject to most American Jews. Those interviewed for *The Jew Within* were happy, even eager, to join and extend conversation on this matter. They liked talking about God; 75 percent of those surveyed believed that belief in God was either "essential" or "very important" to their own sense of being Jewish; 52 percent said it was "essential" for a "good Jew" to believe in God, and 33 percent more said it was "desirable"; 56 percent responded "definitely yes" to the question "Do you believe that there is a God?" and another 27 percent said probably yes. Most surprising of all, perhaps, 36 percent definitely believed "God watches over you in times of danger," and 32 percent more believed this was probably the case.[70]

The propensity to take God seriously is not the least of the gifts bequeathed to Jews by Torah, written and oral. It is one of the resources on which the Jewish community has historically depended to keep Jews hanging onto it, and to each other, for dear life. Sociology has long dominated American Jewish conversation about community, for good reason. It may be time for communal leaders and Jewish thinkers alike to pay renewed attention to theology: normative conversation about God, obligation, and the goods that Jews should be providing for one another and the world.

Notes

1. Robert Bellah, *Habits of the Heart: Individualism and Commitment in American Life* (New York: Harper and Row, 1985), pp. 20–21.
2. Mordecai M. Kaplan, *Judaism as a Civilization: Toward a Reconstruction of American-Jewish Life* (Philadelphia: Jewish Publication Society, 1994), p. 5.
3. Ibid., p. 15.
4. Ibid., p. 178.
5. See Mel Scult, ed., *Communings of the Spirit: The Journals of Mordecai M. Kaplan*, vol. 1, 1913–1934 (Detroit: Wayne State University Press, 2001).
6. Kaplan, *Judaism*, p. 8.
7. Ibid., p. 10.
8. Ibid., p. 15
9. Yehezkel Kaufman, *Golah ve-nekhar*, 2 vols. (Tel Aviv: Dvir, 1962). On Kaplan's encounter with the book, see Scult, *Communings*, pp. 511–12.
10. Kaplan, *Judaism*, chs. 25–26.
11. Mordecai M. Kaplan, *The Meaning of God in Modern Jewish Religion* (Detroit: Wayne State University Press, 1994), p. 9.
12. Ibid., p. 6.
13. Kaplan, *Judaism*, p. 386.
14. I owe this insight to a paper presented by my colleague Steven Zipperstein at a conference marking the seventieth anniversary of the publication of *Judaism as a Civilization*, held at Stanford University in 2004.
15. Kaplan put the matter this starkly only in a later work, originally published in 1948: Mordecai M. Kaplan, *The Future of the American Jew* (New York: Reconstructionist Press, 1967), p. 445. It does appear, however, as we will see, in *Judaism as a Civilization* as well.
16. Kaplan, *Judaism*, p. 196.
17. Ibid., p. 178.
18. Ibid., pp. 215–16.
19. Ibid., pp. 227–34.
20. Ibid., p. 282.
21. Ibid., p. 283.
22. Ibid., p. 285.
23. Ibid., p. 286.
24. Ibid., pp. 287, 289.
25. Ibid., p. 288.
26. Ibid., pp. 290–94.
27. Ibid., pp. 294–96. On the kehillah experiment see Arthur A. Goren, *New York Jews and the Quest for Community: The Kehillah Experiment, 1908–1922* (New York: Columbia University Press, 1970).

28. Ibid, pp. 297–98.
29. Ibid., p. 299.
30. Ibid., pp. 291–92.
31. Kaplan, *Future*, p. 107.
32. Ibid., pp. 114–15.
33. Ibid., pp. 116–22.
34. Moses Mendelssohn, *Jerusalem*, tr. Allen Arkush (Hanover, N.H.: Brandeis University Press, 1983). Kaplan makes frequent reference to Mendelssohn in *Judaism as a Civilization*; see the index entry, p. 578.
35. Joseph Soloveitchik, *Halakhic Man*, tr. Lawrence Kaplan (Philadelphia: Jewish Publication Society, 1983). The Hebrew original can be found in Joseph Dov Halevi Soloveitchiki, *Be-sod Ha-yahid ve-ha-yahad*, ed. Pinchas Peli (Jerusalem: Orot Publishers, 1976), pp. 37–188.
36. On this notion see David Hartman, "Halakhah as a Ground for Creating a Shared Spiritual Language," in *Joy and Responsibility* (Jerusalem: Ben Zwi-Posner Publishers, 1978), pp. 130–61. See also Gerald J. Blidstein, "On the Jewish People in the Writings of Rabbi Joseph B. Soloveitchik," *Tradition* 24:3 (Spring 1989): 21–43.
37. Robert Paul Wolff, *The Poverty of Liberalism* (Boston: Beacon Press, 1968), pp. 162–95.
38. For the recent English translation see Joseph B. Soloveitchik, *Fate and Destiny: From the Holocaust to the State of Israel* (New York: Ktav Publishing House, 2000). The Hebrew original can be found in Soloveitchik, *Be-sod Ha-yahid*, pp. 331–400.
39. Ibid., pp. 43–49, 54, 57–60. The distinction between camp and congregation is developed, in *Lonely Man of Faith* (1965), into the divide separating the utilitarian "Adam I" community and the "covenantal faith community" of "Adam II." The latter is likewise sustained by love, its smallest unit being the love binding husband and wife.
40. Emil Fackenheim, *God's Presence in History* (New York: Harper Torchbooks, 1970), pp. 67–98.
41. Joseph B. Soloveitchik, *The Lonely Man of Faith* (New York: Doublday, 1992), pp. 1–27.
42. Ibid., pp. 28–33.
43. Ibid., pp. 28–43.
44. Ibid., pp. 45–54.
45. Ibid., p. 73.
46. Indeed, note Heschel's complaint in an address first delivered in 1957 that "Jewish thinking during the last three generations has had one central preoccupation. Speaking of the Jewish problem, we meant the problem of the Jewish people. The group, the community and its institutions, received all our attention. The individual and his problems were ignored. . . . The time has come to pay heed to the forgotten individual. Judaism is a personal problem." He continued, "I see only one way out of the trap of institutionalism: a new emphasis upon the personal aspect of being a Jew. By the emphasis upon the personal I mean a relatedness to the center of one's being, a relatedness to one's intimate problems, such as joy and anxiety,

the sense of futility, insecurity, or the search for meaning." Abraham Joshua Heschel, "The Individual Jew and His Obligations," in *The Insecurity of Freedom* (Philadelphia: Jewish Publication Society, 1966), pp. 191–93.

47. See Borowitz's significant wrestling with the demands of autonomy and covenant in Eugene Borowitz, *Renewing the Covenant* (Philadelphia: Jewish Publication Society, 1991).

48. Sociologist Samuel Heilman, in a paper as yet unpublished, reads this as a commitment by modern Orthodox Jews—unlike Haredim—to participate fully in both the Jewish *and* the modern worlds. See Samuel C. Heilman, "The Changing Nature of American Jewish Orthodox Belonging." See also Lawrence Kaplan, "Revisionism and the Rav: The Struggle for the Soul of Modern Orthodoxy," *Judaism*, 48:3 (Summer 1999): 290–311.

49. Joseph B. Soloveitcik, "The Community," in *Tradition* 17:2 (Spring 1978): 16, 18.

50. See Robert Williams, *Hegel's Ethics of Recognitions* (Berkeley: University of California Press, 1997).

51. Charles Taylor, *Sources of the Self* (Cambridge: Harvard University Press, 1989).

52. Soloveitchik, "The Community," pp. 19–22.

53. Ibid., pp. 23–24.

54. Ibid., pp. 98–107.

55. One such effort, very much in the spirit of Kaplan's project, was Salo Baron, *The Jewish Community: Its History and Structure to the American Revolution* (Philadelphia: Jewish Publication Society, 1945). For one summary of the varieties of Jewish communal organization throughout the ages, as well as recurring patterns evident in those varieties, see the article "Community" in the *Encyclopedia Judaica* (Jerusalem: Keter, 1971), vol. 5, col. 808–29.

56. Steven M. Cohen and Arnold M. Eisen, *The Jew Within: Self, Family and Community in America* (Bloomington: Indiana University Press, 2000).

57. On the appeal (and problematic character) of tradition see Arnold Eisen, *Rethinking Modern Judaism* (Chicago: University of Chicago Press, 1998), chs. 6–8. See also Cohen and Eisen, *The Jew Within*, chs. 4–5, and the survey data presented on pp. 214–18.

58. On the appeal (and problematic character of) mitzvah, see Eisen, *Rethinking Modern Judaism*, pp. 10–12, and chs. 1–3, 8. See also Cohen and Eisen, *The Jew Within*, chs 1–2, 8, and pp. 96–99. I myself have tried elsewhere to elaborate on what this might be, suggesting ways of beginning "on our side" of the encounter with God—the tablet on the left, as it were, on which the last five commandments are inscribed—as well as on the "right side," with experiences of God of the sort that Heschel sought to encourage. See Arnold Eisen, *Taking Hold of Torah* (Bloomington: Indiana University Press, 1997), ch. 2. The subject is of course central to much of the Jewish thought written since Mendelssohn, including that part of it written in America.

59. See for example question 4p. on p. 216: 9 percent agreed strongly, and 38 percent agreed, that "I have a special responsibility to take care of Jews in need around the world."

60. All these data can be found in Cohen and Eisen, *The Jew Within*, pp. 214–18.

61. Judith Plaskow, *Standing Again at Sinai* (San Francisco: Harper and Row, 1990).

62. See Abraham Joshua Heschel, *Man Is Not Alone* (New York: Farrar, Straus and Giroux, 1991), p. 231. See also Arnold Eisen, "Re-reading Heschel on the Commandments," *Modern Judaism* 9:1 (Feb. 1989): 24–25.

63. Cohen and Eisen, *The Jew Within*, p. 218.

64. On this matter see Arnold Eisen, "Israel at 50: An American Jewish Perspective," *American Jewish Year Book* (1998): 47–71.

65. Ahad Ha'am, *Selected Essays of Ahad Ha-'am*, ed. Leon Simon (New York: Atheneum, 1970), p. 194.

66. See in particular ch. 5.

67. For related reflections on this point see Arnold Eisen, "Theology and Community," in *Imagining the Jewish Future*, ed. David A. Teutsch (Albany: SUNY Press, 1992), pp. 247–60.

68. Soloveitchik, *Lonely Man of Faith*, pp. 53–66.

69. Kaplan, *Meaning of God*, ch. 7.

70. Cohen and Eisen, *The Jew Within*, pp. 214–19.

Index

Acculturation. *See* American culture and Jewish identity

Adler, Rachel, 244, 246

Adler, Selig, 42–43

Advancing Women Professionals (AWP), 235

Affiliation, 5, 73–87, 89*n*34. *See also* Membership; Synagogues

Agunah, 237

AJRC (American Jewish Relief Committee), 55

Allport, Gordon, 82

Alter, Robert, 295

American culture and Jewish identity: adoption of American values, 255–56, 257; and civil religion, 309–10; and ethnic economy, 30–31, 40; femininity conception, 115, 204; individualism of, 304; and institutions, 52–54; vs. Israeli culture, 323; Jewish mothers' impact on, 213; and literature, 253–54; modern context for community, 319; and myth of unified community, 254–55; Orthodox issues with sports, 120–34, 135*n*9, 138*n*26, 139*n*36; and patriotism, 95–97, 99–105; and radio broadcasts, 182–83; and Satmar board game, 171–72; Satmar women's exposure to, 160–61, 170–71; transformation of European Jewish culture, 4–5, 6; and transnational activities, 49, 62–64; and women's identity, 191–208, 209–10*n*18. *See also* Suburban context

Americanization: and imagined community, 254–55; individuality and collectivity balance, 255–68; and transnationalism, 47–54, 59, 62–64

American Jew as Patriot, Soldier and Citizen (Wolf), 98

The American Jewess, 194–208

American Jewish Committee, 97, 100–103

American Jewish Congress, 245

American Jewish Relief Committee (AJRC), 55

Am Yisrael Chai, 316

Anderson, Benedict, 6, 20, 254

Anker, Laura, 217

Antin, Mary: Americanization narrative, 255, 256–57, 258, 259–60, 263; and multilingual legacy for Jews, 288–89, 301

Antisemitism, 60–61, 222, 224, 228–29, 276. *See also* Holocaust

"The Art of Banality," 151–52

Ashkenazic Jews, 15

Ashton, Dianne, 12

Assimilation: and ecumenism in radio broadcasting, 181–82; and Jewish military service, 93, 95; Jewish mothers' focus on, 218–19; religious education of girls as defense against, 238–39; and suburban paradox, 69, 77–78, 80–81, 82, 85. *See also* Americanization

Atherton, Lewis, 30–31

Authority: community basis in charismatic, 322; and early American communities, 4–5, 6, 9, 16–17; rabbinical vs. yeshiva students', 130, 134; and relief agency politics, 58–59; and suburban Judaism, 80; traditional vs. Zionist, 125; women's claims to public religious, 236–37, 239; and women's home religious role, 17–18, 164

Autonomy of individual, 317, 325

Auxiliaries, women's, 112–15, 234–35

AWP (Advancing Women Professionals), 235

Bais Rukhel Satmar girls' school system, 160

Baron, Salo, 6

Bat mitzvah, 236, 237

Baum, Charlotte, 12

Becoming Mexican American (Sanchez), 31

Beis Yaakov schools, 238

Bellah, Robert, 304

Bellow, Saul, 296

Belonging, sense of: and community based on Sinai experience, 320–22; and gratitude, 326–27; sports as key to students', 124–25; and suburban vs. urban context, 77; through ritual and observance, 77, 316, 327

Benjamin, Judah, 98

Berg, Gertrude, 182, 216

Education *(continued)*
  Yiddish school alumni, 282; values
  education through board game, 156–57,
  161–72
Eighth Assembly District, New York, 36,
  38–39, 142–43, 146–48, 149
Eisen, Arnold, 266
Elizabeth, New Jersey, 122, 128, 133
Ellwood, Robert, 77
Eltinge, LeRoy, 97
Emmanuel, I. S., 10–11
Emotive vs. civic versions of Jewish identity,
  258–67, 281, 283
English language, 273, 288
Entrepreneurs, Satmar women as, 170
Equality for women, 195, 196, 209–10n18,
  233–35, 245
Erlikh, Handl, 156, 161–62, 162–69
The Eternal Light, 181–82
Ethical monotheism, 308
Ethnic economy, 31–44
Ethnicity: ethnic solidarity vs. individual
  identity, 258–60; and music's spanning of
  classes, 179; and Yiddish, 293. *See also*
  Identity
Ethno-cultural imagined community,
  305–13, 319, 324–25, 329
European Jewish culture, 4–5, 6, 39–40,
  93–95. *See also* East European Jewry
Everything is Illuminated (Foer), 297
Exile and Estrangement *(Golah-ve-nekhar)*
  (Kaufman), 307
Ezrat Nashim, 240

Fackenheim, Emil, 323
Falk, Marcia, 239
Families: as center of Jewish identity, 19;
  as community basis, 221, 323–26, 328;
  intermarriage, 11, 18, 280, 283; large
  Satmar Hasidim, 158–59, 169–70;
  mother's role in character formation,
  212–29; and museums as community,
  145; and suburban affiliation, 79–80; and
  urban vs. suburban context, 72
Farband school, 271, 276–77, 278
The Far Euphrates (Stollman), 297–98,
  300–301
The Feast of Freedom (Rabinowicz), 241
Federation of Polish Jews, 60, 61
Feinstein, Rabbi Moses, 131

Femininity, Christian model of, 191–208
Feminism, 232–46
Film festivals, 178
Finkelstein, Jacob, 57, 59, 60–61
Flatbush School, 132, 133
Fleischman, Abraham, 74
Foer, Jonathan Safran, 297
Folkways approach to Jewish practices, 306,
  321
Forgiveness and guilt as connection to
  community, 326
47th St. Photo, 170
Frank, Ray, 201
Franks, Abigail Levy, 13
Fraternal orders, 53
Friedman, Debbie, 236
The Functions of Social Conflict (Coser), 233
The Future of the American Jew (Kaplan),
  312

Gaines, Kevin, 200
Gamm, Gerald, 11, 14, 34–35
Gehinnom, 163
Gellner, Ernest, 254
Gender: and attachment to Yiddish culture,
  274; Christian model of femininity,
  191–208; and consumer roles in ethnic
  economy, 37–38; feminism's impact
  on Jewish community, 232–46; and
  landsmanshaftn, 52; and liturgy, 179,
  239; moral lessons for girls, 156–72;
  separation of in sports, 120–34; and
  suburban context, 215. *See also* Women
Generational issues: home as focus for
  continuity, 18; and intergenerational
  community, 324–25; Jewish mothers'
  value transmission role, 215–19, 221–24,
  228; Jewish women and Christian
  women's culture, 192; and leadership lock
  by older generation, 89n34; and move
  to suburbs, 72, 75, 79; and multilingual
  legacy, 286; and new media, 176–77
Geographical definition of Jewish community, 9–11, 18–19, 72. *See also* Suburban
  context
German language, 290, 298
Gersh, Harry, 71, 73–74, 76
Getting Comfortable in New York exhibition, 148–50
G&G delicatessen, 35, 70–71

Memorial Day commemorations, 108–9
Memorials for Jewish war service, 105–11
Memory and community, 86
Mendelssohn, Moses, 313, 326
Mendlowitz, Rabbi Shraga Feival, 123, 126
Mercantile life and Jewish community
  oscillations, 7–8, 9–11, 16–17
Mesifta High School Athletic Association,
  130–31
Mesifta Tifereth Yerushalayim (MTY), 123,
  130–31
Mesifta Torah Vodaath (TVD), 123, 126,
  127–28, 129
Messianism, 173n20, 184–85
Metropolitan Jewish High School League
  (MJHSL), 126–28, 131–32, 138n26
Metropolitan Museum of Art, 142–46,
  147–48
Metropolitan Yeshiva High School League,
  121
Michel, Sonya, 12
Mikve Israel, Congregation, 8, 16
Military service, Jewish. *See* Patriotism
Minsker relief societies, 56–57, 62
Minyan and early American communities,
  3–4, 8, 26n49
Mirroring Evil: Nazi Imagery/Recent Art
  exhibition, 150–52
Mirsky, Mark, 70–71
Mishkan Tefila, Congregation, 14
Mitzvot and traditional imagined community,
  314, 321
Mizrachi, 125
MJHSL (Metropolitan Jewish High School
  League), 126–28, 131–32, 138n26
Mobility, socioeconomic, 76, 82, 149, 213, 227
Mobility of early American Jewish
  merchants, 7–8
Modernity's impact on Jewish identity and
  community, 146, 305–13, 316, 319
Modesty *(tzniut)*, 120, 128, 132–34, 165,
  168–69
Monopoly game, Satmar derivation of,
  156–57, 161–72
Montreal, Canada, 16
Monuments to Jewish war service, 105–7,
  109–11
Morawski, Ewa, 33
Moses, Adolph, 200–201
Moses, biblical leader, 322

Mothers as teachers of Jewish identity,
  212–29
Movies, silent, 177–78
MTY (Mesifta Tifereth Yerushalayim), 123,
  130–31
Multilingualism in Jewish community, 273,
  286–87, 288–89, 301. *See also* Language
Museum Opening Committee, 142, 143–44
Museums, 141–53, 154n34
Music and Jewish engagement with media,
  178–80
Mutual aid associations *(landsmanshaftn)*,
  47, 49, 51–61

Naming ceremonies for girls, 240
Narrative community, 40–41, 318, 319, 328
National Council of Jewish Women (NCJW):
  challenges for, 206; and Christian
  feminine activist culture, 197, 198–99;
  establishment and mission of, 194–95;
  and feminism, 233, 244; impact on
  synagogues, 207
National Federation of Women's Clubs, 198
Nationalism, 20
National Jewish Welfare Board, 103, 105
National Shrine to the Jewish War Dead, 111
Nation as community, 254, 261, 264–65
NCJW (National Council of Jewish Women).
  See National Council of Jewish Women
  (NCJW)
Neighborhood Guild, 142–43
New Age Judaism, 230–40, 241
New Amsterdam, 3–4, 7–8
Newman, Louise, 202
Newport, Rhode Island, 8, 9, 15, 181
New York City: commemoration of Jewish
  military service, 108–9; early communal
  life in, 3–4, 5–6, 7–8, 10–11, 15–16;
  ethnic economy, 36, 38–39; and "Jewish"
  accent, 287–88; museums as community
  in, 141–53, 154n34; Orthodox sports in,
  124–34; and restrictions of urban ethnic
  neighborhood, 72; Temple Emanu-El, 193
*New York Jews and the Decline of Urban
  Ethnicity, 1950–1970* (Lederhendler),
  85–86
New York Times, 151–52, 152
Nickelodeons, 177
Nordau, Max, 125
Novick, Pesach, 57

Religion *(continued)*
    Jewish identity, 225; and Soloveitchik's
    imagined community, 314–19; and
    suburban Jewish life, 70, 75–76; tradition
    vs. innovation in, 261; women's authority
    in, 17–18, 164, 236–37, 239; and Yiddish
    secular schools, 272, 279, 280–83. *See
    also* Christianity; Denominations; God;
    Ritual and observance; Synagogues
Religious schools, 80, 191, 282
Reminiscences (Wise), 41
Revel, Bernard, 124
Revolutionary War, Jewish service during,
    99–100
Reznikoff, Charles, 295
"A Rhode Island Refuge" (Wishengrad), 181
Richmond, Virginia, 16
Riesman, David, 82
The Rise of David Levinsky (Cahan), 255,
    258, 261–64, 288
Ritual and observance: and American sports
    culture for Orthodoxy, 120–34, 135n9,
    138n26, 139n36; as basis for imagined
    community, 314; bat mitzvah, 236,
    237; and belonging to Jewish identity,
    77, 316, 327; cantors, 179–80, 236; and
    child-centered suburban Judaism, 80;
    ethnic enclave economy as supporter
    of, 32–33, 36–37; feminism's impact
    on, 236–37, 239–41; funerals, 294; and
    Hebrew, 293–94; home-based, 17–18, 19;
    and intergenerational community, 325;
    and isolation of early American Jews,
    3–4, 8, 9, 17, 26n49; Kaplan's cultural
    view of, 308; kosher dietary laws, 9,
    38, 165–66, 276, 283; and lessons of
    Satmar monopoly game, 165–66; radio
    broadcasting's simultaneity of, 182;
    Sabbath, 165, 166, 206; Sinai experience
    as basis for community, 320
RJJ (Rabbi Jacob Joseph School), 129–30,
    131–32, 139n36
Roosevelt, Theodore, 96
Rootedness and early American communi-
    ties, 14–16
Rosenbaum, Joan, 151
Rosenblatt, Yossele, 180
Rosensaft, Menachem, 151
Rossman, Evelyn, 77, 80, 81
Roth, Philip, 287–88, 289, 294, 296
Runyon, Damon, 98

Sabbath, 165, 166, 206
Salome of the Tenements (Yezierska), 42
Salvation, Kaplan's secular version of, 305–6
Samuel, Wilfred, 14, 15
Sanchez, George, 31
Sarna, Jonathan, 5, 20
Sarzedas, Abraham, 10
Satmar Hasidim, 156–72, 173n20, 23
Satu Mare, Hungary, 157–58
Savannah, Georgia, 8
Schachter, Herschel, 236
Schiff, Jacob, 101
Schneerson, Rabbi Menachem-Mendel, 183,
    184
Schoener, Allon, 146
Schwab, Flora, 198
Secularism: and Kaplan's version of salva-
    tion, 305–6; and mothers' transmission of
    political ideologies, 224–25; and religion
    as Jewish identity, 281–83, 329–30;
    Yiddish schools, 272, 279, 280–83
Segregation of Jews, suburban vs. urban,
    81, 85
Self-fulfillment vs. covenantal obligation,
    317–18
Sephardic Jews, 15
Shapiro, Edward, 83
Shapiro, Karl, 295
Shared experience: as basis for community,
    315–16, 318; *halakhah* as language for
    community, 314–15, 321; of responsibil-
    ity, 318, 326. *See also* Holocaust
The Shawl (Ozick), 290
Shearith Israel, Congregation, Montreal, 16
Shearith Israel, Congregation, New York
    City, 4, 7, 10–11, 15–16
Sheftall, Levi, 13
Sheftall, Mordecai, 9, 100
Shkop, Rabbi Shimon, 123
Sholem Aleichem Folk Institute, 271, 272,
    275–76, 277–78, 279, 280
Sholtz, Jacob, 53–54
Silent movies, 177–78
Simon, Kate, 215
Sinai, community of Israel gathered at,
    320–22, 328
Sin and guilt as connection to community,
    326, 328
Singing, liturgical, 179–80, 236
Sisterhood of Personal Service, 193
Sklare, Marshall, 79, 214–15